The
Triumph
of the
Ordinary

**Depictions of Daily Life
in the East German Cinema,
1949–1989**

JOSHUA FEINSTEIN

The Triumph of the Ordinary

The University of North Carolina Press

Chapel Hill & London

© 2002
The University of North Carolina Press
All rights reserved
Designed by Richard Hendel
Set in Charter and Meta types by Keystone Typesetting, Inc.
Manufactured in the United States of America

This book was published with the assistance of the William
Rand Kenan Jr. Fund of the University of North Carolina Press.

The paper in this book meets the guidelines for permanence
and durability of the Committee on Production Guidelines for
Book Longevity of the Council on Library Resources.

Library of Congress Cataloging-in-Publication Data
Feinstein, Joshua.
The triumph of the ordinary : depictions of daily life in the East
German cinema, 1949–1989 / by Joshua Feinstein.
    p. cm.
Based on the author's thesis—Stanford.
Filmography: p.
Includes bibliographical references and index.
ISBN 0-8078-2717-7 (cloth: alk. paper)
ISBN 0-8078-5385-2 (pbk.: alk. paper)
1. Motion pictures—Germany (East)—History. I. Title.
PN1993.5.G3 F37 2002
791.43'0943'1—dc21   2001059826

Excerpts from the screenplay to *Die Legende von Paul und Paula*
by Ulrich Plenzdorf quoted by permission of Suhrkamp Verlag.
© Hencheverlag 1974; all rights reserved by Suhrkamp Verlag,
Frankfurt am Main.

cloth   06   05   04   03   02   5   4   3   2   1
paper   06   05   04   03   02   5   4   3   2   1

To my parents, Edith and Leonard

CONTENTS

A section of illustrations follows page 136.

ACKNOWLEDGMENTS

This project would not have been possible without the kindness and encouragement of many people. In Berlin, I received invaluable assistance from Günter Agde, who not only devoted numerous hours explaining to me the world of East German filmmaking but also helped arrange contacts with artists. In addition, I am very grateful to Heinz Kersten, Erika Richter, and Ralf Schenk, each of whom took time out to discuss my research with me. Manfred Behn and Hans-Michael Bock of the Hamburg Cinegraph were very helpful to me, too, during the initial research stage of the project. Other experts on GDR culture and society who were also generous toward me include Gerd Dietrich, Günter Erbe, Michael Rohrwasser and the late Hartmut Zimmermann. I also thank my friend Rick Le Vert for a number of leisurely but highly profitable discussions about GDR film.

Interviewing filmmakers and former officials was the most fascinating part of my research. For their time, patience, and almost unfailing willingness to entertain difficult questions, I am very much indebted to Frank Beyer, Annekathrin Bürger and Rolf Römer, the late Heiner Carow, Gerd Golde, Christel and Roland Gräf, Egon Günther, the late Alfred Hirschmeier, Rudolf Jürschik, Peter Kahane, Gabriele Kotte, Wolfgang Kohlhaase, Kurt Maetzig, Jochen Mückenberger, Helga Schütz, Konrad Schwalbe, Rainer Simon, Klaus Wischnewski, Günter Witt, Dieter Wolf, and Herrmann Zschoche.

A number of generous grants facilitated research leading to the dissertation on which this book is based. A Bundeskanzler scholarship from the Alexander von Humboldt Foundation made my research in Berlin during the 1992–93 academic year possible. The National Endowment for the Humanities, the Andrew W. Mellon Foundation, and the Institute for International Studies at Stanford assisted me during the write-up phase of the work. A Mellon award from the Stanford Center for European Studies enabled me to take an initial trip to Berlin during the summer of 1991.

Additional research necessary to expand and revise the initial dissertation project was made possible by grants from the Alexander von Humboldt Foundation and the Zentrum für Zeithistorische Forschung in Potsdam. My stay in Potsdam, while short, was among the intellectually most fruitful phases of my work. I am particularly indebted to Simone Barck, Thomas Heimann, Siegfried Lokatis, and Martin Sabrow for their interest in my project as well as their many insightful suggestions. During this stage of the work, I also benefited greatly from discussions I had with Oskana Bulgakowa, Ina Merkel, and Dietrich Mühlberg.

Throughout my research, I enjoyed the use of well-run and efficient archives. Among these was the Stiftung Archiv der Parteien und Massenorganisationen der ehemaligen DDR im Bundesarchiv, where Herr Lange's dry wit helped my work go faster. At the Bundesarchiv Filmarchiv, I appreciated the patience of my projectionists, Herr Berger and Frau Teschner, who uncomplainingly sat through some seemingly endless films with me. I am also grateful to Herr Müller and his staff at the Bundesarchiv Potsdam, now located in Berlin-Lichterfelde, who made it possible for me to use unprocessed collections. Herr Thau of the Institut für Theaterwissenschaft at the Freie Universität Berlin kindly allowed me access to his department's extensive video collection. In addition, the library staff at the Konrad Wolf Film School in Babelsberg showed great kindness to me during the many hours I spent using their very fine collection. Finally, I am very thankful to Frau Seidler at the now long defunct DEFA Betriebsarchiv, who went out of her way to assist me during a period of difficult transition for her staff.

During my studies at Stanford, I benefited from a superb dissertation committee. My adviser, James Sheehan, always made time from his busy schedule to read my chapters quickly and kept me on track with his wise suggestions. Mary Louise Roberts flattered me with her enthusiasm and her insightful comments. Russell Berman helped me negotiate difficult interdisciplinary issues inherent in my work. Norman Naimark and Paul Robinson were also generous in their assistance even though they were not official readers. I further wish to thank Keith Baker and Hans-Ulrich Gumbrecht for their interest in a topic that lies far from their own areas of expertise. My research also owes much to Henry Lowood, erstwhile curator of Stanford's German-language collections, and Sonia Moss, surely one of the world's most diligent interlibrary loan specialists.

At other institutions, I am particularly grateful to Barton Byg, director of the DEFA Research Center and Library at the University of Massachusetts at Amherst, who has been consistently generous with both substantive advice and logistical help throughout the project. Eric Rentschler of Harvard and Anton Kaes at the University of California at Berkeley have also been of considerable assistance. Marc Silberberg of the University of Wisconsin at Madison and his student Stephan Sodovieri were similarly very kind in sharing with me their insights on the East German cinema.

Finally, James Melton, Judith Miller, Mathew Payne, and Douglas Unfug all aided in making a year I spent as a visiting faculty member in the History Department at Emory University a very enjoyable and intellectually profitable experience.

At the University of North Carolina Press, I am fortunate to have had Lewis Bateman and Charles Grench as editors on my side in steering the project toward publication. I am also appreciative of Paul Betz and Ron Maner for their diligence in preparing the final manuscript. Two anonymous referees through thoughtful and insightful criticism also helped me achieve a more focused and efficient narrative.

Among my friends in Germany, I wish to thank Robert Boldt, Martin Oestreich-Gooch, and Tanja Lenuweit, all of whom have helped me out in innumerable ways over the years. I also owe much to the friends with whom I completed my graduate studies at Stanford, including Amir Alexander and Jutta Sperling. Finally, there is my wife and fellow historian, Patricia Mazón, who has supported me in this endeavor with the patience and love of one who truly knows.

Buffalo, New York
November 2001

ABBREVIATIONS

APO	Arbeitspolitische Organisation (vocational-political organization or cell within a BPO)
BPO	Betriebspolitische Organisation (factory political organization or SED group within each large factory)
CDU	Christliche Demokratische Union (Christian Democratic Union)
CPSU	Communist Party of the Soviet Union
DEFA	Deutsche Film-Aktiengesellschaft (German Film Corporation)
DFF	Deutscher Fernsehfunk ([East] German Television Service)
DVV	Deutsche Verwaltung für Volksaufklärung (German Central Administration for People's Education)
FDGB	Freie Deutsche Gewerkschaftsbund (Free German Union Alliance)
FDJ	Freie Deutsche Jugend (Free German Youth)
FRG	Federal Republic of Germany
GDR	German Democratic Republic
HV Film	Hauptverwaltung Film (Central Film Administration)
KAG	Künstlerische Arbeitsgruppe (artistic work group)
KPD	Kommunistische Partei Deutschlands (German Communist Party)
MfK	Ministerium für Kultur (Ministry of Culture)
NÖS	Neues Ökonomisches System (New Economic System)
SBZ	Sowjetische Besatzungszone (Soviet Occupation Zone)
SED	Sozialistische Einheitspartei Deutschlands (Socialist Unity Party of Germany)
SMAD	Sowjetische Militäradministration in Deutschland (Soviet Military Administration in Germany)
Stasi	Staatssicherheit (state security police)
UFA	Universum Film Aktiengesellschaft
VEB	Volkseigenes Betrieb (state-owned enterprise)
VVB Film	Vereinigung Volkseigener Betriebe Film (Cartel of People's Film Enterprises)
ZPL	Zentrale Parteileitung (Central Party Leadership, part of a BPO)
ZK	Zentralkomitee der SED (SED Central Committee)

The
Triumph
of the
Ordinary

INTRODUCTION

BACK TO THE FUTURE

On the night of November 9, 1989, the Berlin Wall fell. For the first time in over twenty-eight years, the German Democratic Republic (GDR) allowed its citizens to cross freely into the Federal Republic of Germany and West Berlin. Spontaneous celebrations erupted as hundreds of thousands streamed over the borders.

In the first weeks after the fall of the Wall, the fate of the GDR was by no means decided. Reform of the existing system rather than immediate unification headed the political agenda. Indeed, many prominent intellectuals as well as representatives of the Citizens' Movement (Bürgerbewegung) expected the GDR to forge a new path between capitalism and socialism. If this option ever existed, however, it did not last long. Crowds pressing for accelerated change switched from shouting "We are the people!" to "We are one people!" Soon their slogan became "Germany, united fatherland." By the time the "Round Table"—consisting of opposition groups and representatives of the official parties and mass organizations—started working on a new constitution on December 7, others were already abandoning the idea of the GDR altogether. A week later, the opposition group "Democracy Now" presented a three-stage plan for national unification. The Christian Democratic Union (CDU)—a former "bloc" party that had been fully complicit with Communist rule—was quick to follow suit. On December 17, its newly appointed leader, Lothar de Mazière, called for capitalism and a confederation with the Federal Republic as a stepping stone toward German unity.

On January 14, 1990, the last Communist head of state, Hans Modrow, still denied that a fusion of the two German states was even an issue. By February 1, though, even he had changed his position. Having just returned from a visit with Mikhail Gorbachev, Modrow first announced that the Soviet leader had no objections in principle to German unity and then proposed his own ten-point plan for achieving that goal. On February 10, it was West German chancellor Helmut Kohl's turn to meet Gorbachev, and only three days later Kohl and Modrow were in Bonn discussing a currency union. If any doubts remained about how the public felt about these developments, they were dispelled by the unexpected landslide victory of the CDU in the GDR's first free parliamentary elections on March 18, 1990. Popular support for the continued existence of an East German state was now unquestionably a chimera. Ironically, many of the public figures who still identified with this lost cause had been prominent critics or outright opponents of the old Communist regime.[1]

Parallel with these momentous events, another set of more modest occurrences was under way. Less than one week after the fall of the Wall, on November 16, 1989, the State Film Approval Board (Staatlicher Film-abnahmekommission), under pressure from an independent committee of the Association of Film and Television Workers (Verband der Film- und Fernsehschaffenden), consented to the release of several films banned twenty-three years previously. The first of these to have an open showing was *Spur der Steine* (Trace of Stones) on November 26. A few weeks later, *Das Kaninchen bin ich* (The Rabbit Is Me) was shown at the East Berlin Academy of Arts. Over the course of the next few months, six other films whose fate had been similar premiered publicly.

What links all these films is the Eleventh Plenum of the Central Committee of the Socialist Unity Party (SED), which took place from December 16 to December 18, 1965. Originally, this meeting of several hundred leading comrades of the East German Communist Party, its highest body, was supposed to proclaim a new summit in socialist economic organization, the "second stage" of the "New Economic System" (NÖS). The Party leadership, however, deemed cultural policy more pressing and devoted a large portion of the Plenum to the savage criticism of several artists and their works. No group felt the repercussions from these attacks more than the film industry. While only two films were directly discussed at the Plenum, the following year saw far-reaching changes at the only East German feature film studio, DEFA. Leading functionaries lost their jobs; directors and screenwriters had their careers interrupted. Institutional reforms led to stricter control by the Ministry of Culture and the Party. In addition to three films banned the previous year, eight film projects—a half-year's production—became the object of prolonged controversies and were broken off near completion. State-organized thugs rioted during the premiere of a ninth film, *Spur der Steine*—an expensive, highly promoted production that had been long anticipated by Party leaders, film artists, and the general public alike.[2]

Early reviews of the once-banned films frequently emphasized their continuing relevance to the present political situation. Reporting for *Die Freiheit* (Halle), Marlen Köhler described the following scene at one of the first viewings of *Spur der Steine*:

Now the people have reconquered their art through a peaceful revolution. And—fateful irony!—one of two copies of the film that currently exist was shown Sunday at SED district headquarters. The desire to see *Spur der Steine* and . . . then have a talk was great. The first viewer to participate in the discussion spoke about the film's amazing topicality after twenty-three years, about how we still have the same problems as back then . . . initiatives from below that hit up against frozen power structures, obsolete ideas about morality, dogmatism, careerism, and ass-kissing.[3]

The East German press also found other forbidden films remarkably current. The *Lausitzer Rundschau* described *Das Kaninchen bin ich* as "a politically provocative film . . . a film of subtle psychological effects and outstanding acting achievement [that] . . . even after two and a half decades [has] lost nothing of its fascination."[4] After seeing the same film, another reviewer asked, "What would have been possible if all these prohibitions had never existed!"[5] Wilfriede Eichler from the *Berliner Allgemeine Zeitung* described a third film, *Karla*, as "of continuing relevance" and observed, "I was overcome by sadness in face of what was kept away from us back then through the banning of such encouraging examples."[6]

Even before the March 1990 elections, reaction toward the Plenum films still trickling into theaters was changing. Commentators increasingly emphasized the films' irrelevance. Writing in April, a reviewer for the *Sächsisches Tageblatt* judged one of two films directly criticized at the Eleventh Plenum, *Denk bloss nicht, ich heule . . .* (Just Don't Think I'll Cry), rather harshly: "The laboriously patched-together version of this DEFA-flick does not approach *Spur der Steine* or *Das Kaninchen bin ich*. Actually [the film] is only a self-justification of DEFA, the sad reflection of a distant past. Because [the protagonist] Peter's error is also that of the director . . . mistaking the humanity of Peter's surroundings for the humanity of the social system. Therefore Peter sheds a tear at the end—socialism has him again."[7]

Other reviewers expressed similar thoughts in connection with films that arrived at theaters after the March elections. In May, the film *Berlin um die Ecke* (Berlin around The Corner) was described as "already quite distant."[8] In June, an article about *Karla* appeared in a Berlin tabloid under the headline, "Pertinent, but Too Late."[9] By October, a reviewer assigned another film, *Wenn Du gross bist, lieber Adam* (When You're Grown Up, Dear Adam), the status of a "living DEFA museum."[10] The *Wende*—the "turn" or transition from one society to another—was complete. The GDR had ceased to exist and with it the specific system of discourse defining its life and politics. The Plenum films had become relics of a vanished land or perhaps one that never was.[11]

In retrospect, there was something uncanny about the urgent relevance assigned to the Plenum films at the time of the *Wende*. The director of *Spur der Steine*, Frank Beyer, may have had a premonition that their moment of fame would pass quickly, that they were marking the conclusion rather than the start of an epoch. At the end of November 1989, when asked how he felt about the films' rehabilitation, he told a reporter: "Besides satisfaction, I also feel sorrow. If it's true what the viewers . . . told me, namely that the films are still relevant, that means then too that the conditions in this land still have not changed, as we expected [them to do] twenty-three years ago."[12]

This very sense of stagnation and arrested development was without a doubt a major factor in the popular rejection of the GDR. Still, the society that greeted the Plenum films after their Rip van Winkle sleep had changed a great deal. A casual glance at many textbook accounts of the GDR may leave the impression that little varied over the state's forty-year history. The same party and ideology and even to an astounding degree the identical functionaries held sway from beginning to end. The few dramatic events that did occur generally concluded with the reestablishment of the status quo ante. Even so, perhaps the only factor that remained truly constant was the reality of massive political oppression. East Germans had not stopped living and thinking; nor had their society entered a time warp. Like their Western counterparts, Easterners were not immune to such postwar trends as the sexual revolution, evolving tastes in entertainment and fashion, or environmentalism. In addition, the state reacted to these changes and was also the object of its own specific dynamic. Official self-understanding, institutions, and mechanisms of social and political control, indeed the state's very sensibilities, experienced constant transformation.

Despite the GDR's demise, the historical study of East Germany remains urgent. National unification has proven to be a long, drawn-out process. Any assessment of the German Federal Republic today is missing the point if it reduces the legacy of socialist rule to continuing economic woes and the grumblings of a disenchanted minority. The fall of the Wall also meant the end of West Germany. The East German past is now part of a new national history, or perhaps even a broader European one, whose contours are still emerging. On a more theoretical level, the study of the GDR can contribute much to the understanding of a central category in any nation's history: identity. The rapid disintegration of the East German state should not overshadow its apparent success during the seventies or the continued persistence of a distinct understanding of self and society in the Federal Republic's five "new" states. Finally, with the end of Europe's political division, there is a pressing need throughout the West to re-examine Cold War myths. A more differentiated understanding of former socialist societies will contribute to a fuller appreciation of Western ones as well.

This book proposes to contribute to a better historical understanding of East Germany by examining its cinema. At the center of my investigation is a group of films that depict daily life in the GDR, set in the context of the movie industry's institutional history and its changing relationship to politics and society. I am particularly interested in three sets of issues. The first is the construction of collective identity in a society lacking the mythic origins of nationhood. Unlike the Federal Republic, the GDR was not able to assume credibly the mantle of previous German states. Thus the regime devoted considerable resources to fostering identification with the new society through film and other artistic means. In effect, the Party was attempting to repeat a key aspect of nineteenth-century nation-building, the positing of a unique culture as the basis for collective self-understanding. A second, related question of great significance to this study is the GDR's response to the profound changes that occurred internationally in personal values, popular tastes, and mass media during the postwar era. These developments undermined the regime's attempt to construct a uniform and comprehensive collective culture. Instead of promoting respect for authority and social harmony, the youth culture that arose during the fifties and sixties called attention to the hypocrisy of modern institutions and celebrated rebellion. Further complicating the situation were the assumptions contained in official discourse about the family and the sexes. Film and other media in the GDR drew on a system of representation in which the constitution of state authority and attitudes toward gender and generational conflict were mutually dependent. Finally, I am concerned with the place of art in socialist society. Indeed, my research suggests that film and the arts generally, despite their highly regulated nature, did offer an avenue for social communication. At the very least, they served a mediating function between the sphere of officially tolerated personal and cultural expression and impulses emanating from a society that, despite conformist pressure, remained essentially diverse.

Although this study provides at least a sketch of the entire history of the East German cinema from 1945 through and beyond 1989, its primary focus is on the period between the late fifties and early seventies. These years saw developments that redefined what it meant to belong to East German socialist society. Among these was Nikita Khrushchev's admission of grave Stalinist errors at the Twentieth Congress of the Communist Party of the Soviet Union (CPSU) in March 1956. This event set off a process of critical reevaluation of the socialist project throughout the East Bloc, and the GDR was no exception. Of even greater significance for Germany was the construction of the Berlin Wall on August 13, 1961. This action emphasized the Ulbricht regime's willingness to sacrifice national unity in favor of establishing an independent socialist state. While most East Germans opposed this action, many artists and intellectuals accepted it as necessary to assure the GDR's stability and the establishment of a just social order. With the mass exodus toward the West halted, they reasoned that the regime could now create the prerequisites necessary for fundamental change by relaxing its internal vigilance. On balance, however, the sixties saw the dashing of such aspirations. The Eleventh Plenum in December 1965 brought an abrupt end to reforms that had followed the Wall's construction. Three years later, the crushing of the Prague Spring by Soviet tanks in August 1968 became an international symbol for the bankruptcy of socialism's utopian potential. Nevertheless, these events, as gravely disappointing as they were for GDR intellectuals, helped set the stage for an ideological shift with profound social consequences in the early seventies.

The cinema was an active participant in the redefinition of East German society that accompanied the political developments of the sixties. A major hypothesis of this study is that the Eleventh Plenum films, regarded as a group, were caught between two basic patterns for constructing East German identity. Beginning in the early seventies, films depicting the lives of common citizens were increasingly described as *Alltagsfilme*—"films of everyday life." Their earlier counterparts, in contrast, were known as *Gegenwartsfilme*—"films of contemporary life." While some caution is advisable in applying the terms to the cinema—both were employed by filmmakers and critics somewhat promiscuously, and they do not refer to distinct film genres[13]—the shift in vocabulary is highly significant. The latter designation implies a strong sense of historical progression: the present as a mediating stage between the past and the future. *Alltag*, while it does not exclude the passage of time, emphasizes ahistorical existence, the diurnal. In a different society, the distinction between these two ways of perceiving time might have been academic, but in East Germany it meant a great deal. The Party's ideology, the country's economic organization, and indeed the entire ordering of society through the state

6

were based on a progressive vision of history. Suggesting that time did not move forward was subversive; nevertheless, by the late sixties, even the Party itself was toning down its millennialism. By the time Erich Honecker succeeded Walter Ulbricht as head of state in 1971, the attainment of Communism, which in the late fifties still was seemingly just around the bend, had been postponed indefinitely. Before the seventies were through, the regime had declared the GDR a nation unto itself and actively encouraged such traditional activities as *Heimatpflege*, or the preservation of local identity and history.[14] In short, as the GDR became older, its official self-understanding became increasingly conservative. The legitimacy of the social and political order depended less on the future promise of universal emancipation and more on the cultivation of a collective identity, whose origins, like that of a national community, were supposed to be self-evident.

What united virtually all DEFA films set in the GDR was a complex set of filmic idioms—character types, dramatic locations, emplotment, and so on—used to define socialist reality. Inventing a character's biography or depicting such typical places of social interaction as the workplace or the classroom invariably involved making wider statements about the whole utopian project of socialism. Thus my emphasis on daily life does not announce claims about the actual fabric and texture of existence in the GDR but rather interest in the changing significance attached to living in the GDR. Similarly, this study does not approach identity as a clearly determinable constant but instead as a complex and volatile set of discursively defined relations. As the cultural studies scholar Stuart Hall has emphasized, "The nation-state was never simply a political entity. It was always also a symbolic formation—a 'system of representation' . . . with whose meanings we could identify and which, through this imaginary identification, constituted its citizens as subjects."[15] In this vein, my project sets out to explore the symbolic field on which both the East German state and its inhabitants drew to define themselves and contest issues. For the sake of convenience, I will refer to this system as the GDR's "civic imaginary."

Of course, the GDR was not characterized by open and free discussion. In contrast to most Western societies, the state carefully supervised all media outlets. A small army of censors vigilantly policed all manner of public expression. Certainly, official culture in the GDR offered no general communicative space for freely exchanging autonomous opinions of the type celebrated by Jürgen Habermas in his model of the classical public sphere.[16] Still, the virtual impossibility of direct political criticism in East Germany should not lead to the conclusion that communicative processes

did not play a role in that society's evolution. Several factors are important to consider in this regard.

To begin with, an "official" public sphere existed in the GDR. Like any
state with democratic pretensions, the GDR sought to legitimize itself
through the court of public opinion, even if the latter was transparently
"manufactured" by the press or "choreographed" through rituals of mass
acclamation.[17] Moreover, the regime's attitude toward media was not
entirely cynical. In contrast to the rhetoric of the Third Reich, whose
leaders were unabashed about their use of propaganda as a means of
outright manipulation,[18] socialist ideology purported to value Enlightenment discursive principles. Expressions of this investment included the
insistence that Marxism-Leninism was a scientific doctrine and the central
role that the notion of education played in official culture and rhetoric.
Indeed, the Party itself was organized as a pyramid of critical forums. At
least in theory, each of these, from the Central Committee to the humblest
cell, was expected to convince itself independently of the wisdom of the
leadership's decisions. Indeed, the SED's view of itself as the ultimate
arbiter of enlightened opinion often led to absurd situations. As anyone
familiar with the archives of the SED can attest, an official call for "further
comradely discussion" of an issue was a euphemism for signaling the need
to quash dissent among the Party faithful.

Some of the discursive forums existing within official culture, most notably those formed by expert communities and artists, enjoyed greater
relative autonomy than others. Of these last two groups, the artists are
probably the more significant, since the nature of their work allowed
them to address not only each other but more general audiences. Indeed,
it is often argued that art in the GDR assumed an "*Ersatzfunktion*," or "replacement" function, filling the gap left by media more directly charged
with political indoctrination. Literature, film, and other kinds of art provided opportunities to air in an oblique fashion issues that were otherwise
taboo. Conversely, the Party leadership, through encouragement or condemnation of cultural trends, sent signals about wider political and social
issues.

At the same time, the official public sphere enjoyed at best a very
limited and fragile hegemony. Applying the notion broadly, David Bathrick argues for the existence of a multiplicity of public spheres that existed
in the GDR outside official public life. In his study *The Power of Speech*, he
divides these into two broad categories. The first is defined through Western media, which in the form of radio, smuggled publications, recordings,
or, later, television were generally available in the GDR. Certainly by the
seventies, millions of East Germans followed nightly the same news broad-

casts and entertainment shows as their cousins in the West. Second, Bathrick emphasizes the existence of "various unofficial public enclaves or counter official voices that sought to break into or establish dialogue with the officially dominating voices."[19] During the GDR's final decade, such forums included writers, the Protestant Church, and the feminist, peace, ecology, and gay movements as well as underground culture scenes.

Scholars have long recognized the interdependence between processes of identity and those of communication. A common set of cultural references among individuals is generally a prerequisite for both shared allegiance and meaningful discussion.[20] Thus an underlying premise of this study is the linked evolution in the GDR of collective self-understanding and communicative possibilities. Over time, not only did new media such as television take the place of old ones, but the relationship among the arts changed as well. Some forms of expression once considered subversive, most notably rock music, were partially co-opted by official culture, while others like literature that had once stood very near to the regime became an annoying source of dissent. Accompanying this process were profound shifts in the GDR's "symbolic formation" or "civic imaginary," which both absorbed new elements and saw the reinterpretation of old ones. By the seventies, much state-supported art and literature thematized personal alienation and lost utopian possibilities. Belonging to East German society became a function of *Befindlichkeit*, or locality and milieu, rather than of identification with the regime's future-oriented ideology.

Since unification, historical research in Germany has tended to discount the possibility of meaningful social communication in the GDR. Instead, the focus has been on structures of hierarchical political control. In the tradition of Cold War totalitarianism theory, conservative historians have emphasized affinities between mechanisms of state repression under socialism and those that were in force during the Third Reich.[21] Eager to avoid simplistic and often tendentious comparisons, politically more moderate scholars speak of a "durchherrschte Gesellschaft"[22]—a society permeated by the state—generally interpreting the GDR's collapse instead as a consequence of fundamentally flawed socialist strategies for achieving modernization.[23] Only gradually have more "bottom-up" approaches emerged that explore the communicative possibilities open to ordinary citizens despite the GDR's fundamentally repressive nature. These studies not only stress inherent limits to state power, accommodation, and resistance but also suggest ways East Germans actively participated in the making of their society. In the tradition of West German *Alltagsgeschichte* (everyday history), Thomas Lindenberger, for example, has proposed focusing on the *Eigen-Sinn* (individual meaning) attached by social actors to contested behavior in order to better understand the social worlds GDR citizens inhabited and the practical results of SED rule.[24] Other younger scholars, including Peter Hübner, Ina Merkel, and Michael Rauhut, have demonstrated the highly contested and constantly evolving nature of East German daily life in such areas as the workplace, consumer design, fashion, and popular music.[25]

Recognizing the communicative possibilities that existed within GDR society also facilitates the integration of the GDR into the broader outlines of German national and late-twentieth-century history. Ironically, more than a decade after unification, the East and West German pasts are as divided as ever. Regardless of political bias, existing research emphasizing hierarchical structures of political control posits a normative modern state characterized by an abundance of social communication and a strong civil society. Implicitly, West Germany as a model Western democracy embodies national progress, whereas East Germany's significance lies only in its deficiency and aberrance. In contrast, Uta Poiger, in her pathbreaking comparative study of the reception of American popular music in the two Germanies, emphasizes inquiry into the construction of individual identities, construed as a contested and constantly shifting process, as a means for appreciating the collective dimensions of German experience.[26]

Although the present study does not share Poiger's comparative focus, it furthers the general aim of liberating the history of the two Germanies from the provincialism imposed upon them by the Cold War in other ways. The GDR cinema originally proclaimed itself a radical alternative to conventional commercial cinema, but it was profoundly influenced by this supposed nemesis and was in constant dialogue with both German cinematic tradition and world film. Moreover, East German film evolved in response to new media forms such as television and to changes in popular culture, including the introduction of rock-and-roll music and other elements of an international youth culture of rebellion discussed by Poiger. Finally, the history of the East German cinema suggests that the East German civic imaginary, as a symbolic field informing the construction of both state and individual identities, evolved in a complex fashion comparable to changes experienced in Western society. Certainly, East Germans and their state had to negotiate mutually many of the same cultural upheavals that buffeted the Federal Republic from the fifties through the seventies.

There are several reasons why the cinema provides an apt vehicle for a historical study focusing on identity and communicative processes in East German society. First, the industrial nature of film production has a special resonance in the context of socialism. Like that utopian project, moviemaking combines crass material calculation with a higher purpose transcending immediate necessity. In this sense, the DEFA studio—and the ironies inherent in harnessing an industrial form of organization in the service of an essentially Enlightenment conception of autonomous art—offers a microcosm for all of GDR society. Second, East German film as a medium was influenced by international developments. The sensibilities of both filmmakers and audiences were steadily evolving in ways entirely beyond the control of SED ideologues. Thus the cinema is convenient for investigating the intersection of international aesthetic and cultural trends with the evolution of self-understanding in the GDR. Moreover, from a purely pragmatic perspective, the highly organized and structured nature of filmmaking is significant because of the written documentation it generates, which can afford considerable insight into the concerns implicit in a film's conception. Especially for the GDR, where the state carefully policed all areas of cultural expression, an enormous amount of archival material is available. In many cases, it is possible to trace a specific film through each stage of its production, from the initial idea to final state approval. While these sources hardly guarantee perceptive film analysis, they facilitate contextualized, historical interpretation.

Last but not least, the cinema lends insight into a society's mythic self-understanding, clearly an essential aspect of identity formation. In the same way that westerns have propagated the notion of America's manifest destiny, many East German films were designed to convince audiences of the truth of Marxist eschatology, the inevitable downfall of capitalism and the dawn of a new era. Of particular significance to this study, film provides a key not only to how a given society defines its own past but also to how it conceives of history itself, the relationship among past, present, and future. In the context of the American cinema, Vivian Sobchack argues that the "Hollywood historical epic is not so much the narrative accounting of *specific historical events* as it is the narrative construction of *general historical eventfulness*."[27] More generally, Lorenz Engell emphasizes a basic affinity between filmmaking and the study of history. Both involve the description of movement: "cinematography." The analysis of events into constituent elements, the desire to re-create fluid experience, and the constant interplay between continuity and interruption found in the cinema correspond to many of the issues implicit in historical writing. The latter concerns change affecting an "imagined" community such as a nation; the former concerns visible change.[28]

Unlocking the full potential of films as a historical source is a matter less of positing them as "mirrors" of some preexisting reality than of interpreting them as participants in what can be understood as a GDR-specific civic imaginary. In order better to understand the process that led to the Plenum films, it will be necessary to explore various aspects of this complex system of representation in depth. Accordingly, the chapters of this study are thematically defined. Except for the first and last ones, each is built around the formal analysis of a single film. In addition, there are several other levels of analysis evident in each chapter. The rich archival materials that are available allow me to explore both the films' production history and their reception in depth. I also consider DEFA's institutional development and trace changing strategies for optimizing the creative process while maintaining economic efficiency. Another concern of the study is "cultural policy" (*Kulturpolitik*), or the expectations associated with art and the place of culture in official ideology. An important issue explored in this context is the changing relationship between artists and the regime. Finally, my study reaches beyond the boundaries of film to consider wider developments in popular culture and social trends.

The book's first chapter sets the stage for later ones by summarizing DEFA's first ten years from its inception in 1946 and explaining some of the parameters for my study. Here I argue that the very zealousness functionaries displayed in supervising artistic production was an indication of the tremendous importance their ideology attached to the cultural realm. First, as the literary scholar Boris Groys has argued in a different context,[29] socialism conceived of itself as a poetic process in a romantic sense. "New" individuals were supposed to fashion the society of tomorrow through the force of creative willpower. Thus artists had a crucial role to play in helping to imagine the future. Second, officials assigned art a genuinely emancipatory function. German artists were supposed to help uplift their compatriots emerging from twelve years of fascism and prepare them inwardly for the truth of dialectical materialism. Finally, claiming Germany's cultural heritage provided a means for linking socialism to that country's past, for presenting the GDR as the next stage of national development. These factors resulted in impossible demands on artists trying to depict the present. Ironically, despite the regime's great emphasis on the future, the early GDR cinema's greatest successes generally concerned the past. Up until the late fifties, most movies set in East Germany were such crude political allegories that even orthodox functionaries left screenings disappointed.

My second chapter analyzes Gerhard Klein and Wolfgang Kohlhaase's 1957 film *Berlin—Ecke Schönhauser* (Berlin—Schönhauser Corner) in order to illuminate the relationship between competing realist aesthetics and the constitution of political authority. Released in 1957 and at first enthusiastically received by the press and public alike, the film became embroiled in a debate concerning neorealism. Through its thematization of alienated youth addicted to Western popular culture and its use of techniques stressing film's indexical qualities—such as on-location shooting, use of original decor, and natural lighting—the film offended functionaries. These further claimed its association of East Germany with a decaying Berlin neighborhood resulted in a depressing vision of socialist society. Officials insisted on socialist realist principles in film, or the depiction of exemplary "positive heroes" and the "law-like nature" of history. At the same time, some high-ranking officials conceded that the movie was on the "right path." Indeed, within a few short years, it was generally recognized as a classic. My thesis is that if the film implicitly undermined the Party's progressive pathos, it also credibly authenticated the GDR as a distinct, autonomous society—a very important result for a state whose legitimacy was always fragile.

My third chapter treats *Verwirrung der Liebe* (Love Confused), a 1959 comedy, which I interpret as a meditation on the regime's utopian pretensions and their significance for everyday living. The film concerns two young couples, one from the intelligentsia and one from the working class, who swap fiancées. Its ending, which restores the original constellation of partners, stood in stark contrast to the officially proclaimed "cultural revolution" then under way, which promised to resolve the contradiction between intellect and labor. In addition, the film was one of the first DEFA productions that challenged the Party's extremely prudish morality. A sexually charged student Mardi Gras in the film suggests a sensual alternative to the technocrat's paradise envisioned by the Party leadership. This chapter also provides a convenient place to consider the intersection of art and industry in the studio. The film's director, Slatan Dudow, the Bulgarian-born "father" of the German Communist cinema and Brecht collaborator, cultivated the image of a temperamental artist. Having gone wildly over budget on the project, he became the chief target of an austerity campaign within the studio. One reform enacted largely to improve efficiency was the establishment of "artistic work groups." Over the next few years, these achieved increasing independence and were an important factor that contributed to a more liberal atmosphere at the studio during this period.

In the GDR's civic imaginary, relations within the family inevitably carried metaphorical significance. The East German cinema was populated by fatherly older comrades and rebellious sons. Another typical protagonist was a young woman seeking her way in life. If her emancipation stood for the new order's avant-garde pretensions, her gender referred to a wholeness lost in modern life that socialism was supposed to recover. In Konrad Wolf's 1963 version of Christa Wolf's novel *Der geteilte Himmel* (The Divided Sky), the focus of the fourth chapter, such a character mourns the loss of her lover who has left for the West. I use the film to discuss romance as a vehicle for thematizing the division of Germany as well as personal loyalty to the ideals of socialism. Through its formal complexity, the work reinvigorates this motif, which had been developed in hackneyed fashion in many DEFA movies. Finally, the chapter considers reasons why DEFA directors, who were predominantly male, chose to make films centered on strong female protagonists. The increased prominence of these characters starting in the sixties was consistent with the general shift occurring in the GDR's civic imaginary toward *Alltag*.

The fifth chapter concerns Kurt Maetzig's 1965 adaptation of another important work of East German fiction, Manfred Bieler's *Das Kaninchen bin ich* (The Rabbit Is Me). Like the work discussed in the previous chapter, this film features a female narrator, but its theme is seduction, not separation. Maetzig's film shows a young woman having to decide whether her married lover, a much older Party careerist, is exploiting her. Singled out for criticism at the Eleventh Plenum, the film's directness is rare among DEFA films. A major theme in the work is communication and political authority. The protagonist's brother is jailed for a casual remark; her lover turns out to have been his judge. Drawing on extensive archival records as well as interviews, the chapter analyzes the complex political and institutional factors that allowed the work's production in the first place. I then turn to the Plenum itself, where the regime associated the unreleased work with a variety of cultural trends—such as beat music imported from the West—deemed threatening to the Party's authority.

The study then considers Frank Beyer's *Spur der Steine* (Trace of Stones), a 1966 film that was crucial during the aftermath of the Eleventh Plenum. Transcripts of seemingly endless meetings document heated debate within the studio about the work in the months leading up to its short-lived release. During this period, the studio's fate hung in the balance while artists vainly fought to salvage a series of controversial projects. It is not too difficult to grasp why Beyer's work became the focus for discussion. Not only was it one of the most expensive DEFA productions of the day, but its story was rich in allegorical significance and pathos. By presenting multiple perspectives on a single problem—the moral conduct of an idealistic Party secretary at a construction site—this work fundamentally questioned the possibility of communion between individual and collective destiny predicated by socialism's utopian goals. For filmmakers struggling in the aftermath of the Eleventh Plenum to reconcile their commitment to the Communist regime with their integrity as artists, the work's relevance was clear. In addition, my analysis suggests that *Spur der Steine* represents the equivalent of an "anti-western" within East Germany's civic imaginary. While the picture celebrated the factory as the mythic cradle of socialist society, it raised serious questions about the cost of progress.

The final chapter describes the emergence of *Alltag* films in the seventies. I begin with a short discussion of Jürgen Böttcher and Klaus Poche's *Jahrgang '45* (Born in '45), which was also made in 1966. This picture, despite being banned at the Eleventh Plenum, strongly anticipated the future direction of GDR filmmaking. By the end of the decade, several of the individuals from this project would become associated with "documentary realism," a loose movement among young filmmakers advocating pictures that thematize quotidian life. Surprisingly, the works of this group encountered few political hurdles even though attempts in the past to apply neorealist principles in the East German context elicited strong objections among officials. My analysis then turns to Heiner Carow und Ulrich Plenzdorf's *Die Legende von Paul und Paula* (The Legend of Paul and Paula, 1973). Celebrating private fulfillment over public success by telling the story of a tragically fated love affair, the picture implicitly criticized the exaggerated social discipline and regimentation of GDR society. Moreover, the picture's great popular success suggests the resonance of an alternative East German self-understanding, premised less on the promise of tomorrow than on local identity and a recognizable lifeworld. Drawing on new historical literature and recent sociological data, the chapter's last section then places the articulation of *Alltag* identity in film in a wider social and cultural context, suggesting some of the reasons identification with East Germany has persisted into the present.

The study's epilogue handles DEFA's last decade and a half of increasing frustration and stagnation. The dynamic that had long governed aesthetic and political battles in the East German cinema had now played itself out. Once the regime abandoned its utopian pretensions, there were few windmills left against which filmmakers could safely joust. As economic and social conditions worsened in the GDR during the eighties, pictures set in the present began to show clear signs of routinization; the studio's more imaginative productions now tended to thematize history in a quite philosophical manner and rarely found large audiences. Increasing competition for limited resources further made it difficult for younger artists in the studio. Having long lost its central place in official culture to television, film was also in no position to carve out even a modest niche for itself among the alternative communicative spaces that began to proliferate as the GDR neared its end. Due to the capital-intensive and highly regulated nature of their métier, filmmakers were at a relative disadvantage compared to their colleagues in literature and other arts in terms of the possibilities for dissent open to them. The critical role that the cinema had attempted to play in the sixties had been highly dependent on the role then still assigned artists in the rhetoric of reform socialism as the heroic co-creators of a brave new society. Thus DEFA ignobly stood on the sidelines as the winds of political change once again swept Germany.

One last issue implicitly addressed by this study is the moral implications of state-supported art in a repressive land. While my main focus is a set of films, this investigation is also about a group of artists who helped legitimize the regime. Especially in the fifties and sixties, many directors and scriptwriters saw themselves as members of a socialist avant-garde who through their art would contribute to the establishment of a truly just society. They may have sometimes disagreed with the regime's specific policies, but they had enormous respect for its leaders as veterans of the Communist movement.

In hindsight, the Eleventh Plenum marks for many filmmakers their banishment from Eden, the moment when their disillusionment began, when it first became obvious that their ideals and those of the regime had little in common. As the director Frank Beyer put it: "We [leading functionaries and artists] were all pulling on the same rope. Only afterward did we notice that it was in opposite directions."[30] The total of eleven films suppressed was staggering, probably more than all other banned DEFA works combined.[31] Immediately following the Plenum, the Party initiated an intensive series of purgelike "discussions." Many artists had to choose between their convictions and their careers, their friends and their livelihoods. Most exercised humiliating self-critiques; a few were forced out of the studio.

Even so, East German filmmakers were obviously a highly privileged group. In any land, working in film is a rare opportunity; in the GDR, where access to all forms of public media was restricted for political reasons, it was even more so. Extravagantly paid compared to most of their compatriots, directors and scriptwriters also had the opportunity to travel abroad. Especially during the period of this study, they enjoyed as artists a certain proximity to power. Walter Ulbricht and other Party leaders personally courted them. Even most of the filmmakers who had to leave the studio after 1966 eventually returned or found employment in other cultural institutions.

Indeed, any retelling of East German history involving art inevitably runs up against two controversies that were thrashed out in Germany during the nineties. The first of these is the *Täter/Opfer* (perpetrators/ victims) debate. In the narrowest sense, this designation refers to the difficulties inherent in judging the actions of former informants for the notorious East German secret police, the Staatssicherheit, or Stasi.[32] More broadly, the *Täter/Opfer* controversy concerns the moral ambiguity that pervades any present-day discussion of the GDR. Easy condemnation is no one's prerogative. The vast majority of East Germans must cope with the fact that they more or less willingly participated in the very state that they now claim was responsible for their oppression. Never having faced quite the same dilemma, West Germans can hardly claim to have greater authority for assessing blame. Who, then, was responsible for a system whose victims and perpetrators were frequently identical? And since this question defies an answer, how does the historian then reconcile two perspectives, those of the casualties and of the survivors of socialism, that are antithetical but nevertheless inextricably linked?

The second controversy that provides an inevitable subtext for the present study has to do with the enduring value of East German art. Such prominent writers as Heiner Müller and Christa Wolf, celebrated before the *Wende* in both Germanies, were excoriated in the press after unification. While the charges themselves concerned their actions as individuals, their work, and with it all art produced in the GDR, was implicitly indicted. The long-term implications of the furor are questionable. For example, Wolf defended herself quite effectively against the charge that a brief stint as a Stasi informant early in her career fundamentally compromised her artistic integrity.[33] After all, most definitions of art do not require its production in a pluralistic society, let alone by individuals whose personal conduct is irreproachable.

At the same time, however crude some of the broadsides against East German artists have been, they do point to issues of a far deeper, even terrible, nature. Many artists, including those of a critical bent who suffered dearly for their views, identified with the ideals of socialism and benefited from the system's privileges. Youthful enthusiasm often preceded great disillusionment. Anyone persecuted in the GDR can find ample cause to judge their art harshly. A gap persists between art that even at its most critical was state-sponsored and actual cases of profound injustice that were beyond the pale of artistic representation in the GDR.

Studying East German films cannot honor the injustice done to victims of vicious SED persecution. Still, historians can appreciate such an undertaking for what it can accomplish. Ultimately, what makes the Plenum films fascinating is that they were very much a part of their day. Perhaps for one fleeting moment during the mid-sixties, an alternative progressive vision of East German society seemed realizable. Reform efforts were under way in various realms, including the economy, education, justice, and youth culture. Dissidents such as the physicist Robert Havemann and the folksinger Wolf Biermann had emerged. On the streets, individuals contested social and political expectations by wearing their hair differently, sporting blue jeans, and listening to rock music.[34]

Even if this study treats the films examined mainly as cultural artifacts, as objects of quasi-sociological inquiry, it is necessary to recognize that their original status as art is a factor of great historical significance. In any society, the autonomy of art is more valid as an ideal than as an adequate description of actual conditions. While the forms its dependency assumed were more obvious in the GDR than in other places, art was still accorded a unique importance within that society. Many filmmakers also took their calling as artists seriously. They struggled to find original solutions to conflicting political and artistic imperatives. Ironically, some of the most innovative East German artists, especially during the period of this study, were not those whose estrangement from the government was obvious but rather those whose loyalty to the Party seemed absolute.[35]

Clearly, some Plenum films did go quite far in questioning the underlying legitimacy of Party and state. These display an elusive quality found in few other DEFA productions—an unreconciled sense of violence and frustration—that might explain why, in contrast to many GDR films banned at other times, most of the Plenum films were first rehabilitated after the Wall fell. The experience of the film industry also anticipated future developments in the wider society. The *Alltag* films of the seventies did not pick up in the exact same place where the Plenum films had left off. Still, the vicinity, especially when particular Plenum films are considered, was similar. What had changed in the meantime was official policy, which had become, if not more broad-minded, at least more sophisticated. It was possible, although officially still undesirable, to depict individuals, in film and other media, who were alienated by socialism and whose integration into a wider community was at best an uneasy one. Whether such achievements can free filmmakers of moral responsibility for a regime whose privileges they enjoyed is doubtful, but their story is still fascinating. There were reasons why the Plenum films after twenty-five years of obscurity enjoyed one last hurrah in 1989. This investigation sets out to find out why these works of art once again seemed vital and relevant, even as the land they depicted was about to dissolve forever into the past.

Conquering the Past and Constructing the Future

The DEFA Film Studio and the Contours of East German Cultural Policy, 1946–1956

Accounts of GDR cultural policy tend to describe it as some grand peristaltic movement, as an undulating series of contractions and expansions, of crackdowns and letups.[1] Implicit in such descriptions is the existence of two clearly defined, opposed sets of individuals: critical artists and hard-line functionaries. Not all of the debates, however, can be broken down along these lines. Artists did not always show solidarity, and functionaries sometimes stuck out their necks to defend art they thought was important. Second, one person's crackdown might be another's opportunity for realizing necessary change. If artists generally supported calls for greater inner-Party democracy, they were not immune to metaphors likening the achievement of socialism to a battle situation requiring military discipline. Freedom of expression may have been a recurring theme in the controversies characterizing the East German art world, but artists rarely questioned the state's right to supervise cultural production. Certainly, during the fifties and sixties, even the most critical would have agreed that some censorship was necessary.[2]

Understanding the role the cinema played in the construction and contestation of East German identity requires rethinking the relationship between art and politics in the GDR. Instead of positing these two realms as fundamentally autonomous and approaching their intersection as suspect, as most existing studies do, it is necessary to understand their profound mutual dependence. This chapter undertakes this task by examining the general history of the East German cinema from 1946 to 1956 in the context of Germany's postwar reconfiguration. At the same time, the discussion traces the institutional development of the motion picture industry as well as DEFA's first ten years of films.

Two tensions inform the story of East German art during this period.

The first of these involves art's role in socialist society. Immediately after the war, the Soviet occupiers and the SED assigned art an emancipatory function; by the end of the forties, however, there was disagreement about what that implied. Did raising socialist consciousness mean teaching individuals to think critically about Germany's past and future? Or did it mean fostering a selfless identity with the socialist cause that would inspire heroic feats of labor? On the one hand, Marxism was supposed to be a rational philosophy, whose truths were consistent with reason and science. On the other hand, as the art critic Boris Groys has argued, Soviet-style socialism conceived of itself as a poetic process. "New" individuals were supposed to achieve the society of tomorrow through the force of belief and creative will alone.[3]

The second tension is the GDR's self-definition. Did the new state represent an autonomous society, or was it still embedded in a larger German nation? Were artists participating in the construction of a radically new society, or were they fighting for the soul of an existing one? Implicit in this issue was the status of Germany's cultural legacy. Paradoxically, while the regime exhorted artists to salvage the best of Germany's classical tradition, Party leaders were often highly suspicious of twentieth-century modernist art, even in cases where its creators were Communists. An added complication for the film industry was the Party's ideological hostility toward commercial culture, the cradle of the conventional film industry. The German Communist cinema of the Weimar period had been relatively limited in scope.[4] Some of its figures, most notably the director Slatan Dudow, had survived the war. Still, they were pledged to rebuilding an industry that was essentially commercial in nature. Indeed, many of the individuals who came to play prominent roles in the East German cinema were quite recent converts to the Communist cause.

The most telling symbol of the dilemma facing the new DEFA studios, the necessity of shaping a radically new cinema out of the remnants of a discredited one, was its location, the grounds of the erstwhile UFA (Universum Film Aktiengesellschaft) studios in Babelsberg, a suburb of Potsdam outside Berlin. Founded with the encouragement of the German military during World War I, UFA quickly grew to become the largest commercial film studio in Europe, Germany's Hollywood. While many of the classics of the Weimar cinema had been produced there, the vast majority of UFA's production had been conventional entertainment works, such as "revue" films featuring leggy showgirls dancing in massive formations or historical "costume" films with nationalist messages. These were precisely the type of "escapist" products of "bourgeois false consciousness" that Communist film critics tended to frown upon. During the Third

Reich, UFA became synonymous with the many Nazi propaganda pictures produced there.

From the beginning, DEFA defined itself in clear opposition to the UFA tradition. Still, some years would have to pass before the German socialist cinema would assume contours of its own. During its first decade, DEFA's most notable successes were films set in the past that depicted Communist "antifascist" resistance to Nazism. Artists found themselves particularly hard pressed to fulfill the regime's call beginning in the late forties for pictures that would both celebrate the new order and raise audiences' political consciousness, or what by the end of the decade came to be known as "socialist present-day" films (*sozialistische Gegenwartsfilme*). Ironically, much of the studio's production remained almost indistinguishable from conventional entertainment films until well into the fifties. Obviously, the uncertain parameters of cultural production in the GDR did not help matters. The function of art in socialist society remained subject to sudden and radical shifts as the regime struggled both to legitimize itself before a mistrustful populace and to position itself within the volatile geopolitics of the Cold War.

This situation only began to approach resolution near the end of the fifties. By this time, the GDR was clearly moving toward definition as an autonomous socialist society distinct from the Federal Republic, even if officials still emphasized the ultimate goal of national unification. Equally important, artists and the regime had their first major controversies behind them, and they were becoming accustomed to negotiating the tensions that would define their evolving relationship for the next three decades. Despite the ruthless suppression of independent media outlets at the end of the forties, artists were able to force the Party to acknowledge their role as constructive critics and grant them on paper, if less so in practice, a measure of limited autonomy. These developments profoundly affected how filmmakers approached the task of depicting East German society. Individual directors and scriptwriters were beginning to overcome their initial hesitation toward the regime's call for works depicting socialist society, an undertaking clearly rife with ideological uncertainty. Filmmakers had embarked on a process of developing images that would confirm East Germany as an independent society while challenging the regime's vision of a land moving harmoniously toward the future.

THE SOVIET OCCUPATION: ART AS EMANCIPATOR

The history of the Soviet Occupation Zone (SBZ)—the territorial unit that preceded the GDR from 1945 to 1949—had both cruel and promising aspects. On the one hand, there were forced population transfers, mass rapes, severe economic retribution, inhuman detention camps, and thousands of cases of arbitrary persecution. On the other hand, the arrival of the Red Army for many opponents and victims of Nazism represented liberation. Even for many suspicious of the Soviets, their presence was a new beginning after years of war. Germany's defeat was profound and devastating. Building on the Popular Front (Volksfront) platform first declared by the Communist International in the mid-thirties, the Soviet Military Administration's (SMAD) set about establishing an "antifascist, democratic" order. To prevent the political fragmentation that occurred during the Weimar Republic, the Soviets insisted on the formation of various nonpartisan "alliances" uniting representatives of all social interests. Cooperation between the "bloc" parties was formalized as early as July 1945; they included besides the two traditional working-class parties a Christian, a liberal, and later, at the insistence of the Soviets, a nationalist one. Unions were gathered into the FDGB (Free German Union Alliance) in February 1946, and the youth of the land were organized as the FDJ (Free German Youth) the following month.

Some contemporary reports suggest that the initial popular resonance of Soviet policy may have been considerable. The majority of Germans hated and feared the Russians, but mistrust toward the other allies, especially the Americans, also existed.[5] Indeed, a certain anticapitalist consensus took hold of Germany immediately after the war. Even the first platforms of the conservative West German Christian Democratic Union (CDU) linked fascism with capitalism and called for at least limited public takeover of private economic sectors.[6] Contemporary commentators also noted the similarity in appeal between Nazism and Soviet-style socialism, both of which displayed a penchant for militarized displays of mass unity. Thus the philologist Victor Klemperer, who chose to stay in the East, noted with some concern the continued prevalence of battle metaphors in political speech despite the defeat of Hitler.[7] In addition, the alleged nonpartisanship of the institutions the Soviets established was consistent with traditional German conceptions of the state as the neutral executor of policies dictated by exigency and reason.

In no single realm was the potential affinity between the Soviet occupiers and the defeated Germans greater than in their shared reverence of art. Only days after the unconditional surrender on May 8, 1945, concerts were held in Berlin. The commander of the city granted permission for Berlin theaters to reopen as early as May 16.[8] By July 1945, one American cultural officer surveying the already flourishing Berlin art scene complained to his superiors about "an almost fanatical honoring of art and artists" on the part of the Soviets.[9] To galvanize artists and intellectuals opposed to fascism, the Soviets formed the Kulturbund zur demokratischen Erneuerung Deutschlands (Cultural Alliance for the Democratic Renewal of Germany). The organization's key figure was Johannes R. Becher, the poet and future GDR cultural minister, who returned from Soviet exile in June 1945. Among the seven points of the Kulturbund's initial program were the "destruction of Nazi ideology in all areas of life and knowledge," the "founding of a national unity front of German intellectual workers," and the "rediscovery and support of the free, humanistic, and true national traditions of our people." The organization's practical work included providing material support to artists as well as organizing exhibits and lectures. The Kulturbund's publishing house, the Aufbau-Verlag, brought out more than 100 titles—a total of 2.5 million volumes—in less than two years, no mean feat in a war-ravaged country. In addition, Becher was able to win the sympathies of many non-Communist artists, including the renowned authors Hans Fallada, Ricarda Huch, Arnold Zweig, and Heinrich Mann.[10]

In light of future developments, many commentators have interpreted the initial tolerance of Soviet cultural policy, along with the wider "antifascist, democratic transformation" that had been proclaimed, as a tactical ploy.[11] From the beginning, all claims concerning official nonpartisanship were belied by the practice of filling pivotal positions in the Kulturbund and other institutions with Communists. By the early fifties, when Becher was writing hymns in praise of Stalin and Walter Ulbricht, some of the artists initially welcomed into the SBZ with open arms were being expunged from the official canon for being decadent modernists. At the same time, the attention paid to art during the Soviet occupation was more than a question of strategic advantage. The Soviet administrators and the KPD functionaries who returned from exile and were charged with running the SBZ may have been skilled manipulators of historical truth, but they were also susceptible to their own productions. The pathetic reverence paid by the conquerors to the cultural greats of the vanquished possessed a certain sincerity. Germany was prostrate, the landscape marred by war, the crimes of the Nazis still fresh. As guardians and propagators of Germany's classical heritage, artists were assigned a special role in emancipating their compatriots just awakening from fascism's trance. Artists provided a link between their ailing land and its better self, between national parochialism and universal progress. Like teachers, artists were supposed to educate the German people and instill in them a love for the noblest of values.

Soviet occupation policy was also characterized by simple pragmatism. At least to contemporaries, the division of Germany was anything but inevitable: no one immediately after the Second World War knew the future. The economic organization of Germany and its place in the international order were open questions for all sides involved. By appealing to Germany's own cultural traditions, the Soviets were clearly seeking to make their general policies palatable to as broad a constituency as possible. After all, their Communist clients might soon have to compete in nationwide elections with other parties. At the very least, the SED faced the task of establishing a positive profile for itself that could appeal to a profoundly mistrustful and traumatized populace. A statement by Walter Ulbricht captures well the mixture of high-minded idealism and concern for political advantage that characterized early cultural policy in the SBZ. For him, the classical heritage offered a key for influencing those who might be at first suspicious of the blessings of Marxism. As he told an assembly of fellow functionaries in Brandenburg in June 1945, "It is necessary that you tell the youth something about the role of Prussian militarism and about the lies the Nazis told. Then you have to begin acquainting them with German literature, with Heine, Goethe, Schiller, etc. Do not begin with Marx and Engels. They will not understand that."[12]

The SED never reversed its position concerning the crucial importance of Germany's classical heritage. Similarly, antifascism remained an essential component of the regime's ideological self-understanding and a favorite theme for its artists. Until the very end, the GDR depicted itself as both the better Germany willing to make a consistent break with the past and the one true heir of German cultural traditions. By the time the GDR was founded in October 1949, however, the priority in cultural matters had already shifted away from a humanistic alliance against fascism to the construction of socialism. Artists and others came under increasing pressure to renounce former political and social allegiances and ally themselves with the new order. This trend intensified as the SED underwent a series of purges[13] and organized itself more strictly along Leninist principles stressing the Party's role as the advance guard of the working class. As early as January 1949, the SED, during its First Party Conference, had declared its intent to establish itself as a "Party of the new type." During its Third Party Convention in July 1950, the SED promised to accelerate this transformation. A new song composed for the occasion by the ballad singer, Ernst Busch, was simply titled "The Party That Is Always Right."

Consistent with its new emphasis on directed political mobilization, the SED began to insist that art serve a direct political purpose. Art's pretense of autonomy became fair game for functionaries. In December 1948, Alexander Dymshits, head of the SMAD's cultural section, published an article in the *Tägliche Rundschau*, the SMAD's German-language organ, in which he criticized abstract painting for lacking social relevance. A similar condemnation of "manifestations of decadence [as well as] formalist and naturalist deformations of art" was adopted by the SED at its First Party Conference the following month.[14] At the end of 1949, officials shut down Alfred Kantorowicz's attempt at a pluralist literary journal, *Ost und West*. Spring 1950 witnessed a critique of Anna Seghers's novel *Die Toten bleiben jung* (The Dead Stay Young) for not containing sufficiently positive proletarian protagonists. This so-called "Formalism Debate" reached a high point in January 1951 with the appearance of a second article on the subject in the *Tägliche Rundschau*, "Paths and False Turns of Modern Art." Written under the pseudonym N. Orlow, the article dismissed most modern art as being bourgeois and decadent, while describing socialist realism as the vigorous direction of the future. Famous controversies followed the Orlow piece, including those concerning the opera *Lukullus* by Bertolt Brecht and Paul Dessau and an exhibition at the Academy of Arts dedicated to the sculptor Ernst Barlach.[15]

THE LAUNCHING OF DEFA

In many ways, the early history of the East German cinema reflected the shifts in cultural policy during the SBZ and the first years of the GDR. A period of relative tolerance immediately after the war soon gave way to one characterized by increasingly crude political intervention. The Soviets and their German clients also took a number of quiet measures in order to ensure control of the film industry from the beginning. Nevertheless, too narrow a focus on shifts in official policy can obscure the considerable complexity of the situation. The very vehemence with which functionaries denounced art's pretense of autonomy was an indication of the vital importance their ideology attached to the cultural realm in achieving socialism. Ironically, the artists who came under public attack were almost without exception loyal to the regime, and their works were hardly critical in explicit content. By the same token, even though the formalism debate was a classic example of a Soviet import—a similar controversy that was if anything far more brutal in its consequences was unleashed in the Soviet Union by the cultural minister Zhdanov in 1946—the SED leadership seems to have more enthusiastically promoted its introduction into the SBZ than did the SMAD itself.[16]

DEFA's first years are sometimes referred to as its golden age. For one brief moment rich in promise and possibility, DEFA seemed the designated heir of the German cinema. The first issues of *Neue Filmwelt*, a journal established in the Soviet Zone to promote the reconstruction of the motion picture industry, featured articles by a wide range of authors.

These included established figures in the prewar and Nazi-era German film industry, such as Paul Wegener, Josef von Baky, and Arthur Maria Rabenalt. In contrast, Alfred Lindemann had earned his reputation in the Communist avant-garde cinema of the twenties, whereas others, like Kurt Maetzig, were relatively unknown figures who were about to make names for themselves. All had been asked to respond to the question "Whither German film?" While opinions varied, there was basic agreement that filmmakers could not return to what had been. As Wolfgang Staudte emphasized, "We stand at the crossways. Will the cinema choose the difficult route along narrow ways into the region of art, [while] loaded down with the responsibility of inner responsibility—or will it march once again . . . along the cheap avenue of tawdry effect in the realm of a mediocre entertainment industry?"

The best-remembered productions of the immediate postwar years all had antifascist themes. Chief among them was Staudte's own *Die Mörder sind unter uns* (The Murderers Are among Us, 1946), the first DEFA film to premiere. This work concerns a doctor who returns to Berlin after the war a broken man but, with the help of a woman who survived a concentration camp, finds new strength. The film ends dramatically with the doctor determined to shoot his former superior officer, who was responsible for the murder of innocent hostages during the war, while the woman seeks to stop this private act of retribution. Kurt Maetzig's debut film the following year, *Ehe im Schatten* (Marriage in the Shadows, 1946), represented another attempt to confront Germans with moral lessons from the past. Its protagonists are a young married couple, both promising actors. Although she is Jewish, they remain in Germany after the Nazis come to power because his career is blossoming. Despite increasing pressure, he refuses to divorce her, but also represses the danger of their situation. Finally, they must pay the price for their political blindness and are left no choice but to commit suicide. Yet a third popular film was Erich Engel's *Die Affäre Blum* (The Blum Affair), which premiered at the end of 1948. It was based on the true story of a Jewish manufacturer in Weimar Germany wrongly accused of a murder actually committed by a Freikorps member.

Grand talk of a new cinema aside, all three of these films were aesthetically conventional and displayed many of the hallmarks of German prewar moviemaking, such as the highly stylized use of shadows. The films relied on pathos and melodrama to thematize the recent past. Ironically, the cameraman for both *Die Mörder sind unter uns* and *Ehe im Schatten*, Friedl Behn-Grund, also shot the 1941 UFA Film *Ich klage an* (I Accuse), a film sponsored by the Nazis to justify euthanasia.[17] Also, the composer of *Ehe im Schatten*'s score, Wolfgang Zeller, had written the music for Veit

Harlan's notoriously anti-Semitic film *Jud Süss* (Jew Süss, 1939). If it were not for the fact that they were produced at an entirely different place and time, many early DEFA films could be appropriately compared to the American television miniseries of the late 1970s, *Holocaust*. The Jewish protagonists in the Maetzig and Engel films are in particular depicted positively, yet in a stereotypical fashion, as highly cultivated individuals representing the best of German middle-class values, such as loyalty and honesty. The injustice they experience serves to indict a political order that wantonly deprived private happiness from those deserving it.

There is little in DEFA's early antifascist films that identifies them as specifically Communist. The same statement does not apply in equal measure to all of the studio's productions from its early years. Milo Harbich's *Freies Land* (Free Land), released in 1946, depicts the land reform carried out by the SMAD. Arthur Maria Rabenalt's *Chemie und Liebe* (Chemistry and Love, 1948), based on an idea of the great Hungarian film theorist Béla Balász, is a fantastic parody that ends with its protagonist, a scientist, fleeing the land Kapitalia. Yet, at the time they were first shown, even these works expressed political sentiments whose resonance was hardly limited to Communists.[18]

Overall, DEFA's initial output was quite diverse and displayed varied lines of continuity with earlier German cinema. Georg Klaren emulated expressionist art films of the twenties with an adaptation of Georg Büchner's classic play *Wozzeck* (1947). Gerhard Lamprecht's *Irgendwo in Berlin* (Somewhere in Berlin, 1946) followed in a line of so-called "Zille" films by that director. Named after the great caricaturist of early-twentieth-century Berlin, Heinrich Zille, these presented a sentimental picture of urban lower-class life. Others, including Peter Pewas in his film *Strassenbekanntschaft* (Street Acquaintance, 1948), which warned against the dangers of venereal disease, oriented themselves toward the international cinema, particularly Italian neorealism.[19] DEFA was even in contact with one of neorealism's great masters, Roberto Rossellini, whose *Germany Year Zero* (1947) was originally planned as a coproduction with Babelsberg.[20] As the next chapter explores in greater detail, neorealism resonated strongly with alternative filmmaking traditions in Germany. Both the German left and the Italian movement rejected the glitz and glamour of commercial cinema in favor of pictures attempting to address issues allegedly of more genuine concern to audiences.

THE PARTY TAKES CHARGE

In marked contrast to this thematic and aesthetic pluralism, the studio's early institutional history contains some Machiavellian undertones.

The initiative for founding the studio came from the Soviets. In accordance with the Potsdam Agreement, the SMAD in October 1945 confiscated all property belonging to the Nazi film industry. At the same time, the German Central Administration for People's Education (DVV), part of the governmental structure that the Soviets established in July 1945, began taking stock of the available personnel. Under the supervision of Herbert Volkmann, head of the DVV's cultural section, a "Filmaktiv," or action committee, was formed in October. Its members consisted exclusively of German Communists.[21] On November 22, filmmakers, writers, and representatives from the SMAD, DVV, and KPD met in the Hotel Adlon in Berlin to discuss getting the film industry off the ground.[22] Despite wrecked studios, lacking equipment and short on materials such as film stock,[23] the reorganization of the motion picture industry progressed quickly. A newsreel, *Der Augenzeuge* (The Eyewitness), began appearing regularly under Maetzig's direction starting in February 1946. By March, filming had commenced on *Die Mörder sind unter uns*. In May, the head of the information division of the SMAD, Colonel Sergei Tulpanow, handed over an official production license to DEFA.[24] The site of the ceremony was the new studio's Babelsberg headquarters, the mammoth production facility that only months earlier had belonged to UFA.

From the beginning, the centralized, state-supported nature of the future film industry was clear. DEFA was originally set up as a private firm—hence its acronym, which stood for *Deutsche Film AG* (German Film Corporation)—but the studio was entirely dependent on the SMAD or DVV for financial backing. The possibility of independent revenues was further restricted by the exclusive distribution rights held by the Soviet film ministry. The studio soon also lost whatever nominal legal independence it ever had. Beginning in July 1947, the studio was reorganized so that the Soviets held a majority interest, while the SED had a minority one.[25] In November, an additional contract was signed between DEFA and the SED Central Committee, assuring the latter's right to influence film production directly.[26]

Whether these organizational changes in themselves represented an intensification of political control or merely its normalization is difficult to assess. Whatever the case, if DEFA's dependence on the SMAD and SED became more clearly defined, related measures ensured the studio's greater control over the economic and material aspects of film production. Its reorganization as an SDAG allowed DEFA to take over facilities and equipment previously leased from the Soviets. The studio also became better capitalized,[27] and its supply situation, particularly with regard to raw film material and fuel, improved.[28] At the end of 1948, DEFA further gained the right to distribute its own films.[29]

A clearer sign of fundamental shifts in cultural policy than the studio's restructuring were changes in its top management that began occurring in 1948. From the start, Communists had occupied key posts in the studio—for example, all three of DEFA's original corporate officers were KPD members.[30] At the same time, people who were not Party members also held many important positions. This situation, however, changed as the Cold War intensified and the SED began to increasingly emphasize the Soviet Union as the sole model for German reconstruction.[31] In a *Betriebsgeschichte* (firm or factory history) from the late seventies, Albert Wilkening, who was a fixture in the studio's top management for many years, wrote candidly of the reasons motivating certain replacements in personnel. One of the first people to go was DEFA's production director, Alfred Lindemann, who was replaced by Wilkening himself. According to the latter, the reason for Lindemann's firing was "neglected political and professional self-improvement." Since Wilkening credits himself with having devised DEFA's first production plan that same year, presumably Lindemann was either unable or unwilling to run the studio according to socialist management principles.[32] In the spring of 1949, Sepp Schwab, a hard-line Party functionary if there ever was one, was named to DEFA's board of trustees; when the board was then abolished, he became the studio's sole director.[33] Soon after Schwab's appointment, Wolf von Gordon, who was without Party affiliation, was fired as chief dramaturge—a key studio position that included responsibility for script development—because he was "politically only ready and prepared to accompany us on the antifascist humanist path."[34]

A further indication of the Party's desire to mobilize the film industry for political purposes was the decision made to transfer its supervision from the culture section to the agitation section at SED headquarters in July 1949.[35] After the studio's first two yearly production plans were approved by the SED Politburo itself, a special "DEFA Commission" was set up in 1950 to facilitate closer supervision of the film industry. In addition, the commission seems to have effectively assumed the function of censorship previously exercised by the Soviets[36] and influenced distribution decisions as well.[37] At the end of 1950, the Soviets relinquished their ownership share in the studio. Now both nominal ownership and control of the industry were in German hands.[38]

THE STUDIO'S FIRST CRISIS

Ironically, far from leading to ideological clarity, the shift in cultural policy and the changes within the studio resulted in an atmosphere of confusion. Not only did projects already in production become liable to revision, but script development broke down. Filmmakers were no longer sure what was expected of them, and they probably feared reprisals if they were to commit unwittingly a political mistake. Finding enough filmable ideas became increasingly difficult.[39] A memo of Albert Wilkening from February 1950 is very direct in its assessment of the situation:

> The formation of the production program relied from the beginning on the recommendations of freelance [filmmakers]. . . . While in the initial period these recommendations were brought into production relatively informally, the board of directors began to criticize increasingly the recommendations after the submission of the treatment, the script, or even the finished film. It demanded more or less severe changes. . . . This [behavior] led to a general uncertainty. No one was really sure what the board really wanted.
>
> The DEFA board increasingly represented the position of direct methods with clear, unambiguous, and outspoken messages. The freelance [filmmakers] in contrast preferred the path of indirect messages, because they considered these psychologically more appropriate and better suited to the expressive means of film. It did not remain unknown that [these filmmakers] were regarded by the board as reactionaries or [politically] indifferent.[40]

Not surprisingly, such conditions had catastrophic effects on the studio's efficiency. Having turned out twelve full-length feature films in 1949, the studio managed only eight in 1950. In 1951, output increased again to eleven, but it fell well short of the eighteen foreseen by DEFA's production plan.[41] Moreover, 1952 and 1953 saw the completion of a miserable five films each.[42] Even what little did get released hardly pleased the Party. In a July 1952 resolution, the Politburo lamented that convincingly depicted working-class protagonists were absent from DEFA films.[43] As Politburo member Hermann Axen elaborated a month later, "The quantity and quality of films devoted to the peaceful construction of our economy and our culture stands in no relation to the achievements of our activists, innovators, and our [farmers]."[44]

While the studio itself was not directly drawn into the formalism debates that engulfed other artistic fields during the early fifties, the banning of one of DEFA's most ambitious and best-realized productions to date, Falk Harnack's 1951 adaptation of Arnold Zweig's novel *Das Beil von Wandsbek* (The Butcher of Wandsbek), sent a clear signal. Regardless of their artistic merit, films dealing with morbid themes and moral dilemmas were of little interest to the Party.[45] Political functionaries called for "socialist realism" and insisted on films brimming with confidence, populated by exemplary "positive heroes," and able to convince viewers that socialism was triumphing. Even films that dealt with political themes were rejected as mere "critical realism" or as progressive by capitalist standards but ill suited to aiding in the construction of the new society. Part and parcel of this development was the rapid end to the relative pluralism of DEFA's first years. In addition, aesthetically innovative works, whether they exhibited the influence of Weimar-era expressionism or contemporary neorealism, became politically suspect.

In effect, filmmakers were also being forced to abandon their most successful subject matter: the recent past. At the same time, no clear notion existed of what was supposed to take its place. The Party's demands were vague. Ironically, of eight exemplary movies specified by the Politburo in its resolution, all but one concerned the most immediate postwar era or an earlier historical period. Two films singled out for additional praise for fulfilling the requirements of a "democratic public" were not even set in the GDR, nor did they emphasize the building of the new society. Kurt Maetzig's *Der Rat der Götter* (Council of the Gods, 1950) adapted the history of the I. G. Farben chemical concern for propaganda purposes. Martin Hellberg's *Das verurteilte Dorf* (The Condemned Village, 1951) concerned a fictional West German village threatened by plans for a U.S. military base.

Of course, some films from the early fifties did attempt to depict the struggle for socialism. From the SED's perspective, probably the most benign of these were a series of what were essentially espionage thrillers. Their political message was simple enough. The battle for Germany was one between crafty capitalists from the West and honest workers from the East. The former were determined to do anything in order to deprive the latter of the fruits of their labor and ingenuity. Such movies tended to be cheaply produced, low-priority projects, and DEFA's most experienced directors shied away from them. The one exception, *Familie Benthin* (The Benthin Family), was rushed into production in 1951 at the Party's insistence and seems to have been an unmitigated disaster. Despite scripting by such literary luminaries as Johannes R. Becher and Kurt Barthel, none of the three directors who worked on the movie was willing to accept responsibility for it.[46]

Other films concentrated on individuals making a life for themselves in the new state but gave socialism too saccharine a coating. For example, Richard Groschopp's *Modell Bianka* (The Bianka Pattern, 1951) features "activists" from rival factories who are rewarded for their dedication with trips to the same ski resort, fall in love there, and learn that the secret to socialist competition is mutual assistance. Some of these productions did well at the box office, but official critics condemned them as superficial and inauthentic, a return to the commercial cinematic tradition that DEFA was supposed to transcend. In future years, such productions would also be often cited as examples of "schematism," or the use of simplistic plots in order to convey an ideological message.[47]

Given the extreme tentativeness of the East German state in its first years, filmmakers hardly had much room for experimentation. The regime urgently demanded their participation in constructing a radically new society, but it was fearful of the least challenge to its authority. The one exception to the otherwise bland films set in the GDR from the early fifties confirms this general rule. Initial reviews of Slatan Dudow's 1952 production, *Frauenschicksale* (The Destinies of Women), were effusive, but the film found little favor with the German Democratic Women's Alliance (Demokratische Frauenbund Deutschlands), the official organization representing the very segment of the population Dudow wanted to honor. The alliance's leaders objected that the film's four female protagonists were not typical of the GDR. Their susceptibility to a Western seducer was not representative of the qualities characterizing the Democratic Republic's women.[48] By choosing as his focal point a social group for whom vulnerability was traditionally a virtue, Dudow had found a solution for the problems associated with depicting a social order that could not admit a weakness. Yet even this ingenious approach was not quite enough to satisfy all his critics.

Another reason for the industry's low morale during the early fifties was its own grandiose ambitions. If politically motivated filmmakers and Party bosses could agree on one thing, it was on the glorious future's novelty. The demand for a radically new German cinema remained consistent in official statements and in those of filmmakers throughout the postwar period and the fifties. Nevertheless, the studio was a conservative institution. The Communists had in many respects not so much established a new film industry as patched together the remnants of an existing one. Both the facilities and the personnel were largely inherited from the prewar period. Except for a handful of individuals, DEFA's staff came from commercial film and did not view themselves as members of a socialist avant-garde. Although few alternatives to such expertise existed, this dependence belied the official claim that socialist property relations would immediately yield a different cinematic practice. Furthermore, the regime and the studio's management were themselves keenly interested in economic efficiency. What the functionaries demanded was "art for the masses," or films that would be popular. Room for formal experimentation did not exist. DEFA was already overtaxed in trying to find politically palatable projects consistent with conventional film aesthetics.

An additional problem for DEFA that became evident beginning in the late forties was the loss of personnel to the West. A letter from the director Martin Hellberg sent to Minister President Otto Grotewohl in December 1952 complained that the studio was firing skilled workers right and left.[49] Others presumably departed on their own initiative for better opportunities in the West. DEFA also alienated artists who might otherwise have been willing to work in the East. Falk Harnack offers a prime example: he ended his career in the GDR after the banning of his film *Das Beil von Wandsbek*. At the same time, even though increasing pressure was placed on individuals in the late forties to choose sides in the Cold War, there was no official policy against Westerners. Directors and scriptwriters from the Federal Republic of Germany (FRG) and West Berlin continued to be responsible for many DEFA films, albeit rarely those of high political priority.[50] In fact, the studio's director who was best known internationally at the time, Wolfgang Staudte, was active on both sides of the Iron Curtain.[51] DEFA also continued to employ a handful of skilled workers from West Berlin right up until the Wall was built in 1961. The final push to rid DEFA of Westerners began only in the late fifties.

Despite the crisis that had developed, many of the recommendations contained in the Politburo's 1952 Film Resolution were of a canned, formulaic nature. These included "a systematic and free discussion" within the studio of the conclusions reached at the recent Second Party Conference, the systematic study of Marxist teachings, and an all-out effort to increase the effectiveness of the studio's party organization. The resolution made only oblique reference to the creative paralysis affecting the film industry by chiding writers for regarding "the composition of a film script as beneath their 'literary honor.'"[52]

Nevertheless, the Politburo's resolution admonished DEFA's management to effect the "political-artistic education" of filmmakers not through fiat and bureaucratic means but rather through "principled and comradely persuasion." Specific proposals indicated a willingness to grant the film industry increased autonomy and allow technical experts and artists greater weight in decision making. One measure had both practical and symbolic significance. The DEFA Commission, which answered directly to the Party, was replaced with a Staatliches Komitee für Filmfragen (State Committee for Film Issues). For the first time, competence in aesthetic and political issues was yielded to a state office that took control of the economic and technical aspects of film production and distribution.[53]

Another major move was DEFA's breakup into four *Volkseigne Betriebe*, or state enterprises. Independent studios were now respectively responsible for feature films, newsreels, technical and documentary films, and children's movies. Hans Rodenberg was named head of the feature film studio. An influential adviser to the Party's top brass in cultural matters, he had in contrast to Schwab considerable professional experience in film and theater. Still, these measures were only a prelude. A drastic shock to the entire East German state would have to come before DEFA's situation changed markedly.

JUNE 17, 1953

The film industry was not the only part of GDR society in which efforts at full economic and political mobilization were proving counterproductive. Even as the SED's Second Party Conference announced "the planned construction of socialism in the GDR" on July 8, 1952, the regime's push to establish a self-sufficient socialist economy was running into difficulties compounded by the continuing massive exodus of citizens to the West. In its efforts to achieve its ambitious plans, the Party leadership resorted to desperate measures that antagonized the already put-upon populace. During the winter and spring of 1953 the regime increased taxes and stopped offering affordable food rations to the independently employed. White-collar professionals lost privileges that were originally granted in order to keep them in the GDR. Next came measures that affected workers. Food and clothing prices increased; alcohol prices went up; transportation subsidies were abolished. All the while, the forced collectivization of farmers was in full swing.[54]

With the death of Stalin in March, the SED came under increasing pressure from his successors to relax its course. Signs of popular unrest also made themselves felt as early as April 1953. Undeterred, the regime took May Day as an occasion to announce new production norms that implied a salary cut for many workers. Although the regime at Moscow's behest soon reversed this and other measures in the "New Course" announced on June 9, the damage had been done. On June 16, workers constructing East Berlin's monumental residential avenue, the Stalin-Allee, marched on the Ministerial Council Building.[55] The next day, hundreds of thousands of protesters jammed the streets of Berlin and other cities.[56]

The revolt took the SED leadership by surprise. Ulbricht and others sought refuge with the Soviet military. If the Red Army had not intervened, the GDR would have crumbled. At the same time, the crisis ultimately helped the regime consolidate its power. The New Course's introduction at Soviet insistence at first put Ulbricht's leadership in jeopardy. After the revolt's end, the first secretary improved his position by disposing of two other Politburo members who had attempted to exploit his temporary weakness by calling for inner-Party democracy.[57] Of greater significance, the New Course emphasized the importance of encouraging inter-German relations, a possible sign that the Soviet leadership was once again considering reopening the German question.[58] If this danger did exist, the uprising's failure and the lack of Western intervention confirmed the Cold War's permanence, the essential precondition of the GDR's survival. Any danger that Stalin's death could lead to a major shift in geopolitics was now over. No immediate alternative existed to Germany's division.

As soon as the dust began to settle from the revolt, the regime sought to take the wind out of its enemies' sails by granting concessions. Otto Grotewohl proclaimed, "If masses of workers do not understand the Party, then the Party is guilty, not the workers."[59] Not only did the Politburo push the New Course with enthusiasm, it promised to reorient the GDR's industrial output toward fulfilling consumer needs. To finance these policies, Ulbricht obtained considerable economic concessions from the Soviets. For its part, the SED had to peddle the New Course's reconciliatory language concerning German unity, but that summer when Moscow renewed Stalin's offer of reunification contained in his famous March 1952 note, new conditions made a favorable response from the West even more unlikely than before.[60]

The uprising of June 17 also had major repercussions within the SED despite the purge of Ulbricht opponents that soon followed. In keeping with the New Course, the Politburo proclaimed increased inner-Party democracy and an end to bureaucratic despotism. Prominent artists and intellectuals took these promises at face value, and, for a couple of short months, East Berlin's newspapers and journals contained lively debates about possible reform.

On June 30, the East Berlin German Academy of Art issued a declaration demanding that "the responsibility of the artist to the public must be restored. . . . State organs should . . . refrain from every administrative measure in questions of artistic production and style. Criticism must be left to the public."[61] Three days later the Kulturbund floated a set of proposals containing similar language.[62] On July 14, another influential cultural figure, Wolfgang Harich, published an article in the *Berliner Zeitung* vehemently attacking two art functionaries, Wilhelm Girnus and Kurt Magritz, both initiators of the formalism debate. Harich argued: "It serves realism little . . . when ignorance and ideological uncertainty declare themselves its judge . . . when . . . cultural politicians . . . fall into the hands of careerists . . . [and] seek refuge in repressive administrative measures."[63]

However harsh they may have sounded, these charges were still very much those of a loyal opposition. For example, one of the regime's most prominent critics, Bertolt Brecht, conceded: "It is the task of art criticism to reject political primitiveness. In this respect, our [previous] art policy was not without success."[64] Regardless of their critical viewpoint, most individuals who participated in the debate concerning cultural policy shared the regime's existential angst on June 17. For them, the reactionary forces perceived to be at work in West Germany were more dangerous than the SED's excessive zeal. Even the writer Stefan Heym, a fairly independent voice, emphasized, "On June 17, a considerable portion of German workers fell for a much larger fascist provocation."[65]

Although many artists had clearly chosen sides in the Cold War, they had not clearly endorsed East Germany as an autonomous society. An important demand echoed in many articles and statements was the maintenance of cultural ties with West Germany. In addition, in arguing for a revision of realism as a category of cultural criticism, critics of the regime were generally calling for art that could still transcend political affiliation and address the populace of both German states. Demands for more artistic autonomy, a freer press, and greater recognition of expert authority were often coupled with reaffirmations of German unity as a central political objective.

The regime's initial response was conciliatory toward its artist-critics, but by September the tide was clearly turning. On October 19, Otto Grotewohl told a meeting of cultural figures in no uncertain terms, "We are not of the opinion that the New Course consists of a lazy liberalism. In our opinion, even in the New Course, one cannot forgo direction and clarity."[66] The force of earlier criticism was long spent by the time the regime implemented reforms. The most significant of these was the establishment of the Ministry of Culture (MfK) under Becher's direction, which assumed functions previously exercised by three different "state committees." Whether this move ultimately improved artistic freedom is more than questionable. Initially, though, the new ministry was viewed as a concession to artists, as an institution that would grant them a certain degree of self-regulation through participation in various official panels. At the very least, some unpopular functionaries, most notably Girnus and Magritz, were out of power.

DEFA AND THE NEW COURSE

For the East German cinema, the uprising of June 17 also led to a reevaluation of official policy. The Academy of Art's declaration of June

30 complained that there were simply too few DEFA films and that these lacked thematic diversity. Their appeal was limited to a small population segment, and not enough movies had an "all-German" (*gesamtdeutsch*) character. The regime largely adopted this stance as its own. An editorial in the fall 1953 issue of *Deutsche Filmkunst*, a trade journal published by the State Film Commission, observed, "Precisely the best, the most progressive and numerically largest part of our audience, which works with eagerness and optimism, has had enough of the dry tone in film."[67] The piece emphasized that just as the populace had the right to expect a better assortment of consumer goods, there was a need for a more pleasing palette of cultural offerings.

Another quality observers found lacking in DEFA films was emotion. In September, Walter Ulbricht proclaimed before the Central Committee, "The population . . . demands more films and interesting films, films concerning not only work, but also love."[68] According to the editors of *Deutsche Filmkunst*, DEFA's failure to deliver such movies not only left audiences disenchanted but was out of step with the advance of the new society: "Above all, people's feelings and the quality of their many-sided relations give insight into the new, progressive, and beautiful, or into the embarrassing, backward, and ugly of the obsolete and dying out."[69]

The ideas expressed in this last passage were in themselves nothing new. For example, several articles making similar arguments had appeared in *Neues Deutschland* in February 1953. The chief lament then was that DEFA films about love were wooden and failed to convey the special intensity of this most beautiful of all human emotions under socialism.[70] Still, if June 17 did not lead to a fundamental revision of the regime's goals for the film industry, the uprising resulted in a more pragmatic assessment of its immediate priorities. Greater emphasis was placed on film as a form of entertainment rather than as a means of political agitation. Filmmakers were also cut some slack in their tortured quest for a cinema worthy of the dawning age. In one speech, Otto Grotewohl warned against the ill effects of applying exaggerated standards. While the minister president ostensibly addressed the behavior of press film critics, his words clearly echoed earlier complaints by artists about the regime's cultural policy:

.For months the public has been discussing how to create a cinema [that] can illuminate all human life expressions and make them come to life. We know [that] that is a difficult task for our filmmakers. After the first hesitant attempts at walking . . . are made, an improperly oriented criticism then falls all over [their] serious efforts, destroy[ing] and ripp[ing] them out of the ground. The consequences of treating our films thusly [will be] that those charged with carrying out such tasks [will] put down their tools in discouragement and no longer find the energy to continue their pioneering work in these questions.[71]

At least in one respect, the slackening of ideological rigor evident in Grotewohl's speech paid off handsomely for the film industry. The studio's efficiency increased dramatically during the mid-fifties. In 1954, the output of features rose from five to fifteen films. The following year, seventeen projects were completed. Although DEFA's annual output in the future would occasionally exceed twenty,[72] the studio had essentially achieved its basic production capacity.

Faced with the simultaneous goals of increasing production, presenting better entertainment, and achieving "all-German" appeal, DEFA relied on the tested formulas of commercial cinema. Indicative of this strategy was the studio's decision to engage a great star, Henny Porten, one of the most popular actresses of the silent era, to appear in two films.[73] DEFA's management during this period also had few reservations about working with Western filmmakers. In fact, the MfK explicitly directed it to do so.[74] Not only were individual directors from the Federal Republic hired for specific projects as in the past, but several coproductions with French and Swedish outfits were realized.[75] A few of these "progressive" artists from the West, such as Wolfgang Staudte or Erich Engel, may have wanted to work in the East out of political conviction; commercial considerations, however, likely predominated for most Westerners engaged by DEFA. On the whole, their work qualifies as run-of-the-mill entertainment that, except for some hackneyed social commentary, was hardly distinguishable from much of what was being produced in the Federal Republic at the time. Some of these DEFA productions were "costume films" loosely based on classics of German literature;[76] others were musicals[77] or comedies whose dramatic setting in the GDR was a minor detail.[78]

Another shift in official policy was the purchase of West German films for distribution in the GDR. Within a year, the number of these increased from one to fourteen.[79] Officials almost certainly viewed this move as a means of satisfying a disgruntled populace's need for diversion, but financial considerations also played a role. If the film industry as a whole was to attain any semblance of financial self-sufficiency,[80] movie houses had to be kept full. Films from socialist countries, let alone DEFA's scant production, had little prospect of achieving this result alone. By the same token, officials justified experiments with commercial genres like musicals as a means of import substitution.[81] Over the long run, however, the industry never succeeded in weaning itself from Western movies. If anything, as competition from both Eastern and Western television began to make itself felt in the late fifties, the need for such films became even more acute.[82]

Despite the official emphasis placed on German cultural unity and the importance attached to providing entertainment in the mid-fifties, political agitation as a goal was not abandoned. Art still had to contribute to the defense and realization of a socialist order in the GDR.[83] "Socialist realism" also remained a core theme of official criticism, and calls for the depiction of exemplary, positive heroes and "typical" social relations persisted.[84] Still, DEFA's greatest successes with such depictions were films not set in the new society. By far the most important of these was Kurt Maetzig's monumental treatment of the life of Ernst Thälmann, who was the head of the KPD during the last years of the Weimar Republic and who died a Nazi prisoner. Released in two parts, *Ernst Thälmann—Sohn seiner Klasse* (1954) (Ernst Thälmann—Son of His Class) and *Ernst Thälmann— Führer seiner Klasse* (1955) (Ernst Thälmann—Leader of His Class), this first film biography of a major Party leader had been in the planning stage since 1949.[85] The Party leadership's interest in the work was so intense that Maetzig pitched the final project directly to the Politburo. Combining a visual style deliberately borrowed from such "high Stalinist" classics as Mikhail Chiaureli's *The Fall of Berlin* (1949)—the color scheme was of course dominated by red—with clearly articulated exhortations to political action, the films were hits with officials. Indeed, the movies' high attendance figures likely did not reflect merely the official campaign to encourage viewership. For all their political bombast, the *Thälmann* films were action movies packed with scenes of battle and intrigue.[86]

Another film heavy with historical pathos was Slatan Dudow's *Stärker als die Nacht* (Stronger Than the Night, 1954), which also told a story of sacrifice and martyrdom during the Nazi period. This film's dimensions were not quite as grandiose as the *Thälmann* films, but both projects shared almost identical protagonists: Communist leaders, radiating optimism, whose unshakable belief in the future allows them to transcend the tribulations of the present. Maetzig's and Dudow's films, however, were exceptions. Most films from the same years whose aim was political agitation were poorly realized projects, earning their makers little respect within the industry and failing at the box office. These movies often used established formulas to depict the Cold War or the realization of a better society. Several were set in the West.[87] A couple of movies unsuccessfully experimented with using agricultural collectives as a new dramatic locus.[88]

THE INSTITUTIONAL STRUCTURE OF THE FILM INDUSTRY

The period following the proclamation of the New Course is also significant for the film industry's institutional structure. By 1954, its basic contours, which would endure more or less unchanged until the end of the GDR, had been established. A division of the MfK, the Hauptverwaltung Film (HV Film), or Central Film Administration, took over the responsibilities of the State Film Commission. Headed by a deputy cultural minister, the new agency had responsibility for supervising virtually all aspects of film production and distribution, from manufacturing film and equipment to the management of theaters. In accordance with general goals formulated by the Party, directors of individual enterprises, such as the feature film studio, submitted annual production plans to the HV Film and consulted with the agency as problems arose. The HV Film then devised a master plan for the entire industry and submitted it to the cultural minister. The latter in turn incorporated the plan for film into a general one for culture and passed everything on for approval to the Council of Ministers, the GDR's highest executive body. Such at least was the theory of how the procedure was to work. In practice, it was only one mechanism of economic and political control. The HV Film tended to refer only routine matters to the minister of culture. Of far greater authority was the Central Committee's Kulturabteilung (Cultural Section), whose staff worked under the Politburo's direct supervision. Because the Central Committee's apparatus also supervised DEFA's internal SED organization, the studio's management or individual artists often made use of their Party affiliation to circumvent the HV Film and the MfK entirely.[89]

One of the HV Film's duties was approving completed films for distribution, which was one of the most important mechanisms of censorship. The agency's director chaired the committee that performed this function. Other members included representatives from the ZK, the various studios, the GDR's two official film distributors, and a few artists. Through the plan, the agency also could exercise considerable influence on the thematic composition of the feature film studio's annual production by encouraging more or fewer projects of a certain type or insisting on a certain title's inclusion or removal. While the agency's "production section" scrutinized scripts ready for filming, DEFA's management generally purchased and developed ideas and treatments on its own. Supervising shooting and postproduction was also the studio's prerogative. This arrangement was subject, however, to some revision over the years. For example, in the years before the Eleventh Plenum, the studio director could approve scripts personally without consulting the agency. Films having high political priority, particularly those concerning the history of the workers' movement—in other words, paeans to individual Communist leaders—were also a special case.[90] In this regard, both the HV Film and the studio tended to be cautious and sought frequent consultation with each other as well as with the ZK.

A final element in DEFA's political supervision was undoubtedly the Stasi, or secret police, which constitutes an extremely complex topic in itself. The secret police's objectives and operating methods varied considerably over time. Although much work remains to be done on this topic, preliminary research suggests that the Stasi's presence in the studio increased markedly after the Eleventh Plenum.[91] The known presence of *informelle Mitarbeiter*, or lay informants, and other agents in the studio undoubtedly contributed to an atmosphere of fear inhibiting free expression. Still, it is very easy to overestimate the Stasi's direct influence in decision making. It did not "run" all facets of life in East Germany, even if the agency was one of the state's most powerful and dreaded organs.[92] Certainly within the studio, the Party had enough direct channels at its disposal for gathering information and directing policy to make the need for intervention through the secret police almost superfluous.[93]

NEW HORIZONS AND THE DEPICTION OF THE PRESENT

In the early fifties, the SED's attempt to enlist filmmakers in its forced march toward the future caused a near total breakdown at DEFA. The 1953 crisis chastened the regime and forced it to concede a measure of autonomy to artists. For the studio, the years following the crisis had a salutary effect. Production soared, and the industry came of age as an institution. Organizational patterns became established. Functionaries, studio managers, and artists all had a better idea of what they could expect from each other. Still, the greatest progress came in areas that the regime did not regard as politically vital. The five years required to realize the *Thälmann* films provide only one indication of how jealously the SED leadership watched over projects near and dear to it. While DEFA forged ahead with films that in the Party's eyes were little better than cheap commodities—prized only for their soothing effect on the populace—the important task of contributing to the new society's realization through its filmic depiction remained largely neglected for most of the decade.

Especially during the fifties, art and politics in the GDR sought legitimacy through each other. If Party bosses wished to harness the prestige of art to enhance their own power, artists wanted to feel themselves part of a transcendent historical project that could lend their work objective validity. Of course, despite this harmony of interests between the two groups, their relationship was largely marked by strife. Several factors explain this apparent contradiction. Official policy was never really uniform. It contained conflicting elements enforced by bureaucratic instances with varying agendas. One recurring problem, for example, was reconciling financial and ideological expediency. In addition, there was an underlying paradox routed in art's mission in the GDR. As the Shakespeare scholar Stephen Greenblatt has argued, "Power . . . not only produces its own subversion but is actively built upon it." Representing a transcendent force requires positing opposing obstacles, so that its superior potency can become manifest by overcoming these.[94] Thus East German artists were caught in the uncomfortable position of *having* to challenge the regime's authority. Otherwise, they would not have been able to celebrate the new order that they had pledged to serve.

Given Greenblatt's insight, it is not difficult to understand why East German artists in the fifties would have had far better luck depicting the past than the present. Films set in the past did not expose the existing state to possible betrayal, since the prehistory of the GDR involved the struggle against fascism and capitalism. Viewers could identify with the Communist movement's former self—which occupied the privileged underdog position—without being reminded of sticky questions concerning the East German state's legitimacy, compromised as it was by the recent legacy of the brutal and widely resented Soviet occupation.

The first indications that artists were finding at least a partial solution to the dilemma associated with representing the new order came toward the middle of the decade. A few DEFA filmmakers had success with films that cautiously challenged formulaic conventions for depicting the GDR and its immediate history. The first of these was Konrad Wolf's 1955 movie *Genesung* (Recovery). Its plot ran directly counter to orthodox notions about socialist realism. An exemplary positive hero—yet another Thälmann-like Communist leader—was shown in a position of moral and physical dependency vis-à-vis a character displaying qualities almost antithetical to his own. Another important movie was Kurt Maetzig and Kurt Barthel's *Schlösser und Katen* (Castles and Cottages), produced in 1956. Already unusual in extensively treating the events of June 17, the film is also notable for its treatment of social relations in a fashion reminiscent of the great nineteenth-century realist novels praised by the Marxist aesthetician György (Georg) Lukács. If the work still had its share of evil Western agents and irreproachable activists, it also had a historical and psychological depth lacking in most DEFA films of the day. Its most compelling protagonist was a hunchbacked farmer, whose outward deformity suggested an inner self-debasement more profound than that caused by mere external oppression. In contrast, Gerhard Klein and Wolfgang Kohlhaase's *Eine Berliner Romanze* (Berlin Love Story) of the same year conveyed a pat political message but drew on an aesthetic that in itself was a challenge to DEFA's established practice: neorealism.

By international standards, these works were a long way off from being masterpieces. Still, in the East German context, they were highly significant. Filmmakers were staking out their own claims about what it meant to live in their society. One factor contributing to this development was the stabilizing of the political situation within the GDR. Even if the regime continued to affirm commitment to German unity, it had demonstrated its resiliency by weathering a major crisis. The mid-fifties were also good years in terms of economic development and saw the relaxation of many emergency measures in effect since the war, such as rationing. The state was secure enough to tolerate films that contained subtle challenges to its authority. Of equal significance, talented younger socialist filmmakers, who identified strongly with the new order, were beginning to emerge. Konrad Wolf, for example, had grown up in the Soviet Union and served in the Red Army as a teenager. Others—such as Frank Beyer, Heiner Carow, Wolfgang Kohlhaase, and Günter Reisch—had come of age after the war. For this reason, they felt more at ease in the GDR than many of their elders, whose relationship with the Communist cause and the German nation was often extremely attenuated. Precisely because their loyalty to the new state seemed beyond question, these younger filmmakers were often in a better position to take the artistic and political risks necessary to depict the new order in an effective manner.

DEFA had traveled an enormous distance in ten years. Its mission had changed from overcoming the past to transforming the future. During this period, the studio had cleared away the debris of war, gotten past the severe institutional crisis occasioned by the regime's shift in cultural policy, and finally achieved a semblance of normalcy. Even so, an equally complex decade lay ahead. A new political crisis was about to rock the GDR. Unlike the uprising of June 17, Khrushchev's revelation of Stalinist errors at the Twentieth Congress of the CPSU in February 1956 did not result in dramatic manifestations of popular unrest, but the Soviet leader's frankness caused considerable upheaval within the SED. This time, though, the regime would emerge on the offensive. After nearly four years of wringing its hands over the national question, the Party was poised to turn its energies once again toward achieving an autonomous socialist state. If anything, official slogans had become more radical in the interim. The Party leadership now insisted that a profoundly rooted "cultural revolution," a true communion between art and life, would help the GDR blaze its own path to socialism.

DEFA and its artists would negotiate these political swings with considerable adeptness. For the first time since the immediate postwar period, a genuine intersection between cinematic and political avant-garde pretensions was on the horizon. By the early sixties, the studio had achieved considerable administrative autonomy, and artists enjoyed unprecedented creative latitude. At the same time, the story behind this result is not simple and contains many twists and turns. Even at its best, the cohabitation of art, industry, and politics that defined DEFA was extremely uneasy. An important key for understanding how change was possible is the concept of "realism." The next chapter will examine this contested idea and the 1957 film *Berlin—Ecke Schönhauser* against the backdrop of the Twentieth CPSU Congress.

The Discovery of the Ordinary

Berlin—Ecke Schönhauser and the
Twentieth Congress of the CPSU

*The corner of Schönhauser. . . . The film originally had the
working title, "Where we aren't." The people's police officer . . .
says once, "Where we aren't, our enemies are." . . .*

*But then we were not very happy with the title. It did not say
enough for us. It was too moralizing for us. . . . In any case, [the
final title] was right. . . . We were really surprised then that the
title became amazingly popular, almost like a synonym, and then
later always popped up, independent from our film, as if a certain
color were meant, a certain area in our city. . . .*

*We often stumbled upon some courtyard or some gateway
and said, "We'll come here again sometime." We found that a
story thought itself out easier if you already had a certain supply
of possible shooting locations.*

—Wolfgang Kohlhaase, scriptwriter, 1984[1]

The first few shots of a film anticipate the whole. *Berlin—Ecke
Schönhauser* (Berlin—Schönhauser Corner, 1957) offers a twist on this
truism. The opening shot, an extraordinary one-hundred-second pan-
oramic exposure of the intersection, suggests possibilities too potent for
the rest of the film to capture. Nowhere else in this film about teenagers in
the divided city does an alternative vision of life in the GDR shine through
so clearly. Moreover, the film's makers may even have been aware that the
first image conveyed something that their script could not fully articulate.
According to the screenwriter, Wolfgang Kohlhaase, it was easier for him
to craft words if he already knew the actual physical setting where the
action would play. He and the film's director, Gerhard Klein, would roam
Berlin in search of inspiration, storing scenery in their minds for possible
future use.

If Kohlhaase's statements, made many years after the fact, are accurate, a mysterious process occurred during the production of *Berlin—Ecke Schönhauser*. The film's setting grabbed more and more of the limelight. First, a phrase coined to evoke the location replaced the movie's original title, a political slogan. Then, the new title assumed a significance independent of the art work. Schönhauser Allee is an actual street, but there is no specific corner associated with it. People started employing the phrase "Ecke Schönhauser" as if it had a precise referent. In other words, the film's creators had depicted a specific, recognizable place, which somehow had not quite existed previously. Although the streets and buildings existed before the film crew arrived to shoot on location, there was no easy shorthand for talking about them. The area had no particular resonance, or at least not the one it then acquired through the film. In a sense, art had created life.

In the short term, *Berlin—Ecke Schönhauser* could not have markedly changed perceptions of the GDR or its capital. Still, the film's novel depiction of Berlin anticipated not only future developments within the GDR cinema but also those affecting East Germany's self-understanding generally. Fully appreciating the picture's significance requires situating it in three contexts. The first of these is a political one. Work on *Berlin—Ecke Schönhauser* began in the summer of 1956 in the midst of the ideological turmoil set off by Khrushchev's denunciation of Stalin at the Twentieth Congress of the Communist Party of the Soviet Union (CPSU) in February of the same year. While devoid of even oblique references to this famous event, the film raised questions concerning the GDR's relationship to history, the root of Party authority. The picture posited the existence of an imperfect community in the present rather than the achievement of the Communist millennium as the premise for the socialist state.

The second context of importance to appreciating the film's significance is the shifting of realist aesthetics within the socialist cinema. In fashioning their film, Klein and Kohlhaase consciously emulated Italian neorealism, which dominated the European cinema of the immediate postwar era. For its contemporaries, this movement stood for a rejection of the artifice of conventional films in favor of showing the world in all its unfinished rawness. The school's masters were known for their preference for real locations over studio sets, as well as their substitution of lay actors for professionals. Officials, however, feared that this emphasis on capturing a precinematic reality could easily lead East German filmmakers astray from the dictates of socialist realism, which emphasized transcendent historical truth rather than surface reality. Thus, once the dust from the Twentieth Congress had settled, Party leaders attacked *Berlin—Ecke Schönhauser* as politically revisionist, even though it had achieved excellent attendance figures for a work thematizing socialist society.

Equally important, *Berlin—Ecke Schönhauser* was a response to changes occurring in German popular culture during the 1950s. The picture's protagonists are teenagers addicted to Western music and movies. The viewer first encounters them sporting portable radios while dancing with wild abandon to "boogie" music, a source of consternation to those passing them on the street. As in other DEFA films of the day, these characters eventually turn tame or are punished for their transgression. The leading female protagonist, for example, appears toward the end of the film wearing a dress rather than her usual blue jeans. Still, contemporary critics, including some Westerners, were impressed by the degree to which the picture acknowledged the existence of an independent youth culture. Certainly, its treatment of the characters' "pathological" social circumstances is far more extensive than its portrayal of an alternative socialist milieu for them to inhabit. For this reason, *Berlin—Ecke Schönhauser* represents an early attempt by artists to mediate between the popular trends of the postwar era and the realm of politically permissible expression. Although the regime would eventually grow more tolerant of such phenomena as rock music and the sexual revolution, this result would occur only after a complex process of cultural negotiation, in which the cinema played a significant role.

This chapter has two parts. The first explores how *Berlin—Ecke Schönhauser* presented an alternative vision of socialist society, focusing in particular on the opening title shot's emblematic significance. In this context, I explain in greater detail how neorealism as an artistic stance directly contradicted official aesthetic doctrine. My analysis also shows how the picture, despite its documentary pretense, recycled established, prewar conventions used to depict Berlin in order to present an original image of socialist society. The chapter's second part focuses on the political implications of the picture's revisioning of East Germany. After sketching the impact of the Twentieth CPSU Congress on the GDR regime and its cultural policy, I turn to *Berlin—Ecke Schönhauser*'s role in debates of the late fifties over the future direction of the East German cinema. Which circumstances favored the realization of Klein and Kohlhaase's project, and which ones later caused it to be criticized? What does the controversy surrounding the picture suggest about conflicting expectations concerning cinema and its role in socialist society? What implications did the picture's novel portrayal of socialism have for political authority?

THE DISCOVERY OF THE ORDINARY

Berlin—Ecke Schönhauser's first shot has no diegetic purpose in the film but rather serves as a backdrop for the titles and credits. The film opens on a street corner on a gray, shadowless day, and the camera begins to pan, slowly but relentlessly. A complex, multiple intersection reveals itself. A trolley passes under an elevated train line. People and traffic move through the frame. Perhaps it is early morning. One man drags a heavy cart. Individuals of various shapes and sizes, dressed in different ways, are seen going about their business. There are women with baby carriages or groceries. A couple stands next to a snack counter engrossed in conversation.

The concreteness of the scene is deceptive. There is something equally abstract about the shot. It provides a good example of how realist impulses can easily lead to a fascination with form.[2] As the camera slowly completes its nearly 360-degree pan, the graphic arrangement of the tableau presented to the viewer is in constant transformation. Most obviously, stationary objects glide in and out of view and the angle of the major compositional elements varies. The most striking example here is the elevated train line. At the beginning of the shot, it forms a strong diagonal, whose orientation alternately contrasts and resonates with the movement of traffic and people. A little further into the scene, the el assumes a horizontal position, dominating the top portion of the screen. Pedestrians step through the space underneath—neatly framed by support columns as well as the street in front—in a stream that vanishes into the distance. Still later, the train tracks disappear altogether. Finally, the sense of depth varies. Since the shot was made with the help of a wide-angle lens with excellent deep focus, the viewer's attention is at points free to wander between different planes of action—for example, between what is happening in front of and what is going on behind the el. At other points, the camera focuses the eye down broad avenues toward the horizon; in still other situations, the field of vision becomes radically foreshortened and extends only a few yards to a tired building facade.

In other words, the camera, despite being rooted in one place, presents an unstable, constantly changing perspective. The point of observation in fact is situated not much higher than eye level, so that the viewer almost has a sense of participating in the scene being recorded. At one moment, traffic even passes perilously close to the camera. In addition, the shot is simply long in duration. It not only documents a place but also provides a direct representation of time—one hundred seconds snatched from oblivion. This duration before the first edit, in combination with the shifting, compositional flux of the evolving image, has a further effect. Together, they suggest the rich openness of being in the world, as if the camera's circumscription encompassed not only a street intersection but an entire microcosm. This impression is further underscored by the title music, which contains a number of contrasting strains. These include a brassy overture that heralds the film, dancelike music with a rhythmic downbeat evocative of the pace of urban life, and a lyric love theme. Modulating, mysterious organ chords, as well as some jazz bars, emphasize rather than obscure transitions.

If the single street corner, properly beheld, contains such a profusion of possibility, why move on? Ultimately, *Berlin—Ecke Schönhauser* is about learning how to see what is before one's eyes and accepting one's place in life, both in a literal, geographic sense and in a figurative one. The movie's major characters are four teenagers who hang out at the intersection. Their choice between West and East becomes one between the illusion of freedom and participation in a benevolent, if restrictive, social order. They proceed through a series of situations in which they confront different forms of authority. The emplotment suggests that their rebellious attitude is a result of domestic anarchy. All come from families that are in one way or the other "dysfunctional." Dieter lost both parents in the war, and Angela her father. Kohle suffers under a tyrannical stepfather who beats him. Karl-Heinz's family is intact, but his parents are *Kleinbürger* who instill in him materialist values and are then powerless to contain his naked egotism. More than anything else, the protagonists are children of the divided city—or, more precisely, of its urban landscape. Their habitat includes gray streets, cramped lower-class apartments, and the empty space underneath the el where many paths converge and diverge but few people linger.

Together with the contrasting human types and the forms of transportation that appear in the title shot, the succession of vistas suggests two themes that are developed in the film. The first of these is the existence of alternatives. The protagonists' lives are figuratively at a crossroads, most obviously between East and West, but also between their present shiftless lives and a possible future for themselves. The second theme is transformation. Dieter and Angela fall in love and find purpose in the East. Karl-Heinz, lured by easy riches of the West, ends up in jail. Kohle dies a freakish death in a West Berlin youth resettlement camp. The film recounts how Dieter and Angela learn to acknowledge the state's legitimate authority and to recognize their torn environment as home.

If the film's title shot is remarkable for its lack of a sovereign, normalizing perspective on the city, the succeeding images establish a clear political and moral geography. They show Dieter's crossing from West to East Berlin and then arriving out of breath at a police station to announce Kohle's death. This scene frames the rest of the film as Dieter's flashback. He explains Kohle's death to a detective who gives his account the stamp of objectivity by transforming it into a typed police report. Because the film also describes events that Dieter did not witness, the detective can be interpreted as the film's joint narrator.

The film can be divided into five major segments. (Although this division is my own, the titles used are derived from the original dialogue.) The first, "A little dare," begins with Angela's mother throwing her out of their cramped apartment for the evening in order to entertain a gentleman caller. Having no place to go but the street, Angela encounters Dieter and joins a group of youths underneath the el dancing to rock music. Here Karl-Heinz dares Kohle to smash a streetlight in for a West German D-mark. This action leads to the first confrontation with the police, who haul the youths off for interrogation.

The second sequence, "I have no friends," starts by comparing how Dieter and Karl-Heinz spend their day. While the latter conducts business with gangsters in West Berlin, the former performs a minor feat of heroism at work, a construction site. That evening the two youths meet Angela and a second woman at a dance hall. Here Dieter backs out of a previously agreed-upon plan with Karl-Heinz to steal their companions' identity papers for sale in the West. Undeterred, Karl-Heinz absconds with the second woman's papers, leaving his friend to face the consequences. For a second time, the stern yet kind detective is the interrogator. He accepts Dieter's claim of ignorance rather than detaining him. This attitude of trust finds its counterpart in Angela's loyalty. She waits for Dieter outside the police station, and that very night their love is consummated.

In order to underscore the privileged significance of this private event, the theme music, which is otherwise employed sparingly, swells. Dieter and Angela are then shown, after their discreetly denoted lovemaking, walking underneath the el, framed by a series of support arches receding into the distance. These create a sense of linear progression. Nowhere else in the film is space constructed in this manner; but while the couple stride confidently forward, their future is not yet assured.

"And what will happen to me?" is the next major sequence, which further dramatizes the consequences of the lack of proper authority in the youths' lives. Karl-Heinz ends up committing manslaughter when a confidence scam goes awry. Meanwhile, Dieter and Kohle have decided to settle scores with him for his behavior toward them. They corner Karl-

Heinz, who pulls a gun. When it goes off suddenly, Karl-Heinz collapses; and Dieter and Kohle, fearing their friend's death, flee to West Berlin.

The fourth sequence, "I'm having his baby," compares authority in the East and West. Dieter and Kohle are taken to a youth resettlement camp, where a glib official interrogates the former. The words "What do you know?" serve as a sound bridge to a parallel interview between the detective and Angela. While the West German authority figure encourages Dieter to elaborate invented political reasons for fleeing, the East German police elicit a revelation: Angela announces her pregnancy. Another way the difference between the East and the West is developed in this sequence is through the opposition of isolation and community. The mise-en-scène and camera work emphasize the two boys' being alone in the camp, a villa surrounded by a huge, barren yard. They are rarely shown in the same frame with its officials. In contrast, the police in the East are family! Dieter's brother is on the force. He finds Angela wandering alone at night when she leaves home after her mother calls her a streetwalker for becoming pregnant. One scene shows him and an FDJ official from Dieter's VEB rearranging the tiny apartment the brothers share to make room for her.

The final sequence, "We'll stay together," begins with a second interrogation of Dieter by suspicious camp officials. To prevent the possibility of being transferred to another camp, Kohle drinks a mixture of tobacco and coffee—a trick he once saw in a Hollywood film. Instead of merely rendering him ill, the potion kills him. Now entirely alone, Dieter escapes from the camp. The flashback ends with a dissolve to the detective's typewriter. He repeats the words with which Dieter began his account: "And Kohle is dead." Another dissolve transports Dieter to the courtyard of Angela's building. The theme music swells, and the film ends in the same manner as the first major sequence began. Dieter waits for Angela outside her mother's apartment.

As is clear from the summary, the film's plot and thematic structure were hardly subversive of the East German regime. A representative of the state, the police detective, functions as Dieter's mentor and—since Dieter's brother is the detective's subordinate—as his metaphorical father. In addition, the detective—quite literally the voice of law—has the final say in the film. In the last scene, through a voice-over, the detective's offscreen presence absolves Dieter of sole responsibility for his friend's death and admonishes him (as well as the film's implied audience) to remember: "Where we aren't, our enemies are." In other words, Dieter, through his presence in the empty courtyard, serves as a substitute for the absent detective. He has become in effect an extension of the state. Of course, there are additional ways, some more obvious than others, in which the film celebrates East Germany. The hypocrisy and impotence of the protagonists' parents compare unfavorably with the police's concerned yet trusting attitude. Romantic love is a metaphor for loyalty to the state: in the dance hall scene, Dieter must choose between Angela or betraying the GDR by stealing identity papers with the intent of selling them. The West stands for greed and egotism; the East for community. Westerners in the film tend to be either gangsters, slimy officials, or violence-prone youths. And the list goes on.

RECEPTION

Berlin—Ecke Schönhauser's narrative content explains little about its reception. Many examples of GDR art and literature from this period developed similar themes. Virtually all DEFA films from the fifties established a link between realizing personal destiny and allying oneself with the new society. Even at the time, such black-and-white comparisons between the East and West seemed hackneyed. What impressed viewers about Klein and Kohlhaase's work was its visual impact. Both admirers and detractors of the work were concerned with what it "showed," not with what it "said."

On the popular level, *Berlin—Ecke Schönhauser* struck a chord with audiences. With nearly 1.9 million tickets sold within four months of its being released in August 1957, it quickly established itself as one of the more popular DEFA productions of the day.[3] Initial reviews in the GDR press were ecstatic. Critics raved about the film's authenticity and its candid approach to a difficult social problem: alienated youth. *Der Morgen* called the film "courageous, honest, and artistically convincing."[4] A reviewer in *Junge Welt* noted that "the story could be written from life itself."[5] Wolfgang Joho announced in *Sonntag*, "Neither fancy phrases are spoken here, morals given with a wagging finger, nor a failure-proof solution proposed. . . . Kohlhaas [*sic*] . . . and Klein have made a brave foray right into the heart of life for Berlin teenagers."[6]

Readers expressed particular satisfaction that they could recognize their city and its people in the film. E. Lenz wrote in to the evening tabloid *BZ am Abend*, "Not only are the shots from our street genuine, but the actors are true to life." Jutta J. pointed out, "Even our sausage stand is there!"[7] Günter Wolansky told the editors of *Neue Welt*, the state youth organization organ, "This film authentically depicts how youths, influenced through the effects of the war, especially through the torn nature of Berlin, find their way." Silvia Stadtler took issue with another reader who felt the film might harm the GDR's image: "Aren't the negative aspects also true? After all, you cannot just show the good and beautiful while simply ignoring the problems, which we also have in the Republic."[8]

Even Anna Teut, a reviewer for a conservative West Berlin paper, while correctly noting *Berlin—Ecke Schönhauser*'s tendentious message, expressed amazement concerning the film's general honesty: "For years, the land of Herr Ulbricht has condemned punks [*Halbstarken*] to the ideological junk heap as the typical and rotten fruits of rotten capitalism, and now they suddenly pop up beneath the red flag. In the film, there are no more heroes who march in formation with fists [held high], but rather the other ones: those with defiant, don't-mess-with-me faces, who stand around in groups in entryways and on street corners, acting silly and harassing passersby or dancing a hot boogie to a portable radio."[9]

For once, Horst Knietzsch, the film reviewer for the official SED organ, *Neues Deutschland*, was in virtual agreement with a Western colleague. He described the movie in almost the same words that Teut used: "What we see here is an aspect of our everyday life [*Alltag*]. You only need to take a trolley from the Friedrichstrasse Station to Schönhauser Allee. . . . Then we'll meet up with the hero[es] of this film on every third street corner. They stand around the place with unconcerned faces, are silly and rude, and gather about a portable radio playing hot music. Their hands, dug into their pockets, only see the light of day in order to touch up their hair, which is cut like James Dean's, the Hollywood heartthrob."[10] If the GDR's most authoritative movie critic confirmed that the film showed "genuine, unfalsified Berlin," he also crowed for another reason. Knietzsch emphasized that here was finally a work of "international format" that could be compared to the films of René Clair as well as those of Italian masters,[11] an obvious reference to Italian neorealism.

Leading cultural politicians responded to *Berlin—Ecke Schönhauser* belatedly, but their judgment was harsh. In March 1958, Anton Ackermann, the head of the HV Film, likened the work to "pornography" during internal studio discussions. What displeased him was the film's subject matter: alienated youth dancing to rock and roll, the hypocrisy and desperation of ordinary lives, broken homes, parents who beat their children. The picture's young male protagonists—dressed in jeans, leather jackets, and listening to African-American-inspired "boogie" music—were *Halbstarken*, or young punks. These figures had become targets of considerable controversy in both German states. Cultural critics decried the youth imitating rebellious American screen idols such as Marlon Brando in *The Wild One* (1954) and James Dean in *Rebel without a Cause* (1955). In the summer of 1956, a series of riots involving *Halbstarken* broke out, lending credence to the charge that American cultural imports were undermining German society.[12] West Berlin officials went so far as to withdraw production subsidies from the picture *Die Halbstarken* (1956), whose protagonists not only followed Western fashion but engaged in violent crime.[13] While the actual riots were less extensive in the East than in the West, SED officials were particularly concerned about the thousands of young East Berliners who, like Kohle in *Berlin—Ecke Schönhauser*, made a habit of visiting theaters in the city's western half.[14]

The depiction of *Halbstarken* in *Berlin—Ecke Schönhauser* in itself, however, did not disturb East German cultural officials. Certainly, the film hardly broke new ground by showing troubled youths at risk of succumbing to the evil influences of Western culture. All DEFA films about the present featured characters who failed to identify initially with the working class. After all, redemption was a theme that complemented Marxism's emancipatory promise. The regime itself in the fifties emphasized East Germany's socioeconomic plurality. Much remained to be done before the new order would be fully triumphant. What upset Ackermann and others was the predominance of misfits contaminated by Western culture and the vestiges of the past. As one Cultural Ministry official explained, there was too much of the negative and not enough of the positive. The film was like a situation in which "there is a pickpocket in a city with a hundred inhabitants, and the other 99 inhabitants are robbed five times a year. Then these have the impression that the whole city consists of pickpockets. Thus these punks face 90 percent of the working youth, who, however, because they behave normally, do not stand out."[15]

COMPETING REALIST AESTHETICS

What the functionaries decried was not in the film by accident. DEFA filmmakers had flirted with neorealism since the studio's inception. Both the socialist cinema and the Italian movement defined themselves in opposition to the commercial cinema. With the turn toward socialist realism in the late forties, however, the Party had forced filmmakers to condemn neorealism as inappropriate for the immediate political task at hand. The Italian films, it was argued, did not transcend "naturalism," or a fascination with outward appearance. In contrast, a true socialist artwork, capable of inspiring workers to heroic feats of labor, had to probe beneath the surface and reveal the underlying laws governing historical development.[16]

Like most neorealist works, *Berlin—Ecke Schönhauser* presented itself as a meditation on seeing the world. The film associated truth with unadorned reflection, with taking an honest look at oneself. Characters observe themselves in mirrors at key moments in their personal development. Dieter and Angela see their own reflection while dancing arm in arm for the first time. Karl-Heinz finds himself confronted with a looking glass before committing manslaughter. Angela's mother has a similar reckoning with herself while finding the strength to throw her married lover out of her life. Indeed, the one character denied such a moment dies. Kohle seeks his reflection in West German and American films, and his attempt at imitating them—the recipe for the lethal concoction comes from an adventure flick—destroys him. The potential danger of hiding from one's true self is indicated in the film in other ways, too. Before his downfall, Karl-Heinz admires himself in a new leather jacket; Angela, who must contend with her mother's hypocrisy, observes her applying makeup in a mirror.

Even before the first title announcing the film flashes on the screen, an advertisement for the SED Party organ, *Neues Deutschland*, is visible in the opening shot. These bold words heralding a new Germany stand in stark contrast to the gray, unremarkable street scene being presented. Someone familiar with Berlin would have recognized the location as belonging to Prenzlauer Berg, a working- and lower-middle-class neighborhood. From an official perspective, a construction site or the stately bombast of some socialist urban renewal scheme, such as East Berlin's famous Stalin- (later Lenin-, now Frankfurter-) Allee, would have been a far more appropriate emblem for the new society's capital.

In another context, this contrast between image and text might be intended ironically, but, given the rest of the film, it serves another purpose. The words embedded in the opening scene valorize the ordinary and identify the new society with the actual. The fascination with ordinary existence in the city so evident in the title shot and elsewhere in the film is reinforced in other ways, too. The use of high-speed, "grainy" film stock generally reserved for newsreels and of actual locations and decor,[17] the near-natural lighting, the reliance on nonprofessional actors for several roles,[18] the unobtrusive camera style that frequently employs lengthy shots and deep focus, as well as the plot's often loose, accidental causality—all hallmarks frequently associated with neorealism—emphasized film's indexical nature, its supposed ability to record a reality that precedes interpretation. Thus, beginning with its very first seconds, the work made strong assertions both about its own nature and what East Germany was like as a place. The film presented itself to its intended audience as a mirror of the social self, as an opportunity to engage in honest self-reflection.

Understanding the political implication of this artistic stance requires attention to the dominant aesthetic doctrine to which *Berlin—Ecke Schön-*

hauser was responding: "socialist realism." Much existing scholarship implicitly suggests that the doctrine existed as a monolithic orthodoxy by focusing attention on the official ostracizing of radical modernist aesthetics, such as the epic theater of Bertolt Brecht.[19] Nevertheless, the boundaries of permissible expression under socialist realism were never precise and were subject to constant renegotiation even by artists who were not iconoclasts. The best points of departure for understanding the parameters of debate surrounding socialist realism in the East German context during the fifties are ideas associated with two men: the Russian novelist Maxim Gorky and the Hungarian literary theorist György (Georg) Lukács.

Gorky's address before the First All-Union Congress of Soviet Writers of 1934 qualifies as one of the classic formulations of socialist realism. There Gorky emphasized the power of imagination and stressed art's poetic function. He called for works glorifying labor, which would directly contribute to the Communist cause "by promoting a revolutionary attitude towards reality, an attitude that in practice refashions the world."[20] Underlying Gorky's ideas was a moral economy with strong religious overtones. For him, "optimism," or the expression of faith in the new society, was a decisive aesthetic criterion. In contrast, Lukács's aesthetics derived from a profound study of the Hegelian-Marxist tradition. Moreover, his tastes ran toward high culture and the literature of the nineteenth century. For him, the best model for all artistic endeavor was the "realist" novel as typified by Balzac. He believed that for a work to be effective, it had to promote an intuitive understanding of the forces underlying social existence. By leading to a harmony of reason and emotion, art could thus help individuals to recognize their class interest and to ally themselves with the forces of progress.

The debate of aesthetic issues within the GDR film industry during the fifties reflects an oscillation between Gorky's and Lukács's positions. On the one hand, there was the call and desire to create an affirmative image of a brave new society. On the other hand, politically committed artists also wanted works that would lead to a more intellectually grounded identity with socialism. Perhaps because DEFA defined itself from the beginning in active opposition to the conventional commercial cinema of effect and illusion, filmmakers were eager to posit a critical audience, possessing an active intelligence. In addition, many in the industry realized that socialist realist protagonists of the Gorkian type would be hard pressed to compete with the glamour roles of Western stars. Through radio, smuggled print media, and personal experience, East German audiences were aware of West German developments. Compared to the icons of fifties youth culture, such as James Dean or Marlon Brando, even the most charismatic renditions of earnest young socialists must have seemed very out of date. Certainly, such heroes could hardly make audiences forget the great disparity between the miserable conditions in the GDR and those in the Federal Republic, where an opulent consumer culture was already coming into its own.

If nothing else, Lukács was a source for language that artists could use to plead their case. However conservative and antimodernist, his aesthetic allowed art a measure of autonomy from politics. Part and parcel of his emulation of bourgeois high culture was the premise that a work's inherent value depended as much on the integrity of the artist as on the expression of "optimism" in the new society. Nevertheless, applying Lukács's ideas to the depiction of the socialist present had clear problems. How could the nineteenth-century realist novel, whose greatness derived from its depiction of the "dynamic contradictions of social life," serve as an effective model for art in a social order in which these very forces of history had been overcome? Lukács's own answer to this question, in an essay written during the confusion of 1956, was to posit socialism as the first societal type *aiming* to eliminate antagonistic conflict. Socialist realism's purpose would then be to depict and further this difficult process.[21] This reasoning, however, flew in the face of official ideology, which held that only "nonantagonistic contradictions" persisted.

The turn toward neorealism by Klein and Kohlhaase can be interpreted as an attempt to break out of this impasse. Even if not well versed in aesthetic theory, they were still responding to a debate whose terms were deeply influenced by Lukács's and Gorky's formulations of key categories. By emulating the Italian movement, these artists hoped to present the new society in a manner that would be at once affirmative yet credible, celebratory but not saccharine. Even so, the choice of neorealism as a model for depicting the present posed a basic challenge to an underlying premise of socialist realism. Both Gorky and Lukács posited a transcendent reality. Like Hegel, they viewed art as a medium between immediate experience and a higher realm of truth. In contrast, neorealism, at least as it was widely understood,[22] stood for a diametrically opposite proposition, an alarmingly simple one: that the world could speak for itself. All filmmakers had to do was provide the proper mirror for its reflection. Everything else, including morality and political consciousness, would follow by itself if only filmmakers could capture the raw truth living before their eyes. In an often-quoted 1948 article, the Italian movement's most famous critic, the French film historian André Bazin, wrote: "The recent Italian films . . . know . . . never to take reality as a means. To condemn the world does not imply the necessity of bad faith. [These films] do not forget that before being condemnable, the world quite simply *is*."[23] Bazin goes on to emphasize that scripting plays a subordinate role in a film of this type. Like Kohlhaase in the passage quoted at the beginning of this chapter, he suggests that narrative is secondary to where the film is set or what the film visually conveys.[24]

Berlin—Ecke Schönhauser's documentary pretense posed a challenge to the prevailing aesthetic doctrine in East Germany. By suggesting that the camera's ability to record outward appearance was a sufficient guarantee of verisimilitude, the work could be construed as discounting the underlying laws governing history as posited by Marx. Neorealism's favoring of images over words also contradicted a certain bias informing the socialist cinema during the Stalin period, which was notorious for a staid and formulaic visual style. The SED Politburo's 1952 resolution on film, for example, devoted considerable attention to the shortage of ideologically informed scripts. However real this problem may have been, the Party's concern reflected the belief that making a film was a fairly mechanical process of translating a verbal message into images.

There is yet another way in which Bazin proves a useful guide for understanding the implications of applying neorealist principles to the depiction of East Germany. The French critic argued that neorealism arose in Italy precisely because World War II did not come to a neat conclusion there but was followed by a prolonged period of social upheaval, during which the present existed for itself in all its fractured truth, independent of political or national ideology. The Italian films were uniquely *actuel* precisely because they were made in a country that had temporarily lost its mythic past.[25] In *Berlin—Ecke Schönhauser*, too, there is at times a sense of the GDR as a place adrift in the here and now. The lasting effects of the war are palpable but still unresolved. Angela and Dieter have both lost parents through that catastrophe. The one scene at the latter's workplace involves the discovery of an unexploded bomb. During the second encounter between Dieter and the detective, the older man remarks that there are spies and saboteurs working to undermine the GDR. He tells Dieter pointedly, "That also exists, even if you don't believe it." In other words, the protagonists live in a world where the regime's legitimizing narrative, its neat division between present and past, East and West, seems strangely irrelevant.

Of course, the standard that Bazin set for the films he so lavishly praised was impossibly high. Neorealism's great masterpieces were hardly devoid of politics or normative statements. A film such as Roberto Rossellini's *Rome Open City*, for example, obviously contributed to the myth that

Italians, whether Communist or Catholic, had been united by opposition to the Nazis. By the same token, *Berlin—Ecke Schönhauser*'s title shot sets an unattainable standard of impartiality for the rest of the film. The work's significance lies in how it exploits the very tension between the cinema's indexical and illusory qualities, developed throughout the neorealist genre, in order to convey an ideological message. The picture's strategy in this regard becomes very clear if one considers its depiction of Berlin, in many ways the true object of the film.

A NEW CINEMATIC TOPOGRAPHY FOR BERLIN

One way *Berlin—Ecke Schönhauser* achieved its realist effect was by drawing on earlier films about Berlin. Many of the locations employed—gray courtyards, stairwells, cramped apartments—evoke those associated with city life in the Weimar cinema. The significance of identifying the GDR with a traditional urban environment can be better understood by briefly considering some of the ways the German cinema had previously treated the modern city.[26] A number of Weimar films, typified by Karl Grüne's *Die Strasse* (The Street, 1924), thematized middle-class anxieties about downward mobility, depicting the city as a realm of dangerous diversions that threatened to ensnare the individual and subvert the social order. Another set of movies, known as "Zille" movies after the great caricaturist Heinrich Zille,[27] relied on clichéd sites such as tenement courtyards to present an almost idyllic view of lower-class urban life. Yet a third group of works can be distinguished for their overtly socialist or Communist perspective. One of the most important examples here is Slatan Dudow's classic film *Kuhle Wampe* (1931), which attempted to depict, in documentary style, the various spaces workers inhabited. In this film, the city is at once the familiar site of proletarian life and an unforgiving place, since it is dominated by forces beyond the protagonists' control. These attempt to escape capitalist oppression by creating an alternative community, a Communist squatter's camp in a bucolic setting where workers can shape their own environment.

Of course, Berlin had figured in DEFA films from the studio's inception. For some of the first postwar productions, the directors had had the opportunity to use an entirely original motif for the city, one that was both a physical result and a symbol of historical events: the *Trummerlandschaft* (rubble landscape). At the same time, familiar ways of conceptualizing the city also reemerged and found new definition under changed circumstances. Slatan Dudow's first postwar film, *Unser täglich Brot* (Our Daily Bread, 1949), much like his famous Weimar work, posited an alternative space controlled by workers, a cooperative factory, as an island of hope and safety. The street itself is associated with the black market and becomes an area of danger, where a son might rob a father or a respectable woman be reduced to a prostitute. In 1951, Kurt Maetzig's movie *Roman einer Ehe* (Story of a Young Couple) took the next logical step and associated the temptations of the city not only with capitalism but with Berlin's Western half. The Stalin-Allee, then still under construction, represented the radically new social order being established in the East.

Klein and Kohlhaase's two previous films about Berlin, *Alarm im Zirkus* (An Emergency in the Circus, 1954) and *Eine Berliner Romanze* (Berlin Love Story, 1956), similarly associated urban pathology with the West, while presenting the East as a realm of intact social relations. For example, the second work reserves its neorealist effect largely for the Western half of the city. A sixteen-year-old girl from the East falls in love with a boy from the West who tries to impress her in various ways, including helping her fulfill her dream of becoming a fashion model. When not only this but also the boy's economic prospects turn out to be illusory, she brings him home to her solid, working-class family. The film's final shot, much like the privileged moment in the "I have no friends" sequence, features the young couple striding confidently into their future along a street that concentrates the viewer's attention toward the horizon.

What distinguished *Berlin—Ecke Schönhauser* was a partial inversion of how previous DEFA films had mapped the cinema's qualities onto Germany's geography. Earlier DEFA productions obviously had never associated illusion with the East, but they depicted the GDR as a place where dreams—or at least the aspirations of the working class—came true. The West was the realm of harsh facts where hopes of a better life were bound to be dashed. Klein and Kohlhaase's work did not so much fiddle with the capitalist side of this equation as subtly revise the socialist one. The GDR's superiority expresses itself less in utopian potential than in present reality, in its thereness. The film's protagonists become disabused of Western fantasies, but what they are offered as a substitute is the realization that their own lives are already sufficient. While the GDR is depicted as a benign social order, the film's progressive pathos is relatively muted. The work's emphasis is on return and acceptance rather than advance.

Oddly enough, the only clichéd landmarks used in the film are Western ones: Bahnhof Zoo (the Zoo Train Station) and the Kurfürstendamm (a famous commercial avenue) near where it passes the ruins of the Gedächtniskirche (a memorial to the destruction of World War II). Standing in close proximity to each other, they collectively embodied West Berlin's commercial dynamism and perseverance in the face of adversity as well as its empty glitter, criminality, and easy morality. The film exploits these sites for their symbolic value, leaving little doubt about which associations the viewer should make—the famous attractions serve as backdrops for transactions between Karl-Heinz and his gangster associates. In contrast, the locations in East Berlin used in the film lack the same specific political and historical associations. The area where most of action takes place is residential and away from the city's center. Klein and Kohlhaase could just as easily have chosen another part of the city for their project. What distinguishes the Eastern half of the city in the film is its lack of distinction.

The construction of interior space varies in the two halves of the city, too. There is a preponderance of domestically coded space in the East, while the scenes in the West tend to present space in a disjointed fashion that emphasizes confrontation and isolation. A good example is Dieter's first interview with a Western official that occurs in the "I'm having a baby" sequence. First, the camera cuts from the official to Dieter and back again. Then the camera slowly pans between the two, pausing in between, to rest on an empty part of the room as the interview continues offscreen. A parallel occurs in the same sequence, when Dieter and Kohle are shown settling into their dormitory at the resettlement camp: a bunk bed standing between them compartmentalizes the room. Only when a third youth invades their privacy are the two shown in the same frame.

Neither half of Berlin is depicted in a particularly flattering fashion, and the film offers little respite from the city's grayness. There are no vistas or wide-open spaces. Windows open onto courtyards. Even Dieter's and Angela's lovemaking occurs in the rather unappealing stalls of what might be an open-air market after business hours. Still, the film hardly presents the city in a claustrophobic fashion. Emptiness and isolation are far more threatening than enclosure and congestion. After all, the slogan "Where we aren't, our enemies are," which the detective proclaims in the final scene, calls for the city's occupation, not its abandonment. In the film's moral economy, escape is a dangerous illusion. The one scene that takes place outside Berlin is Karl-Heinz's apprehension, which occurs in a forest alongside a highway. The youth resettlement camp where Karl-Heinz and Kohle end up is housed in a suburban villa to which an establishing shot lends all the charm of the Norman Bates residence. Particularly barren is the building's yard. Here, several youths physically abuse Dieter for desiring to return home to the East. One shot, remarkable for its starkness and verticality in a film whose visual style rarely calls attention to its abstract composition after the title shot, shows the youths standing against a gray sky with a leafless tree in their midst.

If space in the West seems open but is actually imprisoning—Dieter has to break out of the resettlement camp—the opposite is true in the East. The urban landscape may seem restrictive, but it is actually rich in possibility. The *Ecke*—corner of the city—to which the film continually returns may seem ordinary, but it is special in its own quiet way. The final shot shows Dieter in the courtyard of Angela's building. Such a setting has rich resonances in German film and popular culture, both as a focus of lower-class life and as a metaphor for the city's confining nature. The mise-en-scène of the film plays upon the latter register of associations. The courtyard is barren and empty. Nevertheless, Dieter's return fills it with a web of social relations. He looks upward with expectation toward Angela's apartment. The detective's sonorous voice resonates, and the theme music swells. Dieter and Angela's love, the child within her womb, and the life before them are all signs of a gentle yet powerful becoming. Even so, the film avoids final closure. There is no last embrace between the lovers. Angela's presence is indicated only by the opening of her window. The camera then follows Dieter in a single sweeping motion as he returns to the archway of the building. The screen fades to black with an image of him standing in the archway. Seen from behind, Dieter in essence has become one with the audience. He views what they have been observing in one fashion or the other throughout the film: the intersection in front of Angela's house.

THE POLITICAL IMPLICATIONS OF REVISIONING SOCIALISM

If *Berlin—Ecke Schönhauser*, as a conscious emulation of neorealism, presents itself as a meditation on seeing, then the metaphor of sight can also be useful for understanding dramatic events informing the film's production and reception. According to one political slogan current during the later Ulbricht regime, GDR citizens were to see their society with the "eyes of a planner and builder." Only then would they appreciate the grand perspective socialism offered them. This architectural analogy was an apt description of how the Party conceived its role. As the vanguard of the working class, it was supposed to possess a uniquely privileged vantage on history that allowed it to plot the future's unfolding. The construction of socialism was to follow from precise blueprints—the notorious "five-year" plans—devised by a consciousness capable of overseeing and anticipating the entire process.

The two great political events affecting East Germany in the fifties challenged the Party's transcendent observer position in different ways.

The June 17 uprising sent a message to the regime that the GDR's already greatly put-upon populace would not carry out its dictates submissively. What seemed logical and obvious from on high often appeared nonsensical closer to the ground. In contrast, the Twentieth CPSU Congress in February 1956 represented a calculated admission by the Party that even its commanding vantage was limited. In his famous "secret" speech, Khrushchev deliberately set out to destroy what he called Stalin's "cult of personality." The Soviet premier complained, "Such a man supposedly knows everything, *sees* everything, thinks for everyone, can do anything, is infallible in his behavior."[28] An end to "dogma," "democratization" within the Party, and greater recognition of nonpolitical expert opinion were all deemed necessary for continued progress. Guaranteeing the socialist project, it was conceded, required the recognition of areas of opacity and uncertainty where ideology alone was not a faultless guide.

Berlin—Ecke Schönhauser's offense to political authority lay in its admonition to *see* East Germany in a fashion distinct from that implied by official ideology. Still, defining *Berlin—Ecke Schönhauser*'s relation to these events is not an easy task. In all likelihood, the film would never have gotten off the ground if not for the Twentieth CPSU Congress,[29] but the project generated little controversy until well after its debut in movie theaters. The first documentary trace of the film is its scenario, which was approved by the studio in July 1956.[30] The political confusion of the day hardly seems to have impinged upon the film's production schedule.[31] Official reception began to sour decisively only after the film had completed its strong run.[32] In addition, *Berlin—Ecke Schönhauser* seems almost willfully opaque toward political events. Indeed, the references that date the film concern American pop culture. Angelika, for example, tells Dieter that her ideal boyfriend would look like James Dean. Thus teasing out the work's full significance as an intervention in the wider contestation of East German society requires a number of steps. The first is a brief rehearsal of the political aftermath of the Twentieth Congress in the GDR as well as its impact on the film industry. My analysis will then turn to the controversy among filmmakers and functionaries concerning the production itself. *Berlin—Ecke Schönhauser* was only one of several films that came under official attack during a "Party Activists' Congress." Held during the first half of 1958, this series of internal meetings at the studio concerned the purpose of the GDR's cinema. A nuanced reading of the discussion reveals a rather complex process of negotiation among artists, the studio's management, the HV Film, and the Party. However great their ideological misgivings, officials came to recognize that Klein and Kohlhaase's picture achieved something found in few DEFA productions: the suspension of disbelief. If the work failed to present the GDR as the brave society of tomorrow, at least it offered an image of East Germany that seemed authentic and credible—a result of obvious utility for a state whose legitimacy was always in doubt.

THE IMPACT OF THE TWENTIETH CPSU CONGRESS ON THE GDR

The immediate effects of the Twentieth CPSU Congress were far less dramatic in the GDR than in other East Bloc states. News of Khrushchev's revelations of Stalinist crimes began seeping in from the West around March 18. These reports undoubtedly fueled popular discontent. Throughout 1956, there were isolated strikes and protests.[33] The official disavowal of the "Great Leader's" aura of infallibility came as a particular shock to the SED's own rank and file, many of whom began openly to question the Party's leadership. Still, the Ulbricht regime displayed an uncanny ability to stay out in front of the situation. The SED moved quickly to denounce the "cult of personality" and "dogmatism." Summer brought the rehabilitation of various functionaries and the amnesty of 11,000 prisoners. Even so, the regime managed to avoid an official "discussion of errors." In stark contrast to their counterparts in Hungary and Poland, East German intellectuals were never in open revolt. Many of them perceived de-Stalinization to be more of a Soviet than a German phenomenon. As in 1953, they believed that the Party's power had to be maintained if a new and better Germany was to rise from the ashes of fascism.[34]

After the Soviets crushed the Hungarian uprising in November, Ulbricht was able to backpedal on inner-Party democracy and move against those who had supported "revisionism." At the same time, the Party leadership stopped short of a complete return to the status quo ante. Particularly in terms of economic planning, the Twentieth CPSU Congress was consistent with the Ulbricht regime's own goal of stimulating growth without repeating the mistakes that had led to the June 17 uprising of 1953. Even before 1956, officials had discussed moving away from Stalinist planning that stressed heavy industry—a disastrous policy for a territory whose traditional strength lay in light manufacturing—and allowing individual economic sectors greater autonomy.[35]

Of equal significance, the SED, without explicitly abandoning German unity as an immediate goal, had already begun to advocate mutual recognition between the two German states. Larger developments aided this shift in diplomatic position. In particular, West Germany's decision to join NATO in 1955 led not only to the founding of the Warsaw Pact but also to Moscow's recognition of East Berlin's sovereignty as well.[36] This period further witnessed a shift in Moscow's main foreign policy objectives regarding the GDR. Realizing that the Federal Republic's integration into the Western alliance could not be reversed, the Soviets increasingly sought to guarantee the GDR's viability in the framework of long-term accommodation with the West. Meanwhile, Ulbricht was able to exploit the 1956 crisis in order to improve his position relative to Moscow by outmaneuvering two rivals within the Politburo who enjoyed Khrushchev's favor.[37]

With its position strengthened in the aftermath of the 1956 crisis, the SED's leadership prepared to rejoin the ideological offensive for the first time since the June 17 uprising of 1953. The new campaign had clear implications for cultural policy. Once again, officials emphasized art's poetic function in language reminiscent of Gorky's famous formulation of socialist realism. At the SED's Fifth Party Congress in July 1958, Ulbricht promised that East Germany would surpass West Germany's standard of living by the end of 1961. Attaining this ambitious goal would require nothing less than a "cultural revolution" capable of overcoming "the still evident division between art and life." The time had come for artists to join workers at factories and for workers to start cultivating their artistic talents. Only then could the "further elevation of socialist consciousness" so necessary for "completing the construction of socialism in the GDR" be achieved.[38]

THE EFFECT OF POLITICAL EVENTS ON THE FILM INDUSTRY

The film industry was hardly immune to the shock emanating from the Twentieth CPSU Congress. In April 1956, a special meeting was called for all Party members employed at the feature film studio. There the movie director Konrad Wolf and DEFA's Party secretary Herbert Zank officially informed their colleagues about Khrushchev's "secret" speech. They were met by reactions that included both outrage and confusion. One woman asked, "How is this possible?" She then criticized fellow Party members for failing to come to the defense of falsely arrested comrades in the past. Others complained about the corruption of Marxism-Leninism through the introduction of religious dogmas propagated by Stalin, whom Gerhard Klein said should be posthumously expelled from the Party. Another man concluded, "If we had been in the position ten years ago to speak about these things in an open and honest manner, then some honest comrades, some workers would not have become enemies of our first workers' and peasants' state."[39] This questioning of Communism's past had definite consequences for political authority in the present. In June, Anton Ackermann, the head of the HV Film (the state agency in charge of the studio), complained to Karl Schirdewan, the ZK secretary in charge of cadres, that "among the film artists the tendency toward alienation from life, from the Party, and our state is growing. They place themselves more and more in the rarefied atmosphere of arrogance, of the personality cult of the artist . . . of hostile reaction toward even the gentlest of criticism."[40]

Such an atmosphere quickly led to calls for reform and greater autonomy for the film industry. In June 1956, the directors Konrad Wolf and Martin Hellberg complained to fellow members of the Filmmakers' Club about delayed premieres, completed films being altered by officials fearful of the least controversy, and the unavailability of older and foreign films for study.[41] Simultaneously, Kurt Maetzig renewed an earlier proposal for the establishment of artistic production groups. These were supposed to serve at least two purposes. On the one hand, they would assure the collective nature of the creative process by providing artists with a forum for mutual cooperation and criticism. On the other hand, the new groups would help solve organizational problems plaguing the studio by allowing artists to assume directly much of the financial and political responsibility.[42]

Maetzig's plans were by no means entirely utopian, as there was often a convergence during this period between economic and artistic interests in the studio. Both filmmakers and managers had reasons to resent state interference, which not only set limits on artistic expression but also wreaked havoc with production schedules. Moreover, by the beginning of 1956, the accommodation between economic and artistic objectives that had allowed the studio to dramatically increase its production over the prior two years was in jeopardy. The Fourth German Writers' Congress of January 1956 had marked a clear end to the "New Course" as far as cultural policy went. An article by Anton Ackermann that appeared the same month in the industry's trade journal, *Deutsche Filmkunst*, made it clear that the time had come for the filmmakers to rededicate themselves to their ideological mission.[43] Almost simultaneously, the studio came under heavy criticism from the Party's Central State Control Commission, which issued a report in which a number of wasteful practices were alleged. These included inefficient planning and paying underemployed actors inflated salaries, as well as hiring authors for projects that were never realized.[44] A chronic problem plaguing DEFA was a shortage of filmable material. As the commission's report emphasized, fulfillment of the current year's plan was in question for exactly this reason.

The Twentieth Party Congress took the wind out of the SED's incipient ideological offensive. The studio management reacted simply by ignoring the directives of DEFA's supervising agency, the HV Film. At the end of

April, Ackermann wrote the studio's acting director, Albert Wilkening, threatening the studio with legal action for releasing films into production without the HV's prior approval.[45] Ackermann's bark, however, was worse than his bite. For much of 1956, the studio seems to have functioned in a state of quasi autarchy.[46] Even after the political tide had turned, the HV director struck a conciliatory stance. In the May 1957 issue of *Deutsche Filmkunst*, Ackermann conceded that there was no point going "from one extreme to the other" and that "of eleven years of DEFA's development, the middle third [were characterized by] retardation through administrative interference, etc." Suggesting a virtue of what others would regard as a vice, the HV director emphasized: "Now [administrative] instances are no longer inhibiting art, but an 'inner censor' [is functioning]. . . . It is a question of recognizing mistakes and correcting these. And that's something a true artist does."[47]

The immediate aftermath of the 1956 crisis clearly favored the studio. In January 1957, a directive of the Cultural Ministry formalized the feature film studio's greater autonomy by granting it and its three sister enterprises—the studios for documentary, popular-scientific, and animated film—the right to develop and approve scripts on their own initiative. The HV's political and artistic supervision was limited largely to approving a "thematic plan," an overview of proposed projects at the beginning of each production season. This had previously often been little more than a wish list of movies desired by the Party. Now the initiative was supposed to lie with the studio, which would consult with artists and come up with a feasible list of projects. Filmmakers would also be allowed to form the artistic production groups Maetzig had advocated, although the responsibility to be assigned to them was only vaguely indicated.[48] At about the same time, the MfK announced the formation of individual Film Approval Commissions (Filmabnahme Kommissionen) for the various studios, whose members would consist mainly of artists and critics.[49]

Impressive as these concessions were, the studio had little time to savor them. As early as May 1957, ZK Secretary Paul Wandel summoned DEFA's top management, Minister of Culture Becher, and Ackermann to a meeting in order to express grave disappointment with the studio's proposed production plan. Wandel complained of a "nearly complete lack of film themes that [concern] essential aspects of the social life of our workers' and peasants' power, the important developmental processes of our socialist reality."[50] By the summer, signs of the impending ideological "offensive" were unmistakable. In October, a cultural conference emphatically reasserted the Party's prerogative in artistic matters. Wilhelm Girnus, a functionary who had played a notorious role during the formalism debates of the early fifties, reminded artists that "cultural issues are issues of power." Girnus reduced the relationship of politics and art to a simple formula: "Science and art must contribute to the strengthening of socialist state power, and socialist state power must do its part [to ensure] that socialist culture really becomes the *single dominant* culture."[51] Official talk of "cultural democratization" that had persisted well into the first half of 1957 was over.

The HV Film needed little prodding concerning the interpretation of these signals. Ackermann returned quickly to the "bureaucratic" methods that he had recently forsworn. By the winter of 1958, several leading filmmakers were so incensed about conditions in their industry that they threatened to complain to Ulbricht and Minister President Grotewohl directly. During a meeting of a studio advisory board, these artists lamented, "We find ourselves as Comrade artists in a situation like blind truffle pigs: we search and search, then if we find something, we are suddenly jerked backward—you must not!—or: you may!—Why, because?—that we find out later, or not at all."[52]

THE PARTY ACTIVISTS' CONVENTION

As these events within the film industry were unfolding, *Berlin—Ecke Schönhauser* was enjoying its excellent run. None of the generally positive reviews in the GDR press hinted that the film was about to become the object of controversy. The forum in which official criticism of the film occurred was a "Party Activists' Convention" (*Parteiaktivtagung*) that spanned five separate sessions during March and April 1958.[53] Attended by leading artists, management, and MfK and ZK apparatus functionaries, these discussions were part of a wider effort by the regime to set a clear cultural agenda after a prolonged period of ideological indirection. The Party Activists' Convention was to pave the way for an industry-wide film conference in July, which in turn was to be held in preparation for the Fifth SED Party Conference later that month.

Going into the Activists' Convention, functionaries were concerned about two related but distinct tendencies they discerned within the studio: direct Western influence and "revisionism." In January 1958, Siegfried Wagner, the functionary in charge of the ZK's cultural office, sent a letter to Erich Wendt complaining of DEFA's lack of an ideologically informed policy regarding coproductions with capitalist film companies as well as the easy access to the studio that Western artists enjoyed.[54] Wendt assessed the situation in a somewhat different fashion. He wrote back complaining that the problem was not the presence of Western artists, but rather that "the West is in the heads of our artists."[55]

Characteristic of the problem of direct influence that Wagner emphasized were three film projects by Western filmmakers. The common accusation against all these productions was their similarity to commercial movies. Hans Heinrich's *Meine Frau macht Musik* (My Wife Makes Music, 1958) followed in the tradition of the German "revue" film—roughly equivalent to a chorus-line musical. Its unlikely plot concerned the discovery of an East Berlin housewife by an Italian singer, who over her husband's objection turns her into a nightclub singer. Artur Pohl's *Die Spielbank Affaire* (The Casino Scandal, 1957) was set on the French Riviera. In order to counteract the glamorous locale, DEFA ended up releasing the production in black and white rather than color.[56] Finally, Ernesto Remani's *Die Schönste* (The Most Beautiful), the only one of these three films to be banned, was also set in the West. It concerned two boys of different economic backgrounds who make a bet concerning whose mother is more beautiful. The most serious charge leveled against the work was its reconciliatory treatment of class differences and by extension of the East/West conflict.[57]

In contrast, *Berlin—Ecke Schönhauser* was included in a group of productions that showed evidence of "ideological softening." Made by socialist directors and set in the GDR, the so-called "Berlin" films nevertheless failed to deliver what the Party leadership desired: the image of a new society marching toward the future. The pictures ranged from a second self-conscious emulation of Italian neorealism, Heiner Carow's *Sheriff Teddy* (1957), to a detective thriller by Joachim Kunert with a socialist moral, *Tatort Berlin* (Crime Scene Berlin, 1957).[58]

Another project charged with revisionism at the Activists' Convention was Konrad Wolf's *Sonnensucher* (Sun Seekers, 1959/1971). Easily DEFA's most direct response to de-Stalinization, the film was just beginning to generate controversy. After finally being approved by the SED Politburo, it was banned at Soviet insistence shortly before its planned premiere in October 1959.[59] In contrast to the various Berlin films, this work hardly lacked progressive pathos. What gave officials occasion to pause was its setting: the Wismut Uranium mine during the early fifties, when conscripted German laborers worked directly under Soviet supervision.

The common standard against which all films criticized at the convention were judged was socialist realism. In *Berlin—Ecke Schönhauser*'s case, the implication of its neorealist style certainly did not escape the attention of functionaries. They were well aware that the aesthetic premises informing the film deviated from official doctrine. In his opening remarks at the first session, Anton Ackermann lamented that the work represented "a retreat from Gorky's realism to Zola's naturalism"—the latter author being

69

for Lukács an illustration of the inevitable decline of bourgeois realism. Ackermann likened the film to pornography.[60]

Closely allied with the question of representation was the issue of the "reality" posited as the object of that process. As noted above, functionaries complained about the preponderance of alienated teenagers in *Berlin—Ecke Schönhauser* as well as the relative lack of solid, class-conscious representatives of the proletariat. Why did the film not pay more attention to the workplaces and institutions that defined the new society? As Alexander Abusch explained, the question of "inner proportion" was not just a "teaspoon theory . . . [of whether] you add something here or take away there [from a film]" but instead a matter of "inner saturation." The issue boiled down to whether a work expressed awareness of the "battle situation" in which Communists found themselves with the "class enemy," "the great national and international, life-and-death conflict between capitalism and socialism."[61]

This strong language might seem like a call for agitational art, but functionaries were not demanding films that glorified the GDR just because they would be more effective as propaganda. If that had been the case, there would have been even less room for debate than there was. Officials did not deny outright that problems still existed in the GDR. Anton Ackermann, whose criticism of artists was especially stern, was fully willing to concede that life in the West *appeared* to be better. "There is much nicer fashion than here at home. The shoe buckles and display windows are much prettier." "But," he hastened to add, "the whole world order there is going under, and our world is rising up." What was really at stake was a matter of having the proper eyes, for, as Ackermann attested, "blindness is a sickness of the decaying class. Today, the seers are the class of the future, the working class."[62]

Closely allied with the call for images truly infused by the truth of a society progressing toward the future was the desire for "positive heroes." Siegfried Wagner from the ZK's cultural section rejected the idea that the "most interesting people in the GDR" were the "petty criminal, the failure, the enemy, the *Kleinbürger*, the *Spiesser* [philistines], who develop toward socialism." Wagner wanted to know what had happened to "the normal, class-conscious worker, who develops through the various development stages of socialism as a normal person."[63]

Filmmakers contested such criticism. They did not so much question the premise of the attacks leveled against their work as plead for a fairer assessment of their accomplishments according to the same criteria. They insisted that artists and filmmakers shared the same absolute commitment to the Communist cause. Klein told his critics, "I think you are making it too easy for yourselves when you argue: the artist comrades are turning their backs on the beauty of life! No, they are fighting so that all people will recognize this beauty in their lives."[64] Similarly, Kohlhaase averred, "I, for my part, fully accept the question framed at the [October 1957] Cultural Conference: what serves the Party is good; what harms it is bad. That is an unambiguous criterion and judgment of works of film art."[65] Ironically, Konrad Wolf, who was in the midst of a project destined to be banned, used some of the most militant language heard at the convention to articulate the task facing the film industry. For him, artists and functionaries were participating in "a very complicated ideological battle, which our Party has begun." This situation required them to "occupy the right battle positions together, clean [their] weapons . . . and aim them at the target." For Wolf, the overriding issue was "the fire power of our art."[66]

However emphatic, the artists' declarations of loyalty and common purpose could not obscure differences of opinion among the Activists' Convention's participants. Kohlhaase proposed that the most important issue facing filmmakers was "how you can make the individual aware of the historical role which he plays."[67] Even if most participants at the Activists' Convention would probably have agreed with this statement, there remained the question of how this goal could best be achieved. Artists emphasized that not only was it important for films to convey the correct message, but they had to do so effectively. Kohlhaase himself pointed out that "an important political theme that does not turn into a film success is a public defeat," which would only increase audience resistance toward DEFA productions.[68] Slatan Dudow argued, "We confuse very often the concept 'political film' with the words 'pursuing politics with films.'" In his opinion, one proof of real success for the studio would be an "outwardly unpolitical film" that would have "tremendous political ramifications."[69] Gerhard Klein made a similar argument by asking: "What is more important? Depicting hate toward the enemy or encouraging [it] in the viewer?"[70]

As is evident in both Dudow's and Klein's remarks, a basic question underlying much of the debate during the Activists' Convention was the relation between a film and its audience. The dominant metaphor for discussing this problem was education and was inseparable from the conceptualization of state authority itself. In his opening remarks to the Activists' Convention, Ackermann declared, "What's most important during the construction of socialism is the education of new people . . . and here the cinema as socialist art has to make its contribution."[71] The purpose of state authority was to instruct and uplift, helping the objects of its power to see the world with the same eyes as the vanguard of the working class.

Again, artists did not attempt to challenge such a basic paradigm outright but instead defined their own positions within its terms. They essentially pointed out that films, if they were to be conceived as learning materials for the *Volk*, hardly needed to be didactic in order to accomplish their purpose. In particular, Dudow questioned the function of the "positive hero." Should such a figure simply display heroic qualities?[72] Closely allied with the issue of how films were supposed to affect viewers was the question of who these viewers actually were. In the scriptwriter Kurt Stern's opinion, it was important to make films that would satisfy not only "the most progressive and most active comrades" but also "the indifferent," "the unsatisfied," and even "those who are still against us."[73]

Functionaries were concerned with the very directness with which *Berlin–Ecke Schönhauser* depicted the state in its role as educator. In their opinion, the film's youthful protagonists failed to negotiate the transition from dependency to maturity in an appropriate manner. Their personal development did not occur "organically" as part of a wider social process, but rather resulted from a naked confrontation with authority. Ackermann complained that "the strong, emotional, lasting effect of the film" resulted neither from some "positive transformation" nor from its affirmative conclusion. Rather, the HV director pointed out, "What you notice about a film is . . . that which is most impressively depicted, and here that is doubtlessly the negative occurrences. The only positive [elements] . . . are police officers."[74] Similarly, Alexander Abusch asked, "How did it come about that the development of socialism is depicted there only [through] . . . the too good and too wise . . . figure of the people's police officer?" Why was not there a single "reasonable, politically conscious person from the working class" in the film?[75]

Of course, *Berlin–Ecke Schönhauser*'s very theme, youth alienation, was rich in metaphorical resonance. Klein and Kohlhaase tried to justify their project as a response to actual sociological conditions, but this argument was disingenuous.[76] Since the GDR conceived of itself as the society of the future, the support of the young for the state was axiomatic. *Berlin–Ecke Schönhauser* challenged such political premises less in its depiction of disenchanted youth per se—obviously a few victims of corrupting Western influence were necessary to justify the Party's vigilance[77]—than in the resolution of the conflict between its protagonists and state authority. However tame its plot, the film failed to deliver the image of the new society the Party demanded. Its protagonists hardly correspond to those who were supposed to populate the brave new world. The detective is a kindly man, not an inspiring one. It is his patience, not his revolution-ary élan, that wins the day. Few grand words are spoken. There is no great demonstration of socialist solidarity. The new order, represented by a few figures of authority, is an almost alien presence within Berlin's cityscape. The city of the future, the true present-day reality of socialism, is conspic-uous only through its absence.

The metaphors articulated in *Berlin—Ecke Schönhauser* also defined the discussion of the studio's role as a socialist institution and its relation-ship with the state. Determining DEFA's degree of relative autonomy was a matter of political pedagogy or parental guidance. During the fall of 1956, Maetzig justified his proposal for artistic work groups in language that cast himself and other artists in the role of adolescents. "The previous relationship of parents and children" between functionaries and artists may have had its advantages but had become outmoded. Maetzig as-serted that "the children are gradually becoming adult and can grow into responsible persons only if they are delegated authority and accorded trust."[78] At the Activists' Convention, Maetzig claimed that these words now made him "turn red" in shame because of their presumptive tone.[79] Still, he professed having hurt feelings. While he acknowledged HV Di-rector Ackermann as a mentor, the director complained of having been treated like a "a dressed-down school child . . . to whom the teacher is speaking."[80] Ackermann, for his part, was also repentant. He conceded that he failed as director of the HV Film in "establishing the proper or-ganic relationship between greater or even full independence in the stu-dios and the educational function of the state."[81]

Indeed, artists succeeded during the Activists' Convention in casting themselves in the role of abused pupils. Ackermann was the real loser in the affair. In his opening remarks, he promised to whip the studio into shape by ridding it of the last remnants of Western influence and curing artists of their defeatist, revisionist attitudes. By the convention's third session three weeks later, Ackermann had conceded personal defeat. Ackermann, who had criticized one film earlier in the convention for lending credence to the Western cliché that "the Party sacrifices its func-tionaries [like] one stuffed-shirt after the other,"[82] now made a pathetic statement of resignation: "HV directors come and go, and so I am going now." Apparently still unrepentant, Ackermann added, "But, dear Com-rades, you often forced us [that is, the HV Film] to our knees. . . . That was not a healthy atmosphere." He hoped that his successors would not have to put up with what he had, including the taunt "When Ackermann ar-rives, art dies."[83]

Without attacking the Party's transcendent authority, artists depicted themselves as honest comrades having to contend with an inflexible, narrow-minded bureaucrat impeding progress. Unlike Ackermann, they could claim opposition from the start to the DEFA films that the Activists' Convention condemned as being no better than commercial kitsch. Short-term economic priorities had not seduced them into sacrificing longer-range artistic and political objectives.[84] Moreover, filmmakers at the convention shed few tears over the expulsion of their Western colleagues from the studio. Kurt Maetzig declared, "One thing is clear, a bourgeois wing in DEFA production is not possible."[85] Gerhard Klein was of the opinion that the studio should produce only films that "serve our revolution . . . our life today . . . [and] anyone who disagrees can leave."[86] In his opinion, the time had finally come for filmmakers to "wake up" and "become an avant-garde again."[87]

Pleas such as Klein's made implicit reference to the cinema of other East Bloc countries, where a great artistic revival was under way. In the Soviet Union, filmmakers were self-consciously emulating the formal innovation that had characterized their cinema in the twenties. In Poland, directors such as Andrzej Wajda and those of the "Lodz school" were producing visually devastating films about their country's recent past. DEFA directors had to be cautious in referring to these developments because many works by their East Bloc colleagues were considered suspect in the GDR. Still, artists could complain about short-sighted bureaucratic practices impeding the unfolding of a true socialist cinema. Slatan Dudow argued that functionaries cared only if a script contained "the necessary social message" and thus failed to consider equally important factors such as visual impact. He reminded his listeners that the socialist cinema's great masterpiece, Eisenstein's *Potemkin*, had been a silent film. The time had finally come for DEFA to make up for years of neglect and harness the cinema's "most elemental power."[88]

Overall, the Activists' Convention's outcome was quite positive for the studio. Its director, Albert Wilkening, who took heat for advocating coproduction for economic reasons, exercised some self-criticism but continued in office.[89] DEFA's one major casualty was its chief dramaturge, Rudolf Böhm, who was accused of entering into close personal relations with Westerners at the studio.[90] Filmmakers themselves acknowledged errors and promised to try harder next time, but they generally escaped worse humiliation. One of the more extensive self-criticisms came from Maetzig, who distanced himself from his earlier call for artistic production groups. In particular, he tried to refute the claim that he had been inspired by practices in the Polish film industry—a damaging accusation considering the "revisionist" course that events took in Poland after the Twentieth CPSU Congress. Even so, Maetzig's proposal, which apparently was shelved quickly despite initial MfK promises, would be on the verge of actual implementation before the year was out.[91]

Of course, artists hardly routed Ackermann through the force of argument alone. For one, the HV Film director did not enjoy real prestige within the Party. Once regarded as the SED's leading ideologue, he had been expelled from the Politburo in the aftermath of the 1953 crisis. A number of broader developments also worked to the artists' advantage. One lesson of the Twentieth CPSU Congress was that Marxist ideology, whatever its own pretensions to science, did not supersede all other forms of expert knowledge. Closer to home, one result of the June 17 uprising and the New Course was at least pro forma acknowledgment by the regime of art's autonomy. In addition, artists' complaints about the HV Film's leadership style fit in well with the rationale behind broad economic reforms then under way. In order to increase the effectiveness of the planning process, central administrations like the HV Film were being replaced in various industries by Vereinigungen Volkseigenen Betriebe (Cartels of People's Enterprises, VVB). These middle-level agencies were supposed to allow various branches of the economy to become quasi-autonomous, self-regulating entities that would relieve the state of direct responsibility for lower-level decision making.[92] So the Activists' Convention concluded not only with Ackermann's firing but with the abolishment of his position. His deputy, Hermann Schauer, became the head of the newly formed VVB Film. Ironically, the VVB Film lasted only a few years, after which the HV Film was reinstituted.

The tide would also not have turned against Ackermann if artists had not had the support of other functionaries on many questions. On the last day of the Activists' Convention, Alfred Kurella, who as a Politburo candidate was the highest-ranking official in attendance, came down on the side of the filmmakers by emphasizing the "autonomous laws of film." He pointedly praised the Soviet film *The Cranes Are Flying* (Mikhail Kalatozov, 1957), a work that marked the Soviet cinema's radical departure from the staid film practice of the Stalinist era. Kurella saw little point in prolonging the discussion of *Die Schönste* and other DEFA films by Western filmmakers. These were clearly trash in his estimation. What he wanted the industry to consider was why "essentially good films" like *Berlin—Ecke Schönhauser* were still marred by "decisive mistakes."[93] By the time the film conference took place in July, Abusch, despite certain reservations, ended up praising Klein and Kohlhaase's work as nothing less than "a brave advance in the present-day thematic."[94] While the deputy cultural minister still insisted that neorealism as a method for depicting socialism resulted at best in "superficial pseudo-truth," he was willing to concede that GDR filmmakers could still learn something of value from their Italian peers.[95] So even as the Party was embarking on a cultural revolution that stressed art's poetic function in the Gorkian sense, two of its top cultural politicians were cautiously allowing for the validity of other realist stances within the film industry.

CONCLUSION

Khrushchev's famous secret speech before the Twentieth CPSU Congress signaled a revision of the socialist project's utopian self-understanding. For the East German cinema, the 1956 political crisis had ramifications both institutionally and artistically. Even after the regime regained the upper hand in the situation, filmmakers were able to wring concessions from the state concerning the studio's relative autonomy. As the reception history of Klein and Kohlhaase's work demonstrates, functionaries were willing partly to ignore clear deviations from socialist realist principles, as long as filmmakers seemed to be approaching the elusive goal of presenting compelling images of the new society. Complex negotiations were under way concerning the film industry's implicit pact with the state and its role in the new society.

By associating the GDR with "ordinary" experience and nonofficial youth culture, *Berlin—Ecke Schönhauser* anticipated the East German *Alltagsfilme* that began to appear over a decade later. In a sense, the work introduced an element of indeterminacy into the studio's mission. Were artists supposed to translate ideological premises into images or posit a preexisting East German society whose existence was guaranteed by something other than politics? In 1958, officials were wary of associating the GDR too closely with the here and now. As Ackermann's fate at the Activists' Convention suggests, the consequences of such a move for their own authority were too unpredictable. What role would remain for the Party if the land it governed was already self-sufficient, if its progeny already stood on their own? Thus officials insisted that East Germany's reality lay not on the phenomenological surface open to universal inspection but with the spirit of history. Epiphenomena like the rise of a new, independent youth culture were not worthy of extensive treatment, as they were not truly a part of the great transformation under way. A number of years would have to elapse before officials would appreciate fully the political value of positing a society existing outside of official culture or of cultivating the type of "authenticity" achieved by Klein and Kohlhaase. For the time being, their film was an interesting failure, and its promise, however powerful, was vague and undefined. The regime continued to seek refuge in the future's unfolding. East Germany "in the raw" was still too tenuous a place, its "everyday" actuality too treacherous an ally.

Slatan Dudow published his own thoughts on the eve of the Film Conference in *Neues Deutschland*. Here he lamented, "The populace want[s] to see itself on the screen—with its daily cares and joys, with the countless incidents and ensnarements. . . . We [filmmakers] have not put our listening ear on the pulse of life. We have not directed our observing glance to the everyday." Dudow hastened to add that, of course, "our everyday changes very quickly, unstoppably at very high speed." For this reason, as the Party's new Cultural Revolution platform demanded, it was necessary for artists to constantly renew their contact with workers, to share their lives with them.[96] In short, the veteran director allowed for no necessary contradiction between recording a random moment of existence and capturing history in the making. The two tasks should be identical. Whatever its faults, *Berlin—Ecke Schönhauser* succeeded at the first of them. The trick was to accomplish both simultaneously. During the Activists' Convention, filmmakers pleaded for time and patience. Allowed space to develop, their art would infuse the quotidian with the eternal truth of socialism and render the phenomenological transparent to the laws of history. In the end, functionaries took artists more or less at their word, but the debate was far from over.

3

A Case of Love Confused?

Slatan Dudow's *Verwirrung der Liebe* as a Meditation on Art and Industry

Slatan Dudow's *Verwirrung der Liebe* (Love Confused, 1959) is a light and fanciful romantic comedy. Featuring imaginative sets, sensuous interludes, and a lively score, it is quite different from *Berlin—Ecke Schön-hauser*. If the earlier production emphasized film's indexical quality—its supposed ability to capture a precinematic reality—Dudow's work had more to do with the realm of fantasy, dream, and desire. Instead of taking issue with what the GDR was like in the present, *Verwirrung der Liebe* addressed the regime's utopian vision, the grandiose "Cultural Revolution" proclaimed at the Fifth SED Party Congress of July 1958. The central tenet of this platform was that the working class had to "storm the heights of culture" in order to achieve its historic mission. As Walter Ulbricht explained at a labor congress the following year, "You cannot work at the factory in socialist fashion and then do something completely different at home." Workers had to abandon "old habits" and become participants in a new national culture in which everyday life would be instilled with the creative power of art. Thus the time had come for men to stop playing skat in bars while the women stayed home and darned socks. Instead, the whole family should be spending the evening in the theater raising their socialist consciousness![1] In keeping with the Cultural Revolution, Dudow's goal in making *Verwirrung der Liebe* was to "point out new aspects of our society, to uncover [its] special brightness [*Heiterkeit*]" and to show how "beauty and joie de vivre" had become "active social factors" in the new state.[2]

Despite these lofty intentions, much of the controversy surrounding Dudow's work was rather prosaic. Before its release, functionaries questioned the inclusion of a nude bathing scene. This issue proved so sensitive that Walter Ulbricht and his wife, Lotte, screened the film privately in order to decide the matter. Once the objectionable scene was reshot with swimsuits, the film enjoyed a strong run in movie theaters. Dudow's difficulties, though, were only just beginning. First, a rather heated debate concerning the film broke out in the press. Readers wrote to major publications both praising the film lavishly and attacking it harshly. Then the director became the target of an internal studio investigation of cost overruns on the project. An extravagant personality, the Bulgarian-born "father" of the German Communist cinema was notorious for his inability to follow a schedule or budget. Since a major reform effort was under way within the DEFA feature film studio, the time was inopportune for immoderation. In keeping with the officially proclaimed Cultural Revolution, the goal was to reconcile the artistic and industrial aspects of moviemaking. Higher economic efficiency, better-quality movies, and political objectives were all held to be attainable if art and life could be effectively integrated in the process of production itself. Dudow—his enemies contended—epitomized the prima donna who demanded privileges and ignored financial constraints. Thus he embodied the past rather than the future.

But what could skinny-dipping possibly have to do with industrial efficiency? And why would the attention of the SED's first secretary, the most powerful man in the GDR, be required to decide whether a film could include nudity? It is my contention that these questions are apt ones for understanding the juncture DEFA, and more generally the East German socialist project, had reached by the late fifties. First, the picture is indicative of the great distance the German Communist movement had traveled culturally since its formation during the Weimar Republic. As a personage, Dudow was a living link to the avant-garde, often libertine, cultural traditions associated with the left during the Weimar Republic, in which nudism was a significant element. Aesthetically staid, his picture exhibits little of the modernist energy associated with the art of that era. Still, Dudow developed a definite critique of the strange admixture of wild utopian aspirations and *kleinbürgerlich* norms for personal behavior that characterized official culture under Ulbricht. Second, the controversies surrounding *Verwirrung der Liebe* suggest ways that the language of the Cultural Revolution informed the actual construction and contestation of the studio as a site of cultural production. While Dudow became a target of criticism, other filmmakers successfully argued for internal organizational reform of the studio on the basis of the Party's platform.

Of great importance for understanding the issues at stake in the film and its reception is the notion of "socialist morality." The Party's highly conventional moral expectations for its members were closely allied with its call for a Cultural Revolution. For the Party, both were part of a more general project of aesthetic education, whose ultimate goal ironically often came down to little more than greater industrial productivity. The greater their artistic and ethical sensibility, it was held, the more GDR workers would internalize the Party's precepts and voluntarily submit to both political and workplace discipline. At the same time, the Cultural Revolution still drew on an idealistic conception of art as a moral and emancipatory force. Thus filmmakers and others tried to envision a more complex process of emancipation through art. For them, the success of the socialist project depended, in the abstract, on the growing autonomy of individuals and, more directly, on granting institutions like DEFA a measure of self-control, even quasi self-governance. According to this view, socialist morality was a question of inner responsibility as much as external duty. The Party should lead but also have trust in others, or at least in fellow socialists, to follow on their own accord.

After briefly sketching Dudow's unique stature within the East German cinema, the chapter's first section employs a method from literary criticism, archetypal analysis, to interpret the film as a meditation on the relation between the utopian and the real with direct bearing on the regime's Cultural Revolution platform. My analysis then turns to *Verwirrung der Liebe*'s official reception and the discussion of the film in the press and shows how these debates reveal a spectrum of varying attitudes toward the practical significance of the SED's ideological aspirations. At the heart of this debate was the status of the regime's ambitious goals for socialism. Were these merely a pretext for the rigid enforcement of societal norms, or had the new society already developed sufficiently to allow new freedoms? The third section considers the controversy concerning cost overruns on *Verwirrung der Liebe* as an example of how the obvious incongruity between ideological objectives and socialism's actual practice played itself out in the studio. This incident reveals a highly fractious institution. Even for an industrial organization such as DEFA that was dedicated to an art form, transforming the process of labor into aesthetic endeavor was a utopian undertaking. Artists, management, and workers approached their shared undertaking differently and in unreconcilable ways. Finally, the chapter briefly traces DEFA's institutional history through the early 1960s. In many ways, the discursive force driving the studio's institutional development during this period was the attempt to remedy the types of issues evident in the cost overrun controversy. Ironically, *Verwirrung der Liebe* itself honored the Cultural Revolution as an ideal but raised questions about its application. The work insisted that the realms of necessity and freedom, to paraphrase Friedrich Engels's famous definition of Communism, could not be prematurely bridged. Hence Dudow may have antic- ipated that any overly zealous attempt to suspend the contradiction be- tween art and industry might end, as the studio's reform efforts did with the Eleventh Plenum, in debacle.

DUDOW AND HIS FILM

Slatan Dudow may not have been an immortal, but he was the closest to one that the East German cinema had to offer. In both literature and drama, the GDR succeeded in attracting internationally recognized, émi- gré artists, whose names recalled the glory of Weimar art. For film, though, there were no personalities of the same stature as Johannes R. Becher, Bertolt Brecht, Anna Seghers, Friedrich Wolf, or Arnold Zweig. The one person who came close was Dudow. Other leading DEFA direc- tors of his generation—Erich Engel, Martin Hellberg, Kurt Maetzig, Wolf- gang Staudte—first attained prominence in film after the war. In addition, the only one of them who enjoyed an international reputation as a film- maker, Staudte, never worked exclusively in the East or settled there. In contrast, Dudow's engagement with both cinema and the Communist cause extended back to the 1920s. Arriving in Berlin from his native Bul- garia in 1922, he studied theater, worked as a film critic, and partici- pated in Communist drama groups. For a while, he was a chorus member in Erwin Piscator's legendary theater company and later worked with Brecht as an assistant director. His career making films began in 1929 through participation in the production of several Communist documen- tary shorts. In 1931, he started work on his own feature-length film about unemployed workers, *Kuhle Wampe, oder Wem gehört die Welt?* (Kuhle Wampe, or To Whom Does the World Belong?). With scripting by Brecht and Ernst Ottwalt and music by Hanns Eisler, this became one of the most enduring artifacts of Weimar radical culture.

Dudow's postwar pictures never lived up to the great promise of his early masterpiece. His later productions were major by DEFA standards but of scant significance outside the GDR. Even so, Dudow remained a reflective artist. His theoretical articles, if limited in scope and number, demonstrate a lively intelligence. His work is also remarkable for its the- matic continuity over a period of more than thirty years. From Weimar, through French and Swiss emigration, up to his death in 1963, Dudow as a playwright and filmmaker returned frequently to two issues. The first of these was the daily experience of workers and later of GDR citizens as a site of progressive social transformation. This theme extended from *Kuhle Wampe* through Dudow's first two DEFA films, *Unser täglich Brot* (Our Daily Bread, 1949) and *Frauenschicksale* (The Destinies of Women, 1952), and to his last (unfinished) picture, *Christine* (1963). The second issue that fascinated Dudow was humor as a means of promoting political consciousness. This aspect of his work is evident in certain scenes in *Kuhle Wampe*, as well as in works completed in exile, including the film *Seifenblassen* (Soap Bubbles, 1935).[3]

Shortly after his return to East Germany in 1947, Dudow published an essay titled "Comedy and Its Social Function." Here he attempted to sketch out a dramatic theory in which humor fulfilled a role comparable to the category of *Verfremdung* (estrangement) in the ideas of his mentor, Brecht. In both cases, the desired dramatic effect involved a moment of self-estrangement for the audience, so that its members might see themselves as socially determined objects.[4] For Dudow, the value of humor had to do with its ability to make theatergoers or movie viewers recognize the absurdity of their own situation:

> Who actually laughs in comedy? Ridiculousness is a situation to which a person does not gladly confess; I would almost say that he is rarely capable of becoming conscious of his own ridiculousness. Where do we find a person who voluntarily puts his own ridiculousness on display? Even so, he wants to learn something about his own insufficiency, and, if possible, also have a laugh. The best way for him [to achieve this] is through a third party. In this [figure], he recognizes his own weakness and laughs about his own ridiculousness. And if the ridiculousness in the depicted individual becomes one with the ridiculousness of the corresponding society so that the laughter about both becomes a unity, then comedy achieves its perfection.[5]

Dudow's first DEFA project was very much in accordance with this belief in the liberating power of laughter. Titled *Weltuntergang* (End of the World), the work was a grotesque parable addressing the German populace's fear of change in the immediate postwar period. The project remained incomplete, presumably because the studio judged the work inconsistent with the official shift toward socialist realism in the late forties.[6] Whatever the exact case, the cultural political climate of the early fifties left relatively little room for the type of subversive humor that Dudow advocated.[7] In fact, the filmmaker realized only one openly satirical project at DEFA, and this was set in the Federal Republic. In *Der Hauptmann von Köln* (The Captain from Cologne, 1956), Dudow adopted the premise of Carl Zuckmayer's famous play *Der Hauptmann von Köpenick* for Cold War purposes. The movie concerns a waiter whom a veterans' association confuses with his namesake, a notorious war criminal. Far from having negative repercussions for the protagonist, this error causes him to become the toast of Cologne. His future seems assured until the real captain shows up to claim his share of the *Wirtschaftswunder*.

In Dudow's postwar work, only *Verwirrung der Liebe* makes equally evident his love for comedy and his desire to depict the progressive transformation of workers' lives under socialism. The reasons why these themes tended to remain separate in his other films are not difficult to surmise. Other DEFA directors had attempted to set humorous stories in the GDR, but the antecedents they provided were hardly encouraging. Judging from his available statements, it is almost certain that Dudow dismissed most of these films either as kitsch alien to socialism or as ideologically "schematic" works that failed cinematically.[8] More significantly, according to Dudow's own theoretical premises, writing a comedy was equivalent to "holding court, whether about people or social conditions, and laughter is the final and highest instance of judgment."[9] Any film made in such a spirit and set in the GDR clearly ran the risk of official displeasure, since the Party reserved for itself the right to appraise the new society's progress.

To understand the limitations Dudow was working under, it is useful to consider the insights of "archetypal" analysis, which suggest that only a narrow range of comic possibilities might have satisfied Dudow's brief as a loyal socialist filmmaker interested in the humorous depiction of the new society. In his famous analysis of the "structural principles" of literature, Northrop Frye describes the basic plot of dramatic comedy as involving a frustrated lover who revolts against paternal authority: "At the beginning of the play the obstructing characters are in charge of the play's society, and the audience recognizes that they are usurpers. At the end of the play the device in the plot that brings hero and heroine together causes a new society to crystallize around the hero, and the moment when this crystallization occurs is the point of resolution in the action, the comic discovery."[10] Frye further distinguishes among six phases or structures of comedy, which span the distance between irony and romance. The first five of these, Frye argues, correspond to "a sequence of stages in the life of a redeemed society."[11] In the first phase, this order is shown "in its infancy, swaddled and smothered by the society it should replace." In the third phase, the new reaches maturity and triumphs. By the fifth phase, it is already "part of a settled order which has been there from the beginning, an order which takes on an increasingly religious cast and seems to be drawing away from human experience altogether."[12]

Dudow could hardly have made an ironic comedy about the GDR verging on open satire. As Frye notes, such comedies tend to emphasize obstructing characters rather than scenes of discovery and reconciliation. As far as the SED was concerned, the GDR already was a redeemed society where the forces of progress had seized power and antagonism between the generations was obsolete. Thus it would have been subversive for Dudow to produce a film that made light of older figures embodying existing authority by sympathizing with the travails of younger characters representing a new, just order. At the same time, a comedy suggesting a static society outside of history would also have been impermissible. Officially, the GDR was a country on the move, whose leadership was in tune with the real needs of the populace. The director therefore had to come up with a plot that landed clearly to the right of the third phase, or on the side of Frye's scale closest to romance, but one that did not stray too far from the middle of the yardstick. What essentially remained was Frye's fourth phase of comedy. In contrast to the other archetypes that leave the alternative to the existing society only vaguely defined, this one plays itself out on two planes. The plot commences in the "normal world" of obligation and social convention, proceeds into a "green," arcadian one associated with boundless fertility and wish fulfillment, reaches its resolution, and returns back to the "normal world." Even if the second world is ultimately abandoned, passing through it charges the action with "the symbolism of the victory of summer over winter" and fulfills "the archtypical function of literature in visualizing the world of desire, not as an escape from 'reality,' but as the genuine form of the world that human life tries to imitate."[13]

In order to understand how *Verwirrung der Liebe* exhibits the structural characteristics Frye associates with the fourth phase of comedy, it is necessary to consider the movie's plot in some detail. The four main protagonists are two young couples. Dieter and Sonja study medicine and art respectively, while Edy and Siegi are workers. The film begins in the first pair's "normal" world. Dieter is introduced attending a lecture; Sonja participating in a painting class. Their lives are constrained by obligations associated with time. Both are rushing to meet each other after class, but other commitments interfere with their rendezvous. Dieter is already late for the amateur FDJ "agit-prop" group he directs. Sonja has to help prepare a "carnival" party, which the art students are hosting.

The first introduction to what Frye describes as the "green" world occurs when Sonja, Dieter, and other guests arrive at the party and change into costume. Earlier, Sonja tells Dieter, "I bet you will not be able to recognize me," and her words prove prophetic. Dressed in Bacchanalian garb, Dieter wanders through a warren of colorful, imaginatively decorated rooms. In one chamber, partygoers dressed as angels dance to serene harp music. Another space is filled by celebrants who, prodded on by devils, dance to jazz with wild abandon. Dieter enters a room labeled "Castel D'Amour" by sliding down a chute, and two women successively accost him with full kisses on the lips. Alcohol flows freely, while imaginatively clad revelers smooch left and right.

The action takes form when the debauch fails to achieve an orderly conclusion. Dieter and Sonja have agreed to a midnight rendezvous, when all of the partygoers will reveal their identities. As the moment approaches, Sonja watches Dieter mistakenly pursuing Siegi. The removal of the masks reveals his error, but he kisses Siegi all the same. Sonja leaves the party in distress.

A dream sequence follows in which Dieter's academic anxieties become entangled with his romantic confusion and scenes from the carnival. One of his professors assumes the pose of Alexander von Humboldt in the famous statue in front of the university in Berlin. He tosses an apple toward Dieter. Siegi, clothed only in fig leaves, takes a bite from the fruit. Sonja appears in her carnival costume. The camera zooms in on her, only to have her countenance change to Siegi's.

The next morning, Dieter wakes to the irritating sound of an alarm clock, arrives late for his class in surgery, and suffers his professor's sarcasm. The next scene shows him successfully begging forgiveness from Sonja.

This initial reestablishment of normalcy proves tenuous. The first taste of the realm of desire has had its effect. The film's second major segment begins with a comic chase scene. Dieter sees Siegi pass by on a bus and takes off in wild pursuit in a cab, finally catching up with her in the subway, as the train she has boarded pulls out of the station. Guileless as he is, Dieter reports the incident in detail to Sonja, who by now is hardly unaffected by her boyfriend's behavior. Seeking mental repose, Sonja takes a sabbatical from her studies and volunteers to work in a factory.

At her newfound place of employment as a lathe operator, Sonja meets Siegi, whom she invites to model for a painting. The next segment begins with Dieter arriving at Sonja's apartment and immediately noticing Siegi's portrait. Sonja now decides to force the issue. She sets Siegi up by inviting her to a concert and giving the second ticket to Dieter. By now, Dieter's life is also in disarray. His agit-prop group is angry with him, and his schoolwork has suffered, too. Thus, when Siegi proposes that they escape these obligations by going to the Baltic Sea together, he jumps at the chance.

This decision brings Edy into play. Dressed in work fatigues, he visits Sonja at her apartment to inform her of their respective lovers' vacation plans. Sonja feigns nonchalance but accepts Edy's invitation to a second concert. A series of shots emphasizes the beauty of the concertgoing experience as well as the opulent hall of the East Berlin State Opera. While they are taking their seats, Edy proudly tells Sonja the exact number of bricks he laid as a mason working on the recently rebuilt edifice.

With chords from Beethoven providing a transition, the action returns to the "green" world. Edy and Sonja are seen riding on his motorcycle down country lanes and visiting the Elbe valley, while Dieter and Sonja camp out on a Baltic beach. Sonja and Edy then visit Dresden's Zwinger Museum. They pause in front of a portrait of a reclining nude as Sonja explains: "During the Renaissance, one regarded mortal beauty as a virtue. . . . Beauty itself served to elevate humankind. It communicated a sense of self-worth." The next shots show Dieter and Siegi frolicking in the waves and then embracing in the dunes. Just in case anyone might miss the point, the scene concludes with waves breaking on the shore. Sonja and Edy are then shown going swimming in a secluded pond together, another stock image sometimes employed in DEFA films to denote sexual intimacy.

The film's fourth segment involves the attempt to incorporate the new constellation of partners into their "normal" world. One scene shows Siegi telling Sonja of her engagement to Dieter; another one features Edy awkwardly proposing to Sonja. Scenes featuring every possible pairing of the four protagonists—Edy and Dieter even have a drink together—emphasize reconciliation. Edy proudly shows off his artist fiancée to his fellow workers, and Siegi's mother provides some comic relief by pretentiously announcing to her neighbors that her daughter is marrying a doctor. To celebrate this newfound harmony, Siegi proposes a double wedding to Sonja.

The movie then enters its last segment and quickly builds toward its moment of comic discovery, which coincides with its festive conclusion. Parallel shots show Sonja and Siegi in bridal costumes walking through the archways of their respective tenement buildings to be whisked away by a modest convoy of gleaming cars, all of East German manufacture. As these proceed through the city, shots alternating between two couples make it clear that all is not well. Second thoughts, hinted at in the previous segment, now lead to a complete reversal of the action. Siegi asks Dieter if getting married means that she will never be able to kiss Edy again. Edy demands to know from Sonja if she loves him, and she responds that he should have thought of this question earlier. The cars stop, and the brides trade places.

Thus the film returns to the original constellation of partners. A student marries a student; a worker a worker. The normal world of obligation reestablishes itself. The effect of the story is clarifying rather than subversive. As if to emphasize the salutary effects of the protagonists' excursion into the green world, the last segment begins with a shot of Dieter, who repeatedly arrives late or unprepared to lectures, applying himself to his studies with new energy. Siegi, whose flirtatious ways antagonize Edy, submits finally to matrimony. Edy, an amateur boxer with the unfortunate habit of thrashing Siegi's other male acquaintances, learns to curb his temper outside the ring. Sonja receives new inspiration through working at the factory and her encounter with Edy. The triumph of a youthful yet established order is indicated in other ways, too, during the film's final scene. Two shots show a police officer directing traffic: his initial bewildered expression changes into an approving smile as he observes the exchange of brides. Siegi's mother is outraged with her daughter for giving up her chance to marry a doctor, but Sonja's father, a factory director who was once a worker, gives the whole affair his blessing. Thus spontaneity and verve allied with benign authority triumph over the last vestiges of petit bourgeois pretension and the film fades to black to the sound of a triumphant wedding march.

THE SWIMSUIT SAGA AND THE CULTURAL REVOLUTION

The authority figures in real life were not as magnanimous toward this celebration of youthful exuberance as those depicted within the work itself. Above all, officials objected to the film's sensuality, which they perceived to be a threat to socialist morality. After an initial screening on August 26, 1959, the Approval Commission under the direction of MfK State Secretary Wendt described the work as a "well-executed entertainment film." Particularly noteworthy was its optimistic premise and its creator's attempt "to demonstrate that *joie de vivre* is also at home in the GDR." At the same time, the commission concluded that the film "brackets out actual social problems and contents itself with depicting the relationships between young people . . . [leading to] a few complications and a happy end." Of greatest concern was the carnival sequence, which, it was feared, would not appeal to the sensibility of the "vanguard" but rather to "the so-called average taste of the public." Similarly, the commission members did not object to nude-bathing scenes on principle but raised the question of whether these would distract the public's attention from the work as a whole. Thus the body decided to withhold approval of the film in the version presented and recommended reducing the lengthy carnival sequence.[14]

The commission's findings were only the first stage of deliberations on the matter. Even a high-ranking functionary such as Wendt does not seem to have been fully equal to the task of disciplining the famous director. On September 26, the studio informed the commission of the completion of several cuts to the carnival sequence, totaling less than one minute, but did not mention the nude-bathing scene.[15] Wendt, apparently frustrated by the commission's failure to censor these explicitly, arranged for a viewing of the film by Alfred Kurella. Although the head of the Politburo's Commission on Cultural Matters took Dudow's side in the dispute, his decision was suddenly reversed.[16] With only days remaining before the film's scheduled public preview on October 10, Dudow hastily set off to the Baltic to reshoot the questionable scene.[17]

Even so, the saga of the missing swimsuits was hardly over. The film's general release was planned for November 13. In the interim, Dudow made one last-ditch effort to retain the nude-bathing scene by framing it as a second dream sequence. Presumably also around this time, Dudow met with Cultural Minister Alexander Abusch and the director Konrad Wolf. Dudow countered Abusch's objections to the racy scenes by claiming that Abusch himself had appeared as a nude extra in a sequence of *Kuhle Wampe* celebrating physical culture! Wolf pointed out that Abusch had also published articles in the twenties advocating nudism.[18] In short, both directors demanded an explanation of why an activity that the Party had advocated under capitalist conditions had to be treated as a taboo now that the German working class had become master of its own destiny. Thus the matter arrived before Ulbricht, who, after viewing the film privately with his wife, Lotte, insisted on proper attire.[19]

On one level, this controversy may have represented little more than a clash of sensibilities. The regime's leaders were notorious for their conventional and prudish taste, while Dudow had the reputation of being a rake,[20] a man of the senses, who might have simply rejoiced at the sight of naked bodies. Still, nude bathing had a certain history and significance in the GDR. In his memoir of a childhood spent as an American in East Germany during the fifties, Joel Agee describes the cultural politician Johannes R. Becher's obsession with stamping out the practice at Ahrenshoop, the picturesque artist colony situated on the Baltic coast.[21] In the seventies, *Freikörperkultur* developed into a mass phenomenon, and to this day East Germans pride themselves on being less inhibited on the beach than their Western compatriots. Nudism in the GDR, it has been argued, had less to do with the sexual revolution than with a search for a cultural idyll free of societal restraints. The phenomenon's acceptance cut across demographic categories, and stereotypical enthusiasts were "average" families rather than hedonists or hippies.[22]

Of course, in 1959, these developments in popular culture lay mostly in the future. Dudow's fervent interest in depicting nude bathing has to be seen in the context of the radical traditions of the Weimar period. The vehement opposition voiced by GDR officials, many of whom in their youth may have been advocates of nudism, was a sign of the profound transformation of the German Communist movement over the previous thirty years. A party that had once existed in close proximity with a rich and imaginative counterculture had become the jealous master of a state. Revolutionary exuberance now took a backseat to technocratic rhetoric and autocratic methods. Dudow's pointed exchange with Abusch suggests that the director knew precisely why he was including a little flesh and other scenes suggesting a "bohemian" mode of existence in his film. These scenes evoked an earlier period when being a German Communist had as much to do with a lifestyle of rebellion and protest as it did with submitting to Party discipline.

Pretentious as they are, Sonja's words on the elevating nature of physical beauty in the art museum scene immediately preceding Dieter and Siegi's romp on the beach were supposed to be taken seriously. Preserving the integrity of this sequence was so important to Dudow that he insisted on returning to the Baltic to reshoot the bathing sequence for a third time even after the film had previewed![23] If barred from using actors in the nude, he wanted the next best thing: ones whose clothing status would be rendered indiscernible through the use of backlighting. Indeed, the association of aesthetic experience, sensual abandon, and youthful exuberance constitutes a major subtext of *Verwirrung der Liebe*. The film's most noteworthy sequence, the carnival, takes place on sets constructed on screen by the art students. A similar motif is Sonja's use of concert tickets as a pretext for bringing Dieter and Siegi together, and classical music provides the transition from the city to the idyll of the vacationing couples. Thus art and love both provide an alternative to the realm of duty and obligation.

There are further components to the green world. The story takes place in summer, which is not only the most appropriate season for a romantic tryst but also the traditional time for school and family holidays. The film exploits the division between labor and leisure in an unusual way as well. For Sonja, volunteering in a factory provides respite from her troubles with Dieter and her frustrations as a student. Finally, the work presents consumerism as a field of self-realization. In the first segment, Sonja and Dieter meet in front of the main East Berlin department store, the "HO" on Alexanderplatz. After Edy proposes marriage to Sonja, she dashes out to a conspicuously well stocked store to buy groceries for dinner, for which she chooses an expensive wine to mark the occasion. In addition, Siegi and

Sonja return to the HO to help each other select wedding presents for their grooms.

Thus, in addition to emphasizing love and art as privileged realms, the film draws on rather conventional notions to construct a sense of freedom and individual autonomy. In each case, acting out one's desires ultimately does not subvert the normal world of obligation but redeems it. By the same token, the association of art and sex with consumerism and holiday recreation elevates the latter pair nearly to the level of aesthetic experience and reigns in the subversive potential of the former pair. Last but not least, the depiction of Sonja's factory furlough, or *Arbeitseinsatz*, in this context blunts the radical edge of "production ideology" expressed in the officially proclaimed Cultural Revolution. During the Weimar Republic, various Communist writers emphasized the industrial workplace as a uniquely privileged place of progressive consciousness formation; one of them was Ernst Ottwalt, who collaborated with Dudow and Brecht on *Kuhle Wampe*. In *Verwirrung der Liebe*, however, Dudow transforms the key premise of this earlier literary tradition into just another facet of an established order, an aspect of social existence whose significance and function is comparable to school holidays.

In many ways, what functionaries did not object to in Dudow's film is as remarkable as what did attract their ire. The work's characters are typed in a fashion that carried an obvious political significance. Dieter and Sonja represent the "intelligentsia"; Edy and Siegi the proletariat. Of the men, Edy is the more imposing—and physically taller—figure. While Dieter's flightiness leads to the love confusion in the first place, Edy is a man of a few words and a boxer, willing to fight off rival suitors with his fists if necessary. Of the women, Siegi combines good looks and a flirtatious soul, while Sonja is a serious—at times calculating—person, whose main attribute is her talent as an artist.

Given the emphasis of the official political language on labor as an aesthetic process capable of overcoming the last vestiges of social stratification, any film featuring such characters could hardly escape interpretation as a direct political parable. The Party's relationship with the educated elite was a long-standing problem. During the first years of the GDR, the regime had done its best to lure and retain expert talent with high salaries and generous economic inducements; this policy, however, went against the ideological grain and was a cause for resentment among the populace. Indeed, the long-range objective from the beginning was to replace the "old intelligentsia" with a new one comprised of workers and their children. To achieve this aim, the majority of university places were reserved for students who could demonstrate their proletarian origins, and special "Worker and Farmer's Academies" (Arbeiter- und Bauernfakultäten) were provisionally set up.

By the late fifties, representatives of the "fresh blood" (*Nachwuchs*) so desperately sought by the Party were beginning to assume positions of responsibility in the new society; in the interim, however, official objectives had grown more ambitious. At least rhetorically, Party leaders now declared the very opposition between intellectual and physical labor an impediment to the victory of socialism. One of the high points of the Cultural Revolution was an April 1959 writers' conference that took place at the vast Bitterfeld Electrochemical Complex—today one of the worst ecological disaster sites in Europe. Here, Walter Ulbricht criticized what he described as "the old notions of many workers, who say, 'planning and economic management, etc., those up there run that already; and cultural policy—those up there are in charge of that.'" Thus the first secretary admonished his audience "to plan together, work together, and rule together." Artists had a key role to play in this "great ideological transformation, this forward development."[24] Economic and cultural progress were mutually interdependent. Already workers at progressive factories like the Bitterfeld facility "stand at their machines, master the complicated process of production, constantly further educate themselves, read . . . professional literature . . . [and] to an ever increasing degree high literature." Out of workers, who under capitalism were only "the object of reactionary cultural policy," were developing individuals "who creatively participat[e] in the further development of [the GDR's] entire cultural life."[25]

No great amount of imagination was necessary to interpret *Verwirrung der Liebe*'s final scene as a direct affront to this vision of a society embodied by an aesthetically inspired, multifaceted *homo faber*. The return to the original constellation of partners at the end of the film, it can be easily argued, reinforces the gap between utopian desire and social reality that the regime claimed to be narrowing. The metaphorical implications of a student marrying a student, and a worker a worker, would seem to contradict the official emphasis on eradicating the differences between intellect and brawn, labor and aesthetic experience. All the same, functionaries charged with supervising the film's production apparently were unconcerned with the film's resolution. The question of its seemliness arose only after the work's release. A minor furor about the film erupted in pages of four major publications: *Junge Welt*, the daily organ of the FDJ; *Sonntag*, the weekly organ of the Kulturbund; *Die Wochenpost*, another weekly paper primarily devoted to cultural issues; and *Forum*, a weekly addressing students. Even well-meaning reviewers expressed puzzlement concerning the significance of the film's conclusion. Horst Knietzsch, the authoritative film critic for *Neues Deutschland,* despite some reservations, generally praised the work. Still, he asked, "Would it have not better corresponded to our life if the mason had married the art student and the formula 'shoemaker stick to your soles' had not been applied?"[26] Many letter writers agreed. A student from Halle wrote, "This ending is rather bizarre in our socialist society today, because precisely the opposite of that which the film expresses is being attempted."[27]

At their harshest, commentators charged Dudow with having created a film that was alien to socialism's new reality. Several pointed out that Sonja's private apartment—which in a Western film would hardly have drawn attention to itself as extravagant—represented an unattainable luxury for the vast majority attending university in the GDR.[28] One reader was skeptical that a socialist student would waste money on cab fare, as Dieter did, to chase after a woman he had met only briefly at a party.[29] Several letter writers attested to the discrepancy between the behavior of actual East German students and those shown in the film. One argued, "In *Verwirrung der Liebe*, we experience students celebrating carnival, flirting, not paying attention in lecture, and otherwise not [being] particularly serious. Is that typical of us?"[30] H. Oehlschlägel could not understand "how Dieter can be such a bum. . . . It is inexplicable to me that his fellow students, who are with him almost everyday, [would] tolerate such work habits."[31] A. Rafeld suggested that the film had little to do with socialism and could have been set in any country. She further accused Dudow of borrowing gags from prewar UFA films.[32]

Verwirrung der Liebe's proponents argued that the work, far from being unrealistic, succeeded in depicting aspects of the new life in the GDR neglected in other DEFA movies. Despite his objections to the film's conclusion, Horst Knietzsch, in his *Neues Deutschland* review, honored Dudow's attempt "to demonstrate in an amusing fashion the victorious strength of socialist life through the taken-for-granted beauty of our everyday existence."[33] The critic elaborated that the director "wanted to portray young people who approach the aesthetic ideal of our age. . . . [For him] it was a matter of developing a way of depicting the young, harmonic person in socialist society."[34] In *Der Morgen*, Christoph Funke crooned about "the love of our young people today . . . which is not free from misunderstanding and mistakes . . . but knows no tragic consequences, because it is rooted in a socialist order."[35]

Commentators also differed in their assessment of the various characters. One reader described Edy as the "likable mason [displaying] honest pride in having participated in the construction of the State Opera

House."[36] In contrast, another letter writer thought the depiction of workers in the film was condescending. First, he wanted to know how Sonja became a skilled lathe operator so quickly. Second, he thought Edy came across as an "admittedly good-natured, but thoroughly primitive and naive person."[37]

Other film viewers had misgivings about the depiction of Siegi. M. Kühnhakl asked, "Is it not an insult to the army of our office workers if one depicts their representative as so primitive and brainless as Siegi?"[38] Conversely, several letter writers deemed Sonja decadent and bourgeois. Nevertheless, others were willing to adopt a more indulgent attitude toward the film's female characters. H. Siebers, in his letter to *Sonntag*, described the main protagonists as "genuine children of our socialist society." Siegi might seem superficial, but he asked her critics to consider "how many young people appear untroubled, even though they take their work seriously."[39]

With a more sophisticated argument, the *Forum*'s film reviewer, Winfried Junge, defended the characterization of Sonja. According to him, her reaction to Dieter's disloyalty showed her as a true member of the new society. In a similar situation, "a girl of petit bourgeois sentiment" would fall prey to primitive jealousy. Sonja, though, does not feel "betrayed." "Why should she? . . . Is she nothing without him, is she not an autonomous individual [*Persönlichkeit*], who lives and creates her own life?" Thus her bringing together of Dieter and Siegi does not occur out of resignation but out of self-confidence and a desire for clarity. Junge concluded, "She can afford to play fair. Quite simply from the feeling of equal rights."[40]

There are, of course, several ways of interpreting the extensive discussion of *Verwirrung der Liebe* in the press. The numerous letters against the film could have represented an orchestrated campaign of harassment against Dudow, but this possibility seems unlikely. First, the film attracted 1.9 million viewers, an impressive figure by DEFA standards. Presumably, the regime would have taken other steps and hindered distribution if it judged the film subversive. Second, the letters and articles favoring the film, as well as Dudow's publication of a spirited rejoinder, suggest that the controversy may have indeed represented a rare example in the GDR of more or less open debate. The parameters for discussion were circumscribed. Participants had to assume the attitude of loyal East German citizens and judge the work in terms of its contribution to the brave new society's unfolding. Still, there was obviously considerable room for disagreement. In a state dedicated to the appearance of political harmony, the controversy around the film provided an occasion for individuals to take a position and argue with each other about what their society was about.

Central to debate concerning *Verwirrung der Liebe* was an issue very basic to the language of politics that defined the GDR: socialism's utopian aspirations. Those attacking the film insisted not only on the future triumph but on the actual validity of the regime's vision of total harmony. For this reason, they rallied around the charge of insufficient realism. East Germany and the Party's definition of the new society were identical. Walter Ulbricht's words had the force of reality. In contrast, those defending the work were hardly taking issue with the SED's official program, but their attitude toward the cinema was different. They were willing to tolerate a discrepancy between art and reality as well as between utopian ideal and lived experience. They readily recognized that Dudow's film was not supposed to provide an exact image of a perfect socialist society but belonged to a certain cinematic genre with its own restraints. Indeed, two of Dudow's most enthusiastic boosters, the cultural editors of *Forum*, argued as much. In their view, his film represented "something unusual for the viewer not used to easily digested, but nutritious fare." Realism for them was "hundreds of meters of film of students sweating over their books, but good, true-to-detail milieu depiction, lively people, and youth." Thus, they raved, the work had the potential of becoming "one of the best propaganda films (light genre) for the multifaceted life of our republic."[41]

Official attitudes toward the film are more difficult to generalize. As indicated above, the discussion leading up to the work's release was limited in scope. There is no record that functionaries attempted to change the film's conclusion or extensively criticized the depiction of the protagonists. Instead, they fixated almost exclusively on two issues: nudity and the carnival sequence. At least in part, very specific concerns were behind these objections. The Democratic Republic's first legal nude beach had received grudging approval in 1956,[42] and the regime seems to have been fearful that the film might encourage further nudism.[43] There was even an actual carnival hosted by art students that got out of hand.[44] So, to a certain degree, officials judging the film might have been responding to relatively minor issues incidental to the film itself.

In a wider sense, the regime's objection to the film's sensuality had to do with its interest in promoting "socialist morality." In fact, during the 1958 Fifth SED Congress, Ulbricht proclaimed "Ten Moral Commandments." These emphasized "clean and proper living" as a prerequisite for being a true Communist.[45] Of interest here is less the quasi-religious form of this declaration than the linking of political commitment to private morality. For the Party leadership of the fifties, the GDR's march toward the future depended on the irreproachable conduct of each of its citizens. Outward conformity to a rather conventional code of behavior was a sign of inner belief and loyalty to the Communist cause. Ironically, the inclusion of a carnival scene in *Verwirrung der Liebe* may have been strangely appropriate. In contrast to Catholicism, Communism did not have on its calendar of celebratory days an inversion festival, a ritualized subversion. Through his film, Dudow was in a sense trying to compensate for this omission. More fundamentally, he was suggesting that socialist élan was not equatable with adherence to official ethical strictures. In his public defense of the film, he noted, "Everyplace you hear complaints about the lack of morality among young people. That is only partly true. How often do you meet youths with strong ethical sensibilities, . . . nevertheless, they commit errors?"[46]

Perhaps the same attitude that led functionaries to obsess over details such as a nude-bathing sequence caused them to ignore more fundamental objections to the film. If the SED regime had one saving grace, it was pragmatism. Despite Ulbricht's promise at the Fifth SED Congress that the GDR would surpass the Federal Republic in per capita consumption within thirty months, official growth projections were never so outlandish. The Cultural Revolution may have promised endless horizons by reconciling the poetic powers of art and labor, but, at least within the film industry, functionaries knew what was feasible in the short term. If nothing else, *Verwirrung der Liebe* was reasonably engaging and showed the GDR in an attractive light. The film answered a call by the regime for light entertainment of a socialist character that dated back to at least 1953. The work also clearly filled a gap in DEFA's overall program for 1959, which was shaping up very poorly. Even though DEFA could report a rare surfeit of "present-day" films set in the GDR, it was anticipated that most of these would bomb at the box office. Thus officials, even if they had their reservations about Dudow's film, probably realized that the industry had few alternatives to offer.

Whatever the case, Dudow insisted on reserving the last laugh in the public discussion of the film. In his rejoinder in *Forum*, he assumed a magnanimous attitude toward those who criticized *Verwirrung der Liebe*. "Some find the conclusion kitsch, others conventional," the director noted. For him, though, the very discussion generated by the scene demonstrated its success as "a 'happy end' that occasions a reflective attitude." Thus the film achieved the effect he had intended: "The one laughing is at the same time the one being laughed at." The director conceded that "no one, of course, accepts this consequence gladly." Even so he reminded his readers, "We still must look after merriment, this strange plant, carefully, for it is indispensable for us and our society."[47] Alas, the director badly misjudged the power of his art. Not everyone found his film amusing. A minor scandal about cost overruns incurred during its production was about to show how very fragile Dudow's position was. Although the director ultimately escaped the controversy unscathed, signs of hostility against his person and what he represented as an artist were unmistakable.

THE COST OVERRUN CONTROVERSY AND
TENSIONS WITHIN THE STUDIO

The controversy about cost overruns on *Verwirrung der Liebe* began even before the work's official premiere. In October 1959, Karl-Eduard von Schnitzler, a radio commentator who later became notorious in both Germanies for his pompous delivery, published an article in *Deutsche Filmkunst* criticizing Dudow for expensive delays on the film. The critic insisted that all films, regardless of director, had to be completed on schedule for the studio to function properly. According to Schnitzler, DEFA workers were already quietly complaining about a special "Dudow slush fund" to cover losses on his films. The arrogant behavior of Dudow and other artists contradicted the spirit of socialism and endangered the principles of "internal plant democracy."[48]

Schnitzler apparently was acting on his own initiative. The Central Committee Cultural Section had scant sympathy with the critic when he complained about Dudow's publishing an acerbic ad hominem rejoinder.[49] As far as Arno Röder, the ZK apparatchik most directly responsible for the film industry, was concerned, an open fight between "two leading comrades" served no purpose and only brought profit to the "enemy." Already the Western papers were gleefully reporting the incident. Röder did not feel that the controversy surrounding *Verwirrung der Liebe* warranted higher-level attention. In a summary prepared for his superior, Alfred Kurella, he emphasized, "We are not interested in losing Comrade Dudow for the film industry." DEFA was continuing an in-house investigation of the cost overruns, but Röder had already bluntly instructed the studio's party secretary not to bother him with the matter.[50]

If Schnitzler's polemic did not have the Party's endorsement, the resentment within the studio he described in his article was genuine. In his memo, Röder complained to Kurella of "a sectarian group within the studio, which has contributed to broad anti-Dudow sentiment."[51] Certainly, there were reasons to be upset with Dudow. *Verwirrung der Liebe* had exceeded its original budget of 2,309,500 marks by over 925,000 marks.[52] These unanticipated expenditures had contributed to DEFA's not meeting its annual plan for 1959. This failure not only compromised the studio's good name as a socialist enterprise but also meant that many of its workers had to do without annual bonuses for that year.[53] While Dudow's project was hardly the studio's only headache, his flamboyant personality and thick Bulgarian accent[54] probably made him a convenient target for resentment.[55]

Indeed, the conclusions of an initial internal studio report concerning the project were extremely critical of Dudow. The film's high costs were a function of the extremely long period required for its completion. Whereas a production schedule approved by DEFA's management in January 1958 foresaw 118 days of shooting over approximately a seven-month period, the project ultimately required 148 days over eleven months.[56] According to the report, these delays were attributable to Dudow's work habits and an obsession with artistic perfection that was incomprehensible to his collaborators.[57] The director's extravagance manifested itself in other ways as well. Instead of making maximum use of DEFA's workshops, Dudow contracted out work to art students. Delays resulted in nearly twice the planned outlay for extras.[58] The carnival sequence took twelve days longer to shoot than originally anticipated. Even though each day over budget cost nearly 25,000 marks, most of the additional footage obtained ended up in the waste bin.[59]

Dudow responded to this criticism with his own analysis of the cost overruns, which placed the blame mainly on DEFA's management. Dudow complained that he had been forced to rush the film into production in order to help meet annual plan objectives. For this reason, shooting commenced on August 31, when the season for shooting outdoors was far too advanced. The resulting weather delays alone totaled 300,000 marks.[60] Other problems arose once indoor work began because of poor-quality studio services. Sets were rarely available for prior inspection, so time was lost figuring out shots that should have been planned in advance.[61] Further delays occurred because sets had to be repaired, costumes replaced, props found, and studios properly heated. Finally, Dudow had unkind words for his production director, who, in his estimation, was the actual source of misunderstanding about the project.[62]

Eventually, Dudow got the better of his critics. A report prepared by the agency supervising the studio, the VVB Film, blasted the studio's management, particularly Wilkening, for failing to anticipate and correct problems on the project.[63] In addition, a special commission of the studio's internal Zentrale Parteileitung (Central Party Leadership, ZPL) recommended formal disciplinary measures against *Verwirrung der Liebe*'s production director. In contrast, the commission merely admonished Dudow to do a better job promoting "a healthy work atmosphere in a comradely fashion with the production director" on his next project.[64]

Not all DEFA directors found conforming to a budget as difficult as Dudow did. Some, such as Maetzig, even had a reputation for efficiency. Still, the controversy surrounding Dudow's film represented only an extreme manifestation of long-standing tensions within the studio. In many ways, DEFA as an institution had a split character. As a film studio, its most important constituency was made up of its artists. Even if management and the Party had the last say, the studio's ultimate success and failure depended on retaining and cultivating gifted filmmakers. Before the Berlin Wall was built, DEFA was in direct competition with Western studios for talent; the danger that an artist might take off for the West was always present. At the same time, the studio was also a socialist enterprise, where the proletariat was supposed to control the means of production. The SED insisted that workers were the ones who were really in charge. Nevertheless, the state-sponsored union in the studio lacked the respect of both the workers it represented and the management with which it was supposed to operate in a comradely rather than an adversarial fashion.[65]

Worker resentment toward artists had a long history in the studio. Whereas most DEFA employees lived on modest wages, directors and scriptwriters during the fifties could earn as much as 100,000 marks on a single film. Many actors received generous monthly retainers regardless of whether they actually worked. Another cause of discontent that continued until the end of the decade was the presence of filmmakers from the West who received hard currency payments.[66] Moreover, artists not only were DEFA's best-paid employees; they also included the most influential and best-connected individuals in the studio. For example, even some of the studio's highest-ranking officials complained that they were unable to take stronger measures to contain costs on *Verwirrung der Liebe* because Dudow would have circumvented their authority by appealing to their superiors.[67]

Artists also played a more visible role within the studio's internal Party organization than other groups. Dudow, for one, was a long-standing member of the ZPL. At least during the fifties and early sixties, a far higher percentage of directors and other artists belonged to the Party than was the case with workers. The SED's own general statistics from this period show that "office workers [*Angestellte*] and intellectuals" constituted a disproportionate part of its membership rolls compared to simple workers.[68] In addition, Party membership, if not mandatory, was an important prerequisite for a high-level career in an ideologically sensitive organization such as a film studio. Filmmakers presumably faced greater pressure and had greater incentive to join the Party than studio employees involved in technical tasks did.

The studio's factory political organization (BPO) also provided a convenient structure for monitoring and influencing the political attitude of artists. Each SED member belonged to an Arbeitspolitische Organisation (APO), or a cell organized by profession. These cells met regularly to consider current events or the situation in the studio. The studio's party secretary would then periodically prepare a summary of the APO discussions for review by either the SED's Potsdam district office or the ZK's cultural section.

Such reports often complained about "politically deviant tendencies" among artists. The problem that workers presented to the Party was, however, of a different order altogether: indifference and skepticism. If SED officials were upset with artists for being too eager to express a political opinion, they were hard pressed to find ways of drawing out the workers at all. In one report, the party secretary lamented: "Despite much effort the political mobilization could not be satisfactorily achieved in various areas of the stage, lighting, technical support, etc. . . . In the past, only insufficient measures were undertaken by ZPL and APO leaders in order to increase party strength both quantitatively as well as qualitatively. For example, of 249 stage workers only eight are comrades; of 193 in lighting only twelve are; of 149 in the copying lab seventeen are."[69] According to the Party secretary, DEFA employees avoided "measures and political discussions for [the purpose of] increased production" by arguing that the studio's long-standing script shortage made their own efforts to increase efficiency moot.[70] Why should they bother improving their own work methods if the studio's artists were having difficulty coming up with enough viable projects anyway?

A VVB official investigating *Verwirrung der Liebe* reported that workers complained of a "double standard" in the studio's treatment of artists and themselves. Still, she concluded that "there was no sense asking [workers] about this in giant meetings because they have noticed over time that they will then be tripped up from behind in their work."[71] Worker dissatisfaction also seems to have expressed itself at times in behavior verging on luddism. One BPO report noted the need to constantly improve workers' "socialist consciousness" because "often available materials [and equipment] are so carelessly handled that losses occur where they are absolutely unnecessary."[72] In his analysis of *Verwirrung der Liebe*'s cost overruns, Dudow was also hardly the first or the last director to complain about shoddy workmanship. For example, several years ear-

99

lier, the surly attitude of developing lab technicians had prompted Konrad Wolf to write a furious letter to the HV Film. When the director complained that the print of a nighttime scene had come out too light, the "colleague light measurer" claimed there was no need to correct the problem since he himself "had read newspapers by the sea at night." Other lab workers, having scratched negative footage, were so brazen as to suggest that the director travel to West Berlin to have the damage repaired.[73]

It is difficult to assess the significance of the problems Dudow and Wolf reported. Were such incidents so routine that they rarely occasioned comment, or were they fairly extreme manifestations of discord between artists and workers? That the studio hardly functioned harmoniously is clear. There was a considerable discrepancy between expectations and perceived reality as well as little sense of shared purpose. If an artist like Dudow was involved in an aesthetic endeavor with a sense of how the whole of it should come together, other studio employees, the majority of whom saw a film at most through a few of the many steps associated with its production, presumably approached their work like any other job. They wanted to maximize their compensation and keep their routine as regular as possible. As Dudow complained in his cost overrun analysis, workers often earned more on bad films than on good ones. They had no interest in what they were producing.[74]

In a Western studio, such issues, if discussed at all, would have been at most a problem of employee morale; DEFA, however, purported to be a socialist concern. Its workers were supposed to be engaged in something more than the mere manufacture of a commodity. Through the process of collective production, studio employees were attaining a higher level of consciousness and bringing the dawn of the millennium ever nearer. The controversy surrounding *Verwirrung der Liebe*'s filming highlighted the absurdity of DEFA's mission. Meeting the plan had spiritual, even mystical connotations. Failure in this regard was an affront to the whole socialist project. Yet success was largely measured in terms of bookkeeping minutiae, which had little bearing on the industry's economic viability,[75] let alone the quality of the films actually produced or industrial production's status as a transcendent process. The workers' own interest in meeting official objectives was largely financial.

Officials were well aware of this discrepancy. Indeed, in the early sixties, when DEFA came under increasing competition from television, they embraced an ambitious program of organizational reforms that promised the achievement of a truly socialist film studio, where art and industry would be one. Key to the reforms was the introduction of Künstlerische Arbeitsgruppen (KAGs), or artistic work groups, as a means of improving the studio's financial and artistic performance. Although couched in the language of the Cultural Revolution, the objective of the KAGs gradually allowed filmmakers to increase their autonomy from direct political supervision.

DEFA'S PATH TO THE FUTURE?:
BRIDGING THE GAP BETWEEN INDUSTRY AND ART

By the late fifties, DEFA was thriving as never before. Production was at record levels, with a total of thirty films completed in 1959.[76] The studio could also report significant progress in meeting ideological objectives. For the first time ever, its management could claim that a healthy majority of movies satisfied the important task of depicting life in the GDR.[77] At the same time, filmmakers were carrying on DEFA's established traditions of "antifascist" and "anti-imperialist" works with notable success. Konrad Wolf's *Sterne* (Stars, 1959), concerning the ill-fated love of a Wehrmacht soldier in occupied Bulgaria and a Jewish woman awaiting deportation, garnered a special prize at the Cannes Film Festival.[78] A very different film, Gottfried Kolditz's *Weisses Blut* (White Blood, 1959), attracted an exceptionally large audience with its slick depiction of the decadent West through the eyes of a likable young Bundeswehr officer suffering from radiation poisoning. In addition, DEFA was experimenting with new genres. Kurt Maetzig's science fiction drama, *Der schweigende Stern* (The Silent Star, 1959), based on a Stanislaw Lem novel, attracted a considerable audience, as did two other films by Günter Reisch, *Maibowle* (Spring Punch, 1959) and *Silvesterpunsch* (New Year's Punch), both musical comedies set in a chemical factory.

Despite these accomplishments, the studio was in no position to rest on its laurels. Officials were well aware that the vast majority of movies bearing DEFA's imprimatur were mediocre at best. Films set in the GDR itself, despite their rising number, were particularly weak. As DEFA's management readily conceded in a 1959 report concerning the studio's future objectives, "The artistic-ideological mastering of proper intentions by a considerable proportion of films remains unsatisfactory."[79] Many works tended to have plots that were "schematic" and "superficial." Despite repeated efforts, filmmakers had failed at the task of "bring[ing] onto the screen the figure of the German worker as the builder of socialism in the GDR in [the form of] unique, unmistakable characters."[80] Two years later, a Politburo resolution included virtually identical complaints. It found that the majority of "present-day" films did not "correspond to ideological-artistic needs of our audiences." The conclusion that the SED's highest functionaries drew from this circumstance was hardly inspiring:

"Not second-rate films, but rather the great number of bad films, harm DEFA's reputation."[81]

The Party's own efforts to guide the studio's production by specially commissioning films for specific political celebrations or programs hardly helped matters. One work typical of the whole series of specially commissioned works, or *Auftragsfilme*, from the late fifties and early sixties was Johannes Arpe's *Erich Kubak* (1959).[82] This film told the story of an older worker who does battle with thick-headed managers in order to improve efficiency at the quarry where he works. Initial reviewers, realizing the importance the Party attached to the movie, praised it lavishly. Only Horst Knietzsch, the film critic for the SED's official organ, *Neues Deutschland*, dared utter the truth: the movie was not very good. The critic was even harsher in his assessment of a second film celebrating the regime's renewed efforts at rural collectivization, Frank Beyer's *Eine alte Liebe* (An Old Love, 1959). This featured a female counterpart to the Kubak character, a woman whose tireless devotion to the collective farm she directs makes her husband feel neglected. According to Knietzsch, both works were "schematic" and "unconvincing." They failed to capture "the poetry of socialist life." About all he could do was praise good intentions and counsel patience.[83]

The economic challenge facing the studio was at least as great as the ideological and artistic ones. By the beginning of 1959, 360,000 television sets existed in the GDR,[84] and film attendance was already in decline.[85] Even if DEFA's own balance sheet did not depend directly on box office revenues, the studio had to compete with a new institution, the Deutscher Fernsehfunk (DFF), or German Television Service, for scarce resources. For example, the studio was forced to cede its second-largest production facility, the former Tobis studios in Berlin-Johannistal, to its fledgling rival. Despite this loss, DEFA had pledged itself to increase its production to thirty-eight films a year by 1965. Finally, the studio's managers, like their counterparts around the globe, had concluded that the best strategy for their industry to withstand the onslaught from television was to emphasize qualities unique to the cinema by rendering the viewing experience as absorbing and sensually intense as possible. This objective in turn required the development and increased application of expensive technologies such as Totalvision and even 70mm cinematography. So DEFA found itself in the unenviable position of having to justify major investments to modernize inadequate facilities when audience size and the cinema's general importance were in decline.[86]

In the aftermath of the June 17 uprising in 1953, DEFA had been able to turn around a disastrous organizational situation by de-emphasizing ideological goals in favor of more modest economic ones. Similarly, the industry responded to the 1956 crisis by hiring West German directors to produce entertainment films as well as by increasing the percentage of Western films shown in the GDR's cinema. By the end of the decade, such a quick fix was no longer possible. First, the ideological offensive that had been under way in the GDR since the latter half of 1957 made cooperation with Westerners extremely difficult. Second, DEFA clearly had to respond to television's challenge by proving the unique worth of its product. As the GDR film industry's situation grew more serious, officials tended increasingly to stress the mutual interdependence of economic and ideological goals. The communion of art and industry went from being a vaguely defined ideal to an active principle for formulating concrete policy. The time had finally come, it was argued, to rid the studio of the last vestiges of capitalism and make it into a truly socialist enterprise. Management, workers, and artists all had to learn new means of cooperation and accomplishing tasks. DEFA would either solve all its woes—be they economic, ideological, or artistic—through a miracle of collective organization and communist élan or fail on all counts.

In many ways, DEFA's universal panacea, its secret weapon in its quest for financial solvency, artistic achievement, and political influence, was the institution of the KAGs. As discussed in the preceding chapter, these artistic production groups had been a topic of periodic debate within the industry since at least 1953. In the past, officials had resisted calls for them by artists, fearing that reorganizing the studio into production groups might lead to a breakdown of centralized political and economic authority. As late as the spring of 1958, upper-level functionaries had denounced the proposal in no uncertain terms. It is unclear what exact circumstances led to the regime's reversal by the end of that year, when steps toward implementing KAGs were already under way. Whatever the case, the expectations associated with these new institutional structures were seemingly unbounded.

In an article assessing the industry's prospects on the eve of the GDR's tenth anniversary, the head of the VVB Film, Ernst Hoffmann, emphasized that "the battle for the conquest of the audience" could be won only with "good and honest films." For this reason, KAGs assumed "an eminent meaning" in the next stage of the GDR cinema's development. Hoffmann predicted that such teams of directors, scriptwriters, dramaturges, production managers, and technical personnel would function as the "growth cells of socialist collective work." By bringing together those involved in all aspects of movie production, the KAGs would facilitate the appraisal of "the quality of films produced, artistic achievement, and economic expenditure as an inseparable unity." In addition, socialist film-makers would "multiply their successes as soon as they learn[ed] from workers how tasks [could] be solved more quickly and more easily in creative collaboration."[87] In short, the contradictions between creative spontaneity and financial contingency and between aesthetic experience and industrial organization would be suspended. Art and life would be one.

Obviously one reason that KAGs as an institution reaped such elaborate praise was ideological. The proposal fit in remarkably well with the aims of the regime's cultural policy. As such, it was only one of a number of initiatives being pursued within the studio in conjunction with the officially proclaimed Cultural Revolution. Others included sabbaticals for artists to spend time observing factory life, artists inviting worker brigades to visit the studio, the "adoption" of collective farms by the studio, established scriptwriters assisting "writing workers" (*schreibende Arbeiter*), and artist collaborations with amateur theater and performance groups.[88]

Unlike these other measures, the KAGs implied not only a gesture of solidarity between artists and workers, a symbolic sop to the regime's ideology, but also an actual overhaul of the studio's structure with considerable consequences for the exercise of authority. One of the main reasons for proposing the groups in the first place was the recognition that the studio's centralized management structure created bottlenecks that hindered further growth. In particular, increasing film production had made it virtually impossible for a single individual, the chief dramaturge, to supervise and approve every scenario, treatment, and script.[89] Decisive steps were necessary to increase the number of well-conceived scripts available, whose long-standing shortage, officials believed, was the root cause of the high incidence of low-quality productions.[90]

The KAGs were supposed to remedy those problems by creating forums where artists would, in effect, learn from each other through mutual criticism. Each group also had its own contingent of accountants and dramaturges, whose early involvement in projects was supposed to guarantee that financial and ideological objectives would be thoroughly integrated into the creative process. Obviously, certain safeguards existed to ensure central supervision. Dramaturges, whose role in the studio may in some ways be likened to that played by editors in a commercial publishing house, met regularly with DEFA's top management to discuss common objectives, and the studio director retained final say about which scripts would be released into production. Even so, the artist collectives were allowed considerable latitude in the initial stages of a project. Since script development was an expensive and lengthy process, this concession was of great significance. Studio managers and higher-level functionaries were far more loath to reject a finished script that represented, depending on the prominence of the writer and the rights involved, an investment of tens or even hundreds of thousands of marks than a roughly sketched scenario.

There was also talk that the KAGs might eventually become financially quasi-independent from the studio and that the size of each group's budgets would one day depend on the box office success of their respective films. Indeed, by 1965, concrete steps were already under consideration for implementing such a proposal,[91] when the Eleventh Plenum led to an abrupt return to more centralized management. Most of the KAGs, which had grown from an initial three to seven in number, continued in name, but they now were little more than dramaturge teams. Fearful of losing political control and the possible consequences of allowing artists too much autonomy, the Party did not hesitate to abandon the ambitious attempt at instituting artistic collectives. Still, the seriousness with which the DEFA had pursued KAGs as a concrete reform strategy is measurable through the progressive decentralization of studio management during the early sixties.[92]

At the beginning of the decade, however, the Eleventh Plenum was still a long way off. The studio was embarking on an ambitious reform program, of which the KAGs were the most significant but by no means the sole component. Well aware of the type of problems that had arisen during the filming of *Verwirrung der Liebe*, film industry officials implemented further policies with an eye toward establishing greater harmony between industry and art. Payment of directors' salaries now became dependent on their meeting deadlines and budgets in a timely fashion. Efforts were made to interest technical workers in the artistic and ideological aspects of filmmaking by showing them rushes of work in progress.[93] Above all, an attempt was undertaken to mobilize workers through the Party, the FDJ, and the state union in greater numbers, in the hope that political élan would result in more efficient and effective production. Finally, significant personnel changes were made at the end of 1961. Albert Wilkening, deemed a competent manager but lacking the requisite political leadership qualities, was demoted once again to production director. Jochen Mückenberger, a young ZK functionary, replaced him as studio director. A new Party secretary was appointed.[94] These joined the new chief dramaturge, Klaus Wischnewski, who had started at the studio the previous year.

Such efforts were not in vain. As early as the winter of 1961, the studio's Party secretary could report with enthusiasm to his superiors that "undeniably a new creative atmosphere has developed in the studio through the bringing together of artistic talent. Productive debates about works in progress are constantly taking place in the groups."[95] Indeed, even today many filmmakers remember the KAGs as genuine sites of artistic collaboration, and the years leading up to the Eleventh Plenum were arguably DEFA's most creative and diverse. The film historian and former dramaturge Erika Richter, for example, has described this era of the studio's history as "amazingly multifarious in [terms of] themes, subjects, and stylistic variety" when compared with later years. In her estimation, "The early sixties for many directors and authors were a period of uninhibited testing of their possibility and talents, and they dared original and risky ventures."[96]

The itch for experimentation expressed itself not only in the political boldness of some of the Plenum films but more broadly in a wide variety of movies ranging from musicals to adventure films and satires. For the first and probably only time, DEFA was on the verge of developing a true popular cinema, replete with a number of engaging stars such as Angelika Domröse, Erwin Geschonneck, Manfred Krug, Jutta Hoffmann, and Armin Müller-Stahl.[97] One of the more outlandish films made during this period was Günter Reisch's *Ach, du fröhliche . . .* (Oh, You Merry One, 1962). This East German equivalent of *Guess Who's Coming to Dinner?* told the story of an old comrade, a factory director, whose daughter brings home a fiancé openly disenchanted with the GDR. The work is also perhaps the only pre-1989 DEFA film ever to contain a satiric reference to the Stasi—a strange irony indeed because after the *Wende* its author, Hermann Kant, was revealed to have been a secret police informant himself. Another comedy with a quite original premise was Frank Vogel's *Der Mann mit dem Objektiv* (The Man with the Lens, 1961), which concerned a time traveler from a future socialist utopia who visits the GDR and is shocked by its backwardness. At the same time, Frank Beyer established himself as one of the studio's leading directors with a trio of antifascist films, including the internationally well-received *Nackt unter Wölfen* (Naked among Wolves, 1963), based on a novel by Bruno Apitz concerning a child hidden by concentration camp inmates. Yet another director who came into his own during this period was Ralf Kirsten, whose specialty was light entertainment. His greatest success was *Mir nach, Canaillen* (Follow Me, Scoundrels, 1964). For better or worse, this work was a worthy addition to a certain genre of comic historical adventure films, featuring busty women in tight corsets and sword-fighting cavaliers, the prototype of which was the Gina Lollobrigida classic *Fan Fan la Tulipe* (Christian-Jacque, 1952).[98] Even on economic grounds, there was reason for hope at DEFA. In 1964, the studio could report for the first time in several years that two of its films were among the top ten box office successes in the GDR. Average film attendance was also up considerably, from 500,00 to 640,000.[99] In 1965, DEFA even reversed the overall decline in attendance at its films.[100]

Obviously, the KAGs were not the only factor responsible for these developments. Even at their prime directly before the Plenum, there was a certain discrepancy between the KAGs' theory and practice. Although seven KAGs eventually were established, many sporting heroic Communist monikers such as "Red Circle" or "Concrete," not all attained a critical mass of engaged members. The most successful groups were also generally those which attracted existing talent. In addition, the KAGs never embraced technicians or common studio workers but were generally limited to directors, scriptwriters, dramaturges, and production managers. Even before the Plenum, the groups' main function was script development. Camera operators, set designers, and actors played at best a peripheral role in some groups. Technical service divisions of the studio—such as the stage crew, lighting, props, or the set shop—continued to be centrally organized.

In short, the KAGs only very imperfectly approximated the union of labor and art envisioned by the regime in declaring a Cultural Revolution. Their success probably had far more to do with the studio's decentralization, the somewhat relaxed cultural political climate after the construction of the Wall, and the enlightened tenure of studio director Mückenberger than with the application of socialist principles. It was obviously no accident that previous proposals for artist collectives in the studio had coincided with the great political crises of 1953 and 1956. Regardless of the language in which the KAGs were clothed, their ultimate effect and purpose was relaxed political supervision and greater artistic autonomy. For whatever reasons, the regime at the end of the decade was ready to grant from a position of strength what it had previously considered only under shaky circumstances.

Curiously, Dudow himself was not particularly enthusiastic about the KAGs. During the 1958 Activists' Convention, he roundly criticized Maetzig for having floated the proposal and proudly noted that he himself, even at the height of the 1956 crisis, had resisted the idea.[101] Dudow may simply have been protecting himself from criticism at the expense of a fellow artist; *Verwirrung der Liebe*, however, suggests that his dislike for the KAGs might well have been principled. After all, the film insists on the very barrier the KAGs promised to abolish, the one between the green world of desire and everyday existence, utopian aspirations and pragmatic possibility. Despite his reputation for being an extravagant artist,

Dudow may have been enough of a realist to recognize that antagonism between art and politics was unavoidable. Certainly, he had probably seen enough in his long and varied career to realize that filmmakers given too much rope could easily hang themselves. Whatever Dudow's position on this matter may have been, *Verwirrung der Liebe* was a comedy in which the protagonists' passage through an unattainable realm of boundless possibility ends not in disappointment but in the redemption of their normal world. By contrast, DEFA's experiment with artistic collectives would end if not in outright tragedy—the nobility of the heroes is questionable—then in bitter frustration and estrangement at the Eleventh Plenum.

CONCLUSION

A disciple of Brecht, Dudow believed in the power of art to stimulate political consciousness. Even if *Verwirrung der Liebe* was formally conventional, the director was clearly interested in using humor to encourage East Germans to step back and see their society in a different light. As my interpretation suggests, the issue at which Dudow took aim was socialism's utopian aspirations. His picture honored the Cultural Revolution proclaimed by the regime more as an ideal than a social fact. By assigning the union of intellect and brawn, symbolized by the bride swap in the picture, to the realm of desire rather than reality, Dudow seems to have been reminding his audience that the attainment of true socialism was for the time being only a goal—a beautiful vision of harmony and freedom—not a normative model that could be enforced by fiat.

Determining the relation between ideological ambitions and actual life was of obvious significance in a millennialist state. Insisting on the identity of the two justified calls for increased social discipline. Thus many commentators in the press complained that the characters in *Verwirrung der Liebe* did not conform to the regime's standards for model citizens. Similarly, many in the studio resented Dudow's flamboyant personality and his disregard for financial discipline and other restraints to which everyone else had to submit.

Even so, official toleration of the picture suggests a pragmatic attitude toward the exercise of power. At the very least, *Verwirrung der Liebe* was an entertaining film that showed the GDR in a favorable light. Dudow may have been a living reminder of the radical modernism of the Weimar era that the Party had come to disown, but his latter films were conventional in form and consistent with postwar Communism's cultural conservatism. No longer in opposition but now the zealous master of an embattled state, the SED favored *kleinbürgerlich* values emphasizing discipline and order as embodied in Walter Ulbricht's Ten Moral Commandments. Ultimately, the appearance of order and harmony implicit in *Verwirrung der Liebe*'s classical structure took precedence over doctrinal niceties in official eyes. Party leaders fixated on the nude-bathing and carnival scenes, which seemed to endorse an undisciplined, bohemian lifestyle, but ignored the film's ending, which arguably challenged the Cultural Revolution platform.

While the regime's insistence on the possibility of harmonic progress was generally repressive, it could on occasion legitimize change. In this way, filmmakers were able to use the language of the Cultural Revolution in order to justify the establishment of artistic work groups (KAGs) in the late 1950s. Over the next few years, this reform gradually allowed artists a measure of autonomy from political interference and greater influence in the studio's management. The KAGs were also partly responsible for the cinematic revival experienced at DEFA during the early sixties. As subsequent chapters describe, some directors would use newfound creative latitude to explore cautiously the fissures lurking behind the official facade of monolithic social unity. Integral to this process was the development of an alternative image of East German society as a means of reconciling uncomfortable issues with continuing loyalty to the GDR. In this new vision, the utopian realm of desire celebrated by Dudow in *Verwirrung der Liebe* would not disappear altogether, but it would become increasingly subordinate to the exigencies of everyday life. The analysis now turns to a picture that addressed one of the greatest taboos in East German society: the human costs of the Berlin Wall.

Straddling the Wall

Socialist Realism Meets the Nouvelle Vague in *Der geteilte Himmel*

4

Der geteilte Himmel (Divided Heaven, 1964) is a film about Germany's division and a woman's loss of her lover. A repeated motif in the film is a starkly symmetrical shot of a highway bridge crossing a valley. In the corner of the frame is a small house. Here the film's protagonist, Rita, rests as she recovers from a nervous breakdown that followed her decision not to flee the GDR to be with her fiancé. Metaphorically, the film is about Rita crossing that bridge, having almost fallen into the rift separating one Germany from the other. Two blunt visual refrains in the film reinforce this theme. The first shows a double row of trees bordering a road; shot from beneath at a near-perpendicular angle, the trees neatly divide the sky, thus illustrating the film's title. The second refrain consists of a series of shots relating the immediate incident that precipitates Rita's convalescence. She collapses on the track between two converging railway cars.

Der geteilte Himmel represented the response of two of East Germany's most promising talents to one of the most vexing episodes in that state's troubled history: the construction of the Berlin Wall in 1961. The film's scriptwriter was Christa Wolf, a woman who would become highly renowned as an author in both Germanies. Her first major work, the novella on which the picture was based, had made her an important literary figure in the East. The regime recognized her accomplishment with the prestigious Heinrich Mann Prize, as well as by naming her a candidate member of the Party's highest body, the Central Committee. The film's director, Konrad Wolf (no relation), was arguably East Germany's most distinguished filmmaker. Still not quite forty, he already had a number of major works to his credit, including one that received a special prize at the Cannes film festival. In 1965, his peers would elect him president of the (East) German Academy of Arts.

The two artists' collaboration proved significant for the East German cinema in several respects. First, *Der geteilte Himmel* seemed to be in step with the great cinematic renewal that had been under way in both Eastern and Western Europe since the late fifties. As one reviewer wrote, the work represented a "leap onto the level of modern film" for the GDR cinema after a number of "failed or only half-successful starts."[1] Second, the picture encouraged GDR filmmakers in their quest for original and effective films about their own society. While the number of works set in the GDR had risen greatly in the early sixties, their quality remained spotty at best. Finally, *Der geteilte Himmel* proved extremely popular, becoming one of the ten biggest annual box office draws in the GDR, a rare accomplishment for a DEFA picture.[2]

Nevertheless, the film ultimately did not achieve all that its makers had set out to do. Indeed, it is difficult to see how any picture would have been able to fulfill the ambition of integrating the pain and the shock associated with the Wall's construction into a master narrative celebrating the East German state. Rita's story is overburdened with metaphoric significance. The highly stylized photography used to dramatize her disorientation and mourning sits uneasily with the work's more conventional plot. As some contemporary audience members pointed out, her reasons for leaving Manfred are so overdetermined that her passivity and breakdown become inexplicable.[3] That may explain why two important collaborators on the work, cameraman Werner Bergmann and set designer Alfred Hirschmeier, later complained that the picture was stylistically flawed.[4]

Der geteilte Himmel qualifies as a very self-conscious attempt to reformulate the significance attached to living in a socialist society. The work represented the attainment of an intermediate stage in the development of East German identity. As described in the introduction, DEFA films from the fifties and sixties set in the GDR were known as *Gegenwartsfilme* and tended to depict East Germany as a society on the move. In contrast, the *Alltagsfilme* of the seventies showed an essentially static place. In these later works, characters identify with East Germany not as the realization of socialism's universal mission but rather as a specific and unique place. In *Der geteilte Himmel*, both of these patterns of identifying with East Germany are equally present. The film explores the distance between a tangible yet incomplete present and a perfectible yet absent future, positing an intuitive identity with the former as the guarantee of the latter's eventual realization. The GDR's superiority finds expression in the protagonist's subjective feelings. Her inner attachment to the new society rather than objective manifestations of historical progress guarantees socialism's triumph.

Clearly the construction of the Wall in 1961 profoundly affected the development of East German identity. That event not only guaranteed the GDR's territorial integrity but demarcated it as a society. Understanding *Der geteilte Himmel*'s significance as a contemporary response to the Wall and as a developmental step in the history of East German cinema will require several steps. First, it is necessary to consider the film both on its own terms and in relation to other pictures. After providing a thematic overview, I will briefly compare the picture to two Western films that influenced it, Alain Resnais's French masterpiece *Hiroshima mon amour* (1959) and Herbert Veseley's West German adaptation of Heinrich Böll's *Das Brot der frühen Jahre* (The Bread of the Early Years, 1960). Resnais's work, along with François Truffaut's *The Four Hundred Blows* (also 1959), marked the beginning of the French nouvelle vague. As will be shown, *Der geteilte Himmel* represented less an attempt to import Western avant-garde impulses subversively than an effort to harness them in the service of the new society. The chapter then turns to the general situation within the East German film industry by considering the events at DEFA in the direct aftermath of the Wall's construction. A discussion of the reception history of the two Wolfs' film is followed by a review of cultural and political developments in the early sixties and their effect on DEFA film-makers. Finally, the chapter outlines a basic trend in the GDR cinema that the picture foreshadowed: the increased prominence of female protagonists in DEFA films of the seventies and eighties. This development was in keeping with the general shift from *Gegenwart* toward *Alltag*, from an alliance with the future to an embrace of the subjective and particular.

DER GETEILTE HIMMEL

Two events separate past and present in *Der geteilte Himmel*: the failure of Rita and Manfred's relationship and the building of the Berlin Wall. The lovers' final meeting occurs just days before that historic event. Still unsure of what she wants, Rita travels to West Berlin to see Manfred. Confronted with the choice of a comfortable middle-class existence there or a difficult yet more rewarding life in the East, Rita intuitively opts for the latter; nevertheless, the decision devastates her. Without directly depicting the Wall's construction, the picture draws an implicit analogy between the magnitude of her tragedy and the disruptive nature of that event.

As befits a film thematizing loss and disintegration, *Der geteilte Himmel* begins by presenting a confusing array of fragments, bits and pieces of the city of Halle shot at eccentric angles. Interspersed with these are motifs, such as those discussed above, that stand in either direct or metaphorical relation to Rita's story. In many ways, the film's guiding principle is the therapeutic function of narrative. The picture is structured around a series of seven flashbacks. By remembering and ordering the past, Rita assimilates the shock she has experienced and finds the strength to return to her interrupted life. Indeed, to help her on her way, an alter ego, the mature and resonant voice of the picture's female narrator, offers her advice and direction.

The interpolation of the various motifs serves a second purpose as well. This device frames the flashbacks and, in doing so, emphasizes their fragmentary nature. By the same token, the brief scenes set in the present that show Rita convalescing provide the viewer with only the barest outlines of the dramatic situation. For example, the first of these, shot largely from the viewpoint of her sickbed, emphasizes Rita's isolation, the distance between her and other individuals. The scant dialogue provides false clues about the action to follow. A doctor tells Rita's mother that there is nothing wrong with her, while her mother insists that there was no man involved. As the film progresses, however, each of the seven flashbacks reveals progressively more of Rita's story until past and present converge and she resumes her life. Thus, in the film's last sequence, images of Halle again flash on screen. In contrast to the opening images, the streets are populated, and Rita is seen actively moving through the crowds. Her story has merged with those of others and has become that of the new society.

Despite the implicit emphasis in the film's opening on rupture and discontinuity, the script for *Der geteilte Himmel* has a complex, carefully woven plot, a brief summary of which will facilitate further analysis. The film can be divided into seven major segments corresponding to Rita's flashbacks. The first flashback is set in her home village. There she encounters two men who facilitate her journey to the local metropole, Halle, and the larger world it represents. The first man is Manfred; the second is a representative of the new society, Herr Schwarzenbach, who recruits her to study at a teacher's college.

The next flashback concerns Rita's arrival at Halle. Here her life is neatly divided into two distinct parts. One is associated with the place where she lives: the villa of Manfred's bourgeois parents, the Herrfurths. The other main locale of Rita's new life is the railcar factory, where she begins to work as part of her training to become a teacher attuned to the needs of the working class. In both arenas, Rita observes generational tension. Manfred detests his father as a hypocrite, who arranges himself as comfortably with the Communists as he once did with the Nazis. The conflict at work is similar. In this case, however, the opportunist is a young man, Ermisch, the foreman of the socialist work brigade Rita joins. His nemesis is Meternagel, an older comrade of sincere conviction, who objects to Ermisch's practice of cooking the brigade's books in order to obtain larger financial bonuses for its members.

The film's next segment contrasts Rita's private and public life. Her flashback begins with a crisis at the railcar factory due to a shortage of materials. A general workers' meeting takes place. The factory's dynamic new director, Wieland, explains that there is only one solution for the factory's woes: "Everyone does as much as he honestly can." An interlude within this segment shows Rita and Manfred driving off from Halle on a beautiful, sunny day. Their romantic outing assumes a different character when they run into Wieland. He turns out to be an old acquaintance of Manfred, and the two men become quickly absorbed in a political debate. The next part of the segment shows Rita's brigade becoming embroiled in a new crisis: Meternagel challenges his co-workers to increase their daily production quota voluntarily. The flashback then ends with Rita and Manfred once again attempting to assert the primacy of their personal relationship. Looking out over the sleeping city from the attic they share atop the Herrfurths' villa, they pretend that they are adrift all alone in a small boat.

The fourth segment begins with the film's female narrator's voice noting: "Eight months later the boat has sunk, and they stand on opposite shores." Rita and Manfred's relationship begins to unravel. Manfred, who has just finished a doctoral degree in chemistry, is frustrated in his career because a factory refuses to adopt a new manufacturing process he has devised. Rita encounters an ideologically pedantic instructor, Mangold, who terrorizes her classmates at the institute. Manfred's response to her concerns casts doubts on his character. While Schwarzenbach encourages her to fight for what she feels is right, Manfred tells her to keep her nose out of trouble. This noncommittal attitude on Manfred's part extends to their relationship. When she asks him whether he loves her, he answers simply, "It's O.K."

The next segment suggests a role reversal between Rita and Manfred. She begins to usurp his position as the more mature partner in the relationship. While Manfred is away promoting his manufacturing process, Rita must face a difficult test alone. A classmate is threatened with expulsion after her parents leave for the West. Rita defends her with the help of Schwarzenbach in front of a commission run by Mangold. Finally, Manfred learns that his proposal has been rejected for a second time. Thus, as Rita experiences her success in aiding her friend, his fortunes falter.

By the sixth segment, Rita's convalescence is complete. She returns to the city, to the now barren room she once shared with Manfred. A jump shot then introduces Rita's flashback. Manfred tells Rita, "The foundation of history is the misfortune of the individual." This statement is symptomatic of Manfred's inability to feel part of something that transcends his individual person. In the next scene, his self-exclusion from the new society grows ever more apparent, while Rita experiences a moment of transcendence with her fellow socialists. She invites him to join her on a test run of a new passenger car. As Wieland and Meternagel service the equipment, he argues with them about whether Germany is ready for socialism. His claim is that their country's culture is too Western, too individualistic, to adopt the collective-oriented culture of the Soviet Union. The train stops in a field, and a passing farmer on a tractor announces that the Soviets have a man in space. Images of a rocket taking off interrupt the action. While the others stand silent in astonishment, Manfred cynically suggests that the Soviets' interest in space is purely propaganda.

The following scene relates Rita's discovery of Manfred's flight and her journey from Halle to West Berlin. Finally, in the last segment, Rita assumes the position of narrator. Although the previous segments are supposed to represent her recollections, only at the end of the film does she actively relate her experience to others. Rita describes to Schwarzenbach the day she spent in West Berlin with Manfred. The following two scenes contrast the two realms of her personal experience, private life and work, developed earlier in the film. First, she meets Manfred's father in the barren room the lovers once shared. The disintegration of the bourgeois aspirations of the Herrfurth family is indicated both by the mise-en-scène and by Herr Herrfurth's plaintive question, "Why does my son hate me?" Then Rita visits Meternagel, who is ill in bed. She tells him, "They won't get the better of you." Thus Rita assumes the torch from her ailing comrade.

Der geteilte Himmel's thematic structure was fairly conventional for film and fiction in the GDR. The organizing principle of Rita's story is *Bildung*, or personal improvement and character formation. She leaves the precincts of her childhood, joins life in a wider world, and becomes an adult. Similarly, *Erziehung*, or education and discipline, is a major theme in her story: Rita is training to become a teacher. Throughout the film, a comparison is drawn between different forms of authority. While Manfred's weakness of character is ultimately attributable to his middle-class background and the hypocrisy embodied by his father, Rita's strength derives from the mentors she finds: Meternagel and Schwarzenbach. Socialism's superiority and its ultimate success are shown as dependent on a proper teacher-student relationship, one based on mutual trust and honesty. For example, after Rita tells Schwarzenbach about her journey to West Berlin, he comments, "They told us that too much trust ruins people. For the first time, we are now mature enough to face the truth." The film implicitly argues that socialism in the GDR, as an educational process, has progressed far enough to express ideas that the regime previously suppressed.

Der geteilte Himmel also elaborates the classic production trope in socialist literature, which treats the workplace as the privileged site of progressive consciousness formation. This theme is most evident in the subplot, developed in the second segment, involving the crisis at the railcar factory. The director of the enterprise, Wieland, tells his workers that increasing production is a matter of an honest attitude; what stands in the way of this goal in Rita's brigade is the past. Meternagel, the elder comrade, must struggle against the indifference and hostility of the rest of the brigade, a motley crew, whose members include at least one former Wehrmacht officer. The war has left them, just like Manfred, cynical and selfish.[5]

Rita's status as the only woman in the brigade is significant. In one scene, the brigade's members gather around a table in a bar to celebrate Ermisch's birthday and the "sly pencil" with which he overcalculates the brigade's output. One man begins telling a dirty joke when he sees Rita and stops. The disruption of this sinister fraternity through her presence in the workplace is thus emblematic of socialism's ambition to transform industrial labor from an alienating process into one instilled with higher meaning and purpose.

Reinforcing the picture's thematic structure is a strong overlay of naturalist imagery. The narration, accompanying the images of Halle at the beginning and end of the film, likens urban life to an organism: "The city breathed in those days more heavily than otherwise. . . . The air weighed heavily upon us, and the water tasted bitter." A parallel motif of the film associates the type of hollow bourgeois respectability embodied by the Herrfurth family with death. The second sequence begins with Manfred giving Rita a tour of his parents' villa, whose various chambers he describes as the "living coffin," "eating coffin," and so on. The mise-en-scène of the Herrfurth house is lugubrious, and the camera used to describe it is static and slow. In contrast, the factory where Rita works is introduced through a rapid montage sequence, featuring the morning shift of workers converging on factory gates, sparks flying, and metal being forged. Of course, the most prominent use of organic imagery in the work is its title. Both Germany's division and Rita and Manfred's separation is likened to the sundering of the sky, the rupturing of something intrinsically whole, the cosmos.

The film's naturalism assimilates even the Soviet space shot, perhaps the ultimate symbol of socialism's orientation toward the future and technology. The action in the sixth sequence is interrupted by a shot of a rocket lifting off, which is then followed by images that explicitly compare the physical attitudes of Soviet space center technicians with those of Rita and her colleagues. As the camera then pans across the sky, a male voice repeats the words of Yuri Gargarin comparing the heavens, as viewed from his spacecraft, with the black earth of freshly plowed fields and the stars with newly planted seeds. For the only time in the film, Rita's inner monologue is heard, and her words echo those of the astronaut.

Rita's and Manfred's lives diverge because he cannot comprehend this subterranean solidarity in which she participates. Manfred, the skeptical man of science, is repeatedly shown engaged in arguments with other male protagonists trying to justify rationally his political position. In contrast, Rita's decision to return to the GDR after visiting Manfred in West Berlin occurs in an intuitive and spontaneous fashion. Like her relationship with Manfred, her loyalty to the East is grounded in a way more fundamental than reason. Having to dissolve one of these basic bonds in favor of the other is an existential matter that occasions a nervous breakdown. Only through the slow process of recovery is Rita able to articulate specific reasons for her choice of the East over Manfred. Even these, however, are emotional ones.

The film posits the existence of a quasi-natural community in the East as the ultimate guarantee of the socialist project. This premise is especially clear in the sequence at the end of the film where Rita visits Manfred in West Berlin. Highly stylized images of that city flicker over the screen as Rita's voice explains: "A lot pleases you but you don't really enjoy it. . . . You feel terribly alone . . . worse than [being] abroad, because one speaks the same language." Rita and Manfred are then seen dining at a famous West Berlin restaurant, Café Krenzler. An exceptionally stark mise-en-scène combined with high-contrast photography lends this locale a static air. In another shot, a giant advertisement featuring a woman holding a laundry detergent box looms between Rita and Manfred as the two try to converse.[6] Elsewhere, the former lovers are shown against the gridlike pattern of an international-style building.

Rita's remark concerning the common language of the two Germanies is significant. Language, of course, is one of the classic hallmarks of the nation as a "natural" community. In his vain attempt to persuade Rita to stay with him, Manfred asks her: "Listen to a few names. Lake Constance, the Rhine, the Black Forest. Isn't that Germany, too?" Obviously, for Rita, these places do not represent her country, her *Heimat*. Even so, far from questioning the idea of organic community, both the film and the original novella suggest that its authentic realization can occur only in the East.

Der geteilte Himmel's healthy admixture of naturalism was typical of many earlier GDR works; one need look no further than the writings of Anna Seghers, an important model for Wolf. The positing of some form of organic *Volksgemeinschaft* in the East was also not unusual. A certain *Zivilizationskritik* of the West is clearly evident in official pronouncements from the fifties as well as in East German literature and film of the time. The West stood for the mindless logic of capitalism and all of modernity's supposedly corrosive effects on family and gender relations; the East for community, family, and morality. In short, the working class as a mythic construct easily assumed the same qualities that conservative ideologies often associated with the *Volk*.

In many ways, the film's aesthetic conception conflicts with its normative message. *Der geteilte Himmel* clearly reflected the rich stylistic currents that characterized European filmmaking in the early sixties. One film with which it clearly resonates is Alain Resnais's *Hiroshima mon amour* (1959), and Konrad Wolf himself acknowledged similarities between the two films.[7] Both feature quasi-documentary footage of a specific city intermingled with diegetically motivated shots. In addition, the East German picture makes use of elliptical editing techniques pioneered by Resnais. Each work dispenses with establishing shots and other devices designed to orient viewers. Anachronistic images follow each other without introduction: for example, the jump shot noted in the penultimate sequence. In addition, *Der geteilte Himmel* employs freeze-frame photography in one sequence, a technique rarely found in mainstream films before the nouvelle vague.

On a thematic level, Christa Wolf's novella and the film fable that Marguerite Duras wrote for Resnais also share similarities. Both concern tragically fated love against a grand historical background. Moreover, each emphasizes female subjectivity and memory. The literary scholar Barton Byg has argued that these films address "the paradox of the female voice when confronted with the unutterable horrors of history." In particular, Byg suggests that the makers of the East German picture were interested in "the fragmentation and the accompanying feeling of suffering and loss of individually produced identity in relation to memory as well as of national identity in relation to history."[8] Byg also places the two films in a general historical context. Building on the work of the French feminist theorist Julia Kristeva, he suggests that representatives of the postwar generation across Europe, regardless of their gender, began employing female voices in film and fiction as a means of thematizing that continent's recent historical trauma. Precisely because of its conventional exclusion from political discourse, a feminine perspective was highly suited for addressing ellipses and gaps in collective self-understanding, for thematizing what memory could not preserve.

Byg perhaps overstates his case in respect to *Der geteilte Himmel*. Although the film certainly attempts to address issues excluded from official discourse, it ultimately insists on containing them within a fairly tame narrative. Thus the work exploits female subjectivity in a twofold manner. On the one hand, the emphasis on Rita's inner experience allows for tacit admission of the Berlin Wall's construction as a disruptive, violent event. It is difficult to imagine a film from this period featuring an older male comrade experiencing a similar sort of existential crisis as Rita's. Her presumed vulnerability, her youth, and her liminal position as a convert to socialism allow her to become a vehicle for questions that otherwise might have been subversive. On the other hand, Rita's subjectivity provides a novel means for legitimizing the new society, for grounding the truth of socialism. As already noted, the film acknowledges the West's greater affluence. What binds Rita to the GDR is a purely personal feeling of belonging, one powerful enough to assimilate the disappointments she experiences.

Again, the comparison with Resnais's *Hiroshima mon amour* is informative. Just as the scriptwriter for the earlier film, Marguerite Duras, insisted on the pedestrian nature of the love affair depicted there, so the impersonal narrator in both the novella and the film version of *Der geteilte Himmel* makes the point that Rita's tale is a "banal story." Nevertheless, the emphasis attached to these two pronouncements differs. In Duras's own words, it is "impossible to talk about Hiroshima. All one can do is talk about the impossibility of talking about Hiroshima." As the film scholar James Monaco explains, "Duras intentionally sets up the dullest love story she can imagine . . . [with the hope] that the banality of the fiction and the outrage of the fact of Hiroshima will provide leverage to talk about talking about the subject."[9] Thus one of the stations in the lovers' nocturnal wanderings through the streets of postwar Hiroshima is the Café Casablanca—reference to the cinema's most maudlin and trivial qualities.

In contrast, the East German film spins its tale without the least trace of irony or self-reflection. The narrator's comment about the banality of Rita's story is disingenuous. Rita's tale is weighed down with metaphoric significance. Her relationship with Manfred is not meant as a trivial love story but rather as a parable for Germany's division. Moreover, the picture in its dialogue explicitly thematizes the distance between the ordinary and the epochal in a way that affirms socialism's master narrative. During their final meeting in Berlin, Rita expresses to Manfred her anxiety that it is possible "to grow used to things that are impossible." She then elaborates with four examples: "That you do not say what you think. That you produce [in the factory] less than you can. That there are already more bombs than you need to destroy the earth. That a man, to whom you belong, can be driven away from you forever and only a letter remains." To this last accusation, Manfred replies defensively: "You confuse everything. Your factory, the bomb, and me." In short, one of the main qualities that distinguishes Rita from Manfred is her intuitive understanding that each individual's life has vital meaning within a grander context. Thus the two lovers' tale is embedded in a cosmic battle between good and evil, between well-meaning people, like Rita and her mentors, and the cynical individuals, like Manfred, who have given up hope.

Another point of comparison between the two films is the unique status each assigns to female memory. Both Rita and her French counterpart have far more immediate, even sensuous, relationships with the past than their male opposites. Seeing the prone body of her present lover in bed reawakens in the French woman the suppressed memory of her first tragic relationship with a young German soldier during World War II, which ended when he was shot by partisans while trying to keep a rendezvous with her. She recalls throwing herself against him and being unable to distinguish not only the moment of his death but even her own body from his.[10] Similarly, Rita tries to recall Manfred's bodily presence: "His face, always his face again. A hundred times she follows every line in this face, which disappears when she tries to grasp it all at once. And the touch of his hands."[11] In contrast, the male counterparts in both films have an attenuated relationship with the past. The French woman's Japanese lover never tells his own story. Similarly, Manfred's prior life is shrouded in mystery. Rita knows that his experience conformed to the general pattern of his generation, but she has few details to go on.

Hiroshima mon amour concerns the impossibility of memory—and the cinema—to comprehend adequately past suffering. The French woman repeatedly confuses and conflates her dead lover with her current one. Only the fear of separation from the Japanese man in her present somewhat dubious love affair allows for some impression of her past pain as well as of the enormity of the atomic bombing itself. The past and the present inform each other in ways that undermine both. In comparison, *Der geteilte Himmel* treats the gradual loss of sensuous recollection in a fashion that is at once cavalier and purely sentimental. On the one hand, the picture virtually fetishizes Rita's suffering. In the opening shot, her tearful face looms large like that of a giant madonna. On the other hand, the work presents the inevitable fading of sensuous memory as just a necessary stage in Rita's convalescence. At points, the impersonal narrator coaches her to forget the past, to let Manfred's image fade, so that she might rejoin the present unencumbered. Rita obeys this advice and becomes a spokesperson for the new order.

It is further worth noting that *Der geteilte Himmel*'s depiction of West Berlin bears a striking resemblance to the 1960 West German film *Das Brot der frühen Jahre*, which is equally derivative in style of *Hiroshima mon amour*. Directed by Herbert Veseley and based on a Heinrich Böll novel, *Das Brot der frühen Jahre* has as its theme the emptiness of postwar Western materialism. Having achieved prosperity as a washing machine repairman, the protagonist Walter is thrown into an existential crisis when he meets Hedwig, a young woman, just arrived from his hometown, with whom he becomes infatuated. As in *Der geteilte Himmel*, the liberal use of elliptical editing and highly stylized static images shot at eccentric angles creates an alienating and disjointed image of the city. Moreover, both works use advertising billboards as backdrops in order to comment ironically on consumerism.

Significantly, the film version of *Das Brot der frühen Jahre* changed the story's setting from the West German city of Cologne to West Berlin and the corresponding location of Walter's hometown from West to East as well. The result of this change is that the Western film, just like *Der geteilte Himmel*, seems to associate authentic existence with the East, Hedwig's and Walter's place of origin and their only common bond. The film version of *Das Brot der frühen Jahre* shares with *Hiroshima mon amour*, however, the self-ironizing tendencies that are absent in the East German film. Walter's sudden and all-consuming love for Hedwig is clearly not reciprocated. While Walter insists that their chance meeting has saved him from a prior inferior existence, Hedwig has difficulty considering their relationship as anything more than a random encounter. Indeed, near the conclusion of the film, she nearly wanders off with the proverbial stranger on a street corner. This and other incongruities undermine the original novel's earnest antimaterialism and place the possibility of authentic existence in doubt. Even so, the stylistic and thematic affinities between the West and East German films attest to the shared influence of certain cultural attitudes—including dissatisfaction with the conventional cinema and a view of the modern city and consumer culture as suspect. In attempting to articulate a new sense of East German identity through bringing *Der geteilte Himmel* to the screen, Christa Wolf and Konrad Wolf were thus not only negotiating political parameters specific to the GDR but also actively responding to developments in both the international cinema and post-war German culture generally.

DEFA AND THE WALL

Rita's experience of Germany's division as a shock must have resonated with the feelings of many GDR citizens. The construction of the Wall on August 13, 1961, was tantamount to a mobilization of the entire population. Tens of thousands, attached either directly to the military and police or to paramilitary "readiness groups" (*Bereitschaftsgruppen*), were awoken on a Sunday morning to effect the operation. Others contributed to the undertaking indirectly by participating in a massive propaganda campaign. A general election was then announced for September, so that every GDR citizen could personally affirm the Party's wisdom. Anyone who refused to join such manifestations of common purpose and unity risked arrest in the largest campaign against political offenses since the uprising of June 17, 1953.[12]

The regime lost no opportunity to stress the historic magnitude of this great collective undertaking. The East German populace was not only protecting itself from the predations of rapacious Western capitalists and militarists; it was saving Europe from war. Nevertheless, the hypocrisy of official rhetoric must have been obvious even to loyal GDR citizens. Few could have been blind to the undertaking's actual purpose of stemming the rapidly mounting tide of emigration to the West. East Germans were being forced not only to participate in the macabre exercise of completing their own prison but to profess pride in the accomplishment.

The aftermath of August 13 within the studio suggests deeply conflicted attitudes among workers and artists. Even in purely logistical terms, the Wall's construction was disruptive of the studio's operations. For years, DEFA had proclaimed its independence from the commercial cinema of the past and present; nevertheless, previous drives to achieve self-sufficiency had not uprooted all vestiges of the prewar infrastructure. The studio was still partly dependent on the West for equipment and expertise. Most significantly, it employed many Westerners; approximately a third of the studio's orchestra members were from the West. Because DEFA's main facility, the Babelsberg studio, was located just a few hundred meters west of Berlin, the sealing-off of the border forced workers from the city's eastern half, accustomed to traveling through the Western zone, to employ a circuitous route around Berlin's perimeter. The considerable added travel time exacerbated the competition between the studio and East Berlin theaters for actors, as it became more difficult for them to return from daytime shoots in Babelsberg for evening performances. There was also fear that experienced technical employees might abandon DEFA for more conveniently located television studios.[13]

Some of the studio's personnel responded to the challenge presented by the Wall by displaying their unwavering loyalty to the Party. In a detailed report, DEFA's Party secretary praised those who promptly answered the call to action on August 13. Some performed "agitational" work, explaining the necessity of the regime's action to bystanders at the nearby "Unity Bridge" linking Potsdam and West Berlin (site of the famous Cold War spy exchanges). Others showed zeal by drafting declarations of support for the Party leadership, as well as by doing political work in order to the win the sympathies of workers who would be returning to their jobs Monday morning. Konrad Wolf granted an interview with (East) Berlin Radio. Two other leading directors spent the night editing a television film of political importance depicting collaborations between American spy agencies and war criminals. In the days after the thirteenth, the KAG "Solidarity" prepared a special agitation film for use in the upcoming elections. A noted scriptwriter promised immediately to get to work on a project commemorating the regime's actions. Other artists, previously not in the SED, now promised to join the Party.[14]

At the same time, not all of DEFA's personnel, let alone all Party members, reacted to the Wall's construction in a such an exemplary fashion. The Party secretary criticized three of the studio's production managers for not responding when summoned to the studio on the morning of the thirteenth.[15] One man left his phone off the receiver and arrived at the studio only after a car was sent for him. Dudow and another leading director, who were both out of town on the thirteenth, had to exercise self-criticism before their Party cell for failing to return promptly.[16] Several actors and actresses refused to sign a public declaration of support addressed to Walter Ulbricht. Their union representative, Erwin Geschonneck, who himself often depicted idealized Communists in film, had suddenly taken a vacation and had not been seen in the studio for some time.[17]

Such signs of dissatisfaction among filmmakers and management were just the tip of the iceberg. Among the studio's 2,300 workers, discontent took forms ranging from simple truculence and bizarre behavior to at least one attempt at organized protest. A woman assigned to the dramaturgy section (Dramaturgie) attempted "to induce in her work area an atmosphere of work stoppage."[18] Another serious incident involved a photographer who appeared in an English military uniform stolen from the costume shop and then ordered his co-workers to take off their Party insignia and to answer to him for their behavior on August 13. The cafeteria staff was accused of spreading rumors heard on Western radio. In addition, the Party secretary complained that discussions in various Party cells had taken a bad turn because reliable comrades were absent from their regular meetings performing other duties.[19] Finally, there were the studio's remaining workers from West Berlin, some of whom continued arriving for work for several weeks after the Wall's construction.[20]

The performance of the DEFA's battle group or "century"—a paramilitary unit supposedly comprising the most politically committed men in the studio—also left much to be desired. First, despite its name, the group was able to muster only sixty-two individuals on August 13. Moreover, once its members arrived at the studio, they were stuck there because the comrade responsible for organizing transportation "was in such a state (alcohol) that he did not understand what was going on." Having finally taken up duty policing the border on August 17, the group then had to deal with "antipathy" toward DEFA on the part of other units. The century also had to send back to the studio five of its own members who balked at the tasks assigned them. Even those who did successfully complete their duty had to contend with others stealing their limelight. As the exasperated commander of the group explained in his report, some filmmakers and actors were describing themselves to the press as "reservists," even though "none of them has ever been seen near our unit and there are no reservists in the battle group."[21]

DER GETEILTE HIMMEL AND THE GDR'S "ARRIVAL"

Given *Der geteilte Himmel*'s attempt to make sense out of such an absurd situation, it is easy to dismiss the film as politically compromised, but such a summary judgment would be unfair. To appreciate fully both the novella and the film, it is necessary to approach them less as self-contained final products than as part of a complex process. In the case of Christa Wolf, the novella is only an early example of her work; she would later revisit and refine many of the themes and issues presented in it. Her subsequent writings would go on to develop a critique of Marxism celebrating female subjectivity as the last utopian possibility in a world dominated by utilitarian reason.[22]

Of more immediate significance for this study, *Der geteilte Himmel* represented an important intervention within the East German political and cultural context of the early 1960s. The work is best seen as an extension of a project begun in a number of books of that time that collectively were known as *Ankunftsliteratur* (arrival literature). Named after Brigitte Reimann's 1961 work, *Ankunft im Alltag* (Arrival in the Everyday), these novels and long stories included early pieces by a number of writers who would rise to prominence in the GDR, including Günter de Bruyn, Hermann Kant, and Dieter Noll, as well as Wolf. Written very much under the influence of the SED's Cultural Revolution platform and the *Bitterfelderweg*, this literature emphasized standard themes in existing socialist literature such as *Bildung* (personal development) and *Produktion* (the industrial workplace as a site of consciousness formation). A distinguishing characteristic of *Ankunftsliteratur* was the presence of protagonists who, like Rita, had to reconcile high ideals with sobering experience. The notion of arrival referred to a sense of now having to confront socialism as it actually exists rather than as a still-distant aspiration.[23] In contrast to many examples of later GDR literature, these works, however, still posited East Germany as a perfectible society, clearly advancing toward the future.

Der geteilte Himmel also seemed to confirm the GDR cinema's own promise. While some critics complained that the film's style was too difficult to follow, reviews were virtually unanimous in their praise of the work's courage in tackling controversial issues and of its open treatment of the new society's "contradictions." Günter Karl, writing in the SED organ *Neues Deutschland*, described the film as a "creative experiment . . . in the best sense of the word." The work "demonstrates the viability of a path [that] through the learning and recognition process of an individual [brings to light] the dialectic of our life, its truth and beauty, more multifariously and conflict-laden than before."[24] Christoph Funke affirmed in *Der Morgen*, "This story concerns all of us. It is after all the story of the conquest of our everyday life, the story of conflicts, as they affect all of us—in the factory, at the university, at home between four walls."[25] Even a reviewer for the *Berliner Zeitung*, who found the film's style pretentious, honored its attempt to treat a "difficult present-day problem."[26]

To understand why many reviewers were enthusiastic about *Der geteilte Himmel*'s relative candor, it is only necessary to consider several earlier films thematizing the Wall's construction and Germany's division that DEFA had produced. These so-called *Mauer* films were notorious flops. A movie made by Gerhard Klein, Karl Georg Egel, and Wolfgang Kohlhaase, *Sonntagsfahrer* (Sunday Drivers, 1963), was the best conceived of the lot; nonetheless, even this farce about a group of *Kleinbürger* who unwittingly decide to flee East Germany on the day of the Wall's construction found little audience echo. Similarly, the presence in the main role of the popular star Manfred Krug was not enough to assure the success of Heinz Thiel's *Der Kinnhaken* (The Knock-Out Punch, 1962). In addition, a pair of films by Frank Vogel met with equally lukewarm responses. Despite innovative cinematography, both *. . . und deine Liebe* *auch* (And Your Love, Too, 1962) and *Julia lebt* (Julia Lives, 1963) suffered from horribly wooden scripts. Along with the Krug movie, they shared the same basic plot structure: a woman who must choose between a flashy yet unworthy suitor embodying Western values and a sincere and caring rival standing for the new society.

Years later, Kohlhaase remarked in connection to *Sonntagsfahrer*, his own contribution to this group, that "every family has something that it does not like to discuss at dinner. In my case, it was this film." As he explained, "We thought we could do something to contribute to the lightening-up of . . . the public mood [after the Wall]. That was a mistake."[27] It is notable that filmmakers undertook the *Mauer* films with little, if any, prodding from officials.[28]

In contrast to the *Mauer* films, *Der geteilte Himmel* seemed to offer a viable expression of artists' commitment to the new society, one that transcended the tired formulas of the past. The picture clearly was a great success for the studio. As noted, it was one of the best-drawing DEFA productions of its day. As had the novella earlier, the film generated considerable discussion in various East German papers. Although some viewers expressed in their letters disappointment with the film's complex narrative structure, others found its style intriguing and effective. In short, the work fulfilled several industry objectives simultaneously. Not only was it popular, but it seemed to engage viewers intellectually and politically. The picture also demonstrated that the studio was capable of producing a work that was more or less in stride with international cinematic developments.

Finally, the film seemed to satisfy that most elusive of goals: a *Gegenwartsfilm* that presented a compelling image of life in East Germany. While the studio had had some success recently with pictures thematizing the past, it still lagged noticeably in works set in the GDR. As a reviewer for the *Neue Zeit* wrote, "Present-day themes in particular are . . . all too often [in DEFA films] depicted in a conventional . . . and inadequate way. Here, in contrast, a form has been found to make visible complicated processes of consciousness with social relevance not only as a rational calculation but also as an emotional experience."[29] Similarly, the director Kurt Maetzig gushed at a special meeting of the Berlin Academy of Arts, "This film will contribute to a great degree in overcoming the naturalism, tedium, and schematism of many East German films." Indeed, by combining formal innovation with a thoroughly progressive political standpoint, the work in his eyes represented nothing less than an "important step on the path to a new stage of the world cinema."[30]

Despite such optimism on the part of Maetzig and others, *Der geteilte Himmel* represented at best a very tenuous arrival for the East German cinema. Whatever progress the studio had achieved over the preceding few years depended on a delicate balance of factors, which, as events would soon prove, could shift to the detriment of filmmakers. Indeed, in its formulation, official cultural policy had changed only slightly since the late fifties. Walter Ulbricht, at the Sixth SED Party Congress in 1963, affirmed many of the same themes he had five years earlier at the Fifth Congress in 1958. Once again he urged the working class to "storm the heights of culture." Although he no longer spoke of a "cultural revolution," his plans for the continuing "development of socialist national culture" had lost none of their utopian grandeur. He defended socialist realism as the high road to the future and condemned modernism as bourgeois and decadent. Only through their collaboration with workers, the first secretary explained, could artists contribute to "our present-day becom[ing] more beautiful than ever before."

Still, this constancy in rhetoric obscured complex developments. A renewed wave of de-Stalinization in the GDR following the Twenty-second Congress of the CPSU in October 1961 must have encouraged artists frustrated with existing cultural policy. Moreover, throughout the East Bloc, there was in progress a discussion of modernism that would reach a high point at a May 1963 Kafka conference held in Liblice, Czechoslovakia. Even if the GDR's delegates there denied the importance of Kafka's work as a model for socialist art, the conference itself was highly significant. As the prominent literary scholar Werner Mittenzwei, himself a participant, noted many years after the fact, the conference "was an expression that after Stalin's death it now seemed necessary to reform socialism, and . . . it revealed in the mirror of literary studies the condition of the reform movement."[31]

In the case of the film industry, a great deal certainly was changing. As discussed at length in the preceding chapter, competition with television was forcing DEFA both to increase efficiency and to improve its final product. To achieve these aims, the regime decided to grant the studio a greater degree of institutional autonomy. By the early sixties, artistic work groups (KAGs) were assuming greater political and artistic responsibility for individual film projects. Thus artists were gaining greater control over the filmmaking process (see Chapter 3).

Of no less importance, film policy was trying to adapt in order to keep up with cinematic developments in other socialist states. DEFA's international reputation was suffering, and the studio had little to show that could compete with the best Czech, Polish, or Soviet films. Official obstinacy was not only frustrating filmmakers but was also beginning to cause the regime considerable embarrassment by undermining the facade of unity within the East Bloc. For example, official resistance to importing an award-winning Soviet film, *Clear Sky* (Grigori Chukhrai, 1961), was overcome only after it became known that a West German distributor had already dubbed the film in preparation for its release.[32] Another cause of continual irritation were films from other socialist countries being shown under the auspices of diplomatic missions even though their import had been officially barred.[33] There was also an economic factor. Other East Bloc countries were hesitant to import DEFA films of questionable quality.[34] Such circumstances contributed to a new inflection in film policy away from efficiency measured in terms of output and toward an emphasis on "quality." In a September 1962 meeting with studio officials, the official head of the film industry, the influential functionary Hans Rodenberg, declared that "mediocre films" were now "the main enemy." This position was a direct disavowal of the Politburo's earlier position: "Mediocre films do not harm DEFA's reputation. The high number of poor ones do."[35]

Officials had a difficult balancing act to perform. On the one hand, the Party leadership seems to have been genuinely committed to the studio's decentralization as the best means for achieving long-term objectives for the film industry. Certainly such an approach was consistent with the regime's general economic thinking at the time. Moreover, films that failed to attract audiences were useless regardless of their ideological content. On the other hand, officials feared that reform efforts could easily be misinterpreted. There was concern that filmmakers might see any enlargement of their artistic prerogative as a patent for free expression. Officials may have grudgingly recognized the East German cinema's need to revamp itself aesthetically, but they certainly did not want artists to imitate the political outspokenness of their colleagues in other socialist countries. This issue took on new urgency in the fall of 1962 when Khrushchev, as part of the renewal of his anti-Stalin campaign, allowed publication of Aleksandr Solzhenitsyn's classic depiction of life in a gulag, *One Day in the Life of Ivan Denisovich*.[36]

A Party Activists' Convention (*Parteiaktivtagung*) that took place at the studio in December 1962 is a good indication of the fine line both the regime and the industry were trying to negotiate. There Rodenberg emphasized: "There was once a time when we said that a film was good because it came from the Soviet Union. . . . Today it is not a matter of transferring Soviet conditions to the GDR. That means [we should not] produce our films like direct copies of Soviet ones, but instead, after a thoughtful and careful analysis, study and appropriate everything new, everything essential."[37] On the one hand, these words were a warning to filmmakers not to follow the example of their Soviet colleagues too closely. On the other hand, Rodenberg's remarks left a window of opportunity open. In the context of other comments at the Activists' Convention, they suggested that artists could expect to enjoy a certain creative leeway, provided their intentions were politically pure. Chief Dramaturge Wischnewski, for example, argued that East German filmmakers could learn from Andrei Tarkovsky's *Ivan's Childhood*, as long as they did not merely imitate it but adopted its insights to fit the GDR's particular situation.[38] By not challenging this statement, higher-ranking officials like Rodenberg were making a considerable concession to filmmakers. The great Russian avant-garde director's first film may not have been as abstract in conception as his subsequent ones, but it already represented a radical departure from socialist realism—in Jean-Paul Sartre's words, it was "socialist surrealism."[39]

Clearly, the regime's tolerance had limits. As Rodenberg said at a meeting with DEFA studio director Mückenberger, "The struggle against schematicism, dogmatism, and superficiality can easily ally itself with unprincipled liberalism and open revolt against the Party's cultural policy."[40] Here the HV Film director may well have been thinking of remarks that had been made during the Activists' Convention. The director Frank Vogel had noted that reading the Soviet paper *Pravda* generally made him "upbeat, happy and optimistic," whereas the SED organ, *Neues Deutschland*, often made him angry. His colleague Frank Beyer similarly had asked why writings of certain Soviet writers, including Yevgeny Yevtushenko, author of a controversial poem titled "Stalin's Heirs," were not available in German.[41]

Even so, functionaries were satisfied with the results of the Party Activists' Convention. A report of the ZK Cultural Section concluded that the discussion there had resisted the tendency "to force a discussion of errors on the Party."[42] Indeed, despite its persistent suspicion of filmmakers, the Party leadership would continue to permit DEFA's institutional decentralization.

In this relatively relaxed climate, production of *Der geteilte Himmel* proceeded without significant hitches.[43] Konrad Wolf's worst difficulties in completing the film seem to have been of an organizational nature. Morale among his production staff was low; many of its members found the structure of the script too complicated and were skeptical about the film's prospects.[44] In contrast, DEFA's management seems to have had no major reservations about the project.[45]

It would be a mistake, however, to interpret the way in which the project proceeded as a sign that artists found accommodation with the state easy even under the improved conditions that prevailed in the early sixties. One of the most controversial DEFA films actually released in the early sixties was *Der Fall Gleiwitz* (The Gleiwitz Incident, 1961), made by Gerhard Klein, Wolfgang Kohlhaase, and Günther Rücker. This film presented itself as a precise reconstruction of the attack on a German radio station that the Nazis staged in September 1939 in order to provide a pretense for invading Poland. What disturbed officials most was the film's style, which combined the pretense of a quasi documentary with highly stylized photography. The work did not engross it viewers in its plot but rather encouraged a distanced, reflective attitude. While the film was enthusiastically received within the studio and lauded in the press, the Politburo complained that its makers had allowed formal considerations to take precedence over political ones. Other officials faulted the work for lacking a clear message and even glamorizing the Nazis.[46]

A great number of themes remained taboo for filmmakers. For example, another Christa Wolf project, titled *Ein Mann kehrt heim* (A Man Returns Home), did not proceed beyond the initial treatment stage because of its controversial subject matter: an individual's readjustment to the GDR after years of exile in the Soviet Union.[47] Another project, *Wind von vorn* (Headwind, Herman Nitschke, 1962), was broken off during filming ostensibly on account of the incompetence of its makers. The actual reason probably was the extreme minimalist style the young filmmakers working on the project were trying to develop.[48] Easily the most dramatic example of a project that failed for political reasons was Konrad Petzold and Egon Günther's film *Das Kleid* (The Suit, 1961). Adapted from the Hans Christian Andersen tale "The Emperor's New Clothes," this absurdist parable of GDR society featured a walled city.[49]

Tensions between artists and the regime were more obvious outside the film industry. Frequently cited examples of repression from the early sixties include the firing of Peter Huchel in 1962 as the editor of the journal of the German Academy of the Arts, *Sinn und Form*, for defending modernism and publishing pieces by Western intellectuals, including Paul Celan and Sartre. Stephan Hermlin, who as head of the literature section of the Academy of the Arts had similarly encouraged new artistic directions, was forced to step down in 1963. In the theater, various plays were banned, including Heiner Müller's *Die Umsiedlerin* (The Refugee Woman) in 1961 and Peter Hacks's *Die Sorgen um die Macht* (Worries about Power) in 1962. Two television films, *Fetzers Flucht* (Fetzer's Flight) and *Monolog für einen Taxifahrer* (Monologue for a Taxi Driver), both written by Günter Künert and directed by Günter Stahnke, also failed to see their debuts that year.

In short, *Der geteilte Himmel* would prove the exception rather than the rule. The picture seemed to provide a model for harnessing avant-garde impulses in a way compatible with official expectations. Its success encouraged other filmmakers to take risks and experiment formally. Nevertheless, in attempting to find an alternative to socialist realist aesthetics, even politically loyal artists, such as Christa Wolf and Konrad Wolf, had embarked on an odyssey that would take them far afield from their original mark.

THE TRIUMPH OF FEMALE PROTAGONISTS

Der geteilte Himmel belonged to a small flurry of DEFA films from the years leading up to the Eleventh Plenum focusing on the experience of a single female protagonist. These included *Septemberliebe* (September Love, Kurt Maetzig, 1961), . . . *und deine Liebe auch* (Frank Vogel, 1962); *Christine* (Slatan Dudow, 1963), and *Lots Weib* (Lot's Wife, Egon Günther and Helga Schütz, 1965). Although these works were not the first DEFA pictures to feature female protagonists, their relative concentration at this point of the studio's history is significant. Moreover, several such works, including *Der geteilte Himmel*, were different from earlier East German pictures in having a highly subjective narrative structure. Of the films banned in the aftermath of the Eleventh Plenum, two fall into this last category: Kurt Maetzig's *Das Kaninchen bin ich* (1965) and Herrmann Zschoche and Ulrich Plenzdorf's *Karla* (1965/1966).

As noted, this turn toward female subjectivity had an international resonance. Besides Alain Resnais's *Hiroshima mon amour*, other important films from this period that are constructed around a female protagonist include Jean-Luc Godard's *Vivre sa vie* (1962) and Milos Forman's *Loves of a Blonde* (1965). Seen in broad perspective, such female characters were a continuation of a cinematic trend, which began with neorealism, toward more intimate films and away from the genre pictures typical of commercial moviemaking. Exploring the world through such figures allowed filmmakers to question the certainties of the postwar era, to insist on realms of experience that were discordant with the political and social myths of their societies.

Of more immediate concern to this study, the trope of the young woman seeking her way in life possessed a specific valance within the system of representation used by artists to depict East Germany. If her emancipation stood for the new order's progressive pretensions, her gender referred to a wholeness lost in modern life that socialism was supposed to recover.[50] Indeed, as Elizabeth Heineman has noted, the GDR celebrated the role of single, independent women in socialist society. In stark contrast, commentators in the Federal Republic during the fifties saw such women as a troubling reminder of the demographic gender imbalance that resulted from Germany's catastrophic battlefield losses during World War II.[51]

Thus it is not surprising that DEFA filmmakers would have been drawn to young women protagonists seeking self-realization and emancipation. Slatan Dudow's *Frauenschicksale* (The Destinies of Women, 1952) celebrated East Germany as a refuge for four women fleeing the same Western Romeo (see Chapter 1). Another early example of such a figure appeared in *Bürgermeister Anna* (Mayor Anna, Hans Müller, 1950), which was based on a play by Konrad Wolf's father, Friedrich Wolf. The plot here concerns a spunky young woman who becomes the mayor of a small village. She must contend not only with sinister wealthy farmers representing the capitalist past but also with her own fiancé, a returning prisoner of war, who at first reacts coolly to her new responsibilities.

Similar characters from other DEFA pictures from the fifties include Erika in *Das kleine und das grosse Glück* (Happiness, Small and Great, Martin Hellberg, 1953), Lena in *52 Wochen sind ein Jahr* (52 Weeks Are a Year, Richard Groschopp, 1955), Lutz in *Sonnensucher* (Sun Searchers, Konrad Wolf, 1958), and Inge in *Reportage 57* (János Veiczi, 1959).

Few female characters in the East German cinema of the fifties were as central, however, as those in *Frauenschicksale* or *Bürgermeister Anna*. Generally, they occupied subsidiary roles or were but one of several main figures.[52] The men still tended to be the more compelling characters. Indeed, the character that best typifies the East German cinema of the fifties is the mature and resolute male comrade, as exemplified by the protagonist in Kurt Maetzig's two-part dramatization of the life of the prewar Communist leader Ernst Thälmann.[53] Several actors specialized in such roles, notably Günther Simon, Erwin Geschonneck, Erich Franz, and Wilhelm Koch-Hooge. Simon rose to prominence as Thälmann's interpreter. Koch-Hooge played fictionalized, Thälmannesque members of the World War II Communist underground in films by both Slatan Dudow and Konrad Wolf.[54] Geschonneck portrayed one of the founders of the socialist movement, Wilhelm Liebknecht, in Artur Pohl's *Die Unbesiegbaren* (The Invincibles, 1953) and had heroic male leads in several Konrad Wolf and Frank Beyer films of the early sixties.[55] Franz was adept at playing a somewhat homier, more down-to-earth Communist male, the proletarian *Familienvater*, or family man.[56]

The partial eclipse of strong male protagonists by female figures in the period leading up to the Eleventh Plenum reflected the increased production of *Gegenwartsfilme* in general. The most memorable of the strong male protagonists tended to appear in historical films. Despite repeated calls by officials for more films set in the GDR featuring heroic workers,[57] the ones that were made had mixed success at best. For example, Konrad Wolf's *Leute mit Flügeln* (People with Wings, 1960) featured Geschonneck as a Communist airplane mechanic who, after participating in the resistance, helps in the founding of the GDR aerospace industry. The film opened to weak reviews and was quickly withdrawn from circulation after the cancellation of plans to build an East German jet plane. Another flop was Johannes Arpe's *Erich Kubak* from 1959 (see Chapter 3); the film's multitalented, proletarian *Familienvater*, who is shown tirelessly conspiring to improve workplace efficiency, similarly failed to capture the imagination of audiences.

There may well have been an element of narcissistic identification on the part of male directors and scriptwriters with the female characters in their pictures. One of the clearest examples of this phenomenon comes from one of the two films directly criticized during the Eleventh Plenum, Kurt Maetzig's *Das Kaninchen bin ich*. Here the theme of seduction can easily be read as a metaphor for artists' own uneasy relationship with the state. The young female protagonist has an affair with a judge, who has unfairly sentenced her brother to a harsh prison term for a casual political comment. She then must decide whether the favors he offers her are sincere expressions of sentiment or if he is exploiting her. Maetzig's next film, *Das Mädchen auf dem Brett* (The Girl on the Diving Board, 1967), features a young woman athlete struggling to make a comeback, just as Maetzig must have been doing at the time, since his last film had been banned two years earlier.[58] Although *Der geteilte Himmel* does not present an obvious case of "transference," the work's placement within Konrad Wolf's opus is suggestive. Similarly, Wolf's last major work, *Solo Sonny* (1978), focuses on a female character whose situation must have resonated with his own self-understanding as a socialist filmmaker by that time. Written by Wolfgang Kohlhaase, the picture is centered on a nightclub singer who despite repeated setbacks attempts to stay true to herself as an artist.[59]

Quite strikingly, during the fifties and sixties, all of the directors who made DEFA films featuring women were male.[60] The same holds largely true for screenwriters as well.[61] It seems doubtful that these artists were choosing to focus on female protagonists out of feminist convictions alone. In his earlier films, Maetzig was certainly not above borrowing demeaning conventions for depicting women from the commercial cinema. His *Vergesst mir meine Traudel nicht* (Don't Forget My Traudel, 1956) presents a voluptuous ditz as an orphan of the holocaust, who in one scene prances about at length in nothing but a bath towel.[62] Konrad Wolf was himself the virtual embodiment of the heroic Communist male. Not only did he return to Germany at the end of World War II as a nineteen-year-old lieutenant in the Red Army, having grown up in Soviet exile, but he was respected by his colleagues within the studio for taking courageous, principled positions in political discussions.[63]

Despite the regime's official commitment to equality between the sexes, the GDR as an authoritarian state was deeply patriarchal. Women rarely occupied the highest-ranking political or managerial positions. Although women participated in the work force to a much higher degree than in West Germany, they tended to be concentrated in lower-paying and less prestigious jobs than their male colleagues.[64] Within DEFA itself, the situation was quite similar. In the early sixties, even though women made up 31 percent of the studio's work force, they were virtually absent in trained technical professions and in artistic ones. The studio's top management was also almost exclusively male. In order to achieve greater parity, a 1964 internal DEFA report urged all supervisors to support the advancement of women, but the report was only guardedly optimistic concerning the rate at which progress would be made. It noted that many women were too overburdened by their duties as wives and mothers to assume additional professional responsibilities. Attempts by the studio to alleviate their domestic pressures through such measures as providing on-the-premises laundry and child care had met with only partial success.[65]

The progress toward equality that women in the studio made in future years was limited. The studio's leading artists continued to be predominantly men. Although there had always been a few women scriptwriters active in the feature film studio, women directors did not begin to emerge at all until the seventies and eighties.[66] Only on celluloid did women ever achieve significant parity with men at DEFA. Here the trend that began in the years leading up to the Plenum resumed in the seventies and early eighties. A relatively large number of *Alltag* films from this period featured a woman protagonist.[67] If resolute males represent the most typical DEFA protagonists of the fifties, then single women characters are in many ways emblematic of the studio's later history. The East German cinema's general turn toward the everyday life of ordinary individuals favored female experience. The abandonment of the GDR's utopian pretensions placed a premium on the private and more concrete social realms conventionally associated with women, while it also called into question the mythic dimensions of the political imaginary on which modern male identity often depends.

Indeed, several *Alltag* films concerned older male comrades experiencing existential crises. For example, Roland Gräf's *Bankett für Achilles* (Banquet for Achilles, 1975) stars Erwin Geschonneck as a retiring foreman in a chemical factory facing his own mortality. The film's last shot shows him alone against a barren landscape, trying to cultivate a private garden threatened by industrial pollution.[68] As one critic has noted, many of DEFA's male characters by the eighties seemed to be "joust[ing] with windmills, los[ing] strength, even disintegrat[ing]." In contrast, various women figures were being depicted "going with increased strength and full of optimism through circumstances . . . unfavorable to their own self-preservation."[69] The concrete and the personal now took precedence over the sweeping historical vision that once defined the GDR's purpose as a society. At least in many *Alltag* films, the brave new world of the future appears to be a tired place, populated by individuals whose own concerns no longer hinge on the destiny of the working class.

Of course, Rita in *Der geteilte Himmel* is still a far cry from the female characters appearing in some later DEFA pictures. Her excursion into her own subjectivity is only a temporary detour. Her return to active life is a matter not of accommodation but rather of unqualified commitment to socialist society. She not only feels solidarity with her fellow GDR citizens; she experiences a sense of a shared higher mission. In the film's last sequence, the dying Meternagel gives Rita what amounts to his blessing. As the next images show Rita moving among crowds of people in Halle, the narrator says, "Perhaps they understand now that the fate of the unborn depends on the strength of countless people." In the wider context of East German cinematic history, though, this passing of the torch from an older experienced comrade to a younger woman takes on a quite different meaning: the transition from one set of assumptions about GDR society to another.

CONCLUSION

In an often-cited lecture, the nineteenth-century French sociologist Ernest Renan pointed out that the origin of every nation coincides with an act of violence. Insofar as East Germany ever achieved the attributes of a nation, its violent predicate was the building of the Berlin Wall. Outrageous as it was, that deed underlined the GDR's apparent permanence and autonomy as a society. Perhaps what distinguished East Germany from other countries was that the violence associated with its founding was introverted. The purpose of the Wall was not, as the regime claimed, to exclude external enemies but to restrict the GDR's own citizens from leaving.

Few filmmakers and other East German artists could have been entirely blind to this dilemma, even if they remained committed to the socialist project. Clearly one factor that makes *Der geteilte Himmel* an interesting film is its acknowledgment of the costs of Germany's division. At the same time, the film, like the novella on which it is based, does not seek to challenge fundamentally the regime's legitimizing narrative but rather to deal somehow with the shock of the Wall's construction without offending existing authority. In order to accomplish this goal, the film's creators employed a complex narrative structure as well as an unconventional style inspired by recent developments in the international cinema. These aesthetic moves allowed for an articulation of a subjective, female perspective that was both eccentric to official self-understanding and assimilable within it. Of particular significance to this study, the turn toward female subjectivity was associated with a privileging of the prosaic as a realm of experience and truth.

As events would soon prove, this solution to the creative issues facing DEFA filmmakers was problematic. To begin with, avant-garde impulses and the regime's political expectations for the film industry were clearly on a collision course. Developments in the world cinema such as the nouvelle vague were not easily reconcilable with continuing demands for socialist realism, even if the authorities were prepared to be flexible in their understanding of the GDR's official aesthetic. In addition, artists' commitment to the new society did not necessarily translate into unwavering loyalty to the regime. Filmmakers in the early sixties had reason to believe that their society was advancing toward the future because their own industry was showing signs of improvement. While *Der geteilte Himmel* seemed to confirm this trend, the picture was also an indication of the uneasy accommodation between artists and the regime. Emphasizing subjective experience and favoring the ordinary over the epochal allowed the film's creators to present the GDR in a far more complex manner than was previously possible, but these characteristics also implicitly challenged the regime's millennialist self-understanding.

Günther Simon, who specialized in playing resolute
Communist leaders, rousing his comrades to action as
the title character in *Ernst Thälmann—Sohn seiner
Klasse* (1954). (Courtesy Dr. Irmgard Wenzel)

A publicity poster for *Berlin—Ecke Schönhauser* (1957).

Underneath the el, the gathering place for the
youthful protagonists of *Berlin—Ecke Schönhauser*.

The wayward Karl-Heinz, played by Harry Engel, confronts his own image in *Berlin—Ecke Schönhauser*, a film that presented itself as a meditation on seeing.

Raimund Schelcher as the kindly police inspector, the face of benign authority in *Berlin—Ecke Schönhauser.*

Gitta Lind as an East Berlin housewife turned entertainment sensation in *Meine Frau macht Musik* (1958), a *Revuefilm*, or chorus-line movie, that soared at the box office but was roundly attacked by officials.

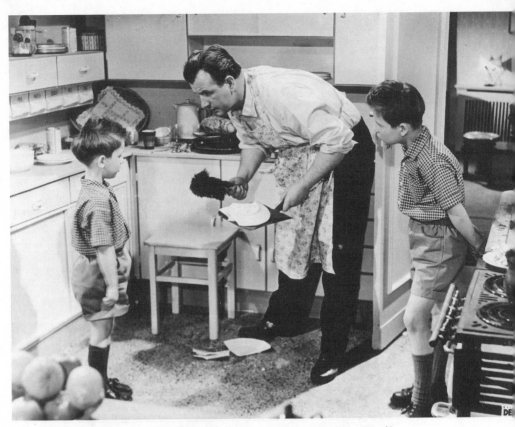

**Günther Simon as the husband in *Meine Frau macht Musik*,
forced to assume domestic responsibilities because of his wife's
glamorous career.**

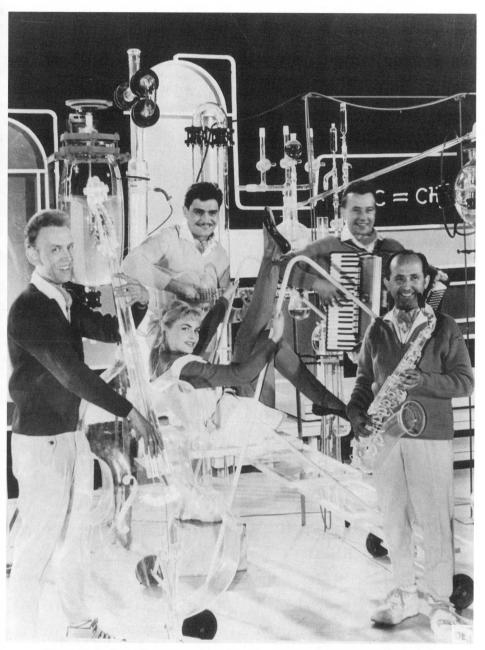

Günter Reisch's *Silversterpunsch* (1960), an engaging attempt at a genuinely socialist musical comedy, set in a chemical factory. (Courtesy Waltraud Pathenheimer)

Renate Blume as Rita, on the job with her all-male work brigade, in *Der geteilte Himmel* (1964). (Courtesy Elfriede Bergmann)

The last meeting at Café Kranzler in West Berlin between the politically doomed lovers, Rita and Manfred (played by Eberhard Esche), in *Der geteilte Himmel*. (Courtesy Elfriede Bergmann)

Angelika Waller as Maria, reduced to working as a barmaid in a questionable establishment in the banned film *Das Kaninchen bin ich* (1965). (Courtesy Jörg Erkens)

State security agents invade the domestic refuge of the proletarian kitchen in *Das Kaninchen bin ich*. (Courtesy Jörg Erkens)

Manfred Krug as the born rebel Balla (center), together with his brigade of carpenters, in the banned film *Spur der Steine* (1966).

**Eberhard Esche as the tormented, adulterous
Party secretary Horrath in *Spur der Steine*.**

**The official inquest concerning Horrath's
immoral behavior in *Spur der Steine*.**

Angelika Domröse as Paula from the dream sequence in *Die Legende von Paul und Paula* (1973). (Courtesy Marianne Damm)

The Polynesian feast, with Winfried Glatzeder as Paul, in *Die Legende von Paul und Paula*. (Courtesy Marianne Damm)

Paul, the spurned lover, camps out in front of Paula's apartment, as the latter converses with a rival suitor, the gallant but ridiculous Herr Saft. (Courtesy Marianne Damm)

The apple feast from the dream sequence in
Die Legende von Paul und Paula. (Courtesy Marianne Damm)

Renate Krössner in the title role, an aspiring night club singer
struggling to succeed despite an indifferent society, in *Solo Sunny*
(1980). (Courtesy Dieter Lück)

5

The Eleventh Plenum and *Das Kaninchen bin ich*

When people have often asked me why this film was
actually forbidden, then I say that why it was forbidden
is . . . relatively easy to understand. Much more difficult
to comprehend is why it could have been made.
—Kurt Maetzig[1]

For East German filmmakers, the Eleventh Plenum of the SED's Central Committee in December 1965 represented a unique juncture in their history. At this meeting Communist leaders launched a scathing attack on artists, singling out the DEFA feature film studio for especially harsh criticism. The total of twelve pictures that the regime banned over the next nine months was unprecedented. A number of these works not only were politically provocative but demonstrated artistic accomplishment as well. Thus, for many involved in the industry, the films' public debut after the fall of the Berlin Wall in November 1989 seemed to redeem decades of struggle and frustration.

Das Kaninchen bin ich (The Rabbit Is Me, 1965) was one of two films directly criticized at the Eleventh Plenum. Looking back from the vantage of nearly thirty years, the director Kurt Maetzig is surely correct in emphasizing that understanding why his picture was banned is easier than appreciating the conditions that allowed for the film's production in the first place. The work's offense to authority was obvious. The literary basis for the picture was a novel of the same title by Manfred Bieler that the GDR Cultural Ministry had already refused to approve for publication. The plot turns on an explosive character constellation: a young woman has a love affair with a judge responsible for sending her brother to jail for a trivial political offense. Because of her brother's conviction, the picture's protagonist must cope with Kafkaesque courts, rude prison guards, and the denial of admission to university.

One indication of the film's complex production history is the biographies of the principals involved. Only Bieler's career conforms to the romantic image of a dissident artist. The young writer emigrated from the GDR soon after the severe criticism he endured at the Eleventh Plenum. In contrast, the much older Maetzig did not have a reputation for taking critical stands. He enjoyed great prestige with the regime for his monumental movie epic celebrating the martyred Communist leader Ernst Thälmann of the Weimar era. This lavishly financed project instantly became a classic articulation of the heroic antifascist ideology that justified Communist rule. Other individuals who supported the realization of *Das Kaninchen bin ich* were also unlikely critics of the regime. For example, before being appointed to his position as studio director, Jochen Mückenberger had served as a Party functionary assigned to the ZK apparatus. His brother, Erich, belonged to the Politburo.

Tightly regulated by the state, DEFA never enjoyed a reputation for political outspokenness. Especially during the twenty years of its history that preceded the Plenum, the studio's production had tended toward either facile propaganda or genre films. Indeed, even *Das Kaninchen bin ich* does not qualify as an unmitigated act of resistance against Communist rule. While its makers were aware of the controversial nature of their project, their persistence in pursuing it did not indicate hostility toward the ideals of socialism or even the regime. The same applies to other Plenum films to the degree that these individually had an overt political purpose. Most of the artists involved certainly regarded themselves as loyal Party members committed to the new society. Many, like Maetzig, had been involved in the production of films glorifying Communist rule. Frank Vogel, the director of the second film directly attacked at the Plenum, *Denk bloss nicht, ich heule* (Just Don't Think I'll Cry, 1965), for example, had within the previous three years completed two rather facile pictures heroizing the Wall's construction. Nevertheless, in this third film he did not shirk from depicting East Germany as a violent, angry society: generational conflict climaxes in a brutal beating amid the ruins of a Nazi ceremonial edifice.

This chapter considers the conditions that facilitated the production of the Plenum films and evaluates their significance within the wider context of East Germany's cultural and political evolution. After surveying developments leading up to the Plenum, my analysis then turns to *Das Kaninchen bin ich*. In depicting the adulterous relationship between a young woman and her brother's judge, this picture broke many taboos. At the same time, the work suggested the possibility of socialism's redemption through a communal solidarity, depicted as latently present in the interstices of the existing state. Honesty and communication are the keys for activating this hidden power. In this sense, ordinary life functions in the film as an antidote to a political realm dominated by abstract historical considerations. Equally interesting is the picture's production history. The decision to proceed with the project depended directly on ambitious plans to reform the structure and goals of the movie industry. Thus even as the work began encountering considerable political resistance, a few officials attempted to salvage it. Finally, the chapter considers the Plenum itself and the discursive logic that allowed Party leaders to assign the unreleased work direct responsibility for a whole array of alleged social pathologies.

THE POLITICAL AND CULTURAL CONTEXT
OF THE PLENUM FILMS

Understanding why artists and officials loyal to the regime risked their careers to realize provocative works of art requires attention to East Germany's cultural and political context. Many participants refer to a similar sequence of political events in order to explain the conditions that inspired the Plenum films. Among these was the construction of the Wall. Many who identified with the GDR found this act perversely liberating. The director Frank Beyer explained to me in an interview:

> I certainly did not perceive the Wall's construction as a victory, as the papers claimed. I experienced it rather as a defeat, [but] as a defeat from which one could recover. . . . They always told us before, we stand here at the very front line of the socialist camp. Here is the borderline, and we are here in the very first trench . . . and, as is known, you don't debate in the front trench . . . you follow orders, you obey. . . . And [thus] I had the feeling after the Wall's construction, now we are no longer in the front trench. Now we can talk with each other in another fashion. We can deal with each other in a critical fashion. We can talk about things that were forbidden before.[2]

In the short term, the Wall did not have the moderating effect that Beyer describes. Efforts to mobilize the population politically as well as an intensification of repression accompanied its construction. Still, a gradual relaxation in official cultural policy made itself felt in the GDR during the early sixties. A renewed wave of de-Stalinization emanating from Moscow followed close on the heels of the sealing of the Berlin border. Even if the works of such figures as Solzhenitsyn remained taboo for them, GDR artists were clearly excited by the success of their East Bloc colleagues. In addition, a new generation of homegrown writers—Christa Wolf, Hermann Kant, and Erik Neutsch, among them—first made a mark for themselves in these years. Within the film industry, change included a more open attitude toward the international cinema and efforts to decentralize the studio through artistic work groups (KAGs).

The continuing legacy of Khrushchev's denunciation of Stalin at the Twentieth Congress of the CPSU in 1956 also contributed to the sense among East German intellectuals that change was imminent in their society. While SED leaders hardly embraced their Soviet colleague's liberalizing tendencies, they found much common ground with him on economic matters. Following the Soviet lead, efforts to decentralize the East German economy had been under way since the late fifties. By 1963, these culminated in the proclamation at the Sixth SED Party Congress of an ambitious New Economic System (NÖS). This grandiose proposal aimed to combine the efficiency of a self-regulated economy with the advantages of central planning. Individual enterprises would enjoy greater autonomy in making decisions, while the Party would assume the role of the invisible hand by manipulating a new set of "levers," such as interest rates on state loans. Bottom-line profit was also supposed to replace raw output as a measure of efficiency. The state would set basic goals for the economy, but lower-level combines and enterprises would determine the details of the plan. Technically trained experts would assume decision-making power from political elites. Workers would benefit from a wage system that would better stimulate and reward individual ability.[3]

From today's vantage point, the technocratic vision of the NÖS seems anything but liberating. To those receptive to the progressive pathos adhering in its rhetoric, however, the scheme stood for change and renewal, even democratization.[4] Its premise was that the first stages of achieving the new society were now complete. Even if Germany was still divided, the working class had consolidated its rule over one part of the land and created basic structures for the future. Hence the time had come to replace the crude inefficiencies of a command economy. Only by taking full advantage of the "technical-scientific" revolution could East Germany overtake the West. As Walter Ulbricht himself emphasized during a 1964 ZK Plenum, "We have as little use for . . . petty, small-minded bureaucratic souls who have lost sight of the new as managers . . . as for old slaves of routine, who do not want to recognize that . . . it is impossible to lead people with old caught-in-a-rut administrative and dogmatic means."[5]

The NÖS had its analog in cultural politics as well: the Second Bitterfeld Conference of 1964. Western scholars have generally interpreted this meeting of leading politicians and cultural figures mainly as a retreat from the rhetoric of the First Bitterfeld Conference, which took place in 1959.[6] But the decision to stage both meetings at the same location was hardly coincidental. The new platform differed from the old one less in terms of aims than in the means proposed for achieving them. There was less emphasis on artists seeking communion with the proletariat by volunteering in factories or on recruiting new talent directly from the ranks of labor. Instead, officials stressed the need to achieve higher quality art that was in keeping with the ever-rising expectations of workers. The conference equally emphasized the need to apply scientific principles to cultural management. Accompanying this call was the promise that the Cultural Ministry would simplify its administrative structures and would involve artists in decision making more actively by establishing special advisory boards.[7] Even if party leaders continued to condemn modernist impulses, their emphasis on "scientific" approaches rather than dogmatic or bureaucratic ones clearly resonated with the language of the Twentieth Congress of the CPSU in 1956.

Developments in other areas also provided artists hoping for reform with reasons for optimism. In September 1963, the Politburo issued a *Jugendkommuniqué* (Youth Communiqué) emphasizing the need to accord young people more trust and understanding. Here the Party leadership warned against "dismissing somewhat uncomfortable questions . . . as bothersome or even as provocations," lest hypocrisy be encouraged.[8] In the legal system, there was the October 1964 amnesty decree, which followed in the wake of two earlier Jurisprudence Decrees supposedly guaranteeing judicial autonomy.[9] The measure further allowed for the creation of committees locally and in the workplace with the supposed intent of allowing citizens to regulate minor matters among themselves.

The announcement of such reforms reinforced developments that had been under way at the DEFA feature film studio since at least 1956. Over the years, the studio had increased its autonomy vis-à-vis the Cultural Ministry. As early as 1957, the studio director had obtained the right to approve scripts for production independently. DEFA had also had success with nuts-and-bolts issues such as annual production planning. The state still set basic annual goals, but the studio was generally free to develop individual projects as it saw fit. Central to the reform process was the introduction of KAGs. Initially proposed even before the Twentieth Congress of the CPSU, these were simultaneously supposed to create a sense of collective socialist élan within the studio, ease the perennial problem of script development, provide artists with more say regarding the industrial aspects of filmmaking, and increase efficiency.

By 1964, the film industry was already gearing up for a new round of far-reaching reforms. The state office responsible for supervising the motion picture industry, the HV Film, envisioned an ambitious overhaul of all aspects of film production and distribution. A complex system of inter-locking contracts codified in the annual plan would still regulate the rela-tionship among the film industry's various branches, but the income of institutions like the feature film studio and the salaries of its employ-ees would depend on actual performance. For example, DEFA would no longer be able to expect a set sum for each film produced regardless of the audience it attracted. Another aspect of the HV Film's plans foresaw a rad-ical expansion of functions assigned to the KAGs, which in effect would gain financial quasi independence from the studio and would compete with each other for funds. Those whose films were successful could expect larger budgets in the future. They would also have the freedom to dis-tribute their own funds among their members' projects as they saw fit. Thus one group might decide to invest heavily in a single lavish produc-tion, while another could choose to take a risk with a promising young talent. Comparable incentive schemes were in the works in the areas of film distribution and the operation of individual movie houses.[10]

While these measures remained largely unrealized, the studio took a number of steps toward implementing them in the period leading up to the Eleventh Plenum, among the most significant of which was abolishing the position of chief dramaturge. This move shifted greater responsibility to the studio's seven KAGs and indirectly to the artists who, along with other studio professionals, participated in their management. The heads of work groups now reported directly to the studio director. While the latter still had to approve a film before it could enter production, each group was responsible for devising its own annual plan, as well as for preparing financial estimates and supervising its own expenditures.[11] An-other reform that would have given filmmakers greater influence in the studio involved tying the bonuses that made up a hefty portion of their income to the quality of their work as judged by a commission consisting primarily of artists.[12]

On other fronts, the HV Film was attempting to broaden significantly the range of films shown in East German theaters. On assuming office in 1963, the agency's director, Günter Witt, allowed the release of several "progressive" films from capitalist countries whose East German pre-mieres had been held up even though distribution rights were already in hand. These included Bernhard Wicki's *Die Brücke* (The Bridge, FRG, 1959), about the vain sacrifice of life by Hitler Youth volunteers in the closing days of World War II, and Stanley Kramer's *Judgment at Nurem-berg* (USA, 1961).[13] The HV Film director also authorized the purchase—if not the release—of politically controversial East Bloc films, including ex-amples of the Czech nouvelle vague such as Milos Forman's *Loves of a*

Blond (CSR, 1964).[14] Moreover, in an apparent attempt to soften leading functionaries' attitudes toward the world cinema, Witt prepared a special film series for them that included the Beatles' *A Hard Day's Night* (UK, 1964).[15]

General developments in East German media are also significant to an understanding of why filmmakers believed their society was capable of fundamental change. The period following the Wall's construction saw increasing official tolerance for entertainment forms that only a few years earlier had been condemned as "decadent." Instead of fighting trends in popular entertainment, the regime cautiously attempted to capture their energy for its own purposes. Thus the 1963 Youth Communiqué, while still decrying Western *"Unkultur,"* conceded that dance was a "legitimate expression of joy and pleasure in life." The document insisted, "Nobody wants to prescribe to young people that they should express their feelings and emotions dancing . . . only in waltz and tango rhythms."[16] To answer the demand for contemporary music, a new radio station, DT 64, commenced operation. Originally set up to serve the spring 1964 *Deutschland Treffen*—a youth convention that impressed even Western observers as "hip"[17]—this broadcast soon developed into a focal point for a thriving *"Beatmusik"* subculture. On the local level, the FDJ's attempts to co-opt this movement led to official sponsorship of "hot" concerts.[18] Another sign of the relatively relaxed spirit of the day was the university student publication *Forum*, which attempted to foster both innovative literature and genuine debate.[19] At the same time, a coffeehouse culture sprung up that provided a venue for *Liedermacher*, or folk-singing cabaret performers, most notably Wolf Biermann.[20]

Television's rapid rise also made the GDR a very different place in the early sixties. The Party seems to have been drawn to the new technology as a means for indoctrination, as an "ideological weapon" in a battle of the ether with the West. Still, no one in the fifties could have fully appreciated the new medium's complex ramifications. Under pressure to fill airtime, East German media pioneers resorted to the same strategies as their colleagues in the West.[21] Even if GDR game shows, variety programs, and the like often had deliberate political subtexts,[22] their diffusion through a high-profile, official medium had subtle effects on East German society's self-understanding. Television's unique strength lay in dramatizing the immediate moment, not in making grand narratives spring to life. Thus television dramas were relatively ill suited for conveying an epic vision of the GDR as a society rapidly advancing toward the future, such as the regime had hoped to achieve during the fifties through film. The very experience of watching a serialized broadcast on a small screen at home was fundamentally different from that of joining a throng of people in a darkened movie theater, one's consciousness absorbed by the sights and sounds emanating from the giant screen.

Partly in response to the introduction of television, the early sixties saw a blossoming of entertainment movies. For the first time, directors specializing in genres such as the musical were now exclusively from the East, since their Western colleagues were no longer welcome in the studio. The films were also more identifiably situated in socialist society. Still, their overt political ambitions tended to be modest. Their primary purpose was to entertain and to demonstrate that DEFA could still compete in these genres. Such works indicated that the dream of a radically new inspirational socialist cinema was slowly giving way to more modest aspirations. As the following chapter will show, the immediate aftermath of the Eleventh Plenum greatly favored entertainment genres.

Individually, the emancipatory potential of developments such as the NÖS and the regime's new attitude toward contemporary cultural trends, let alone East German television, was dubious. In the context of the day, their effect was different. Each contributed to a sense that the GDR was developing into a more mature society, less dominated by immediate political imperatives and willing to tolerate a modicum of individual freedom. Moreover, many loyal to the regime did not interpret this apparent trend as a renouncement of socialism's utopian goals but rather as a signal of their long-awaited redemption. Yet expectations varied widely. An end to dogmatism and narrow-mindedness did not necessarily translate into openness and liberalization. As events would soon prove, the regime's commitment to reforms stopped abruptly whenever its own authority seemed in jeopardy.

DAS KANINCHEN BIN ICH

Das Kaninchen bin ich was a very deliberate response to the political and cultural situation in the GDR. While uncommonly direct in its political criticism, the film hardly aimed to subvert the socialist project. Rather, the picture suggested that the struggle for a new society was beginning to develop a dynamic of its own, independent of the state. The film probably owed its existence to the initiative of a young DEFA dramaturge, Christel Gräf, who introduced Bieler to Maetzig.[23] The director later recalled that what most impressed him about the work was the "very lively, folksy, original figure [of Maria]," the "profound ethical problems," and the "riveting story," as well as the "fabulous dialogue."[24]

The reasons for Maetzig's being drawn to the figure of Maria are not difficult to surmise. The previous chapter has already discussed the special resonance of the trope of the young woman protagonist seeking her way in life within the East German cinema. If women characters' emancipation stood for the new society's alliance with progress, their femininity referred to a lost wholeness in modern life that socialism was supposed to restore. In addition, the marginality and implicit vulnerability of these characters in terms of their sex, age, and station in life made them convenient vehicles for thematizing controversial issues.

Young female protagonists in East German film and fiction also retained a traditional resonance as emblems of their society's moral purity and righteousness. This function is particularly evident in *Das Kaninchen bin ich*. Maria's ability to preserve her integrity as an individual redeems her society. In justifying the proposed project, the film's maker described the protagonist: "Maria, the 'rabbit' . . . should right away win the sympathy of the widest public through her Berlin humor, her brashness, her charm, and, of course, the unshakable manner in which she opposes injustice."[25] That Maria's personal qualities are supposed to correspond with those of her society is clear from Maetzig's résumé of the picture's purpose: "It is the goal of the film to make clear through Maria's experience how socialist democracy has established itself in our republic, and [that] herein lie the sources of strength that allow Maria to recognize that not hypocrisy but truth and rectitude, not superficial nimbleness but steady character are the markings of a socialist."[26] Of course, these statements were written to convince skeptical functionaries of the film's cultural-political utility and therefore are deliberately incomplete. Maria's story was hardly a typical GDR *Bildungsroman*. Maria derives her power as an emblem for her society from her liminality. She embodies the GDR's inner purity, but her outward circumstances are suspect. By the same token, the film shows a society that may be essentially just but is still far from perfect. Moreover, even though Maria's stigmatization and fall from grace are undeserved, the film suggests specific reasons for socialism's ills, such as official arrogance and blindness.

Given Maria's liminal position, it is appropriate that the film's first few shots show her crossing a threshold as she arrives for work as a barmaid. The picture begins with an establishing shot of the street scene in front of Bahnhof Friedrichstrasse, an instantly recognizable East Berlin location. Maria provides the narration. As the camera shows her traversing a back alley, her voice announces, "I'm the rabbit. That one there." As she pushes the swinging door into the actual restaurant, she remarks, "Such is my world . . . the 'Old Bavaria.'" The script describes the space as having "escaped modernization. The furniture is of that shabby wine-red elegance that induces so-called intimacy . . . the interior and the mood produce the impression of a tired, dreary beginning." Adding to the sense of transgressive decadence are two gaudily dressed women with beehive hairdos, who dance listlessly with each other on the dance floor.

As if sensing her audience's shocked reaction, Maria is quick to add that even though this is her world, she does not really belong here. She explains, "But at least it is not too far from home . . . or do you think I was born in this shop? No, I had big ideas. I wanted to study Slavic languages . . . but something kept me from it." The next shot confirms her story by showing a markedly different scene. Maria, now a schoolgirl with braids, kneads bread dough with a heavyset older woman, her aunt Hete, at home in their proletarian kitchen. In contrast to the bar, this space is light and airy. A buzz at the door disturbs this idyll. Two large men from the Staatssicherheit invade the room. Maria's brother, Dieter, has been arrested.

These two short scenes define Maria's liminality quite efficiently. Politically stigmatized by her brother's arrest, she is unable to advance from high school to university. She is sexually suspect because of the dive where she works. The parallel between political and sexual pollution is further developed in the subsequent two scenes. Maria's words "and that was not the only surprise" links the first of these, depicting Dieter's trial, to the next sequence that concerns her deflowering at the hands of a cavalier high school gym instructor.

The film's charm and political punch derive largely from the way it presents Maria's compromised position as a moral asset. Maria's dual role as protagonist and narrator allows adversity and humiliation to function as sources of pride and insight. Particularly important in this regard is the dry humor that she uses to describe her life and ridicule those who patronize her. The use of inner monologue also serves to dramatize Maria's ability to transcend her circumstances. For example, in the second scene, when the Stasi agents ask her to characterize her brother, she thinks to herself, "Dieter is a smart fellow, perhaps a little too smart for the circumstances." Similarly, during the trial scene, she describes her aunt's feelings with affectionate condescension: "Aunt Hete had the easiest time getting over everything. She was quite happy that Dieter had not stolen anything. She thought it involved espionage, and for her spies are people who always have a tuxedo [and] therefore somehow something better."

Maria's sexuality provides another example of how she derives strength from something for which others might condemn her. Bieler's novel in particular includes passages describing her becoming aware of her body as an adolescent. The novel also has her admit to sexual longing and compare the performance of her lovers. Although the film does not develop these themes explicitly, Maria speaks frankly about her sexual history and is obviously aware of herself as an attractive young woman. Emblematic of Maria's self-reliance is the sharp wit she employs to fend off unwelcome advances in the bar where she works. To one customer who declares her love to her, she retorts, "Then we must get married right away." Another man who swears that they have met before receives the answer, "Yes, at a retirees' ball!"

Of course, Maria does fall for a man. Central to the film is the relationship that develops between Maria and Paul Deister, the judge responsible for sentencing her brother. While portrayed with sympathy, Paul embodies qualities that are the opposite of Maria's. A guardian of public order and morality, his personal life is rife with hypocrisy. A man in the prime of his life who projects an image of strength and solidity, he is inwardly vulnerable, dependent, and neurotic.

Paul's saving grace, which causes Maria to fall in love with him, is his willingness to both talk and listen to Maria. Unlike the other men she encounters, he does not try to rush her into bed but courts her slowly. Their relationship develops through a series of strolls through East Berlin, during which the two explain their prior lives to each other. This desire for communication both makes and breaks their relationship. On the one hand, Paul is the only person in the film with whom she can talk. An early scene in the film featuring Maria with her former lover, Uli the gym instructor, is typical of her situation. When she tries to start a serious conversation, he responds by dragging her kicking and screaming into bed. On the other hand, Paul and Maria's relationship is premised on mutual silence about her brother Dieter. It is Maria, and not Paul, who suffers under the burden of this omission, since she must face the dilemma of torn allegiances. When she finally raises the issue of her brother with Paul, he accuses her of attempting to take unfair advantage of him.

Obviously, the problem of communication in Maria and Paul's relationship has political resonances as well. The two protagonists represent different social and political classes. Maria personifies the disenfranchised little people. Her only family is her daffy aunt and a brother in jail. She speaks with a strong Berlin accent and lives in a disreputable corner of town, Oranienburger Tor, an area traditionally associated with prostitution. In contrast, Paul is a "big shot" who lives in Pankow, a district directly associated with the regime's leadership. Moreover, the plot draws an explicit parallel between the relationship's ills and those of GDR society. A refusal to communicate is equated with a fundamental lack of trust between the state and the populace. The school director admonishes Maria to have confidence in the courts, but no one reveals to her the crime with which her brother stands charged. In the Kafkaesque courtroom scene, the judge—Paul—announces the exclusion of the public, but Maria and her aunt are the only ones in the visitors' gallery asked to leave. When Maria then tries to ask Dieter about his wrongdoing while visiting with him in jail, a guard interrupts their conversation.

The romantic idyll of Maria and Paul's relationship contrasts with the repressive mechanisms of state power. This theme is articulated through the difficulties Maria encounters when she attempts to draft a clemency appeal on her brother's behalf to Paul. The film dramatizes her dilemma by juxtaposing images of the couple playfully sailing a small boat with Maria's thoughts while trying to find the right form of address for her request: "Highly Honored Herr Deister . . . Herr Committee Chair, please allow me . . . Dear Paul . . . My Dear Paul . . . you must know what's up with me." In another scene, Maria, upset with Paul's refusal to discuss Dieter's case with her, destroys the harmony of the breakfast table by setting the paper Paul is reading, *Neues Deutschland*, the official organ of the SED, on fire.

The film's title is evidently an allusion to a parable about innocence and evil, represented by a rabbit (Maria) and a snake (Paul or the order he represents). It refers to the inequality of the relationship between the two lovers and more broadly to the skewed distribution of power within GDR society. The picture dramatizes its title in a confrontation between Maria and Paul's wife, Gabriele, whose refinement and proper command of *Hochdeutsch* mark her as a representative of the privileged elite. The latter casually points an air rifle at Maria, whose voice describes the action, "If I say anything now, she'll shoot. We stand there like the snake and the rabbit." An eccentric high camera angle brackets this shot from the film's visual flow, suggesting a decisive moment of insight. The scene itself occurs at a bucolic cottage outside Berlin, in which Paul installs Maria after they become lovers. Gabriele's arrival shatters this romantic idyll. Not only does she bring a real estate agent along to discuss selling the place, but she also tells Maria disturbing news: Paul has attempted suicide.

What shocks Maria most in Gabriele is her calculating attitude. Maria chases her from the house after Gabriele explains her willingness to tolerate Paul's deceit as "compensation" for his difficult responsibilities. Maria returns to Berlin, where Paul makes one last attempt to win her back. He announces his intention to divorce his wife and marry her and his decision to intervene on her brother's behalf. He explains that his harsh sentencing of Dieter occurred out of a false zealousness, which under new political circumstances is now a liability. Thus Maria realizes that Paul's actual purpose in pardoning Dieter is to salvage his own career.

Rather than allow herself to become implicated once again in a tangled web of power relations, Maria opts for her own autonomy, which the film equates with an absolute willingness to seek and admit the truth. The final sequence shows her enduring a brutal beating from her newly released brother for refusing to renounce her love for Paul. After a scene of quasi ritual purification—Maria bathes in the kitchen of her aunt's apartment—the last shots show her setting off on her own through the streets of Berlin, her belongings loaded on a small handcart, a symbol of her authentic proletarian origins.[27] As she proceeds, nonplussed by the taunts of men, her voice is heard in mixed-over dialogue, answering the questions of a university registrar by stating her particulars, each phrase resonant and confident.

In short, *Das Kaninchen bin ich* can be interpreted as a film about East Germany's repressed alter ego asserting itself and demanding a hearing. The picture's sympathies clearly lay not with the Byzantine state but with the folksy verve and wit of the little people, caught between the cracks and without a voice. The creators of *Das Kaninchen bin ich* had clearly set out to make a critical film, if not a subversive one. As the next section indicates, Maetzig and Bieler took pains to show that Maria's development occurs in tandem with her society's progression. Even so, their efforts in this direction were not enough to assure the approval of a picture, a major theme of which is official injustice. Indeed, the image of East Germany presented in the work probably would have provided much fodder for Western detractors of socialism.[28] Moreover, the regime saw no necessity for redemption. In its eyes the new order had no blameless victims, like Maria, whose ability to overcome adversity was a barometer of socialism's success. Finally, this character's very autonomy, her insistence on defining herself in the first person and against convention, was threatening. The Party derived its legitimacy from its position as the avant-garde of the proletariat, society's guide to the future. The regime was not quite ready to admit that the disenfranchised could fend for themselves, especially if this autonomy could be used to criticize its rule.

THE RABBIT AND THE FUNCTIONARIES

In adapting the original novel for the screen, Maetzig and Bieler retained the major conflict—the dilemma of Maria's relationship with Paul—as well as the emphasis on Maria's first-person voice. Indeed, the film's style was largely tailored to complement her dialogue. Particularly during the first minutes of the picture, the rapid montage, the ironic juxtaposition of words and images, and the use of visual gags highlight and reinforce Maria's humorous commentary. For example, when she introduces her first lover as "the type who does not talk a woman into bed but places her there," the film elides a shot of Uli helping her in gym class with one of him carrying her to bed. At the same time, the film also includes more leisurely paced "psychological" scenes, whose purpose is to dramatize the inner conflicts of the characters.[29] If the fast-paced scenes lend a critical and satirical edge, the slower sequences endow the film with a certain gravity, befitting the underlying seriousness of its subject matter: Maria's personal development as a member of East German society.

Even before work on the screen adaptation began, the responsible section of the Cultural Ministry, the Central Administration for Publishing (HV Verlage), had already determined that Bieler's novel required major revisions before it could be approved for publication. Above all, the agency insisted on the "removal [from the work] of the false [political] line that Maria Morzek must succeed amid a hostile environment."[30] Toward this end, officials suggested strengthening the "positive influences" in the work by depicting authority figures more sympathetically. Other recommended changes involving "certain aspects of our life" that were "absolutely too negatively depicted." Chief among these was the justice system. In this regard, it was deemed important to make clear that Paul's personal weakness—not the courts themselves—warranted criticism. In addition, the HV Verlage wanted Maria's own "positive" development toward a socialist consciousness to be clearer. Thus her narrative voice should reflect the "higher point of view" she achieves by having her describe her past experiences more self-critically.[31]

In adapting the novel, Bieler and Maetzig obviously tried to anticipate these issues as best they could without depriving the work of its political charge. One important change involved the elimination of a character named Harry Rutek, a friend of Paul who is a poet. In the version of the novel later published in the West, Rutek articulates for Maria's benefit a broad critique of socialist functionaries as masochistic Faustian figures. In this context, he reaches the conclusion: "Whoever is interested in politics in a state whose highest principle is defending the power of a certain clique is either suicidal or belongs to this clique."[32]

The script elaborated on a passage in the novel involving a second political defamation case that is parallel to Dieter's. This one concerned a character named Gambow who drunkenly insults a member of the National People's Army during a dance held at a village near the lovers' bucolic retreat. Two scenes were added. The first of these depicted an argument between Paul and the young idealistic mayor of the village. While the judge insists on Gambow's arrest, the mayor suggests that airing the case publicly before a conflict resolution committee in the village would be a more appropriate response. The second additional scene dramatizes the hearing, where it is revealed that the provocatory statements arose not out of fundamental hostility toward the state but out of simple frustration with a rectifiable problem. Gambow has been unable to earn a living as a fisherman since a military unit on maneuvers disturbed his pond.

In short, the proposed script eliminated the character articulating the most direct political criticism and added scenes suggesting East German society's ability to regulate itself in a fair and open manner. The elaboration of the contrast between Dieter's case and Gambow's was supposed to demonstrate the film's optimism. This modification also allowed the artists involved to claim that the picture was made in the spirit of legal reforms announced since the Sixth SED Party Congress of 1963. Attached to the original proposal for adapting the novel for the screen was an addendum listing no less than eight official documents and speeches germane to the project. As Maetzig explained in the body of that text, the film aimed to show that "Paul does not recognize the deep meaning . . . of the Jurisprudence Decree, which is a result and expression of socialist democracy and which leads to the founding of resolution committees. . . . The observation of opposing positions of both Paul and the mayor as well as the public discussion . . . [of] Gambow's [case] . . . is an important education for . . . Maria. She recognizes in practice, in life, the unfolding of socialist democracy."[33] Thus if Paul's behavior as a judge was a warning against the arbitrary exercise of judicial power, then the participatory truth-finding process that occurs in the village affirmed the GDR's progressive potential.

At least initially, the revisions had the desired effect. In November 1964, Günter Witt, the director of the HV Film, approved the inclusion of *Das Kaninchen bin ich* in the studio's thematic plan for the coming year. In December, Cultural Minister Heinz Bentzien ruled that the film could be treated as a matter separate from the book.[34] That same month, Bieler and Maetzig submitted the film script to the ministry. The HV Film's subsequent evaluation praised the draft for being much clearer than the original novel in its treatment of "careerism, double-faced behavior, and hypocrisy in the figure of Paul Deister." Instead of calling for specific changes, the report merely emphasized that the "greatest value must be placed . . . during the production [on depicting] the genuine representatives of our society and our state [as a] strong counterweight" to Paul.[35]

Having received a green light, the studio proceeded with the project. Nevertheless, studio director Mückenberger ordered a halt to the production before shooting could commence as scheduled on February 2, 1965.[36] He had received a letter from Witt. Under pressure from the Central Committee's Cultural Section (ZK Kultur), the HV Film director now insisted that script revisions were necessary in order to address several issues.[37] There was continuing concern that the film failed to develop its positive characters sufficiently. Moreover, Witt asked whether "the jargon and atmosphere of many scenes," as well as the "overemphasis on the erotic element," were necessary, since these "covered up the social and human problematic." In particular, he urged changes in several sequences, including the bed scenes and the episode in which Paul's wife confronts Maria with an air rifle.[38]

The HV Film's intervention had little effect. At one meeting, artists from "Red Circle," the artistic work group responsible for the project, showed little willingness to accept criticism. The director Konrad Wolf argued that the studio had already approved the script and accused the agency of trying to subvert the KAG's newly gained administrative competence. A subsequent discussion, involving representatives from the ZK Cultural Section as well as from the state attorney general's office and the Justice Department, was more productive from an official perspective.[39] Still, the resulting changes in the script were relatively minor. The dialogue was now supposed to suggest that Paul was not so much a careerist as a well-meaning functionary overtaken by the rapid pace of events. Thus his character was afforded more opportunity to articulate motives justifying the harsh sentencing of Maria's brother. Other minor line changes were made to suggest more clearly Maria's sympathy for socialism as well as her disapproval of the sports instructor Uli's behavior toward her.[40] Finally, the studio found a new actor, Alfred Müller, to play Paul in the hope that this change would result in a more sympathetic portrayal of the character.[41]

Apparently still under pressure to stop the film, Witt made one last gambit to halt production. In March 1965, his agency completed an evaluation criticizing the final, revised version of the script. This report pointed out that according to the state attorney general's office the film contained a serious legal error. The *Rechtspflegeerlass* was not meant to apply to acts of political provocation or lèse-majesté, such as those committed by Dieter and Gambow. In May, Witt then drafted a letter to studio director Mückenberger demanding modification of the script in order to correct this mistake. Since such a change could not be made without trivializing the film's political purpose, Bieler and Maetzig presumably would have balked, and the picture would never have been completed. But the letter was never sent. Fearing that Mückenberger might use it as a means for saddling the HV Film with responsibility for breaking off the production[42]—and thus expose the agency to renewed charges of bureaucratic interference—Witt tried another tack. He asked Mückenberger to co-sign a memorandum agreeing to the proposed changes, but the studio director refused.[43]

The stalemate persisted throughout the summer and fall. In the meantime, the film neared completion. At the end of September, Mückenberger applied for permission to release the film.[44] After a preliminary meeting between Witt and Mückenberger, a few additional changes proved necessary. Two shots of prisoners marching in formation and guards with dogs at Dieter's prison had to be removed. A line in Maria's dialogue where she uses the pronoun "you" to refer to anonymous forces in GDR society responsible for her situation was modified.[45] Finally, on October 26, the Film Approval Board convened to pass judgment. This time, however, Witt stood up for the film. A few hours before the scheduled meeting, the ZK Cultural Section summoned him to its offices to advise against releasing the picture without having first referred the matter to his agency's Artistic Council, but the HV Film director rejected the recommendation. Instead he argued that discussion of the controversial project should be public. Thus the Film Approval Board allowed release of *Das Kaninchen bin ich*.[46] Maetzig and the studio had gotten their way—or so it seemed.

THE ELEVENTH PLENUM

There is much that a simple chronology of the production history of *Das Kaninchen bin ich* fails to reveal. The fight to win approval for the film was a far more complex process than artists locking horns with intransigent functionaries. The artists' success in lobbying for *Das Kaninchen bin ich* depended in no small part on measures that had already been implemented to increase the film studio's institutional autonomy. During at least one point in the negotiations, the KAG "Red Circle" resisted the HV Film's demands on the grounds that the agency was exceeding its authority. Agency director Witt was also clearly concerned with avoiding the impression of arbitrary meddling. In addition, the officials involved probably had deeply conflicted feelings. Both Witt and his superior, Cultural Minister Bentzien, were relatively young—neither man was much past forty. They were also on friendly terms with studio director Mückenberger and former chief dramaturge Wischnewski, with whom they had climbed the administrative ladder and privately shared ideas concerning the necessity for socialist reform.[47]

However much they may have sympathized with the film's purpose, Witt and Bentzien were also obviously conscious of their own limited power. Neither man had close ties to the Party's inner circle. Even in cultural matters, Witt's and Bentzien's influence could not compete with that of older, more experienced functionaries, such as their immediate respective predecessors, Hans Rodenberg and Alexander Abusch, or the writer Otto Gotsche.[48] Witt's own contradictory behavior—first approving the project, then trying to sink it, but finally authorizing the film's release on his own initiative—gives a sense of the fine line he was trying to negotiate. Another indication of these officials' predicament is a note that Bentzien scribbled in the margin of an enthusiastic September 1965 evaluation of *Das Kaninchen bin ich*: "Out of pure fear of [accusations of] dogmatism, the [ministry's] standpoint is being endangered. Unfortunately all the same no clear recommendations."[49] These words suggest that the minister was concerned that the reform process within his area of responsibility would be undermined if it proceeded too quickly. Adding to officials' confusion were the contradictory signals they were receiving from their superiors. For example, Witt recalls a lengthy meeting with Ulbricht in September after a film premiere where the first secretary encouraged him to continue a patient attitude toward artists and counseled against resorting to "administrative means" in dealing with the studio.[50]

Ultimately, developments within the film industry depended on wider political circumstances. The shift in cultural policy that accompanied the Eleventh Plenum caught officials in the MfK and the studio off guard. Less than two months after his discussion with Ulbricht, Witt received a late night summons to a Politburo meeting where he was criticized.[51] Nevertheless, as late as November 12, *Das Kaninchen bin ich* was still described as a model for future productions during a studio management meeting.[52] On November 23, Mückenberger suggested that the heated discussion surrounding the film might affect other productions, but at this time he still anticipated the film's release.[53] Only on the twenty-ninth did the studio director feel obliged to inform his staff that approval for *Das Kaninchen bin ich* was about to be withdrawn.[54]

It is impossible to say what prompted the Party leadership to use the Plenum, which originally was supposed to be devoted exclusively to the economy, as a forum for attacking artists. Two factors external to the cultural sphere were clearly involved. The first of these was a gradual move away from the NÖS as a course of reform; the Plenum ratified adjustments to the program that had the effect of restoring economic power to the central state.[55] Developments in the Soviet Union were the second factor influencing the Plenum. With Khrushchev's fall from power in October 1964, the pressure for continuing reform throughout the East Bloc had diminished. That developments emanating from Moscow were having an impact seemed to be dramatically confirmed on the eve of the

Plenum with the suicide of Erich Apel, the head of the State Planning Commission and one of the principal architects of the NÖS. Apparently, Apel was distraught over plans to roll back reform as well as over a decision reached at the summit between Ulbricht and Brezhnev in November 1965 to continue conducting trade with the Soviet Union on highly disadvantageous terms.[56]

Even so, the sputtering out of economic reform in the GDR and the change of regime in the Soviet Union provide at best only a partial explanation of the attacks on art that occurred at the Plenum. For one, the Party took pains to avoid the impression of a major economic policy shift. The new measures, far from being packaged as the NÖS's death knell, were supposed to represent its "second phase." Of equal significance, the links between Soviet and East German cultural policy during the sixties remain obscure. A campaign against "skepticism and nihilism" conducted under Khrushchev in 1963 found only a moderate echo in GDR at the time.[57] Moreover, the Eleventh Plenum anticipated the February 1966 trials of the Soviet dissidents Andrey Sinyavsky and Yuly Daniel, which are often taken to mark the end of the Khrushchev-era "thaw."[58] As the case of Czechoslovakia, where reforms continued to accelerate until 1968, also shows, developments within East Bloc satellite states during the post-Khrushchev era did not merely mirror those within the Soviet Union.

In addition, overemphasizing the external determinants of the regime's cultural policy runs the risk of ignoring what the historical actors themselves understood to be at stake. In retrospect, the aspirations of East German artists were hopelessly utopian, but to those who believed in socialism the issues being contested were hardly academic. Implicit in much of the art criticized at the Plenum was an alternative vision of East German society, one that was far from harmonious and where the Party did not always represent the best interests of the new society. These works did not so much attack the GDR from without as criticize it from within. Drawing on the same system of representation that the Party used to define its objectives, they appealed to Communism's allies, not its enemies. Still other artworks tried to explore fundamental questions adhering in socialist discourse through satire and macabre parody.[59] These reasons help explain the unexpected vehemence of the official reaction at the Eleventh Plenum. During the formalism debates of the early fifties, the regime had gone on the offensive against modernist art it deemed useless for the revolutionary tasks at hand. Now artists were finally creating works relevant to socialism, but they were claiming an independent voice.

A documents binder made available to Central Committee members before the Plenum began on December 16 provides considerable insight into official concerns regarding cultural policy. Among the materials provided was a lengthy informational report prepared by the Berlin Party District Office (*Bezirksleitung*). This called attention to "several serious ideological phenomena that have become noticeable in the artistic realm recently." One problem was that some artists "see their task as . . . mak[ing] the Party aware of mistakes and shortcomings and claim thus to advance socialism." Equally troubling was the opinion widely held by artists "that supposedly primitive and oversimplified utilitarian demands are being placed on art by functionaries."[60] A second summary of the political mood among writers and artists, one that presumably was prepared by the Stasi, painted a similar picture. Despite the support of "large parts of the artistic intelligentsia" for the Party, "many statements and individual conversations show that a number of artists have reservations and doubt concerning the correctness of our politics." Two areas of particular concern were identified. First, there was a tendency to dismiss the regime's "assessment of the danger of state monopoly capitalism in West Germany" as exaggerated. Second, the report noted "great uncertainty and fluctuation," even "tolerance toward essentially alien and imperialistic influences," in discussions concerning "problems of the artistic depiction of the present."[61]

Other documents shown to Central Committee members were supposed to provide solid evidence of these assertions. Among them was a copy of an essay by the writer Stefan Heym that had appeared in the Hamburg newsweekly *Die Zeit*. Titled "Die Langeweile von Minsk" (The Boredom of Minsk), the piece argued that the meaning of socialist realism was "to depict the truth, [including] its inherent perspective, which according to the nature of things can only be a socialist one." Despite this disarming hypothesis, officials cited Heym's arguments as an example of how artists were trying to subvert the leadership role of the party.[62] Another artist who earned the Party's opprobrium was Wolf Biermann. According to one assessment, his book, *Die Drahtharfe* (The Barbed-Wire Harp), which like Heym's essay had been published in the West, "contains multiple poems, with which sharp attacks are launched against our state in the name of petit-bourgeois anarchist socialism." The folksinger was taken to task not only for "betray[ing] the good and hopeful [aspects] of his own work, not only the state, which facilitated his highly qualified education, but also the life and death of his own father," a German-Jewish Communist who died in a concentration camp.[63] Other artists whose works were attacked included the playwrights Peter Hacks and Heiner Müller and the writer Werner Bräunig. The document binder also included a report highly critical of management practices at the East German television network, the DFF,[64] as well one damning the editors of a film journal, *Filmwissenschaftliche Mitteilungen*. The editors caused offense by publishing a candid poll of artists' opinions regarding developments in the world cinema and cultural policy.[65]

Among the most interesting items contained in the binder concerned youth policy. Included was a letter to the heads of all Party district offices from Ulbricht describing a disturbance by "a large group of rowdies" that had occurred on October 30, 1965, in downtown Leipzig. Youths had annoyed passersby, disrupted traffic, and insulted police officers. To restore order, local officials had to call in riot troops as well as paramilitary units belonging to the FDJ. The apparent cause of the riot was the circulation of an unofficial broadside that protested the prohibition of beat music. While no actual ban was in place, the Leipzig incident seems to have convinced Ulbricht that such an action would not be a bad idea. In language reminiscent of the Third Reich, he described those responsible for the disturbance as "malingerers and asocial elements, who derive their living from theft and other illegal activities." The first secretary concluded: "It was a mistake on the part . . . of the FDJ to have organized beat group competitions and to have encouraged the notion that Western hits and beat music for us, in contrast to West Germany, cannot have damaging effects."[66] As a follow-up measure, the ZK Executive Committee instructed the interior minister to arrest musicians suspected of criminal activity and place them in labor camps.

What is perhaps most striking is the range of behavior that officials lumped together. Mixed in with the materials provided to ZK members pertaining to the Leipzig disturbance were items documenting various incidents involving insubordinate youth. On one end of the spectrum was a statement signed by 138 Leipzig theater students protesting the futility of nuclear air raid drills on the grounds that such exercises minimized the dangers of war.[67] Someplace between thoughtful political opposition and more diffuse forms of protest were the cases detailed in a report concerning the behavior of Berlin students participating in "volunteer" harvest brigades. For example, fifteen theology students had refused to participate in an election, made statements protesting the Wall, and compared East Germany to South Africa. Another case involved physics and math students who applauded West German politicians appearing in a newsreel during a film presentation.[68] Other transgressions detailed in the documents folder seemed to have involved cases of more conventional criminal behavior. One report described in great detail a case of several students from the Dresden Technical University, again members of a volunteer harvest brigade, who after a game of spin-the-bottle gang-raped a seventeen-year-old female farmhand.[69] There was also a letter from a teacher to an Education Ministry official complaining about the behavior of thirty drunken university students who had tried to storm a dormitory where high school students were sleeping.[70]

In the mind of Party leaders, violent incidents among youths, isolated examples of political protest, and problems with artists were cut from the same cloth. The causes of all these phenomena lay not with the GDR's overly regulated and repressive social order but with the West's pernicious cultural influence. In reading the Politburo's official report, Ulbricht's eventual successor, Erich Honecker, set the tone for the Plenum by declaring, "Our GDR is a clean state [in which] there are unshakable ethical and moral standards. Our Party stands decidedly against the immoral propaganda pursued by imperialists [whose] purpose is to harm socialism."[71]

As the Party's chief ideologue, Kurt Hager, saw it, a "great intellectual clarification" was necessary. First, Hager emphasized that there was room for only one cultural policy. The Cultural Ministry had obviously failed in carrying out the decisions of the Sixth Party Congress and in encouraging progressive socialist tendencies in the depiction of the present. This mission might include helping artists who "temporarily fall into confusion," but it did not encompass toleration for those who "under the banner of 'criticizing shortcomings' spread skepticism in an organized manner."[72] Second, Hager insisted on "a reckoning with alienation theory." Attempts to apply Kafka to the depiction of socialist society demonstrated an ignorance of the GDR's historical development and suggested that certain artists themselves had a "broken relationship to our state."[73] Hager then elaborated his position by emphasizing the great difference in the role of art between the West and the East. He took fundamental issue with the notion that socialist art could content itself with "pure, documentary observation" of reality as well as with the idea that art's essence was critical. Artists in the East had to assume a creative posture and embrace partisanship. Only under the leadership of the Party could they overcome their isolation from the people.[74]

There was little new in Hager's words. Party leaders had traded similar charges with artists on many previous occasions. If anything distinguished the rhetoric of the Plenum, it was the degree to which film and literature were associated with popular cultural and social trends. Officials insisted that artists were willingly enlisting in the service of socialism's enemies. Ulbricht referred to the existence of a planned conspiracy, spearheaded by Biermann, Heym, and the dissident physicist Robert Havemann. As the first secretary explained in his closing remarks to the

Plenum, "The groundwork was taken care of with sex and beat propaganda in order to loosen up the atmosphere for the political struggle. . . . Everything, from DEFA to television and through the Cultural Ministry, was well organized."[75] Erich Honecker went so far as to suggest that the artworks criticized at the Plenum were themselves a cause for "manifestations of immorality and of a lifestyle alien to socialism" such as hooliganism.[76] The fact that the films, theater productions, and books about which he was talking had mostly never reached the East German public did not deter Honecker from reaching his conclusions.

According to the Politburo's logic, the depiction of violence and sex resulted in "reification of [social] conflicts" and "disregard for dialectical development." Works containing such images tended to "deny the creative character of human work" and to depict the "[Communist] collective and leaders of Party and state" as "cold and alien powers."[77] Indeed, many of the ZK members who added their voices to the chorus condemning art at the Plenum conflated the preservation of familial and sexual order with the integrity of the socialist project. Ingeborg Lange, the director of the Politburo's Commission on Women, complained that it was no longer safe to let her teenage daughter watch television. Even a broadcast with an edifying theme such as agricultural collectivization might contain graphic sexual content. In the past, Lange had always pitied parents in the West who tried to raise their children properly, since the media there were full of disturbing images; but now she was asking herself, if "one of the extraordinary advantages [for] families is that we keep a tight reign on these things, why does the opposite occur so often?"[78]

There was little opportunity for artists to defend themselves at the Plenum. Except for the self-criticism of officials such as Witt, the only person who took exception to the attacks was Christa Wolf, but even her circumspect pleas for greater patience and understanding for artists were shouted down. The Party leadership dismissed their opponents' arguments with ridicule. Ulbricht described the claim that "Stalinism has returned again" as an "old trick . . . which is already so worn out that nobody falls for it." The GDR already offered far more extensive freedoms than the West, above all the freedom to participate in the construction of a better society. The Plenum had nothing to do with dictating aesthetics; rather, the issue was politics.[79]

In short, the time had come for artists to mend their ways, submit to Party discipline, and rejoin the march to the future. Ironically, the harsh attacks against literature and film that occurred at the Eleventh Plenum resulted from what artists and the regime shared in common. Both sides believed in the power of art. Unfortunately, whereas many artists thought that critical works might contribute to socialism's reform, leading functionaries were obviously concerned with propagating an image of East Germany as a harmonious and wholesome society. They insisted that they were only asking artists to capture the plain truth visible everywhere—the new order that the proletariat was bringing nearer to completion day by day. But clearly the relation between art and reality for officials was more complex than simple mimesis. At one point in the proceedings, Ulbricht bellowed, "Are we of the opinion that a few artists or writers can write what they want and that they determine the entire course of development of society?"[80] Given the Plenum's harsh and vehement tone, the answer to the first secretary's rhetorical question could only have been that functionaries did indeed believe in art's power to transform society.

CONCLUSION

Das Kaninchen bin ich represented an attempt by artists to participate in the GDR's social and political development by furthering an incipient reform process. In this sense, the picture followed the call, long central to DEFA's self-understanding, for an interventionist cinema, capable of bringing the realization of the future ever nearer. At the same time, Maetzig and Bieler's film attempted to fulfill this function in an unorthodox fashion. Instead of positing harmony between the Party's leadership and the aspiration of ordinary individuals, their picture allied itself with the GDR's own disenfranchised. Its protagonist, Maria, represents this group. Her subjective experience, rather than history's dialectic, serves as the guarantor of truth. As my analysis in previous chapters has shown, *Das Kaninchen bin ich* was not the first DEFA film to privilege such a vantage point, but the work went a step further by using Maria's bottom-up perspective as a means not only for legitimizing the new order but also for criticizing it.

A comparison between Maria and Rita, the protagonist of *Der geteilte Himmel*, helps illuminate this point. As I argued in the last chapter, young female protagonists in DEFA films often functioned as emblems for socialist society. If their emancipation illustrated the GDR's progressive potential, then their gender referred to a lost wholeness in modern life that the new order was supposed to restore. As women, Maria and Rita have as their primary association a domestic realm of prosaic experience removed from politics. It is typical of Maria that she should observe the idealized truth-finding process represented by the village conflict commission from the kitchen of the town pub where the proceedings occur. But here the similarity between the two figures ends. Rita's attributes include interiority, weakness (she is introduced on her sickbed), vulnerability, and sensitivity. Her story is one of recovery, of overcoming her estrangement from socialism, metaphorically represented as illness. In contrast, Maria's most impressive qualities are self-assurance, candor, and confidence. Her tale is one of growing personal autonomy. Similarly, whereas an idealized notion of selfless romantic love governs Rita's relationship with her lover, Maria's sexuality is openly admitted. The latter's sarcasm and wit in discussing such matters underline the discrepancy between societal norms and life's complexity. By extension, this attitude calls into question the all-too-neat moral universe inherent to the Party's worldview.

Das Kaninchen bin ich found both detractors and supporters among officials as it became entangled in a struggle within the Cultural Ministry concerning the direction of socialist reform. The image of the GDR implicit in the film had specific consequences for the constitution of political authority. Despite the HV Film's decision to approve the picture, the regime concluded that its release would set a dangerous precedent. Party leaders, alarmed by incidents of youth violence that in their eyes confirmed not only widespread discontent but even the danger of popular rebellion, decided on the necessity of metaphorically reasserting the state's mastery over society at the Eleventh Plenum in December 1965. Here Maetzig and Bieler's film as well as other works by GDR artists were offered up on the SED's altar. The message was clear. East Germany's march toward the future could continue only under the Party's forceful direction. There was no need for alternative scenarios. Reforms requiring a decentralization of power were unnecessary since social harmony was already a reality. Only a few intellectual misfits still marred the scene, and they could easily be dispensed with.

Yet, despite the vehemence and apparent finality of the regime's verdict at the Plenum, subtle changes within the GDR's civic imaginary were already under way. The prosaic realm embodied by female protagonists like Maria was in ascendance, and the historically informed understanding of the present championed by the regime had gone into partial eclipse. Future years would see a decided turn away from films and other artworks depicting the new society's brave march into the future; moreover, official policy would allow for some depoliticization of the private realm. Party leaders may have been as eager as artists to reconceptualize the relation between utopian aspirations and ordinary existence, between ideology and life. Certainly, the regime was hardly equal to the achievement of grand ambitions. The next chapter considers the Eleventh Plenum's aftermath for filmmakers and suggests the ways in which a new East German identity, based less on the promise of tomorrow than on the acceptance of the here and now, was already in the process of formation.

A Dream Deferred?

Spur der Steine and the Aftermath
of the Eleventh Plenum

The Eleventh Plenum's effect on the film industry was chilling. Artists who only a few months earlier were riding the wave of socialist reform now found themselves political outcasts. Nevertheless, as Marxists, many believed in socialism's own supposed dialectic: the Party's tendency to overcorrect itself and the high human costs of apparent progress. Such a pathos of spiraling development was intrinsic to the reform process and had animated the Twentieth Congress of the CPSU, where Communist leaders had pledged to press on toward the future even while acknowledging some terrible mistakes of the past.[1] Thus many filmmakers hoped the Plenum would be only a temporary setback. Moreover, the Plenum's full ramifications were by no means clear at first. No one was certain which film productions and individuals would be caught up in its wake.

After considering the situation in the studio and surveying the films banned, my analysis turns to Frank Beyer's *Spur der Steine* (Trail of Stones), a 1966 film that became a bellwether case. In the months leading up to its brief release, artists vainly fought to salvage other threatened pictures. It is not too difficult to grasp why Beyer's work became the focus of controversy. Not only was it one of the most expensive DEFA productions of the day, but its story was rich in allegorical significance. By presenting multiple perspectives on a construction site crisis, the film questioned the possibility of communion between individual destiny and collective destiny predicated by socialism's utopian goals. For filmmakers struggling to reconcile their commitment to socialism and its ideology with their integrity as artists, the work's relevance was clear. Arguably, *Spur der Steine* represents the last attempt by an East German director to envision the GDR as a forward-moving society in a fashion that was critical yet affirmative of the socialist project.

THE AFTERMATH OF THE PLENUM AND
THE EAST GERMAN CINEMA

The Party followed up the Plenum with discussions within the studio to assess responsibility for the films already banned and to propagate the new official line. SED ideologue Kurt Hager himself attended several meetings of the APO I, the Party cell comprising leading studio managers and artists. DEFA was clearly in dire straits. The tenor of many speeches was harsh and accusatory. One financial expert, for example, expressed disbelief that the studio had paid the author Manfred Bieler for the rights to *Das Kaninchen bin ich* even after the book had been banned.[2] A director who described himself as Maetzig's protégé accused his former mentor of betraying his own "enduring contribution" to the German cinema, the Thälmann films dramatizing the life of the Weimar-era Communist leader.[3] No one dared dispute the Party's criticism. Maetzig himself conceded that "liberalization is not a viable way for us." His intentions in regard to *Das Kaninchen bin ich* might have been good, but his path was false.[4] In the same vein, the dramaturge Klaus Wischnewski spoke of "a number of false ideological and theoretical positions" that had developed in the studio.[5]

The Party took steps to reassert hierarchical state control over the film industry. In early February a reliable functionary from outside the cultural sphere, Franz Bruk, took over from Mückenberger as studio director. In March, Witt stepped down as HV Film director. Even before his departure, the "Production Section" of his agency under the direction of Dr. Franz Jahrow had begun intervening in questionable productions. In addition, a rollback of recently instituted reforms began. The KAGs lost their independent authority and within a year became little more than vehicles for dividing responsibilities among dramaturges. The goal of establishing self-regulating artist collectives was fully abandoned. Yet another indication of the sour atmosphere after the Plenum was the establishment of a conflict commission, whose mission included recouping the costs of banned productions directly from the responsible filmmakers.[6]

From the regime's perspective, turning the studio around clearly required hard work. The roots of "skepticism" and "pessimism" among filmmakers ran deep. *Das Kaninchen bin ich* was hardly an isolated case. To begin with, there were the other films directly criticized at the Plenum. A work by Frank Vogel, Manfred Freitag, and Joachim Nestler, *Denk bloss nicht ich heule* (Just Don't Think I'll Cry), featured a self-styled *Halb-starker* (punk) who was precisely the type of rebellious delinquent that officials at the Eleventh Plenum had in mind when they warned against the corrupting influence of Western culture. In the opening scene, this character confronts his father, an older comrade in his final alcoholic death throes. Bitter for having been excluded from the Party for cowardly behavior during the Third Reich, the father offers some final advice to his son: that the only point to life is the pursuit of pleasure and money. Another scene in the film depicts the brutal beating of another older Party member, a school principal, by a band of youths in the ruins of a Nazi monument, known as the "Saukropolis" (Pig-opolis). Further underscoring the symbolic import of these scenes was the picture's setting, Weimar, a city distinguished both by its association with German classical culture and by its proximity to the Buchenwald concentration camp. Günther Stanke's *Der Frühling braucht Zeit* (Spring Takes Time, 1965) was also clearly intended to further the reform process in the GDR. Since this film did not thematize rebellion—its hero is a middle-aged engineer falsely accused of sabotage—it did not elicit the Plenum's wrath to the same degree as the other two films. Still, officials complained that the picture's extremely stylized mise-en-scène and camera work conveyed an alienated vision of socialism.[7]

The films criticized at the Plenum were very much part of a trend in East German cinema that had been in the making for several years. The period preceding the event saw the successful release of several films that depicted East Germany in new ways. These included the subject of Chapter 4, Konrad Wolf and Christa Wolf's *Der geteilte Himmel* (Divided Heaven), which attempted to deal with the construction of the Wall as a complex event. Another important film was Frank Beyer's *Karbid und Sauerampfer* (Carbide and Sorrel, 1963), a picaresque comedy about an individual who sets off from Dresden immediately after the war in search of supplies to rebuild a factory. This picture spared no one, including the Red Army, in its satire. The work also subtly undermined official accounts of the GDR's history that emphasized the Soviet Union's and the Party's deliberate shaping of the new society. A second picture that attempted to cast the immediate past in a new light was Günther Rücker's *Die besten Jahren* (The Best Years, 1965), which emphasizes the anguish of a man who, after returning home from war, is entrusted by the Party with progressively more difficult tasks at the cost of his own private happiness. There was also Egon Günther and Helga Schütz's *Lots Weib* (Lot's Wife, 1965), a film about a woman who allows herself to be arrested for a minor offense in order to escape an oppressive marriage with a naval officer. The picture depicts this decision to forgo the material comforts of a hypocritical relationship and defy the norms of respectable society as an act of self-liberation. Like *Das Kaninchen bin ich*, the film was also notable for its open treatment of its female protagonist's sexuality.

Well before the Plenum, HV Film officials had noted a great change in the depiction of the present in DEFA films. One June 1965 report suggested that "films and scripts presently in progress or near completion . . . justify speaking of a new development phase in our cinema." In its estimation, the studio's "decisive efforts . . . in recent years . . . have had recognizable results. . . . The long neglected present-day thematic is being taken up by a number of young artists. In contrast to the situation four or five years ago, when many authors avoided [such themes], they [now] flock to the depiction of exciting problems, taken from the present day of our republic."[8] Using the language of the Bitterfelder Way (*Bitterfelderweg*), the report attributed the change in the studio's direction to a group of young scriptwriters who "know the events about which they write thoroughly from their own lives [since] they have dedicated years rich in experience and work in the service . . . of our republic."[9]

Still, HV Film officials were clearly aware of the potential for controversy. Despite the optimistic tone of the opening paragraphs, their report went on to express serious reservations about the implications of the trends it had identified. One problem with the films in production, it was noted, was the tendency "to intervene in a more or less extensively developed social discussion and . . . to identify issues needing to be addressed, for which solutions have already been found."[10] Officials were also suspicious of "a central motif" in these works, namely, "a type of generalized crisis of confidence" involving "a subjectively honest protagonist who does not understand the objective . . . nature of our revolutionary process." In addition, few of the protagonists had a "secure place, inseparable from [their lives], in a genuine collective." Instead, they labored under the impression that "one does not trust them, that [one] only considers them partly capable of recognizing their place, their task, and their responsibility in our society."[11] Moreover, the works erred in depicting dogmatism as an attribute exclusive to functionaries.[12]

Taken together, these shortcomings resulted in a "weakening of the conflict" portrayed in a film, "a narrowing of the historical dimension," and "a diminution of the big question [*Schrümpfung des grossen Gegenstandes*] itself." The report attributed these tendencies to the limited perspective of artists. Contradicting its earlier finding concerning their wide-ranging life experience, it argued that filmmakers had "weak personal connections to the people, who stand at the focus points of our developments." For this reason, artists had failed in following "great development processes through the years" and instead turned to "empirical material" and "isolated facts" for their creative inspiration. Hence they still found themselves "arduously attain[ing] a perspectival outlook" and "aspiring to the position of the planner and director."[13]

The authors of the report clearly had good political noses. Of the eight films they named, seven were eventually banned. These officials were also plainly correct in identifying the present as the most contested field of depiction within the East German cinema. Of the eleven Plenum films, ten were set in the GDR. In contrast, only one of the four DEFA films from 1966 that were not set in the present was banned. Moreover, of five released films set in the present, two were children's films and two others examples of traditional entertainment genres. Those that passed muster also displayed a bent for the fantastic, extraordinary, and the exotic. One of the children's films, *Alfons Zitterbacke* (Konrad Petzold, 1966), had to do with a man who daydreams about being a sports star or an astronaut. Another work, *Der schwarze Panther* (Black Panther, Josef Mach, 1966), concerned a woman who wants to become a lion trainer. A third film, *Hamida* (Jean Michaud-Mailland, 1966), was a coproduction made with Algerians that condemned French colonialism. Perhaps the most significant film of the lot was *Die Söhne der grossen Bärin* (The Sons of the Great Bear, Josef Mach, 1966). This was the first in a series of highly successful DEFA westerns, filmed either in Yugoslavia or Mongolia and invariably featuring the U.S. Cavalry as the bad guys. As that reversal of convention suggests, the films that escaped the effects of the Plenum were not devoid of political content. Rather, they scrupulously avoided the depiction of essential conflicts within their own society. Or, as in the case of one of the entertainment films, *Reise ins Ehebett* (Journey into the Marriage Bed, Joachim Hasler, 1966), they tried to delimit such conflicts as strictly as possible to an idealized domestic sphere. The premise of this musical was two women on a freighter who successfully conspire to capture the captain and the mate as their husbands.

While the Plenum films themselves were fairly diverse, most of them attempted to break with the conventional depiction of East German society. The HV Film's June 1965 report concerning the depiction of the present correctly identified important characteristics shared by many of the banned films. At least five featured adolescent or very young adult protagonists. Of these pictures, all except one dramatized a confrontation between the main characters and an older Party member representing established authority. Three even employed the same actor, Hans Hardt-Hardtloff, to play the more senior figure. Examples of films dramatizing a crisis of state authority in terms of generational conflict include the two films that bore the brunt of the criticism at the Plenum, *Das Kaninchen bin ich* and *Denk bloss nicht, ich heule*. Two further works developing similar themes were Gerhard Klein and Wolfgang Kohlhaase's *Berlin um die Ecke* (Berlin around the Corner, 1966/1987)—a belated addition to their earlier Berlin pictures (see Chapter 2)—and Herrmann Zschoche and Ulrich Plenzdorf's *Karla* (1966/1990). An eccentric member of this group was Jürgen Böttcher and Klaus Poche's *Jahrgang '45* (Born in '45, 1966). This last picture, which will receive greater attention in the following chapter, was in many ways the prototype for the *Alltag* films of the late sixties and early seventies. Displaying similarities with other Plenum films through its depiction of youthful nonconformity and rebellion, its loose plotline and extreme documentary pretense suggest an attempt to avoid politically laden metaphor altogether.

Two other pictures distinguished themselves less through explicit content than through style. Both contained elements of magical realism. Egon Günther and Helga Schütz's *Wenn Du gross bist, lieber Adam* (When You Are Grown, Dear Adam, 1966/1990) concerned a young boy who receives from a swan a magic flashlight that functions as an antigravity device when aimed at someone telling a lie. The film's political provocation lay in its absurdist dialogue and plotline, which made a mockery of socialist order and institutions. The factory where the boy's father is employed hopes to mass-produce the device and thus finally meet its production plan. The picture reaches a zany highpoint with the arrival of a government minister on an inspection tour. As the film critic Erika Richter emphasizes, the film offers a meditation on the issue of truth. The lamp reveals "the reality of actual power relations," yet at the same time it suggests the dangers of too much knowledge.[14] Kurt Barthel and Christa Wolf's never-completed picture *Fräulein Schmetterling* (Miss Butterfly, 1966) also aimed at shedding a different kind of light on socialist society by combining fantastic elements, such as the flight by one character over the roofs of Berlin, with quasi-documentary footage. This picture considered the plight of two orphaned sisters who attempt to survive on their own in defiance of the authorities. As one official assessment concluded, the film developed a "contrast . . . between the impersonal sobriety of Berlin everydayness and the melancholic, dreamy distance" of the protagonists, but it failed to achieve a "truly dialectical position."[15]

Other Plenum films seem to have fallen victim more to bad timing than anything else. Hans-Joachim Kasprzik's now-lost *Hände hoch—oder ich schiesse* (Up with Your Hands—or I'll Shoot, 1966) was the third in a series of successful but thoroughly conventional films essentially designed to serve as vehicles for the popular comedian Rolf Herricht. Even those who ordered the work banned conceded that it was "optimistic in its message and . . . very funny."[16] If not for the extreme situation in the studio, officials would almost certainly have ignored the seditious potential of the picture's premise: a provincial police detective, Holmes, bored out of his skull because there is nothing for him to investigate. Ralf Kirsten's *Der verlorene Engel* (The Lost Angel, 1966/1971) presents a somewhat similar case. This picture was based on actual events in the life of Ernst Barlach, a sculptor persecuted by the Nazis. Even though the history of Barlach's reception in the GDR was complex—an exhibit featuring his work was the object of official wrath during the formalism debates of the early 1950s—the film dovetailed well with antifascist ideology by portraying a bourgeois artist whose attempt to remain apolitical during the Third Reich ends with his own death. The Plenum, however, rendered any work depicting the persecution of artists problematic. As one HV Film official concluded, "The picture can easily be interpreted [as saying] that the filmmakers themselves want to protest against state interference in artistic creativity."[17] Thus the picture could not be released until 1971.

Directly after the Plenum, the fate of most of the films eventually banned was far from clear. Over the next nine months, artists desperate to win approval for their works entered into drawn-out and fruitless negotiations with the HV Film over possible changes. Still, despite the general grimness of their situation, filmmakers had reasons to hope that the event's ramifications might remain limited. However harsh their attacks on individual filmmakers, officials made a point of stressing the loyalty of the studio as a whole. Moreover, during the discussions in the studio, Hager emphasized that no one wanted to call into question "milestones [that] have already been set" such as *Der geteilte Himmel*. The Plenum was not a matter of "retreat but of advancement." Its purpose was not only to correct "ideological-theoretical mistakes" but also to call upon artists "to consider how the great issues of the further development of the socialist society . . . can be artistically mastered through films."[18] In addition, Ulbricht indirectly absolved the studio in an open letter to Maetzig, who later recalled that the fawning self-criticism that elicited this response had left him feeling as if he had "knelt in shit."[19] Here, the first secretary acknowledged that the filmmaker had not set out to make a picture that "would have found the approval of the most reactionary enemies of the GDR." Ulbricht also expressed satisfaction that Maetzig had been able, "undoubtedly after difficult inner struggle," to find his way back to the Party's position.[20]

Financial factors might also have given filmmakers whose projects

were threatened grounds for optimism. Banned films meant wasted resources and unmet plan objectives. In addition, studio workers would be
antagonized because year-end bonuses depended on the studio fulfilling
its obligations to the state, the primary measure of which was the number
of films delivered. Thus Franz Bruk, on assuming office as studio director,
moved quickly to renegotiate plan objectives with the Cultural Ministry.[21]
If for only appearances' sake, officials had a clear stake in the successful
completion of as many pictures as possible. With the regular rhythm of
production within the industry disrupted, they desired nothing more than
a quick return to normality.

By March 1966, in addition to the three films criticized at the Plenum,
only *Fräulein Schmetterling* had been declared dead.[22] One battle still
remained to be fought before the Plenum's aftermath would be fully
played out. Only with the banning of Frank Beyer's *Spur der Steine* after a
one-week release in July would East Germany's cinematic revival clearly
be at an end.

SPUR DER STEINE

Spur der Steine became a test case for the entire film industry for the
simple reason that both the regime and artists had a tremendous stake in
the picture. For the former, the film promised to provide what it had
always sought from the cinema: a persuasive image of socialist society
progressing toward the future. The plot, derived from a very popular
novel by Erik Neutsch, is set against the backdrop of the construction site
for an immense chemical factory. The most arresting character is the
leader of a work brigade, Balla, a physically powerful man inspiring the
awe and respect of his peers, precisely the type of figure Party leaders
desired as an embodiment of the proletariat and the new society. This
figure undoubtedly impressed many artists, but equally important for
them was the novel's complexity and critical potential. For one thing,
Neutsch depicted Balla as a rebel and a free spirit who wears a pearl in his
ear. No easy convert to socialism, he can be convinced only by sincere
example. Moreover, at the heart of the story is a love triangle involving
Balla, a woman engineer named Kati Klee, and the plant's Party secretary,
Horrath. Although all three characters are sympathetically depicted, it is
Horrath's weakness that fuels the plot. Having betrayed his wife, he lacks
the courage to proclaim the truth and face the consequences, even after
Kati becomes pregnant. This failure leads to complications that threaten
to undermine the whole construction project. In contrast, Balla's love for
the engineer remains unconsummated and pure.

As a novel, *Spur der Steine* was a great success. The progressive pathos adhering in Balla's growing loyalty to the new society was enough to compensate for any troubling resonances for the regime. Despite some criticism—invariably there were complaints about the "negative" depiction of the Party secretary and other characters—the book's reception in 1964 was very positive. In later years, it would become a mainstay of official literature, frequently featured on secondary school reading lists. The same story resulted, however, in one of the most controversial pictures in DEFA's history. After months of wrangling over the project, all was set for a gala premiere. A giant billboard featuring Balla was under construction on Alexanderplatz,[23] the main square in East Berlin. Then at the last moment Party leaders changed their minds and condemned the film as dangerous and subversive. Since publicity preparations had advanced too far, it could not be banned altogether without embarrassment. Still, instead of being released in dozens of theaters simultaneously as originally planned, the work came out in only a handful of poorly marked movie houses. State-organized thugs rioted at a number of performances, and the regime used this violent behavior as the justification for withdrawing the movie from distribution altogether only a few days after its release.[24]

Various factors explain the novel's and the film's different receptions. The story line of the screen version varied considerably from that of the original book, which ran to some 900 pages. Beyer and the scriptwriter Karl Georg Egel, who assisted him on the project, clearly had little choice but to reduce the plot considerably. Moreover, in order to give the picture a clearer dramatic focus, they took a mere reference in the novel to a Party inquest directed against Horrath and made it into a framing device. This change involved a new narrative structure. In contrast to the novel, which employs a single omniscient storyteller, the film is multiperspectival. Individual episodes correspond to the flashbacks of different characters testifying at the investigation. The main purpose of other minor changes was presumably to avoid overly transparent melodrama, but they also had political implications. Although the main characters' futures in both versions are only vaguely indicated, the picture has less closure. Balla does not join the Party. Also, instead of a last pathos-ridden meeting between him and Kati before each sets out to seek his or her fortune, the picture emphasizes even benign authority's inability to rectify all wrongs. The district Party leader, Jansen, concerned about Kati's absence at the inquest, searches her out at home only to discover an empty room. The last shot then shows him alone in the back of his car reading a note in which she explains the reasons for her flight.

These changes resulted in a different inflection in tone between the book and the screen versions of *Spur der Steine*. Epic dimensions were common to both. Very much at the center of the story are the shortcomings of the supposedly omniscient, all-seeing authority inherent in the "Plan," which requires constant correction and initiative from below. In order to prosper, the new order must harness the vital forces that Balla represents. Whereas the novel presents Balla's conversion as a heroic process, the film adds a twist of irony. The leader of the work brigade is reconciled to authority and becomes a convert to socialism, if not to the Party itself, but the new society loses much of its aura.

The difference between the novel and its screen version is comparable to the shift that occurred in American westerns during the fifties and sixties. Westerns from before the fifties tend to present basic elements of American self-understanding—rugged individualism, manifest destiny, the taming of the wilderness—in a fairly unself-conscious fashion, but later examples frequently question the costs of progress and depict their protagonists—be they Native Americans or gunslingers—as the last survivors of an endangered universe.

This comparison between the American and East German cinemas is hardly as outlandish as it might seem on first inspection. *Spur der Steine* displays many elements in common with westerns.[25] No place is this clearer than in the scene that introduces Balla together with his brigade. Like typical heroes from a western, they are presented against the land that they shape and that shapes them in turn, the construction site. Shot in wide-screen CinemaScope, the film emphasizes the expanse and untamed qualities of this lunar landscape. Marching against a sea of humanity streaming toward a political rally, the "Ballas" are dressed in the traditional garb of German carpenters, featuring broad-brimmed hats similar to those of cowboys. Instead of pistols, they carry beer bottles, whose old-fashioned flip-off tops produce a popping noise when the brigade members hold them up high and open them in unison. In a subsequent scene, they highjack trucks carrying building materials as if they were stagecoaches. Balla himself was played by one of DEFA's most popular stars, Manfred Krug, who cuts a fine figure as a lovable rogue. Finally, Balla and his band of outlaws must confront the equivalent of the new sheriff in town, the new Party secretary, Horrath, who has been brought in at the request of plant managers to restore order.

The comparison between Beyer's film and the classic American movie genre becomes even more cogent if the provenance of Neutsch's novel is considered. The book is a typical *Produktionsroman* (production novel). This type of work aspired to occupy a place in the East German civic imaginary similar to that of westerns in American self-understanding.

Novels like Neutsch's had their antecedents both in such classics of Soviet socialist realism as Fyodor Gladkov's *Cement* and in the writings of German "proletarian" writers active in the twenties, including Willi Bredel, Otto Gotsche, and Karl Grünberg.[26] The distinguishing characteristic of all production novels was the positing of the workplace as a uniquely privileged locus of progressive consciousness formation. Such works aimed to dramatize the central tenet of Marxist ideology: the determinant relation between the means of production and individual political consciousness.

After the GDR's founding in 1949, official calls for artworks depicting the construction of socialism and the present took this sort of literature as its model. Nowhere is the development of a worker-related aesthetic clearer than in the rhetoric of the *Bitterfelderweg*. Not only was this platform associated with Gotsche personally, but its aim of encouraging workers to become writers to report about their daily struggles as laborers displayed a strong affinity with the proletarian writers' movement of the twenties.[27] Still, adapting the theme of production to the needs of the new order was not a trivial matter. In Germany, artists sympathetic to Communism were accustomed to creating from an oppositional stance. Their sensibilities tended toward the celebration of struggle and conflict. They were uneasy with works that transparently acclaimed an existing status quo. The difficulties encountered in the East German cinema were as great as or perhaps even greater than those in other artistic realms. As previous chapters have described, the film industry's success with works set in East Germany up through the early sixties had been at best limited. Most notable pictures continued to be set in the past. One important exception, Konrad Wolf's *Sonnensucher* (Sun Seekers, 1959), ended up being banned (see Chapter 2), even though it told a classic production tale.

Thus in many ways *Spur der Steine* represented the culmination of developments that had been under way at DEFA for years. Here once again was a film that the studio hoped would finally help fulfill what had long been the GDR cinema's most cherished yet most elusive goal: an image of the East German present that both confirmed socialism's promise and seemed authentic, a world whose dimensions would be at once mythic and true. Indeed, even before Neutsch's novel had been published as a book (the work first appeared in serialized form), there had been intense competition between DEFA and DFF for the rights. After beating back the television network's bid,[28] the studio approached one of its most talented artists, Frank Beyer, to adapt the work for the screen. Having completed four highly acclaimed films in as many years—including a trilogy of antifascist films, two of which had garnered prizes at the Prague and Moscow film festivals—the young director's prestige among his peers by 1964 was second perhaps only to Konrad Wolf's. DEFA's management also assigned a disproportionately large sum for realizing the project, 2.7 million marks, about three times the budget for an average film.

However great the studio's interest in *Spur der Steine* had been before the Eleventh Plenum, its stake in the project grew even more afterward. First, there were indications that the film might prove immune to the political fallout affecting other productions. As late as November 1965, the response after an initial viewing of a rough cut of the film by officials from the ZK Cultural Section was overwhelmingly positive. Beyer himself even recalls telling friends at the time, "If this pleases all of them so much, I must have done something wrong."[29] Second, the studio hoped to redeem itself with the project. As the dramaturge Klaus Wischnewski explained in a 1990 interview, "After the heavy blow on the heads of artists . . . [there] arose on both sides . . . an urgent need to get back to normal behavior." In his own self-criticism published in *Neues Deutschland*, Wischnewski referred to Neutsch's novel as a "marker" for the studio's future course: "Thus *Spur der Steine* became in a certain sense the flagship that would decide whether things would work again. And it seemed sure to us that if *Spur der Steine* came through, we would also be able to [bring through] some of the other films . . . in its wake."[30]

There is a strange logic in Beyer's film becoming the focus of artists' aspirations. The picture thematized a process similar to the one under way in the studio in the months following the Plenum. As noted, the cinematic version of *Spur der Steine* is structured around Horrath's inquest. Members of the collective supervising the construction of the chemical plant sit in judgment of the Party secretary's behavior and character. Their deliberations then widen to include the question of their own responsibility. Although the actual issues at stake at DEFA bore little resemblance to the symbolically distilled ones contained in the novel, the discursive parameters of artists' self-criticism and of various Party discussions set in motion by the Plenum were essentially the same. Like the fictional characters, studio personnel were engaged in a cathartic ritual, a great confession of sins whose underlying assumption was the identity between truth and progress.

Spur der Steine did not so much question this basic process as to warn against its abuse and degradation. The picture reminded its viewers that socialist morality was a matter not merely of outward conformity but also of inward conviction. Despite his gross misconduct as Party secretary, Horrath is pardoned at the end of the film because his convictions are genuine, and his heart, if not his actions, pure. If his true fault is his failure to have been open about his feelings and thoughts with the Party earlier, then his saving grace is his decision to come clean, even after the crisis occasioned by his affair with Kati has passed. In contrast, other characters in the film such as the ironically named construction manager Trautmann ("trust-man") and Horrath's deputy Bleibtreu ("stay loyal") display a cavalier attitude toward the truth. In one scene, Trautmann counsels Horrath to submit to self-criticism in a secondary matter for purely tactical reasons. Similarly, Bleibtreu, after the Party secretary confides in him about Kati, recommends suppressing the information to save the Party loss of face.

Indeed, the success of the construction site, and by extension the whole socialist project, is depicted as dependent on personal integrity and honesty. This link is effected through the love triangle involving Horrath, Kati, and Balla. Such a constellation was common to many early novels and films about the GDR, but *Spur der Steine* offered an unusually complex variant. In contrast to the standard scenario, it did not focus on a woman's choice between two lovers, one embodying Western, the other Eastern values. Instead, the central relationship is between the two men, Balla and Horrath, one representing the Party, the other the aspirations of dissatisfied workers. While the film only weakly develops the homoerotic subtext evident in much art celebrating labor—the Ballas' bare-chested brawn is rather flabby—the brigade leader, as portrayed by the charismatic Krug, is the most charismatic figure in the picture. Horrath must court him in order to reform the construction site. In this context, the Party secretary's secret involvement with Kati functions as an obstacle. When Balla's jealous suspicions are confirmed after learning of the young engineer's pregnancy, he feels betrayed by Horrath and goes on an alcoholic bender. His subsequent loss of enthusiasm for a new, more efficient production system for which his support is critical then results in a strike among other workers.

In the film, Horrath wins back Balla's confidence, and the inquest clears the Party secretary of essential wrongdoing. Of course, the actual discussions that occurred in the studio after the Plenum had a less salutary outcome. Here, truth-finding procedures assumed a transparent second function: the enforcement of Party discipline. Moreover, in cases where even carefully supervised Party and state mechanisms failed to produce desired results, the regime showed little compunction in resorting to more naked forms of intervention.

THE BANNING OF *SPUR DER STEINE* AND ITS AFTERMATH

Originally, Beyer had hoped to complete work on *Spur der Steine* by the end of 1965. Following the Plenum, the director asked for an extension until February 1966. As he recalled many years later, "I had only one thought in the back of my mind: [get] out of this hysteria and gain time."[31] Still, the mood of leading cultural politicians had not changed considerably by the time they viewed the picture in early March. High-ranking individuals, including Alexander Abusch, Kurt Hager, and Hans Rodenberg, sharply attacked the picture. Not surprisingly, their concerns focused on the figure of Horrath as the embodiment of Party authority. Hager argued: "The role of the Party as a battle group, as a unified revolutionary force, is pressed too strongly into the background. This happens . . . [because] the problem of the moral behavior of the Party secretary comes to the fore. . . . The Party actually appears as an inquisitional force."[32] Similarly, the newly appointed cultural minister, Klaus Gysi, complained: "In the film, the whole development [of socialism] continues on, in part because of, in part in spite of, the Party. On the whole, the Party . . . is a neutral institution." Among the most objectionable aspects of the film, to its critics, was the strike scene. Hager asked, "Do we want to propagate the right to strike? . . . The strike is no way to fight one's own class."[33]

The tone of this criticism was harsh. Even so, by not calling an immediate halt to the production, functionaries left open a window of opportunity. Their common presence at the meeting was also an indication of the great importance still assigned to the film. For his part, Beyer responded to the criticism with eighteen alterations. Among these was the removal of a scene featuring Horrath drinking at home as well as of one showing Balla throwing a hammer at a fellow worker. Similarly, some pointed political dialogue was taken out, including one exchange between the two lead male characters:

> Horrath: Out of three vague sentences one could stitch together for you an entire ideological line, an enemy one, naturally. There were people who understood that so well as if they had studied with Stalin personally.
> Balla: So, little father Joseph Wissarionovitch is responsible for your having made the girl pregnant.
> Horrath: I am speaking about myself, Hannes, I helped write such resolutions, in good faith.[34]

There is no record of Hager's reaction to these changes. He and other leading functionaries adopted a demonstratively hands-off attitude toward the project in the months leading up to its ill-fated release.[35] The matter was referred to the HV Film's Artistic Council. Although this body's membership had been reconstituted after the Plenum, it still included a number of artists who in previous years had vigorously supported reform within the studio, including Beyer himself, Konrad Wolf, Wolfgang Kohl-haase, and Erwin Geschonneck. These members' arguments carried the day on May 12 when the Artistic Council met to pass judgment on the picture.[36] The new HV Film director, Wilfried Maass, who had objected to the film when it was discussed among functionaries in March, informed Hager of the body's position, but the director of the Politburo's ideological commission took no action.[37] Thus Maass reluctantly approved the work.[38]

Just as had been the case with *Das Kaninchen bin ich* seven months earlier, filmmakers had apparently triumphed. At the cost of relatively minor changes, Beyer received approval for *Spur der Steine*.[39] Preparations for the picture's release continued as originally anticipated. Plans were already under way to delegate the picture as East Germany's official entry to the upcoming Prague film festival. On June 16, the film even enjoyed a preview at the annual Workers' Art Festival in Potsdam, an event that the official East German news agency, ADN, described with enthusiasm: "The conversation [between filmmakers and the audience] which followed the successful premier . . . marked the start of a great discussion concerning DEFA's latest film. . . . A construction worker described the film . . . as a film 'which brings us further.' The depiction of Balla by Manfred Krug found undivided approval. . . . Critical comments concerned the insufficient effectiveness of the plant Party organization. . . . The discussion ended with the promise of more events of a similar nature."[40] Yet, even as Beyer and his collaborators were discussing their film with fans, a campaign against their project was already under way. On June 10, DEFA's distributor, Progress, sent out a telegram instructing its theaters to accord the eagerly anticipated film only average publicity.[41] Moreover, despite the ADN bulletin, the ZK Agitation Committee successfully suppressed virtually all reviews written in conjunction with the film's preview, including one lavishly praising the picture by Horst Knietzsch, the cinema critic for *Neues Deutschland*.[42] Even some of the audience members who participated in the discussion after the Potsdam premiere had been planted by the Potsdam SED district office in order to encourage criticism of the film.[43]

The final decision to quash *Spur der Steine* came only on June 28, three days before its official release, when the Politburo agreed to limit the film's run to one week and to halt all publicity.[44] This action was taken after a secret screening of the picture for "leading comrades,"[45] presumably including Ulbricht. Officials took care to nurture the impression that their actions conformed to a truth higher than that of the raw exercise of power. Hence the staging of riots in movie theaters was meant to suggest that the film provoked the rightful wrath of the proletariat. Similarly,

Frank Beyer received a letter signed by twelve workers from Leipzig complaining that his picture had done Neutsch's novel a terrible disservice by fundamentally distorting socialist reality. Written in highly formulaic language typical of functionaries rather than of ordinary citizens, this statement hardly fooled the director, who suspected the hand of the Leipzig Party boss Paul Fröhlich, known for his notoriously conservative views in cultural matters.[46]

At the studio, the banning of *Spur der Steine* was followed by a series of discussions within DEFA's internal Party organization. These had two purposes: the "thorough clarification of the role and essence of the SED as the leading power of social development in the GDR" and the "destruction of all revisionist positions."[47] For the most part, filmmakers toed the line. Those who did not paid the price. By the end of August, the studio's central Party leadership identified Beyer, Konrad Wolf, and the dramaturges Klaus Wischnewski and Günther Karl as the "main representatives and intellectual authors of the false ideological-aesthetic positions."[48] All except Wolf were fired from the studio. Wolf, who as head of the Academy of Arts was too prominent a figure to be treated in such a summary fashion, became the object of considerable pressure. Particularly galling in the eyes of officials was a letter vigorously defending Beyer's film that Wolf had submitted to a Party Activists' Convention (*Parteiaktivtagung*) that took place in the studio in July.[49] The influential director was also suspected of complaining about the situation at DEFA to colleagues in Moscow.[50] The question of his loyalty was deemed so pressing that the matter was referred by the ZK Cultural Section to Erich Honecker, the Politburo member responsible for internal security. Under threat of exclusion from the SED, Wolf finally submitted to the inevitable in early September. Rather than allowing himself to become the object of an inquest conducted by fellow members of the DEFA's internal Party organization—a real-life Horrath—he abandoned what was a lost cause and exercised self-criticism.[51]

THE BEGINNING OF THE END?

Evident in *Spur der Steine* is a desire to situate truth in ways quite at odds with the moral universe posited by official ideology. The lack of closure in the work, particularly Kati's sudden flight, suggests disharmony between individual destiny and collective destiny. Noble heroes become casualties in the struggle for socialism. Even under the Party's leadership, personal virtue goes unrewarded. In this regard Beyer's film displays many similarities with the picture discussed in the preceding chapter, Kurt Maetzig's *Das Kaninchen bin ich* (1965). Both works thematize the inadequacy of rigid moral and legal norms when confronted with authentic experience. Balla, like Maria, the protagonist in Maetzig's film, is simultaneously an outcast from socialism and an embodiment of its genuine life force. A second character standing for authority in each picture, Horrath and Paul respectively, faces the dilemma of enforcing standards that he himself cannot satisfy. Finally, both films accord utopian potential to truth-finding and communication as a collective process. If the privileged locus of this activity in *Spur der Steine* is Horrath's inquest as presided over by Hansen, the benevolent SED district leader, then the village conflict commission represents the same ideal in *Das Kaninchen bin ich*.

Nevertheless, neither of these films fundamentally questioned the forward-looking orientation of socialist society. Their premises still conformed to the notion of *Gegenwart*—the present as a mediating state between past and future, or the conviction, as expressed by the narrator at the end of Konrad Wolf and Christa Wolf's *Der geteilte Himmel*, that "the fate of the unborn depends on the strength of countless people." In many ways, filmmakers had as much invested in socialism's progressive pretensions as the regime. Especially for those who first achieved prominence or had come of age during the first decade or so of the GDR's existence, artistic identity was closely bound up with the role assigned them in official ideology as *Mitgestalter*—co-creators—of the new order. Thus, even in their criticism, many filmmakers were trying to contribute to socialism's unfolding. In this regard, official complaints about artists at the Eleventh Plenum were probably accurate. They were challenging the Party's leadership role. They really did hope that their works might change East German society.

In many ways, a number of the Plenum films, and *Spur der Steine* in particular, were the last of their kind. Although other DEFA pictures had been banned in the past and would be in the future, never again would East German filmmakers see their art as a means of influencing directly the future course of their society. Later films that proved politically controversial either addressed specific problems or thematized socialism's general stagnation without purporting to offer any alternative.[52] Thus *Spur der Steine*, it can be argued, represents the last attempt by an East German director to present a critical vision of the GDR that still affirmed it as a dynamic society. Still, the Plenum's finality and its significance as a turning point in the development of the East German cinema are far more apparent in hindsight than they were at the time. The event did not so much shatter utopian pretensions entirely as contribute to their more gradual abandonment. Indeed, as the enthusiastic reception of *Spur der Steine* nearly a quarter of a century after its banning would attest, the embers of socialist faith for some would continue to smolder for many years, only to blaze briefly with the hope of a new beginning for the GDR after the fall of the Berlin Wall.

The next chapter discusses the displacement of utopian beliefs from the realm of history and politics to the quotidian that occurred within the East German cinema of the late sixties and seventies. This new solution to the dilemmas involved in depicting socialist society would be closely associated with wider trends in the GDR under the Honecker regime. Nevertheless, whatever accommodation was achieved between art and politics in the cinema would prove tenuous. Despite short periods of renewed optimism, the relationship between artists and the regime would continue to worsen. Moreover, under the unrelenting onslaught of television, the cinema's political function was clearly in eclipse. These developments found reflection in pictures that either mechanically followed tired conventions for depicting socialism or increasingly thematized social estrangement.

The Triumph of the Ordinary

East German *Alltag* Films of the 1970s

7

     Even at the time of the Eleventh Plenum, some filmmakers, particularly younger ones just establishing themselves in the studio, were already abandoning the task of depicting a society rapidly moving toward the future. Among the works banned in 1966 was a film that was aesthetically more radical than *Das Kaninchen bin ich* or *Spur der Steine*, even if it lacked their overt political ambition. In many ways, Jürgen Böttcher and Klaus Poche's *Jahrgang '45* (Born in '45, 1966) qualifies as the first East German *Alltagsfilm*. It differed from earlier pictures set in the GDR mainly in its attempt to dispense with an essential moral realm informed by official ideology and to allow the immediacy of ordinary existence almost complete autonomy. Its plot was not much more than a dramatic situation. The main characters are a young couple, Al and Li, whose marriage is on the rocks. With their divorce pending and four days of vacation to kill, Al wanders from one episode to the next trying to decide whether he should really move out. The same questions and themes occur again and again. Various friends and relatives ask why he is leaving Li, to which he invariably replies, "It's just not working. That's our business." Repeated attempts at reconciliation fail. Al ogles other women and runs into an old flame. His boredom even leads him to stop in at work, an auto repair shop, where the personnel director encourages him to give the marriage another shot, as a good socialist comrade should. Yet, despite this advice, what seems to bring Al and Li back together is less an act of conscious will than the same ennui and vague longing that led to their troubles in the first place.

Jahrgang '45 had many precedents within the East German cinema. Among the most significant of these considered extensively in the second chapter is Gerhard Klein and Wolfgang Kohlhaase's *Berlin—Ecke Schön-*

hauser (Berlin—Corner Schönhauser). Not only are both films set in the same Berlin neighborhood and focused on similarly passive protagonists, but they also clearly favor the cinema's indexical nature, its supposed ability to record a preexisting world, over its escapist and illusory qualities. As earlier chapters have shown, since DEFA's founding in the forties, East German filmmakers had flirted with Italian neorealism, a movement that promised an alternative cinema predicated on real life rather than celluloid fantasy. By the early sixties, techniques for emphasizing documentary pretense were common to many GDR films, including some with plots that were little more than transparent political allegories.

Even so, *Jahrgang '45* went further than these other pictures not only in the directors' rigorous preference for actual locations and natural lighting conditions but also in the lack of a clearly articulated political theme. In contrast to pictures like *Berlin—Ecke Schönhauser* or *Der geteilte Himmel*, everydayness did not supplement or compete with a narrative driven by ideological logic. If romantic love in earlier films had served as a vehicle for thematizing socialist commitment, then all that was left in Böttcher's film were the shards of a metaphor. Similarly, the film's political content was nonexplicit and ambiguous. On the one hand, it expressed a certain narcissistic fascination with a recognizable lifestyle and setting. On the other hand, the juxtaposition of barren urban landscapes with the sensual disorder of summer greenery, the theme of sexual longing, and visual refrains, such as birds in cages and Al observing Li and others through glass panes, suggested feelings of estrangement, frustration, and entrapment.

My analysis begins with the political and institutional factors in the film industry after the Eleventh Plenum that, despite the banning of *Jahrgang '45* in 1966, allowed for the completion of several films sharing a similar aesthetic stance starting only two years later. The young artists responsible for these works claimed to represent a new artistic direction for DEFA: "documentary realism." While the movement as such quickly petered out, the innovations associated with it, particularly its call for films dramatizing ordinary life rather than epochal developments, were typical of the general direction of the East German cinema of the time. Many older directors were already embracing such subject matter independently.

Alltag's heyday arguably came with several works produced in the early seventies. Among these was Heiner Carow and Ulrich Plenzdorf's *Die Legende von Paul und Paula* (The Legend of Paul and Paula). Produced in 1972, this film was a box office hit and for this reason provides a good vehicle to gauge the significance of the *Alltag* films in a wider social and political context. The success of such pictures both anticipated and was dependent on the broad ideological and political changes associated with

Erich Honecker's succeeding Walter Ulbricht as first secretary of the SED in 1971. Equally significant, the image of East Germany articulated in many *Alltag* films found a genuine and lasting popular resonance. Indeed, the continued popularity of such works as *Die Legende von Paul und Paula* and recent sociological data suggest the persistence of unique social and cultural attitudes among former East Germans even after national unification. *Alltag* films thus helped to articulate an alternative East German self-understanding, which functioned as a means of resistance to, and of accommodation with, the conformist pressures of the socialist system.

FROM THE BANNING OF *JAHRGANG '45* TO THE RISE OF DOCUMENTARY REALISM

At first, officials do not seem to have known quite what to make of *Jahrgang '45*. Cultural Ministry officials, although puzzled by the lack of strong dramatic structure, concluded that "the script nevertheless contains no incorrect political-ideological views."[1] Given the studio's tremendous problems with meeting basic economic plan objectives directly after the Plenum, such innocuousness was welcome. The film's problems began only when the studio director Bruk viewed the initial cut and ordered an immediate halt to the project. In October 1966, the state agency supervising the film industry, the HV film, seconded Bruk's decision. While the basic story might have yielded "a perhaps unpretentious but unambiguously partisan" picture, the office blasted the artists for approaching the material with such "a profoundly indifferent, skeptical-subjective attitude" and found "that the desired partisan message for socialist society is turned into its opposite." In particular, officials were upset about the character of Mogul, a retired neighbor of Al and Li who is featured prominently in the film. They complained that even though the script indicated he was an "old antifascist . . . who satisfies his need for social engagement through volunteering," the film showed "an old man, undistinguished, poorly dressed, and without any magnetism." Equally troubling from the agency's perspective was the depiction of a "social milieu" that was "far removed from characteristic traits of our socialist reality." The settings were "sad, unfriendly, dirty, and ill kept." "A back courtyard, a basement apartment . . . an ugly, weed-infested heap of debris" dominated the screen. It seemed as if the filmmakers had taken "almost embarrassing care to avoid awakening friendly impressions."[2]

For its makers, the banning of *Jahrgang '45* came as a considerable shock, since their work did not have the same obvious political pretensions as Plenum films like *Spur der Steine*.[3] Nevertheless, this outcome is hardly surprising considering the Plenum's immediate impact on film production. For the next several years, pictures attempting to depict the present in a nonconventional fashion did not fare well. As it had once before during the period following the June 17 uprising of 1953, the studio took refuge in bread-and-butter entertainment or "genre" films. This trend continued throughout the late sixties, which saw a profusion of detective thrillers, comedies involving mistaken identity, and historical costume films, as well the first DEFA western, the wildly popular *Die Söhne der grossen Bärin* (The Sons of the Great Bear, 1966).[4] As in the fifties, intellectually ambitious productions tended to be dramatically situated in the past. These included Konrad Wolf's autobiographical war film, *Ich war neunzehn* (I Was Nineteen, 1968); Egon Günther's *Abschied* (Farewell, 1968), based on the Johannes R. Becher novel of the same title; and Heiner Carow's *Die Russen kommen* (The Russians Are Coming, 1968). One indication of the continuing tension in the studio was the banning of this last work and the suppression of Günther's picture after an abbreviated run.

Even the few explicitly political *Gegenwartsfilme* set in the GDR from this period had a curiously historical orientation. The episode picture, *Geschichten jener Nacht* (Stories from That Night, 1967),[5] depicted the construction of the Wall from the retrospective vantage of four fictional participants. The premise of Heinz Thiel and Horst E. Brandt's *Brot und Rosen* (Bread and Roses, 1967) was a delegate to the Seventh SED Party Congress in 1967 who recounts his life to a young woman reporter.

As the sixties ended, the studio came under considerable pressure to produce *Gegenwart* films consistent with ideological objectives.[6] With clearer lines of authority having been established in the film industry in the wake of the Eleventh Plenum, officials hoped that filmmakers would now prove more responsive to political imperatives. In addition to replacing the studio's top management and calling a halt to reforms within the studio (see Chapter 6), the regime further encouraged the HV Film to become involved increasingly in the daily operations of the studio. For the first time since the late fifties, the studio director lost the authority to commission scripts independently. The HV's artistic production section was even supposed to involve itself at the earliest stages of the creative process, a practice that in the years preceding the Eleventh Plenum had been largely curtailed because of bitter complaints from artists.[7] Increasingly, officials held up the East German television network, DFF, as a model for the film industry. Subject to more direct political control through a special state committee directly responsible to the Party, the DFF was more efficient than the film industry in producing "agitational" films designed to propagate the official viewpoint. Moreover, its artists, used to working under the far different financial and creative constraints of their media, were less prone than their DEFA colleagues to embarking on expensive and controversial projects.[8]

Such efforts were not fruitless. By the close of the decade, officials could point to several competently made *Gegenwart* films that fulfilled the Party's ideological objectives for the film industry. Among these were Horst Seeman's *Zeit zu Leben* (Time to Live, 1969) and Siegfried Kühn's *Im Spannungsfeld* (Force Field, 1970). Both of these were "production" stories, dramatizing the workplace's central importance as an arena for achieving socialist consciousness. The one element distinguishing such works from earlier production films were their heroes. These tended to be the "planners and directors" of Ulbricht's "technical-scientific revolution" proclaimed at the 1967 Seventh SED Party Congress rather than the simple workers of earlier pictures.[9] Seeman's film, for example, concerned a distinguished, older comrade who learns that he is incurably ill. Instead of retiring as his doctor advises, he decides to devote the little time he has left to one last task: the modernization of a dilapidated factory. In the process, not only does he inspire its workers with new confidence, but he wins back the respect of his errant son. Other comparable productions from the same period included Ralf Kirsten's *Netzwerk* (Network, 1970) and several episodes in a collaborative effort commissioned to honor the GDR's twentieth anniversary, *Aus unserer Zeit* (From Our Time, 1970). Some proved quite popular. The most successful of them, *Zeit zu Leben*, attracted more than 2 million viewers over its complete run,[10] a very impressive figure, even assuming it was bolstered by officially sponsored attendance drives.[11]

Nevertheless, the relative success of these production films is deceptive. During the late sixties, the discrepancy between official expectations and the general direction of the East German cinema was, if anything, growing. In contrast to Seeman and Kirsten, most leading filmmakers tended to avoid traditional *Gegenwart* films. In depicting their own society, older and younger directors alike were increasingly eschewing epic stories about achieving socialism for more intimate ones purporting to describe prosaic problems faced by ordinary individuals. Indeed, even the films discussed in the preceding paragraph were not immune from this trend. Their success with audiences probably had more to do with their melodramatic qualities than with their ability to inspire socialist élan. However idealized, the image of the GDR conveyed in such pictures was not quite as outlandish as that found in comparable pictures from the fifties or early sixties. Gone were the Stakhanovite characters advancing socialism through Herculean feats. The heroes in a typical Horst Seeman film were engaged less in the rapid construction of a new society than in the continual improvement of an existing one. Professionally dedicated yet also seeking fulfillment within the family, they were exemplary role models rather than proletarian supermen.

Far more indicative of the general direction the East German cinema would take in the seventies than production stories like *Zeit zu Leben* were works by younger filmmakers associated with "documentary realism." This movement was not a particularly cohesive one, and the idea behind it quickly lost currency as its adherents began to go their own way in the mid-seventies.[12] Nevertheless, documentary realism followed a discursive logic that had long influenced developments within the East German cinema. On the one hand, filmmakers' fascination with neorealism and the indexical qualities of the cinema was nothing new. Their persistence in this direction in the face of official criticism throughout the fifties suggests the power of such an aesthetic stance as an alternative to socialist realism. Under the pretense of striving for authentic depiction, artists could resist official demands for works conforming to an idealized image of socialist society. On the other hand, officials, while they could attack individual pictures, were hard pressed to reject the aims of a realist cinema, since the regime desperately sought legitimization through confirmation of its practical achievements.

Several of the documentary realists had cut their teeth on *Jahrgang '45*, a film that would continue to serve as a model for this generation. Besides the picture's scriptwriter, Klaus Poche, and its cameraman, Roland Gräf, who would go on to direct his own films, others who can be loosely grouped together here include the directors Ingrid Reschke, Rainer Simon, Lothar Warneke, and Herrmann Zschoche, as well as the scriptwriter and novelist Ulrich Plenzdorf. Among the most influential *Alltag* films of the early seventies were Lothar Warneke's *Dr. med. Sommer II* (Dr. Sommer No. 2, 1970) and Roland Gräf and Klaus Poche's *Mein lieber Robinson* (My Dear Robinson, 1971). Comparable works included Herrmann Zschoche's *Weite Strassen—stille Liebe* (Long Roads—Silent Love, 1969), Ingrid Reschke's *Kennen Sie Urban?* (Do You Know Urban?, 1971), Rainer Simon's *Männer ohne Bart* (Men without Beards, 1971), and Siegfried Kühn's *Zeit der Storche* (Time of the Storks, 1971). While these pictures rarely achieved the conceptual rigor of *Jahrgang '45*, they shared a similar aesthetic stance. To varying degrees, all eschewed ideological narrative in favor of a subtler, if still politically premised, truth situated in the texture of daily experience.[13] *Dr. med. Sommer II*, for example, concerns a young doctor who begins a residency at a small-town hospital. Here he faces a variety of challenges, including an overbearing chief surgeon sharing the same last name. The picture reaches a dramatic high point with the suicide of a patient with an incurable illness, an event occasioned by the younger Sommer's perhaps excessive candor.

However clichéd this last plot element may have seemed, *Dr. med. Sommer II* exhibited little of the melodrama associated with Dr. Kildare movies or modern-day hospital television series. Dr. Sommer has no romantic interest. About the most the film offers in this regard is a visit to the beach with a nurse with whom he enjoys a strictly platonic relationship. They spend their time together discussing the meaning of life in socialist society. By the same token, the operating sequences in the film do not function as dramatic focal points as in conventional pictures about medicine. Using footage from actual procedures shot by the picture's crew at East Berlin's famed Charité Hospital, these scenes convey a rather routinized impression of medicine. Their purpose is to document authenticity as much as it is to entertain. Moreover, the picture's pacing is deliberately slow, the editing sparsely applied, and the camera static. In an interview shortly after the film's premiere, Warneke implicitly acknowledged the consequences of his aesthetic choices while justifying them with an ideological credo: "I affirm [the Italian neorealist scriptwriter] Zavattini's conviction that every moment is endlessly rich, that boredom is the most superficial reaction to everydayness. . . . In our circumstances, this [aesthetic stance] has political meaning; the individual becomes a conscious subject. . . . In this way, the film is capable of showing to what degree Communist principles have become inner human requirements, what, as Lenin put it, has become habit."[14]

ALLTAG TRIUMPHANT

Remarkably, *Dr. Med. Sommer II* and other "documentary realist" films encountered little political resistance. While DEFA's management feared, not without reason, that their slow pacing and dramatically diffuse plotlines would bore and alienate audiences, higher-level cultural politicians did not intervene.[15] Such tacit approval represented a considerable transformation in official attitudes. Only a dozen years earlier, the attempt in Gerhard Klein and Wolfgang Kohlhaase's *Berlin—Ecke Schönhauser* to apply neorealist principles to the depiction of the present had occasioned considerable controversy.

Indeed, throughout the sixties, there were signs of the new aesthetic accommodation on the horizon. In 1964, Warneke published a master's thesis, "The Documentary Feature Film," that articulated in advance the artistic position implicit in the films of the late sixties.[16] The official reception of Kurt Maetzig's *Das Mädchen auf dem Brett* (The Girl on the Diving

Board, 1967) is also significant in this context. Concerning the crisis a competitive high diver faces when she loses the nerve to jump, the film had obvious political value for a regime that prided itself on athletic accomplishments. At the same time, the film shared certain qualities with documentary realist films in terms of the intimate dimensions of its story, pacing, and photographic style. Some of Maetzig's colleagues in the studio had even taken the suppression of *Jahrgang '45* as an indication that his film might also be quashed.[17] Nevertheless, the film received a gala premiere with Ulbricht himself in attendance, an event that signaled the director's rehabilitation after the criticism he suffered at the Eleventh Plenum.[18] Clearly, over the years, the regime had grown more accepting of intimately conceived and personal films, provided they did not challenge socialism's master narrative.

Nevertheless, the regime's attitude toward the greater emphasis on *Alltag* in DEFA films remained for many years one of grudging tolerance. Officials might have been relieved that filmmakers were avoiding controversy, but the Party still would have preferred agitational films. Internal studio documents from the late sixties repeatedly note the lack of pictures in production treating "central problems of social development."[19] In a veiled reference to strained relations between artists and officials, a report of the Central Committee's Cultural Section emphasized widespread "subjectivity in the judgment and evaluation of films" and the lack of "criteria that correspond to the growing needs of the entire society." Equally troubling was the infiltration of "artistic representational techniques from the late capitalistic-modernist cinema."[20] Officials were also concerned about filmmakers' refusal to acknowledge television films featuring transparently political narratives as models for their own work.[21]

Only with the ascension to power of Erich Honecker in May 1971 did artists have reason to believe that the restrictive political climate ushered in by the Eleventh Plenum might finally be over. Their hopes found seeming confirmation when the new first secretary in December 1971 famously proclaimed, "If one proceeds from a solid socialist position, there can in my opinion be no taboos in the area of art and literature."[22] Other changes in policy initiated by Honecker suggested that the Party was seeking to define a new direction for socialism in the GDR, one that would deemphasize utopian ideological goals in favor of more practical social ones. Having already given up the goal of overtaking the Federal Republic economically, the regime stressed socialism's alleged advantages as a more humane social order than capitalism. Central to the shift in the SED's platform was the call for a society dedicated to personal self-realization, captured in the slogan "The individual is the focus" (*Der Mensch steht im*

Mittelpunkt). In economic policy, the new inflection meant more importance being attached to consumer needs and housing. Similarly, the regime now saw cultural policy in a different light. Artists were no longer
being asked to help create the new society; instead, they were merely to
entertain and stimulate its inhabitants. One obvious precondition for the
Party's political shift was the normalization of relations with the Federal
Republic and the West, which culminated with the signing of the Berlin
Agreement in June 1972. At least in the eyes of its leaders, the GDR had
arrived as a society.[23]

In this way, the stage was set for the emergence of *Alltag* in the early
seventies as an increasingly central concept among East German artists
and thinkers. By then, the term had acquired considerable popular and
quasi-official currency as well. As one 1973 article on the aesthetics of
labor in the influential intellectual weekly *Sonntag* noted:

> Everydayness seems to have always been identical with the boring and
> monotonous. For this reason, genuine, meaningful human existence
> has never seemed accessible in the prose of *Alltag*. Now, however,
> literature and art compete to uncover the poetry of "ordinary *Alltag*."
> The interest in everyday subjects and processes is general. We often
> find headlines in papers and illustrated magazines such as "Out of the
> *Alltag* of the Republic," "Passing the Test in *Alltag*," "The Arts in Social-
> ist *Alltag*," "From the *Alltag* of Socialist Jurisprudence," etc. . . . In
> concern for everyday activity, a healthy skepticism toward idealized
> exceptions combines itself with a decisive orientation toward that
> which animates millions of people every day and everywhere.[24]

Of course, this new emphasis on *Alltag* in East German art and literature
came at the expense of the GDR's progressive aspirations. Nevertheless,
the regime tolerated, even encouraged, this development. Kurt Hager declared before the Nineteenth Party Plenum in 1972 that "today the great,
the historically and personally meaningful grows precisely in *Alltag*." The
SED's chief ideologue hastened to add that a true art "matures out of deep
understanding of the historical and human content of our socialist development."[25] Even so, *Alltag* had become a notion that cultural politicians were eager to co-opt.

Such favorable political conditions reinforced developments long under way in the East German cinema, and the seventies soon became
Alltag's heyday at DEFA. Not only did everyday-life films dominate the
studio's production, but they became aesthetically and thematically more
diverse, running the gamut from socially engaged art films to comedies
deeply rooted in traditional commercial genre films. Several main direc-

tions are distinguishable. Although some directors, notably Warneke and Roland Gräf, continued to build on the tradition of documentary realism, producing for the most part intimately scaled, carefully crafted films with intellectual and political pretensions, other artists sought wider audiences. Herrmann Zschoche, for example, directed a number of generally well attended films dealing with teenage sexuality and coming of age. Typical examples of his work include *Liebe mit sechszehn* (Love at Sixteen, 1974) and *Sieben Sommersprossen* (Seven Freckles, 1978). In contrast, Roland Oehme specialized in comedies that varied from light entertainment to the grotesque. His most popular films were *Der Mann der nach der Oma kam* (The Man Who Replaced Granny, 1972), premised on the idea that a male housekeeper would take over for a grandmother within a household, and *Einfach Blumen aufs Dach* (Just Put Flowers on the Roof, 1979), a work that somehow managed to poke affectionate fun at the politically charged issue of social stratification in the GDR.

Equally significant was another development: older, established artists began increasingly to thematize the ordinary. These included Konrad Wolf, who, after completing in 1971 an epic historical film, *Goya* (about the Spanish painter), took up the same basic theme of artistic patronage in a vastly different context. Together with Wolfgang Kohlhaase, Wolf made *Der nackte Mann auf dem Sportsplatz* (The Naked Man on the Athletic Field, 1974). This picture depicts a middle-aged sculptor of no particular renown whose social estrangement becomes obvious when a statue he completes on commission from the local soccer club meets with derision. Similarly, Frank Beyer, finally able to return to the studio in the midseventies, collaborated with Jurek Becker on a picture, *Das Versteck* (The Hideout, 1978), about a divorced couple unsuccessfully attempting reconciliation. During this period, the director Heiner Carow also came into his own with three highly successful films about personal relationships, the most popular of which, *Die Legende von Paul und Paula*, is discussed extensively in the next section of this chapter.

Among the most significant pictures produced in the first half of the seventies were two directed by Egon Günther. *Der Dritte* (Her Third, 1972) concerns a single mother in search of the right man. Although its protagonist, a mathematician who works in a modern factory, outwardly conformed to the type of hero desired by the regime, the film is less about the new society than a woman's experience in learning to express her needs and desires. Indeed the picture's open treatment of sexuality offended members of the ZK's Women's Section, who sensed lesbian undertones in the relationship between the film's two main female characters.[26] *Die Schlüssel* (The Keys, 1974), directed by Günther and written by Helga Schütz, is unquestionably one of the most fascinating and aesthetically complex DEFA pictures. Concerning a young East German couple vacationing in Poland, the film juxtaposes their personal story with scenes evoking the enormity of the recent past and the troubled nature of German-Polish relations. While the explicit treatment of historical and political questions went far beyond that found in most *Alltag* films, the film's makers went to excessive lengths to assure quasi-documentary exactitude, including the staging of a trolley accident in Cracow that elicited an actual emergency crew response.[27]

As the example of *Die Schlüssel* suggests, one problem inherent in describing the *Alltag* films of the seventies is that they never represented a precise category, a problem compounded by the somewhat promiscuous use of the term within the film industry. Still, what united the pictures described above, despite their great diversity, was their implicit construction of East Germany as an actual, if imperfect, place. If the images contained in the majority of *Alltag* films were in fact idealized—the protagonists exemplary, the living conditions better than those enjoyed by most GDR citizens—the pretense of the films was the normalcy, indeed the banality, of their subject matter. Though inescapably embedded in the society that produced them, these films are less directly concerned with socialism than with basic life issues: love, coming of age, and death. Thus *Die Schlüssel* depicts the death of one of its two lover-protagonists, an abrupt event that in the thematic context of the film allows life's existential uncertainty to resonate with Germany's ruptured past.

DIE LEGENDE VON PAUL UND PAULA

No film suggested the promise of a genuinely popular but socially engaged cinema centered on *Alltag* more than *Die Legende von Paul und Paula*. The collaboration between the director Heiner Carow and the scriptwriter Ulrich Plenzdorf came about literally by accident: a tragic car crash that claimed the life of the promising young film director Ingrid Reschke. As her studio mentor, Carow agreed to assume responsibility for the film, a project she had begun with Plenzdorf. Likewise, the choice of Angelika Domröse for the title female role was hardly a deliberate one. According to Carow, he sent the actress the script with no particular expectations and began to consider her seriously for the role only after she insisted on playing it.[28] Whatever the exact case may have been, the happenstance was fortuitous. One of the most popular DEFA pictures ever made, *Die Legende von Paul und Paula* would bring Carow his greatest triumph as a director, establish Plenzdorf as a leading scriptwriter, and turn Domröse into one of East Germany's most recognizable stars.

Even though his film would come to typify the *Alltag* pictures of the seventies, Carow himself did not identify with the documentary realists. Having made his first films in the late fifties, he belonged to an older generation of DEFA directors. Moreover, he disagreed markedly with the aesthetic stance propagated by his younger colleagues. Although Carow had been drawn to neorealism as a young man, he was concerned that documentary realist films lacked the narrative depth and emotional energy necessary to engage broad audiences. The hyperrealism of these works in his opinion came at the sacrifice of artistic creativity.[29] By contrast, as Carow claimed later in an interview, his and Plenzdorf's main objective in fashioning their film was to win an audience: "Now we have to try and see if we can't get people into the theaters." Clearly impatient with the tendency toward abstract theorizing in GDR film culture, the director added, "One should say simply: I enjoy it and find it beautiful. That's probably the most important answer that you have to give yourself, whether [the story] interests you at all, whether it can excite you."[30]

This defiantly unreflective attitude was in many ways disingenuous. Certainly, Carow's opus betrays a pronounced political and social engagement similar to that of many of his colleagues at DEFA. Still, his comments were consistent with the tenor of *Die Legende von Paul und Paula* itself. A love story, the picture celebrates emotional honesty grounded in an awareness of life's existential nature. At the same time, the work makes no bones about its own artifice and the cinema's escapist function. Although the setting, contemporary East Berlin, is hardly idealized in its depiction, the film's pretensions of verisimilitude are limited. As the title announces, the story presents itself as a "legend," in the sense of a fairy tale. Thus the picture begins with a kind of prologue that uses both images and song to suggest a theme, even a moral, for the action to follow. The first shot shows an old apartment building, which then implodes. As the titles roll over a cloud of dust rising from the site, lyrics, sung by the popular East German rock band the Puhdys, are heard:

> Wenn ein Mensch kurze Zeit lebt
> Sagt die Welt, dass er zu früh geht
> Wenn ein Mensch lange Zeit lebt
> Sagt die Welt, es ist Zeit, dass er geht
>
> Jegliches hat seine Zeit
> Steine sammeln, Steine zerstreuen
> Bäume pflanzen, Bäume abhauen
> Leben und Sterben und Friede und Streit

Meine Freundin ist schön
Als ich aufstand, ist sie gegangen
Weck sie nicht, bis sie sich regt
Ich habe mich in ihren Schatten gelegt[31]

The next shot then shows the male protagonist, Paul, throwing rubbish out of a window, including dishes, the breaking of which in Germany is traditionally associated with weddings. Another imploding building flashes on the screen, this time clearly contrasted with a modern apartment block rising around it. Finally, Paul displays a photograph of himself and Paula wildly embracing, their clothes in tatters, to a small crowd of laughing construction workers and neighborhood children. Only at the end of the film does it become clear that the prologue is actually a "flash-forward," showing the bereft Paul clearing out Paula's apartment. Nevertheless, the short sequence of scenes not only efficiently establishes the cyclical nature of human existence but also prefigures the importance the picture will attach to emotional and romantic fulfillment versus other measures of happiness and success.

Indeed, as a love story, *Die Legende von Paul und Paula* is not only unbearably trite, it is deliberately so! Although living across the street from one another, Paul and Paula go about their lives independently for years without finding happiness. Paul has a model career, but his marriage to Ines, a very attractive yet utterly boorish woman, is a failure. Paula seeks romantic fulfillment, but her poor choice of men leaves her a single mother working as a cashier in order to feed her two children. One evening, overcome with drudgery, she leaves them behind in her apartment and escapes to a singles club, where she meets Paul, who has similarly fled his family. After a night of wild passion, they agree to keep their fling a secret. Paula tells Paul, "We'll let it last as long as it lasts. We'll do nothing for or against it. And we won't ask each other too much, just our names."[32]

Of course, this attempt to contractually manage passion quickly unravels. Whereas Paula desires nothing else than "simply to be happy," Paul feels a sense of obligation toward family and work. When he refuses to spend more time with her, she leaves him. Only the death of Paula's toddler son in an automobile accident brings them back together again; this time, however, it is Paul's turn to insist on the importance of true love, since Paula is contemplating marriage to another admirer, Herr Saft, a gallant but somewhat ridiculous older man, who offers economic security. Paul responds by waging a comic campaign of attrition, sleeping outside her apartment door and shadowing her on outings with Saft. The final resolution occurs after Paul's colleagues from work try to convince him to return to his wife. Arriving home with a bottle of champagne in hand, he makes a valiant effort, even choosing to ignore Ines's lover hiding in the closet; however, the hypocrisy is too much. So, Paul marches across the street to Paula's apartment. In a scene characterized by mock chivalry rather than machismo, he breaks down Paula's door with an ax and overcomes her feeble protestations; the couple is finally reunited.[33]

Alas, happiness such as theirs is too perfect to endure. Paula knows that bearing another child might kill her. Nevertheless, she must have a child by the man she truly loves. In the last scene, she excitedly returns from a visit to her obstetrician, as a narrator's voice explains, "Paula did not survive the birth of her child." The next image is of her apartment building, the last old house on the block, imploding. The picture's final shot then shows Paul, together with Paula's children, his own son, and their new baby, in a new apartment. They are sleeping in Paula's bed under the photograph, familiar from the film's prologue, of the two lovers wildly embracing, while the theme song's lyrics about life's cyclical nature are heard one last time.

Even though the subject matter and the self-ironizing fairly tale elements in *Die Legende von Paul und Paula* emphasize existential truisms about the human condition, the picture is just as deliberately rooted in the specifics of East German society and the more general cultural context of the late sixties and early seventies. In no respect is this more apparent than in the film's critique of *Kleinbürgerlichkeit* and conformist behavior in the GDR. Until his final romantic conversion, Paul is depicted as a careerist who structures his life around professional advancement. Every morning, a limousine containing three identically dressed colleagues picks him up for work. Moreover, in contrast to his relationship with Paula, the premise of his marriage is material well-being. Thus Paul's main reason for not divorcing is the effect that such an action might have on his career. Typically, his first date with Ines gets steamy only after he mentions the salary he expects to earn after completing his studies. Another scene shows Paul and his wife in bed after making love eagerly discussing a new apartment and buying clothes. Meanwhile, the camera ironically dwells on an absolutely *kitschig* picture of flying geese hanging in their apartment. The depiction of Paul and his family also has clear political resonances. Paul's position makes him precisely the *Leiter und Planer* (leader and planner) type celebrated in other DEFA films of the same era. Moreover, he is constantly shown in military uniform, either returning from compulsory service or as a member of his factory's *Bereitschaftsgruppe*, or reserve paramilitary unit, further emphasizing his willingness to submit to the discipline of official culture.

In contrast to Paul, Paula is hardly a model socialist citizen. Her job is anything but high-powered, and her primary aspiration is escape from her workaday routine. Indeed, she lives above a movie theater, the noise of which permeates her apartment. One scene contrasts her, as she laboriously drags heating coal inside from a pile dumped unceremoniously outside her building, with figures featured in glamorous publicity stills hanging in front of the theater. Judging by her previous taste in men, Paula is also more in touch with contemporary cultural trends than Paul. Early in the film, as he falls for Ines, Paula becomes involved with a hippie, Colly, the father of her second child. Their relationship ends when Paula returns home from the maternity ward only to find him making love to another woman as rock music blares in the background. Above all, Paula's main attributes are fantasy and a free spirit. At no point are Paula's qualities clearer than in the film's central love scene. Here, she welcomes Paul into her apartment, whose ingenious decor contrasts sharply with the sterile furnishings of his own residence. While he struggles to extract himself from his military uniform, the flower-adorned Paula turns her bed into the site of an elaborate picnic featuring exotically prepared food.

In short, Paula, through her resourceful imagination, creates for Paul a romantic idyll, insulated from public obligations associated with work and civic duties such as military service. In contrast to Paul's marriage with Ines, their relationship is not emblematic of social reproduction but stands for the possibility of private escape from the pressures of conventional existence. Indeed, the theme of their tryst is vaguely Polynesian, with Paula wearing flowers in her hair and serving food on skewers— Plenzdorf even specified (presumably canned) pineapple in the script. However, if Paula's imagination, enthusiasm for life, and equally exuberant sexuality suggest freedom from the discipline and conformism of official culture, she also represents an attitude toward life, even identity, more authentically rooted both in the organic continuity of human existence and the specific traditions of German popular culture.

This second aspect of Paula's character is most apparent in a fantastic vision, ostensibly experienced by Paul, which is interspersed within the central love scene. Noticing a picture of Paula's grandparents, Paul asks her about her family. She explains that she is descended from a long but now defunct line of rivermen. Indeed, her name is the same one given to all women and barges in her family. These particulars lead to Paul's dream or hallucination, which Plenzdorf describes in the script as follows:

As Paul opens his eyes again, Paula's bed stands on the deck of a moving Spree River barge. The barge is named "Paula" . . .

Paul *whispers*: Paula! We're moving!
Paula: What I've always wanted—traveling in bed.

. . . .

The "Paula" docks—in the middle of other, long wrecked, barges. . . . On the barges stands Paula's entire clan, all the generations back to the beginning.

Paula *introduces*: This is Paul. I also have a son.

Everyone bows to each other.

. . . A sumptuous feast follows on an infinitely long table in the hull of the "Paula"—sumptuous in any case as far as plates, table settings, etc. are concerned. Otherwise there are only apples. . . . Nevertheless, the mood could hardly be better. Suddenly Paula is on the table. All the guests attempt to obtain a piece of the long bridal veil she wears. It is the only thing she has on. Paula flees across the long table and finds refuge on the middle bulkhead, [where] her grandmothers, great-grandmothers, and great-great-grandmothers stand, smile benevolently, and knit baby things.[34]

Inherent in this phantasmagorical image is nothing less than an alternative understanding of time that contrasted markedly with the regime's transcendent vision of history. Here Paul, who as a family father and a loyal career man embodies conventional virtue, finds himself unable to resist the vital forces that Paula represents. If the premise of his lifestyle up to now has been the promise of steady material advancement in exchange for discipline, then she stands for an understanding of life emphasizing cyclical renewal rather than endless horizons, tradition instead of progress. Thus Paul's vision is organized around a wedding, the rite of passage most closely associated with genealogical replication. At the same time, a comparison is drawn between the two lovers' imagined wedding and the actual one between Paul and Ines that occurs earlier on screen. The film reduces this second event to a photographer posing the couple for posterity, suggesting the strained conventionality of their future life together. In contrast, the union between Paul and Paula is the more authentic one, even if its formal validation remains only a dream. Sanctioned by the presence of Paula's ancestors, the celebration occurs on a river, a symbol of life's continuity. In addition, the guests' enthusiastic participation in the celebration affirms the life-giving force of sensual love despite its inherently disorderly nature. Further emphasizing the gap between the worlds the two lovers represent are two colleagues of Paul who appear in the vision. Wearing somber suits, they express obvious displeasure with the wild exuberance of Paula and her clan.

A second type of genealogy, of course, was also at work in *Die Legende von Paul und Paula*. In developing the contrast between the sterility of official culture and the idyllic alternative represented by the lovers' relationship, the picture drew on idioms established in previous DEFA films and earlier German pictures. Paula followed in a distinct line of strong female protagonists in the East German cinema, many of whom have already been discussed in this study (see Chapter 4). For example, one figure whom she resembles quite closely in many respects is Maria in *Das Kaninchen bin ich* (see Chapter 5). Like her, Paula is identifiably proletarian and involved in a relationship with a man of higher social status whose education and professional position remove him from the authentic stream of life. Indeed, the only time Paul is seen "working," he is at a fancy reception his company holds for foreign customers. In contrast, Paula's job as a cashier brings her in constant contact with her customers and colleagues, with whom she enjoys a grudgingly affectionate rapport. Thus, even if Paula's and Maria's relationships carried different metaphorical resonances—Maria's story, for example, was a far more direct indictment of the East German state than Paula's—both stood for a truth located in the lived experience of ordinary people rather than in official ideology.

In addition, Carow and Plenzdorf's film presented Berlin in an alternative fashion consistent with a number of earlier DEFA productions that had called into question the regime's understanding of its capital as a city of the future. The picture does not so much celebrate the replacement of old housing stock with new buildings than record the process neutrally. As already noted, Paula lives in a tenement flat, whose dingy stairwell in several scenes provides the setting for a traditional communality among her neighbors, ever curious about her unconventional life. In contrast, the modern apartment that Paul occupies with Ines is depicted as sterile. The picture also makes little reference to the regime's grand urban renewal projects, such as East Berlin's recently rebuilt main square, Alexanderplatz, frequently shown in other DEFA films from the same period. In short, the film's attitude toward progress as expressed in the ideological reinscription of urban space is at best ambivalent. Indeed, if anything, the lifestyle and the comfortable proletarian sociability that Paula represents appear threatened, an impression heightened by premonitions of her premature death throughout the film. Arguably, the picture is ultimately about preserving what Paula embodies against the relentless pressures of supposed progress.

Another suitable comparison for *Die Legende von Paul und Paula* is Slatan Dudow's 1958 picture, *Verwirrung der Liebe*. As discussed in Chapter 4, Dudow's film is likewise noteworthy for its celebration of sensuality and its extensive dream sequences. In contrast to that work, however, the romantic idyll developed in *Die Legende von Paul und Paula* serves less as a clarifying vision than as a practical alternative to official culture. There is no return to "normalcy" as represented by Paul's previous life with Ines. Instead, Paul's life becomes fundamentally altered. He abandons the conventional, materialistic values associated with his previous life in favor of the vitalistic ones Paula embodies. In other words, to the extent that Carow and Plenzdorf's film encouraged audiences to see their own lives differently in light of Paul and Paula's fictional experience, the guiding utopian vision being proffered was an explicitly private one, at best marginal to the goals and practices of state ideology.

This last aspect hardly escaped notice in the official reception of *Die Legende von Paul und Paula*. Although the project's production and approval process proceeded without significant problems,[35] the picture had the misfortune of being released at a time when the favorable cultural political climate of the early seventies was already deteriorating. According to Carow, controversy began after Harry Tisch, then Party district leader in Rostock, saw the still unreleased film. His complaints ultimately led Honecker to view the film personally at the Cosmos Movie Theater in Berlin the morning before its scheduled opening there on April 29, 1973.[36] Although the film's distribution proceeded normally, its reception in the official press was decidedly cool. Critical reviews appeared both in *Neues Deutschland* and in the youth organization organ, *Junge Welt*. The GDR's most politically authoritative movie critic, Horst Knietzsch, complained that much in the film "was not quite fully fermented." Particularly troubling from Knietzsch's perspective was the figure of Paul, which according to him lacked "internal logic" and was dramatically bland. In contrast, the reviewer allowed, Paula was a "lovable and sympathetic young woman," but even her "inner richness" was sometimes overshadowed by "biological interests."[37]

Ironically, official ambivalence toward the film probably only contributed to its popular success. Honecker's unusual visit to the Cosmos Movie Theater before the film's premiere did not escape notice in the capital, whose denizens were intrigued by the unusual occurrence. Carow reports being surprised to find the cinema already packed when he arrived for the opening. While half of the audience, consisting of officials with invitations from the Cultural Ministry, sat through the viewing stone-faced, the rest of the crowd, aware of the controversy, responded with enthusiasm. Clearly in terms of overall attendance, the picture was a great popular success. More than 1.84 million tickets were sold, an unusually high figure for a film set in the GDR that did not benefit from an organized attendance drive. Indeed, the only East German film that drew a larger audience in 1973 was an entertainment film, one of a series of highly popular DEFA westerns, titled *Apachen* (Apaches, Gottfried Kolditz, 1973).[38]

Existing evidence suggests that audience members on the whole were positively disposed toward *Die Legende von Paula*. Even before the official premiere, Carow, Plenzdorf, Domröse, and other artists took the picture on tour, showing it to approximately ten test audiences. Judging from the "focus groups" selected, which included units of the National People's Army, one purpose of the tour for some studio officials may well have been to find a justification for preventing the picture's release. Be that as it may, the results hardly suited this purpose. Even though officials in charge of two special training classes, one for union officials and another for high-ranking SED officials, insisted that their charges had rejected the film,[39] a studio report suggests otherwise. Its author could hardly hide a note of triumph: "The film pleases the public. . . . Issues were related with which everyone is familiar. . . . In every group, the discussion [suggested] that it is important that the public respect and be drawn to our DEFA productions without our making artistic and political compromises. [*Die Legende von Paul und Paula*] was named several times as an example of how this could be accomplished." The report went on to say that viewers were quite upset with the film's rejection by the official press, noting that various discussion groups had expressed "incredulity and opposition" to reviews in *Neues Deutschland* and elsewhere.[40]

If a small sampling of opinions from the Dresden area is at all typical, theatergoers who saw the picture were also generally enthusiastic. An electrical engineer reported, "I am honestly amazed that DEFA has produced such a down-to-earth, realistic, and nevertheless optimistic film without pathos. I would never have expected this from DEFA."[41] A thirty-three-year-old office worker was of a similar opinion: "The film is really classy. It is just the right thing for young people and expresses the reality of life in our time."[42] A nineteen-year-old student agreed. She noted, "The film addressed me personally very directly. It shows real problems. . . . I would desire more such realistic depiction in film."[43] A twenty-six-year-old laboratory worker remarked that the film's creators "really gave their imagination a free hand."[44] According to one doctor, "The film is made in a modern fashion and very expressive. . . . It does not shy away from sharp points. I found it excellent."[45]

At the same time, several older viewers included in the sample had reservations about the film's relatively open treatment of sexuality and questioning of conventional morality. A fifty-nine-year-old weaver complained, "Despite the theater being full, the film surely did not please everyone. . . . This is not a picture that shows a good marriage to our younger people of marriageable age. There are enough problems in life; they should show something life-affirming."[46] A forty-five-year-old lathe-operator agreed with her: "The ending, the tragic conclusion of the film, really bothered me. Not enough, that unfortunate marriage situations . . . and unsatisfied longings . . . [and] the death of a small child [ruin] the film, but then the death of the young mother as well!"[47] Some younger viewers found the film overdone, too. A seventeen-year-old high school student, perhaps influenced by his teachers, opined, "I cannot imagine that a genuine affection, a true love, would take such a course as depicted in this film. Here, sexuality [is the main characteristic] of both female figures. Are such marriages really typical in our socialist GDR, are they a model for our young people?"[48]

Echoing the official press, disagreement among the audience members sampled tended to revolve around the film's social relevance. Curiously enough, some critical viewers far exceeded official reactions in their rejection of the film's explicit sexuality, suggesting that the picture touched a generational and cultural nerve as much as a political one. Though hardly radical in its sentiments, *Die Legende von Paul und Paula* certainly shared some of the countercultural flair of the late sixties and early seventies. Even if Paul is not a complete *Aussteigertyp*, or "drop-out"—like Paula's earlier paramour Colly—he clearly chooses sensual abandonment over discipline and self-realization and personal freedom within the private realm over convention.

In short, *Die Legende von Paul und Paula* more than perhaps any DEFA film of the day either struck a chord or got under the skin of East German moviegoers. Its popular reception suggested to filmmakers that the work had indeed found its intended audience, that the East German cinema had a natural constituency, which at least in this picture had recognized itself. Still, as was already apparent in the work's rocky official reception, this moment of seeming triumph for DEFA, like so many other ones in the history of East German cinema, was destined to be fleeting. As the next section briefly traces, the ideological accommodation reached between artists and functionaries around the notion of *Alltag* in the film industry was a fragile one. Even though the term's official currency would continue to increase over time, it offered at best a very limited solution to deep-seated political and structural problems.

DEFA'S INEXORABLE DECLINE

The early seventies were good years for the studio. As noted above, *Die Legende von Paul und Paula* was hardly the studio's only success story during this period. Several other pictures whose box office numbers were comparable included the comedy *Der Mann der nach der Oma kam*; *KLK an PTX—Die Rote Kapelle* (KLK to PTX—The Red Choir, Horst E. Brandt, 1971), a bombastic historical film about the famous German Communist resistance group during World War II; and a melodramatic "production" movie, *Reife Kirschen* (Ripe Cherries, Horst Seeman, 1972)—not to mention a whole slew of DEFA westerns featuring the popular entertainer Gojko Mitic.[49] Moreover, the documentary realist movement and works by individual directors like Egon Günther and Konrad Wolf spoke for the artistic vitality of East German cinema as well. Nevertheless, even such encouraging examples could not solve the fundamental structural crisis affecting the industry. Overall attendance continued to fall because of the onslaught of television. Between 1960 and 1970, the average number of annual cinema visits per person in the GDR declined by more than 60 percent from 13.8 to 5.4. By 1980, the figure had dipped further to 4.75 annual visits.[50] As recently as the early sixties, the cinema had unquestionably been a key media in East Germany. By the seventies, its influence was diminished and limited largely to a relatively small segment of the population. As was the case worldwide, East German film audiences now consisted predominately of teenagers and very young adults. By the end of the decade, 70 percent of all moviegoers in the GDR were between fourteen and twenty-five years of age.[51]

As if these trends were not troubling enough, DEFA had to struggle even to maintain its share of the declining filmgoing public. As in years past, the studio faced stiff competition from foreign films, particularly those imported from the West. During the early seventies, which were probably well-above-average years for DEFA, the studio captured at best a quarter of its own domestic market,[52] and even this percentage was likely inflated because of built-in biases toward films from socialist countries in the collection of statistical data. Moreover, even though individual *Alltag* films achieved impressive attendance figures, the vast majority of DEFA films, as was the case with motion pictures worldwide, continued to flop, some selling fewer than 100,000 tickets during their first year of release.[53] Many DEFA films were simply poorly conceived. Filmmakers and management alike continued to complain about the paucity of high-quality scripts.[54] The relative indifference toward attendance as a criterion of success among some of the studio's most talented young filmmakers did not help matters, either. The documentary realist films of the early seventies attracted at best a few hundred thousand viewers each. In contrast, some of the studio's better-conceived entertainment films, such as Oehme's *Der Mann der nach der Oma kam*, still surpassed 2 million during the first year of release.

Finally, the improved cultural-political climate of the early seventies was destined to be short-lived. By mid-decade, the political situation in the film industry was once again approaching bottom. In particular, several *Alltag* projects encountered problems. Siegfried Kühn's *Das zweite Leben des Georg Friedrich Wilhelm Platow* (The Second Life of Georg Friedrich Wilhelm Platow, 1973) was a comedy about a worker who impersonates his son so that he may take part in a training course and learn about new technology that threatens to make his railroad job superfluous. Given the grotesque premise and the depiction of the main protagonist as a disoriented, often unintelligible old man, the work clearly questioned both the desirability and reality of social progress in the GDR. Another case of official intransigence was the controversy surrounding Ralf Kirsten's *Eine Pyramide für mich* (A Pyramid of My Own, 1975). Concerning a prominent middle-aged comrade who decides to revisit the remote town where he served as a Communist activist after the war, this picture's message was hardly subversive. Despite having to confront unpleasant memories suggesting youthful political overzealousness, the protagonist makes life choices that are shown to be vindicated in the end.[55]

Equally troubling to filmmakers was the rejection on ideological grounds of several projects involving the adaptation of recent works of literature by prominent GDR authors, including Günter de Bruyn, Karl-Heinz Jakobs, Brigitte Reimann, and Alfred Wellm. Another disappointment was the curtailed export of Egon Günther's *Die Schlüssel*, a film whose great artistic accomplishment might have helped DEFA's perpetually sagging international reputation. Although the picture's reception within the film industry was enthusiastic,[56] it offended the sensibilities of Polish officials, who claimed that the work showed their country in an unfavorable light. Particularly objectionable were images of a Catholic processional featuring Stefan Cardinal Wyszyński, the portrayal of inefficient Polish officials, and at least one scene suggesting popular apathy toward the official commemoration of the recent past.[57] By 1975, these and similar setbacks had led many filmmakers to conclude, "A climate is developing in which the willingness to take risks is diminishing [while] self-censorship increases."[58] Adding further urgency to this complaint was evidence that viewership of new DEFA films, after some improvement early in the decade, was once again falling.[59]

Still, even if the cinematic revival and improved political circumstances of the early seventies lasted only briefly, one result was apparent: *Alltag* was now the dominant concept informing the cinematic depiction of East Germany. Although artists had been the first to embrace the notion, officials were not far behind. One indication of *Alltag*'s growing currency among the latter group was an article from 1975 that appeared in *Einheit*, the Party's most important journal devoted to ideological questions. Titled "Everyday and the Epochal in DEFA Motion Pictures," the piece was written by Rudolf Jürschik, then a professor at the Party's Political Training School. The piece took issue with the argument that many recent films, despite "greater closeness to reality," lacked what he called "the breath of greatness" (*der grosse Atem*), or a sense of being infused with the spirit of socialism. Quoting Honecker's report to the Eighth SED Party Congress of 1972, Jürschik advanced arguments similar to those that documentary realists such as Gräf and Warneke had already been making for years: "The fact is not sufficiently recognized that important steps are being taken in DEFA films 'to discover in the everyday life of people socialism's great and world-transforming deeds,' something 'that is no easy task.' . . . The better, the more exact and deeply we show and make visible these changes in the everyday life of people . . . the more [audiences] will understand our epoch."[60]

Jürschik vigorously contested the notion that some recent films, even if their themes were of a more personal and intimate nature, were not politically significant. Ethical questions concerning the discovery of an individual's conscious attitude toward life were clearly of collective interest.[61] Jürschik also defended DEFA films, such as Konrad Wolf's *Der nackte Mann auf dem Sportsplatz* (The Naked Man on the Playing Field, 1975), whose box office results were disappointing, as attendance figures were not the best measure of a picture's success at bringing to light the processes of individual and political growth.[62]

In many ways, the publication of Jürschik's article was too little, too late. By 1975, the first bloom was already off *Alltag*, and artists were rapidly losing any illusions they might have had initially about Honecker's new cultural policy. Moreover, Jürschik's viewpoint was never universally shared within the Party. For example, Jürschik's boss, the rector of the Party's Political Training School, Hanna Wolf, was furious with the editors of *Einheit* for publishing his article.[63] Even so, Jürschik's article was indicative of DEFA's general direction in the years to come. Within two years, a new managerial team would take over the studio, led by Hans Mäde, a very agile cultural politician and an accomplished theatrical director. One sign of Mäde's intention to rule the studio in an enlightened fashion was the naming of Jürschik as DEFA's chief dramaturge. Nevertheless, by the early eighties, at least two leading directors, Frank Beyer and Egon Günther, were working primarily in the West. Significantly, an increasing number of DEFA's artistically ambitious works concerned historical themes—the depiction of the socialist present was once again showing signs of routinization. Tracing DEFA's last decade and a half of decline, political estrangement, and artistic frustration, however, will be left for the epilogue of this study. Of more immediate urgency is the topic of this chapter's final section: the general significance of *Alltag*'s cinematic emergence in the broader context of East German history.

ALLTAG IN CONTEXT

Critics have often been quick to dismiss DEFA films as politically compromised works that were out of touch with the basic realities of life under socialism. In contrast, this study suggests that the East German cinema as a socially self-reflective medium was not a complete failure. Not only were DEFA pictures participants in a civic culture specific to the GDR, but they remain important artifacts of that society's evolution. In this vein, the emergence of *Alltag* in the East German cinema represented a dramatic result. Throughout the fifties and beyond, the Party sought films that affirmed the GDR as a bold new social order rapidly advancing toward the future; however, beginning in the late sixties, many DEFA pictures set in the present tended to achieve the exact opposite. They presented East Germany as an essentially ordinary place. On the whole, directors became less interested in dramatizing the march of history than in capturing everyday realities. Several questions are useful for fully understanding the significance of this development. First, what does *Alltag*'s growing currency imply about the changing self-definition and sensibilities of the East German state? Second, how great might *Alltag*'s popular resonance have been? Finally, to what degree did it offer a viable alternative for constructing East German identity?

The rise of *Alltag* as a representational strategy clearly occurred in the context of changing state policy. As scholarship has long recognized, Honecker's ascent to power in the early seventies was accompanied by a clear de-emphasis of utopian goals in official ideology.[64] One area where the ideological shift under Honecker became obvious was the economy. Unlike his predecessor, Ulbricht, the new first secretary did not attempt to meddle with the basic structure of the GDR's hierarchically organized demand economy. There was little talk in the early seventies of decentralizing management, let alone greater internal Party democracy, as had been the case with the New Economic System a decade earlier. Nevertheless, if the regime was not willing to reconsider the question of means, it was happy to revisit that of goals. Thus, instead of emphasizing building toward the future through industrial investment, state planners now paid increasing attention to meeting the immediate needs of household consumers. One emblem of the new policy was the greater availability of both bananas and women's brassieres imported from the West. Another way in which the economic policy change affected ordinary East Germans was in the very conceptualization of consumerism. Under Ulbricht, product design exhibited an almost puritanical streak emphasizing the meeting of more or less uniform needs with sturdy, practical goods meant to last a lifetime. In contrast, a more Western aesthetic of provision characterized the later GDR. At least in theory, the state approached consumption as a means of individual expression, requiring a rich assortment of products that would allow for personal choice and a variety of lifestyles.[65]

Commensurate with this change in consumer policy was a relaxation of the regime's exaggerated moral and personal standards under Honecker. One of the most important examples here was the official attitude toward popular music. As with film, the Eleventh Plenum of December 1965 brought to an end a period of experimentation in official music policy. The regime called an abrupt halt to efforts by the state youth organization, the FDJ, to co-opt the beat movement emanating from Britain into official culture. Perturbed by the role such music had played in the Prague Spring of 1968, Party leaders continued condemning rock as a decadent capitalist manifestation pernicious to socialism. Even so, many lower-level entertainment industry officials were sufficiently prescient to recognize that accommodation with the cultural ferment of the sixties was inevitable. Moreover, the irrepressible nature of the blossoming rock music scene in the GDR and other socialist states not only forced the issue but also seemed to offer a possible alternative to Western imports.[66] As early as 1969, East German radio stations thus began cautiously to invite local talent into broadcast studios. Soon, leading bands were signing record contracts and appearing on television. Further measures included new laws designed to regulate amateur and semiprofessional groups and ensure for them adequate entertainment facilities such as discotheques. An important emblem of the regime's new attitude was the Tenth World Festival organized by the FDJ during the summer of 1973. This featured approximately 200 rock bands from the GDR and elsewhere in the East Bloc, as well as a smattering of politically acceptable performers from the

West. Clearly, a principal motive for the regime's change of heart with regard to rock music was to gain a measure of control over it. Some elements of the Party also continued to resist the genre, which itself always retained a certain potential as a medium of political and social protest.[67] Still, the growing acceptance of rock in the early seventies was a development of profound significance for the GDR's official culture.

Another area where public standards underwent dramatic revision in the GDR in the course of the sixties and seventies was the realm of sexual morality and the family. Before World War II, German Communists had always tried to distinguish themselves from other political parties through their unambiguous advocacy of equal rights for women and progressive social policies, including the toleration of abortion and homosexuality. Once the SED was in power, however, its record on these issues was mixed at best. The new regime not only encouraged women to enter the workforce but guaranteed them at least on paper equal professional opportunity. Even so, abortion remained illegal, and gays and lesbians continued to face discrimination and harassment, although their legal situation improved on paper after 1957.[68] Indeed, official culture throughout the fifties and well into the sixties remained extremely prudish and conventional. The Party demanded great personal discipline from both the populace and its own members. Consequently, it frowned upon all but the most regulated expressions of human sexuality. Perhaps the most notorious example of the SED's sometimes comical zeal in enforcing mundane personal standards was Ulbricht's "Ten Commandments of Socialist Life," which explicitly encouraged all good comrades to lead good, clean lives (see Chapter 3).

In contrast, by the 1970s, official attitudes about sexuality and gender issues were in some respects almost the reverse of those of twenty years earlier. The regime placed remarkably few hurdles in the way of the sexual revolution's arrival in the GDR, at least for heterosexuals. The pill was introduced in 1968, and abortion was legalized in 1972. While pornography and eroticism remained taboo, nudity itself gradually became fairly routine in state-controlled media.[69] Certainly, *Die Legende von Paul und Paula*, although an early example, was hardly the last DEFA production to feature moderately explicit love scenes. At the same time, without abandoning its long-standing rhetorical commitment to encouraging workplace equality, the state instituted a series of unabashedly natalist policies. These included assigning priority in receiving housing to growing households and providing liberal child-care opportunities. The regime even offered financial loans to families that were similar to those available during the Third Reich, repayment of which could be *abgekindert*—or reduced by having children.[70] Single parents could qualify for many of the same advantages and in some respects even received preferential treatment. As Ina Merkel has noted, such measures "paradoxically had two unexpected and contradictory effects. They affirmed the traditional division of sexual roles and had simultaneously the social acceptance of single mothers as a historically unprecedented consequence."[71]

These policies also contributed to attitudes about sexual equality in the GDR that were quite at variance with those prevalent in the Federal Republic. Much to the later bafflement of Western feminists, East German women seem to have been remarkably accepting of the double burden of career and family associated with the 90 percent female participation in the labor force during the later GDR. Similarly, few voices objected to the professional "glass ceiling" that undoubtedly existed for women (see Chapter 4). On the contrary, many women, while regarding gender equality more or less as a given in their society, tended to assign greater importance to their private lives than their careers. Again paradoxically, although female identity seems to have been more closely tied to employment in the East, GDR women cherished values that were less individualistic and more family-oriented than their counterparts in the Federal Republic. Apparently, Eastern women overlooked the discrepancy between the regime's emancipatory rhetoric and the persistence of traditional gender roles because they valued the camaraderie of the workplace over professional advancement. For them, working was less an opportunity to prove their equality by competing with men than an important socialization sphere.[72] Presumably as well, professional success simply did not carry with it in the GDR by the seventies the prestige it did in the West. More generally, developments in family policy and gender relations, like those in economic and consumer policy, were consistent with the general devaluation of the public realm in the later GDR, a phenomenon that this study has argued found its filmic expression in the shift from *Gegenwart* to *Alltag*, or from an image of a society mobilizing toward a common future to one focused on immediate, individual concerns.

Defining the cinema's contribution to these changes touches on a number of issues. The GDR, despite the totalitarian pretensions of the regime, was clearly a complex society consisting of a multiplicity of communicative forums. Not only did various audiences exist for different media forms from both the East and the West, but East Germans came together in different social settings, ranging from the workplace, the classroom, and the interactions of daily life to officially sponsored activities and celebrations. Among these, the cinema represented only one arena for symbolically contesting questions large and small relevant to life under socialism. Still, the case of film is suggestive. At least with regard to the depiction of East German society, cinematic developments seem to have anticipated political ones. As this study has endeavored to show, the articulation of *Alltag* in the East German cinema was many years in the making. Its antecedents extend back at least to the "Berlin films" of the late fifties, most notably Gerhard Klein and Wolfgang Kohlhaase's *Berlin— Ecke Schönhauser* (see Chapter 2). Moreover, as the documentary realist pictures, whose production began already in the late sixties, indicated, tolerance for *Alltag* films began to grow even before the ideological shift associated with Honecker's ascent to power in 1971 was fully articulated. Together, these factors suggest that the cinema's role in politics was not exclusively reactive. At the very least, filmmakers had considerable influence on official policy as it affected their own area of expertise. They did not so much carry out political directives as interpret them. Equally important, film did not merely reflect or accompany changes in official culture and civic discourse; it helped to effect their continuing evolution as well.

Two sets of mechanisms are useful for understanding film's contribution to the changing parameters of GDR society. The first of these is specific to the medium. Filmmakers and other artists were always pushing the envelope of permissible expression. In many cases, this occurred less with the aim of being politically controversial than out of a simple desire to make effective films. In attempting to fulfill the regime's expectations, even the most loyal artists had to take into consideration the limits and the possibilities of the medium. Consciously or not, they were in constant dialogue with German cultural and cinematic traditions. In addition, film's status as a popular medium forced filmmakers to confront evolving tastes and changing cultural trends. Since East Germany's media landscape was never hermetically sealed off, DEFA was in direct competition with Western television as well as with movies imported from the Federal Republic and elsewhere by the state's own official film distributor. In this way, the East German cinema derived a measure of autonomy. However much officials might have desired pictures that would glorify the new order, these also had to be effective. Works that viewers mistrusted or did not want to see were of little political use.

The second set of mechanisms that is useful in explaining cinema's place in East German society and history derives from the medium's participation in what has been called the GDR's "imminent" or officially inherent public sphere. However tightly controlled, "choreographed," or "directed" this discursive space might have been, it still retained a communicative function. Like any state with democratic pretensions, the GDR sought to legitimize itself through the court of public opinion, even if the latter was clearly not autonomous. At the same time, the state's attempt to control virtually all aspects of public expression caused both art and entertainment to assume greater political significance than they traditionally had in Western societies.[73] Similarly, the regulated nature of the socialist public sphere led to a situation in which any innovation in content or form in a medium like film could function as a political sign of the regime's intent, which at the time was referred to as art's *Signalwerkung*, or signaling function. For example, if a previously taboo issue could be broached in a film, then its discussion was usually permissible in other forums. For these reasons, it is often argued that art in the GDR sometimes functioned as an *Ersatzöffentlichkeit*—or "replacement" public sphere—by providing an opportunity for more genuine social communication otherwise unavailable (see the Introduction).

The degree to which DEFA was ever capable of offering its viewers much of a replacement for genuine public exchange is questionable. Clearly, filmmaking's highly technical and capital-intensive nature makes it a poor vehicle for two-way communication under even the best of circumstances. Nevertheless, as the case of *Die Legende von Paul und Paula* makes clear, individual films were capable not only of finding large audiences but also of provoking strong reactions and of stimulating discussion. Equally important, developments in the cinema complemented and reinforced those in other areas of GDR society. On an institutional plane, the studio, far from being a passive object of official policy, was a product of constant political negotiation. As earlier chapters have shown, management fought to maintain a measure of autonomy against central agencies like the HV Film. In addition, artists and other constituencies in the studio could be quite vociferous, particularly where their own direct interests were concerned. On a representational level, the depiction of the East German present evolved in response to international cultural trends and to impulses emanating from GDR society. More broadly, I would argue that official tolerance for *Alltag* films and similar works was indicative of a new accommodation between East Germans and their state, a compromise that reflected years of wrangling and *Kleinkrieg* in a broad variety of social and cultural forums. Other factors, such as growing international recognition of the GDR, were also clearly preconditions for the ideological shift under Honecker, but these alone do not explain the specifics of how GDR society and culture evolved.

Although historical research on East German society is still a developing field, one finding that has emerged is that the GDR was a highly contested place. Stephan Wolle and Armin Mitte have established that the popular response to grand political events such as the June 17 uprising of 1953, the building of the Berlin Wall in 1961, and the 1968 suppression of the Prague Spring was far deeper and widespread than previously suspected. Using the archives of the State Security Ministry, these two historians have documented hundreds of hitherto unknown examples of political protest, including labor walk-outs, leafleting, and dramatic acts of individual defiance.[74] At the same time, recent research has also considered how East Germans coped with the more mundane issues of daily living. For example, Peter Hübner has shown that strikes and work slow-downs concerning working conditions and wages were almost routine occurrences. In contrast to Mitter and Wolle, he finds that these typically led to attempts to mollify the protesters internally at the factory level through concessions and negotiations. Only after such local efforts failed did workplace confrontations tend to become overtly politicized. In addition, the work of other scholars, including Ina Merkel, Michael Rauhut, and Uta Poiger, suggests that East Germans were highly self-conscious and deliberate cultural consumers. Just as in the West, one's choice in music, hairstyle, or fashion was a means of defining an individual lifestyle that often had a political resonance as well. Yet another avenue that ordinary individuals took to express discontent was a very direct and simple one: complaint letters typically concerning the availability or quality of goods and services sent to socialist enterprises and government agencies. Recent research indicates that the volume of these was extremely large and carefully monitored by officials, thus suggesting that even ordinary problems could become a source of considerable pressure for the regime.[75]

The issue of the East German cinema's resonance remains. Although socialism's ultimate failure might suggest that state-supported media such as film had little influence on ordinary citizens, much evidence speaks to the contrary. Even if the SED failed to create a homogenous society congruent with its ideology, forty years of socialism left a lasting impression on its subjects. More than a decade after unification, cultural differences between the "old" Federal Republic and its "new" states remain a topic of great interest. Sociological research and polling data suggest that a divide persists in attitudes and values among the Germans. According to a 1995 survey published in the leading news magazine *Der Spiegel*, while 83 percent of East Germans were supportive of unification, 67 percent of them believed that the *Mauer im Kopf*, or mental wall, was growing higher between East and West.[76] Other studies have purported to establish differences in areas as diverse as personal goals and priorities, social skills, the importance assigned to family life, understanding of recent history, and even sexual performance.[77] Equally significant is the phenomenon of *Ostalgie,* or nostalgia for the GDR. This has taken the form of clubs for Trabant automobile owners, renewed interest in East German rock and roll, loyalty to surviving GDR brand names—so-called *Ostprodukte* such as Spee laundry detergent and Florena soap—and even the persistence of such secular rituals as the *Jugendweihe,* the socialist ersatz confirmation. Indeed, the popular response to a museum specifically dedicated to the preservation of East Germany's material culture has been overwhelming. In 1997, the Dokumentationszentrum Alltagskultur der DDR in Eisenhüttenstadt reported the donation of over 35,000 household and similar items with more arriving daily.[78]

DEFA, or its legacy, has benefited as well from this renewed popular interest in the East German quotidian. Although new DEFA films fared miserably in the period immediately following unification and the studio disbanded, interest in older films revived during the mid-nineties as the culture divide between East and West reasserted itself. DEFA entertainment films, especially those featuring popular stars such as Rolf Herricht, Manfred Krug, or Gojko Mitic, became a mainstay of weekly programming by the two main public television stations in the Federal Republic's "new" provinces, MDR and ORB, with individual pictures garnering as much as 13 percent of the local evening viewership.[79] In addition, DEFA classics have been featured at various Berlin revival theaters. A few pictures, including *Die Legende von Paul und Paula* and *Spur der Steine,* even have something of a cult following among some young Berliners, being favorites at open-air summer viewings and cultural clubs in the eastern half of the city.[80] Thus DEFA, far from fading from popular consciousness in contemporary Germany, seems to be experiencing a second life as a key element of a well-entrenched regional culture.

The interpretation of such examples of belated enthusiasm for GDR life is open to continuing debate in contemporary Germany. Whereas some interpret them as proof of unconquerable division and a genuine sense of East German identity, others are quick to dismiss them as the petulant reaction of a disaffected minority, destined to fade as time passes. More than one commentator has also argued that the conditions for the relative strength of East German identity today arose ironically only after the Wall's fall. Disappointed economic expectations, a feeling of second-class citizenship, and the perception of condescension on the part of supposedly well-meaning Westerners have perhaps accomplished more than four decades of Communist rule.

The appeal of what this study has described as *Alltag* identity is perhaps not that surprising. The type of self-understanding evident in many

East German films and other cultural production from the seventies on-
ward resonates strongly with a traditional sense of *Heimat* or local identity in German culture.[81] This aspect of East German society during the
seventies even impressed the Federal Republic's first official representative to the GDR, Günter Gaus. In his famous characterization of the GDR
as a *Nischengesellschaft*, or society of niches, the diplomat, journalist,
and television personality argued that East Germans responded to the
repressive nature of public life by withdrawing into private spheres, or
"niches," defined primarily by family, friends, hobbies, and similar pre-
occupations. Significantly, elements of traditional *Volkskultur* and *Gemüt-
lichkeit*, or a relaxed and easy sociability, figured prominently in Gaus's
description of these:

> The middle-German [that is, East German] niches are, just like every-
> place else, very diverse in their manifestations. They include . . . plea-
> sure in owning an automobile [with] a Kewpi doll hanging from the
> rearview mirror, self-installed loudspeakers, [and] occasionally em-
> broidered pillows. . . . Or, the niches consist of regular absorption in
> *Hausmusik* [amateur performances of music], held in accordance with
> such a consistent ritual—a dry Hungarian white wine and some sand-
> wiches to start off—that a guest would think that they have been play-
> ing that way for thirty years. The great favorite among the privileged
> niches is the *Schrebergarten*[82] [garden plot], if at all possible with a
> little cottage. At harvest time, the paths in the garden colonies—named
> for old yearnings: "At Home," "Harmony," "Land of Sun"—become pre-
> ferred promenades for those fellow individuals who do not have gar-
> dens. Flowers, fruit, vegetables are displayed in buckets and baskets
> and are sold privately.[83]

Gaus is obviously not an unproblematic source, and other commentators
have objected that his open sentimentality contributed to a rose-colored
vision of the GDR.[84] Indeed, in another passage, he describes experiencing a "tug of memory" (*Erinnerungsschlag*) while driving through the
East, having discovered there a "'German'-landscape," no longer extant
in the West but familiar to him from his prewar childhood. Still, the
currency that Gaus's neologism *Nischengesellschaft* quickly gained among
observers in both Germanies suggests that his description of the GDR as a
society where an old-fashioned sensibility had survived (or perhaps more
accurately had been "reinvented") contained a kernel of truth.

The appeal of *Alltag* among intellectuals was hardly an exclusively East
German phenomenon during the postwar period; the notion was also
very important in West German film circles during the seventies and

eighties. Directors such as Alexander Kluge and Edgar Reitz consciously thematized the distance between quotidian experience and transcendent political events in such films as *Die Patriotin* (The Woman Patriot, Alexander Kluge, 1979) and the series *Heimat* (Homeland, Edgar Reitz, 1984). Professional historiography in the Federal Republic also saw the rise of *Alltagsgeschichte*, a research direction that insisted that the past could be best grasped through the analysis of ordinary lives.[85] More generally, the importance that *Alltag* as a notion assumed in Germany was consistent with a shift among the left in many Western societies after the fiasco of the 1968 student revolts. Disappointment with transcendent political philosophies found expression in the abandonment among activists of broad revolutionary goals in favor of practical objectives, often rooted in daily life, such as those associated with the feminist and environmental movements.

In the context of the East Bloc, a certain parallel is further perceptible between the alternative sense of East German identity that found articulation in film and other art forms during the seventies and eighties and the growing importance of civil society as a political concept among oppositional forces in such countries as Czechoslovakia and Poland during the same period.[86] Even if this intellectual process may not have advanced as far in East Germany as it did elsewhere, the emergence of a competing conceptualization of GDR society should not be overlooked. If processes of communication and identity are inextricably linked, then the positing of an East German identity distinct from that implicit in official ideology was an essential prerequisite for advancing political demands. Many East German opposition figures, even those who had never stood close to the regime, remained committed to a separate East German state during and even after the *Wende*. Arguably, the tragedy for such leaders was that yet a third identity offering very real material and social advantages stood open for their envisioned constituencies. Thus the majority of East Germans, instead of entrusting themselves to an uncertain future under the banner of a reinvented state that in its previous incarnation had never served them well, chose what seemed the far safer route of unification.

These ruminations aside, the case of the GDR cinema indicates that the nagging persistence of a distinct sense of self and society in eastern Germany is premised on a complex history. For better or for worse, the cinema through its representation of the GDR as a specific place participated in the evolution of a civic discourse unique to that society. Films helped articulate the equivalent of what Stuart Hall describes as a nation: "a symbolic formation—'a system of representation' . . . with whose meanings [ordinary individuals] could identify and which, through this imaginary identification, constituted its citizens as subjects."[87] Many East Germans may have only half-heartedly taken part in the identification process that Hall describes here—most probably found greater satisfaction in private pursuits or in Western media outlets—but they could hardly have avoided the influence of state symbols and narratives. Such elements of official discourse were not only prevalent in the media but also instrumental in the very conceptualization of such key areas of human interaction as the workplace and the classroom. Moreover, the rise of *Alltag* in film when seen in its social context suggests that ordinary citizens in turn did affect the evolution of the East German state. Through varied forms of contestation occurring in diverse social arenas, they forced the regime to revise its utopian goals and ultimately to sanction a less restrictive, more accommodating variant of GDR identity that was premised less on belief in some bold tomorrow than on feeling at one with the specific texture of everyday life. That some erstwhile East Germans responded to the economic and social stresses of unification by seeking comfort in the remnants of their former selves is therefore not surprising. Their pattern of seeking protection against the hostile forces of epochal change in familiar, everyday comforts follows established precedent.

Conclusion

The story of GDR film is largely one of frustration and disappointment. DEFA certainly never fulfilled its original ambition of achieving a radically new progressive cinema. The success of filmmakers in meeting more modest goals such as earning the respect of their peers internationally or providing audiences at home with entertaining genre films was spotty. Still, there was one area where the studio arguably accomplished its mission as a state-sponsored cultural institution. For better or for worse, DEFA pictures participated in the making of East Germany. Shaped by political prerogatives, artistic ambitions, and cinematic traditions, they remain important artifacts of that process.

This study has concentrated on one of the most vexing problems filmmakers faced during DEFA's long history: the depiction of the GDR itself. Despite the tremendous official importance assigned to this task, early attempts to dramatize the construction of the new order through film tended to be failures. Artists and cultural politicians alike decried the "schematicism" of works that conveyed political messages in a crude, unconvincing fashion. Both groups desired films that would present an image of East German society that, while confirming the socialist project, would seem credible and "authentic." Yet the GDR's status during the 1950s was too tenuous to provide much creative leeway. Germany's permanent division still seemed inconceivable to many; moreover, the regime was under duress because of the massive emigration to the West and the Soviet Union's desire to keep the German question alive geopolitically. Thus, for many years, the studio's most successful pictures concerned earlier Communist struggles against capitalism and Nazism. Artists were on much surer ground in this narrative space, since the wellspring of socialism's legitimacy in the GDR lay in the myth of "antifascist" resistance.

A distinct image of East Germany gradually emerged in the GDR cinema, but it was not the one that the regime had originally sought. Instead of a heroic, future-oriented vision of socialism, a largely static society came into focus. This result occurred in the context of a wider shift within the East German civic imaginary between what I call *Gegenwart* and *Alltag* identity. From the time of the GDR's founding, the regime had called upon artists to address the *Gegenwart*, or the present, as a mediator between past and future, yet the uniform, progressive temporal advance adhering in this notion contained intractable paradoxes for artists. If the goal of the new order was greater freedom, why then was discipline and submission to Party authority so necessary for achieving it? Moreover, how was it possible to depict a society as simultaneously dynamic and subject to an authority that was unimpeachable and thus timeless? The articulation of properties associated with *Alltag*, or everydayness, occurred in film as well as in other media both as a means of resistance and as an avenue of accommodation with the demands of *Gegenwart* identity. Positing the existence of a preexisting, essentially timeless community satisfied the regime's need for legitimacy while also providing refuge from the Party's forced march toward the future.

While the term *Alltag* first became a rallying cry among East German artists and intellectuals in the early 1970s, this result was the culmination of a long process. Most generally, the formation of East German *Alltag* identity can be linked to the failure of efforts to reform socialism in the wake of Khrushchev's denunciation of Stalin at the Twentieth CPSU Congress in 1956. In the years following this event, film and other artistic media were very much involved in contesting the direction of East Bloc countries. In East Germany, developments in both the cultural realm and politics came to a head with the Eleventh Plenum of the SED Central Committee in December 1965. At this meeting, the regime signaled the end of reforms in areas ranging from economic planning to social policy by roundly attacking artists. This experience hastened artists' disillusionment and the development of an alternative sense of what it meant to belong to their society, one less dependent on history's progressive fulfillment.

This study is not the first to emphasize the gradual abandonment of utopian aspirations in the GDR and other socialist states between the 1950s and the 1970s. Scholars have long recognized the triumph of "real-existing socialism" over earlier, more aggressive ideological stances. My analysis enriches the understanding of this process in East Germany by proposing ways that its society developed and changed not only by political decree but also through processes of social communication involving cultural contestation and negotiation. Filmmakers and other artists may have belonged to a privileged elite, but they were not merely lackeys of the regime. Encouraged by official rhetoric to view themselves as co-creators of the new order, they felt qualified to voice an independent opinion. In particular, Kurt Maetzig's *Das Kaninchen bin ich* (The Rabbit Is Me, 1965) and other films criticized at the Eleventh Plenum provide excellent examples of works made with the express intention of spurring debate. Of even more fundamental importance, East German art helped shape what might be thought of as the GDR's civic imaginary, a symbolic field or set of discourses, which both the Communist regime and ordinary individuals used to define themselves and dispute issues. Even uncontroversial works contributed to the continuing development of this system of representation.

Approaching East German identity through film has proven advantageous in several ways. The cinema, due to its dual status as an industry and an art form, has special significance for studying a state that saw in the modern-day workplace a means of "producing" a new political consciousness and a brave new society. This circumstance also makes it possible to trace how discourses articulated in individual pictures informed the contestation of issues within the studio. Thus I interpret Slatan Dudow's *Verwirrung der Liebe* (Loved Confused, 1959) as a meditation on the regime's declaration of a "Cultural Revolution," which promised to infuse labor with the creative spontaneity of art. Even though actual relations between artists and workers at DEFA were in fact strained, the platform's language justified the formation of artistic work groups (KAGs), a reform that allowed filmmakers to gradually increase their influence within the studio in the years leading up to the Plenum. My analysis suggests a parallel between the discursive parameters of a Party inquest depicted in Frank Beyer's *Spur der Steine* (Trace of Stones, 1966) and the actual purge-like discussions under way at the studio in the aftermath of the Plenum.

The filmic idioms—character types, dramatic locations, emplotment, and so on—employed in DEFA pictures to define East German reality had resonances that extended far beyond the confines of the studio. Representations of gender and generational conflict could assume a striking range of political valences; moreover, this system also evolved over time as East German society itself changed. A good illustration of these points is Konrad Wolf and Christa Wolf's film *Der geteilte Himmel* (Divided Heaven, 1964). By focusing on the subjective experience of its young woman protagonist, the picture was able to thematize a politically explosive issue, the shock associated with the construction of the Berlin Wall. This strategy foreshadowed the partial eclipse of male workers as emblems of socialist society in later DEFA films, a result consistent with a reevaluation of the domestic sphere inherent in *Alltag*'s favoring of the everyday and the ordinary over the epochal. Similarly, my analysis shows how identifying with a preexisting society affected the representation of urban space. The existing city of tired facades and cramped apartments increasingly appeared as a haven against an oppressively rationalized official culture reflected in sterile urban renewal projects. The depiction of more flexible sexual and moral norms also became officially acceptable once the enforcement of strict discipline and uniformity were no longer required as part of a general mobilization of society toward the future.

Furthermore, the cinema facilitates an understanding of the GDR's place in twentieth-century German history. The circumstance of DEFA's inheriting its Babelsberg studios from UFA, the largest motion picture company in Nazi and Weimar Germany, symbolizes the dilemma faced by postwar socialist film. DEFA took pains to distance itself from the German commercial cinema of the past, which filmmakers believed was strongly implicated in the rise of fascism. Nevertheless, the East German studio remained dependent for many years on inherited personnel and infrastructure. Even the works of artists who took DEFA's mission to create a new progressive cinema seriously display strong lines of continuity with the past. In its depiction of urban life, Gerhard Klein and Wolfgang Kohlhaase's *Berlin—Ecke Schönhauser* (Berlin—Schönhauser Corner, 1957) stands clearly in the tradition of "Zille" films, a melodramatic subgenre popular during the twenties. A similar affinity with established idioms from German popular culture is also evident in the crusty *Berliner Witz* (Berlin humor) prominently featured in *Das Kaninchen bin ich* as well as in the self-ironizing melodrama of Heiner Carow and Ulrich Plenzdorf's *Die Legende von Paul und Paula* (The Legend of Paul and Paula, 1972).

Perhaps most surprising is the muted influence of avant-garde Weimar art traditions within the studio. The studio never entirely overcame the legacy of the "formalism" debates of the early fifties that saw the persecution of modernist art as antithetical to the needs of socialism. Even the later works of Slatan Dudow, an erstwhile Brecht collaborator who played a prominent role in prewar Communist filmmaking, were aesthetically staid. As in the GDR generally, conventional taste tended to win out over revolutionary pretensions at DEFA. As the zealous master of the state, rather than an opposition force, the Party was more at ease with *kleinbürgerlich* values emphasizing discipline and order than with the unruly energy of avant-garde art. For these reasons as well, it is not surprising that the studio responded to political crises such as the Twentieth CPSU Congress and the Eleventh Plenum by emphasizing the production of familiar commercial genres such as musicals and detective films. Similarly, the GDR never weaned itself from entertainment pictures imported from West Germany and the United States. Although officials and artists alike during the fifties condemned such works as reactionary kitsch, they did well at the box office and did not challenge political authority. Indeed, by the sixties and seventies, some of DEFA's most popular films, most notably a beloved series of westerns, unabashedly adapted commercial entertainment genres while justifying themselves ideologically with a few crude narrative inversions.

DEFA's tortured relationship with commercial film suggests a further advantage of the cinema as a vehicle for understanding the East German past. As a medium with its own traditions and history, film provides insight into how supranational cultural trends influenced the GDR. In broad perspective, the turn toward *Alltag* occurred in the context of a general shift away from grand narrative in the postwar European cinema that began with Italian neorealism. This movement appealed to socialist filmmakers because of its rejection of the illusionary qualities of commercial cinema. Among the most important DEFA films directly influenced by the Italian school were a series of "Berlin" films by Gerhard Klein and Wolfgang Kohlhaase. As in the case of *Berlin—Ecke Schönhauser*, the official reception of these works in the fifties was ambivalent. Cultural politicians were fascinated by the "authentic" image of the GDR achieved in these pictures but felt threatened by their implicit situating of the truth in surface reality rather than in history's dialectic, as stipulated by the precepts of socialist realism. Nevertheless, only a decade later, the first *Alltagsfilme*, whose creators similarly emphasized the indexical nature of film, encountered no ideological objections. This result was consistent with the gradual de-emphasis of utopian aspirations in the GDR's official culture, which I argue was precipitated by such phenomena as the rise of television, changes in popular entertainment, and the sexual revolution. No film better typifies the triumph of the quotidian in East German culture than *Die Legende von Paul und Paula*. Challenged but not banned by officials, this picture struck a chord with audiences in its depiction of life's most prosaic yet existential dimension—love, death, and procreation—as a refuge from the conformist pressures of socialist society.

DEFA's interaction with the world cinema is also of crucial importance for understanding developments leading up to the Eleventh Plenum. During this period, East German cinema like its counterparts elsewhere came under increasing pressure from television. Artists were able to use this circumstance, together with GDR film's declining international reputation, to pressure officials for leeway to experiment aesthetically. Christa

Wolf and Konrad Wolf's *Der geteilte Himmel* was clearly a response to one of the landmarks of the French nouvelle vague, Alain Resnais and Marguerite Duras's *Hiroshima mon amour* (1959). Other works mentioned in this study were in obvious dialogue with the great cinematic revival that occurred throughout the East Bloc during the late fifties and sixties. Similarly, *Spur der Steine* ingeniously commented on GDR's mythic self-understanding as a socialist society by ironically borrowing elements from a film genre closely associated with another society's exaggerated belief in its own destiny: Hollywood westerns. After the Plenum, DEFA would rarely again attempt such dramatic innovation. Still, as the wave of *Alltagsfilme* beginning in the late sixties suggests, the East German cinema continued to evolve.

Perhaps most significantly, studying East German film provides insight into the complex nature of communicative processes in the GDR. The contested and evolving nature of these—understood broadly to encompass not only overt political speech but also art, entertainment, fashion, consumer choice, and even sexuality—suggests that East Germans participated fully in many of the same cultural upheavals experienced by their Western cousins. Even a state as manifestly oppressive as the GDR could not ultimately stop its citizens from defining their own lives. On the contrary, official culture was under tremendous pressure to adapt to the ever changing realities of lived experience in the GDR.

By contributing to the evolution of the GDR's civic imaginary, DEFA helped to define the changing limits of permissible personal expression. Whereas many works reinforced the Party's image of a disciplined, harmonious society, others celebrated unconventional lives or acknowledged controversial social trends, including the sexual revolution and changes in international youth culture such as rock music. By articulating an alternative sense of GDR identity premised on identification with a recognizable quotidian rather than on an alliance with universal progress, filmmakers and other artists thus facilitated official culture's acceptance of changes already under way in GDR society. Indeed, the rise of *Alltag* as strategy for depicting the GDR—traceable to the Berlin films of the late fifties as well as to works such as Jürgen Böttcher and Klaus Poche's *Jahrgang '45* (Born in '45, 1966) banned in the wake of the Eleventh Plenum—anticipated the regime's ideological shift of the early seventies, which involved both a partial abandonment of utopian aspirations and a relaxation of social discipline. Thus film resonated with, and reinforced, broader processes of communication in the GDR that contributed to profound social and cultural change.

The emergence of *Alltag* as a means of accommodation with the relentless demands predicated by the regime's utopian aspirations may have represented only an imperfect response to a fundamentally repressive order. Even so, tracing this process in the cinema and elsewhere suggests the ways that East Germans participated in the wider outlines of late-twentieth-century history while facing dilemmas uniquely their own.

Epilogue. Arrested *Alltag*?

East German Film from the Biermann Affair to DEFA's Final Dissolution, 1976–1993

DEFA's 1946 founding preceded that of the East German state by more than three years, and the studio outlived its patron by an almost equal amount of time. Still, DEFA was closely associated with the socialist cause, and even ardent defenders recognized that its chances of survival in postunification Germany were slim. In addition, DEFA was economically behind the times. Not only were its technical facilities hopelessly out of date, but an integrated studio uniting all aspects of filmmaking under a single roof was an anachronism. In the West, such institutions had long given way to outsourcing and other methods of eliminating overhead costs. By the end of 1990, the studio had let go half of its 2,400 staff members. With state subsidies quickly evaporating, film production wound down, finally petering out altogether in 1993. By then, a French investment firm had already privatized and rechristened the production facilities as the Babelsberg Studios.

DEFA had reached the end of the road. The new head of the studio's successor, Volker Schlöndorff, envisioned a European filmmaking center of international standing, not some preserve for provincial cinema, be it East or West German.[1] Responding publicly to criticism from his East German colleague Günter Reisch, the famed West German filmmaker remarked, "The name DEFA is colorless and without smell. It belongs, just like the name UFA, to history."[2] Such comments could hardly have reassured Reisch, whose fear was precisely that Babelsberg's new owners did not appreciate the past. He foresaw a return to an escapist cinema of illusion or to the commercial traditions arguably implicit in the rise of fascism and symbolized by the prewar UFA studios, to which DEFA had once attempted to offer a progressive alternative.[3]

Alas, Schlöndorff's implicit comparison between UFA and DEFA was not far off the mark. Both stood for the cinemas of discredited German regimes. Many DEFA filmmakers shared Reisch's regret about their studio's passing, even some like Egon Günther, who had experienced professional frustration in the East and had left for the West many years earlier.[4] Even so, only the most nostalgic could have regarded their previous careers and lives without ambivalence. Thus, in unification's aftermath, many of the same filmmakers whose works had helped legitimize the GDR now turned their talents to revealing socialism's false utopian promises and oppressive nature. With the Wall gone, previously taboo issues became commonplace as artists struggled to find new relevance for their endangered film tradition. Such efforts were nevertheless insufficient to redeem the East German cinema. DEFA was only now catching up with other artistic media in the GDR, most notably literature and theater, where individual artists including Volker Braun, Christoph Hein, and Monika Maron had for years been airing repressed topics such as the police state or the horrendous ecological conditions. In addition, as East Germany became absorbed into the Federal Republic, guaranteed state distribution channels disappeared, and audiences turned elsewhere. DEFA's belated reckoning with East German socialism was too little, too late. Political and social change quickly outstripped attempts by filmmakers to address current events.

The roots of DEFA's malaise lay even deeper. Well before 1989, the studio's modest audience share had been slipping. Moreover, the function of official art, and the cinema in particular, had undergone significant revision in the GDR since the heyday of the studio's political involvement in the 1960s. East German socialism had grown increasingly conservative. Accordingly, art was no longer expected to fulfill a revolutionary role by contributing to the establishment of a radical new society but rather to provide diversion while celebrating an existing society. Thus, even if aesthetic standards in the late GDR were more flexible, state-supported art gradually had lost its importance as a forum for contesting political issues. In contrast to the situation in the fifties and sixties, younger artists avoided official sponsorship, and political dissidents began creating their own channels for communication outside official culture. Leading DEFA artists were only peripherally involved with the alternative politics of the eighties that led to the formation of the Citizens' Movement. Equally troubling, the studio had failed to renew its talent and to find fresh artistic directions. Whereas the *Alltagsfilme* of the late sixties and early seventies seemed to offer artists a fresh start, DEFA's final decade had no comparable aesthetic focal point. These years saw both institutional decline and rising bitterness among filmmakers, especially young, aspiring ones.

After briefly considering several post-*Wende* DEFA films that treated the East German past critically, this chapter surveys the studio's history from the mid-seventies to the late eighties. During this period, the changing parameters of cultural politics as well as economic and organizational factors specific to the film industry made it increasingly difficult for artists to produce even cautiously critical works about East German society. Established directors tended to turn to themes and motifs taken from the past rather than the present, often losing themselves in abstract issues related to the regime's Marxist eschatology. The dream of socially rooted and politically engaged socialist cinema, if not entirely dead, petered out in increasingly formulaic works that rarely found popular resonance. Attempts to define new aesthetic directions, if not absent, invariably faltered. Hopeful new voices fell silent after at most one or two films. Whether DEFA during this period succeeded even as a "provincial cinema"—addressing the parochial needs of a well-circumscribed society—is doubtful. The dynamic that had long fueled the East German cinema in previous eras—the questioning of the regime's utopian pretensions—had exhausted itself.

DEFA RESPONDS TO THE *WENDE*

Ironically, the best-received and most widely distributed DEFA films following the Wall's fall were once-banned productions, such as *Spur der Steine* (Trial of Stones, 1966) and *Das Kaninchen bin ich* (The Rabbit Is Me, 1965), associated with the Eleventh Plenum of 1965. Still, if newer DEFA films played no appreciable role in public discussion of the recent past in postunification Germany, it was not for a lack of effort. Roland Gräf's *Der Tangospieler* (The Tango Player, 1991) is perhaps the best known among the small flood of DEFA films released after the *Wende* dealing critically with the East German experience. Work on the script began in the spring of 1989. Had the film been completed before the fall of the Wall, it would have been a sensation. Based on a novel by Christoph Hein, the picture tells the story of a man who returns home after serving a prison term for a trumped-up political offense. Even though he resists *Stasi* efforts to enlist him as an informant, isolation and despair lead him to accept reintegration into an obviously hypocritical social order. He accepts a university position after the person who previously held it is arrested for protesting the Soviet invasion of Prague.

The state security agency is also featured prominently in a collaboration between Frank Beyer and Ulrich Plenzdorf, *Der Verdacht* (The Suspicion, 1991). Adapted from Volker Braun's novel *Unvollendete Geschichte*, the film concerns a pair of young lovers whose future life together is deliberately destroyed by the state. Similarly, Heiner Carow used both romantic love and the secret police in order to thematize Germany's postwar division in *Die Verfehlung* (The Missed Appointment, 1991). Carow's film portrays an East-West love affair between an older couple, which is denied a happy post-*Wende* resolution after the pressure of *Stasi* persecution leads one of the protagonists to commit a murder. Yet another notable example of *Vergangenheitsbewältigung*, or reckoning with the past, was Egon Günther's *Stein* (1991). The protagonist of this work is a famous actor who withdraws to a villa on the edge of Berlin after resigning from his career in protest of the 1968 invasion of Czechoslovakia. By focusing on how his insular existence then disintegrates in the political maelstrom of 1989, the picture raised larger questions about the legacy and place of art in East German society.

Critical as they were, these works were by prominent directors, whose careers owed much to DEFA. Particularly the films by Carow and Beyer drew on the same conventions of political melodrama common to numerous DEFA pictures. All four pictures tended to elicit sympathy for individual victims, arguably avoiding harder questions about socialism's fundamental failure. Indeed, one critic, Oskana Bulgakowa, complained that Gräf's adaptation of *Der Tangospieler* transformed the distanced "grotesqueness of the novel into a psychologically, milieu-motivated story: [the path from being] an initially innocent victim to a resigned collaborator." Far from condemning its protagonist, the film is "suffused with melancholy, nostalgia, verging on tearful self-pity." Thus, Bulgakowa insisted, Gräf was able to commence the project before the Wall fell because even "the [studio] chiefs did not expect anything earth-shattering." Like the director, "they believed in the reality and historical necessity of the Wall, the invasion [of Prague in 1968], of errors and loyalty" to the GDR.[5]

Implicit in Bulgakowa's argument is the suggestion that the realist style that DEFA directors such as Gräf once cultivated as a subtle vehicle for social and political criticism had become merely another prop for the regime. Certainly, DEFA films played a role in the invention and evolution of East German society. They had, in the words of the American literary critic David Bathrick, participated in the rewriting of the "master code" of East German civic discourse "from within the code itself."[6] To this extent, many directors may have been too much prisoners of their prior productions to accept the GDR's complete absurdity.

The anger of Bulgakowa's criticism also likely reflected her own status as a spokesperson for the self-styled "last" generation of DEFA filmmakers, who largely experienced frustration in their careers before the *Wende*. Indeed, members of this cohort were responsible for two pictures that among all of DEFA's final productions went furthest in brutally lambasting GDR society—works that were at the extreme fringes of, if not perhaps entirely beyond, Bathrick's code.

Jorg Förth's *Letztes aus der DaDaeR* (The Latest from the GDR, 1990) premiered on October 8, 1990, just days after the GDR's official end. One indication of this work's unsparingly critical attitude toward the role of GDR artists can be found in its protagonists, two vain, self-important, and, above all, self-pitying clowns. Played by the picture's screenwriters, the cabaret performers Steffen Mensching and Hans-Eckhardt Wenzel, the clowns wander through the GDR during the last months of its existence between the Wall's fall and unification. The result is an intriguing work that itself constitutes a surrealist document of a social order in dissolution. The various sites featured in the film stand for the utter bankruptcy of the social project and the emptiness of its utopian promise: a prison, the decrepit remains of the Buna Chemical Works, as well as a slaughterhouse. In one scene, the clowns stab each other into submission with medals and commendations awarded to them for their cultural contributions to the GDR as a crowd of elderly men applaud. In another sequence parodying sanctimonious intellectuals, Christoph Hein makes a cameo appearance as a garbageman who laments: "I feel the sadness that the Roman Patricians of the fourth century felt. I feel an unsaintly barbarism rising out of the ground. . . . I have always attempted to live in an ivory tower, but a sea of shit laps at its walls."

Similarly, Herwig Kipping's *Das Land hinter dem Regenbogen* (The Land over the Rainbow, 1992) was unforgiving in its satire of the GDR of the early fifties. Set in the village Stalina, the picture features a family whose exaggerated dysfunction stands for socialism's absurdity. While innocent children, representing the filmmakers' generation, amuse themselves with explosives, the grandfather and father go about organizing rituals honoring Stalin and otherwise terrorizing the village. When the district Party leader arrives, the local women line up to be raped in an outhouse. The film climaxes with a paroxysm of violence as soldiers suppress the June 17 uprising in the village. The last scene then shows a giant bust of Marx standing alone in an endless desert.

Although both Förth's and Kipping's pictures enjoyed a reasonably warm reception in the press and at film festivals, neither found wide distribution or reached a large audience.[7] Their style was unusual, but that was hardly the only factor. Even Gräf's *Der Tangospieler*, a more conventionally structured and equally acclaimed picture, fared only slightly better. These films shared a fate suffered by all of DEFA's post-*Wende* productions: obscurity. Whether with political melodramas or phantasmagorical satire, filmmakers were beating a dead horse. The GDR was finally gone, and with it the social and discursive context that would have made these films politically urgent. Criticism that once might have been explosive was now pedantic; broken taboos were now mere clichés.[8]

FILM AND THE CHANGING
CULTURAL POLITICS OF THE 1970S

The grotesque images of GDR society featured in some of the last DEFA films were an appropriate ending for the GDR cinema. Conditions at the studio had never been good. Still, GDR filmmaking evolved considerably over its initial three decades. In contrast, the studio's last decade and a half were largely years of retrenchment. Although these years saw some aesthetically interesting films—and, in this respect, were likely neither richer nor poorer than other periods in the studio's history—signs of DEFA's deepening malaise were unmistakable. Both the overall number of films produced and the average amount spent per project were falling. The studio all but abandoned entertainment genres such as musicals and westerns in order to concentrate its limited resources in other areas. The situation for younger filmmakers who were trying to establish themselves in the studio in the eighties was particularly bleak. Distrusted by DEFA's increasingly cautious management and lacking experience, they were poorly positioned to compete for shrinking resources. Many remained "directors in training" (Nachwuchsregisseuren) into their late thirties without having a chance to embark on their own projects. The case of Herwig Kipping, the director of Das Land hinter dem Regenbogen, is quite typical. Only after the Wall's fall and at the advanced age of forty-two was he able to realize this work, his first full-length picture.[9]

Equally evident was growing political dissatisfaction among established filmmakers. Youthful idealism had long given way to disillusionment. Some, such as Heiner Carow, preferred to wait years between realizing projects of their own choice rather than accept those proposed by studio management. Others, including Roland Gräf, Rainer Simon, and Lothar Warneke, finding it difficult to realize meaningful projects set in the East German present, turned more and more to themes set in the past. Another bad omen was the growing number of recognized artists once active at DEFA who had either renounced their GDR citizenship or were working primarily in the West. These included the directors Frank Beyer and Egon Günther; the scriptwriters Jurek Becker and Klaus Poche; and the actors Angelika Domröse, Winfried Glatzeder, Jutta Hoffmann, Manfred Krug, and Armin Müller-Stahl.

The so-called Biermann affair signaled a new level of estrangement between many leading artists and the regime that continued throughout the GDR's later years. In November 1976, the regime made use of a concert tour in the Federal Republic by Wolf Biermann as a convenient opportunity to rid themselves of the famed folksinger and dissident, whose history of outspokenness extended back to before the Eleventh Plenum. Party leaders failed to anticipate, however, the vehemence with which others would rally to Biermann's defense. Within a few days, over eighty prominent artists signed a letter protesting the regime's action, which they published in the West German press. This response was in many ways unprecedented and caused great consternation among Party leaders. Never before had so many artists defied the regime in such an open and direct manner.[10] In order to restore discipline among the intellectuals, the regime ordered official artists' groups to organize a series of disciplinary procedures. As had happened after the Eleventh Plenum, dissenters had to submit to ritual humiliation and ostracism. Ironically, many of the signatories who had protested Biermann's forced expatriation accepted for themselves offers by the regime to leave the country. The final result was thus a mass exodus of literary and theatrical talent from the GDR.

The political discussions following the Biermann affair within the film industry were not nearly as extensive as in other forums such as the Berlin Writers' Association. The artists active at DEFA who did sign the petition tended to be authors or actors attached to other institutions.[11] Frank Beyer, the one film director who joined the protest, had not been on the studio's permanent staff since the banning of his film *Spur der Steine* a decade earlier. Still, filmmakers could not have been blind to the affair's significance. The always uneasy but still quite powerful alliance between artists and the regime, first forged in the years immediately following World War II, was breaking down. The socialist state and many of its leading artists had apparently outgrown each other. Even some signatories who chose to remain in the East, most notably Heiner Müller and Christa Wolf, had abandoned a clearly defined socialist position in their work in favor of a more diffuse *Zivilizationskritik*.[12] By the early eighties, many younger authors and artists were avoiding official patronage and institutions altogether, preferring instead informal, underground channels of dissemination.[13]

Signs of a growing cultural-political impasse were evident in the film industry even before the Biermann affair. In September 1975, a group of directors wrote to Kurt Hager drawing the Politburo member's attention to filmic adaptions of four important examples of GDR literature that had been blocked for political reasons (see Chapter 7). The letter went on to suggest cautiously the necessity of overhauling the script development. Specifically, the directors complained that lower bureaucrats were passing off decisions on individual projects to higher officials, who would then simply stonewall filmmakers.[14] The influential director Konrad Wolf pointedly described relations between DEFA and the state agency charged with its supervision, the HV Film, as "desolate, with paralyzing effect." The studio's management had suffered a great loss of authority and was no longer effective.[15]

Although the HV Film's tendency to intervene arbitrarily in the studio's business was a perennial sore point, artists were experiencing new difficulties by the seventies. Gone were the theatrics of the Eleventh Plenum. Confrontations had a less dramatic, more routinized quality.[16] Nevertheless, a number of individuals, most notably Heiner Carow, Egon Günther, and Ulrich Plenzdorf, found it all but impossible to realize projects despite repeated attempts at negotiation and compromise. Especially after the Biermann affair, such conditions led many to seek permission to work in the West. In a 1980 letter to Kurt Hager making such a request, Frank Beyer bitterly complained of being without work for two years despite having extensively pursued at least three projects, all by well-known authors. Comparing his present mood with how he felt immediately after the Eleventh Plenum over a decade earlier, he conceded that he was still officially under contract with the DFF television network. Nevertheless, after the banning of his *Spur der Steine* in 1966, he still had been given some work. "Moreover," the director added, "today I am 48 and notice that my ability to accept humiliations has decreased markedly and is approaching nil."[17]

Beyer indeed had plenty to complain about, as his last two pictures had both experienced political problems. Curiously, both concerned estranged middle-aged relationships, a theme resonant with artists' growing disenchantment with the Party. The television film *Geschlossene Gesellschaft* (Private Party, DFF, 1978) suffered the fate of being broadcast at an unusual hour without prior announcement, and the DEFA production *Das Versteck* (The Hiding Place, 1977) ran into difficulties after both its stars, Jutta Hoffmann and Manfred Krug, left for the Federal Republic. Only after extraordinarily extensive lobbying were officials willing to allow Beyer's film a limited run. Official concern about audience members' expressing sympathy with the renegade actors was nevertheless so great that Kurt Hager and Erich Honecker personally reviewed the minutest details relating to the film's distribution.[18]

Another factor that assumed greater importance during the seventies and eighties was the influence of the State Security Ministry within the studio. The difficult nature of the archival sources and German laws designed to ensure privacy has so far limited research into this question. Still, some preliminary conclusions are possible. Although the Stasi's presence in the studio was long-standing, its role there almost certainly grew considerably in the years following the Eleventh Plenum,[19] which generally saw much more systematic efforts to supervise artistic activity. In the case of DEFA, the secret police by the mid-seventies at the latest maintained an extensive network of informants, including most of the studio's top management and a large proportion of the studio's dramaturges responsible for script development. At the same time, the ministry's influence is easily overestimated. Its role was always clearly subordinate to that of the SED. Nevertheless, the effect of the Stasi on individuals or specific projects that attracted its attention was often devastating. The ministry was capable of going to Kafkaesque extremes to sabotage a person's life or career.

Filmmakers who were subjects of long-term and systematic observation by the Stasi include Frank Beyer, Ulrich Plenzdorf, and Rainer Simon. Plenzdorf, who was prominent not only as a scriptwriter but also as a dramatist and fiction writer, attracted attention through the controversy surrounding his play *Die neuen Leiden des jungen W.* (The New Sufferings of Young W.) and with *Die Berliner Geschichte* (The Berlin Story), an independent attempt to publish an anthology of leading writers.[20] Simon became an object of the Stasi's interest with his 1975 film, *Till Eulenspiegel*, concerning the life of an iconoclastic Renaissance artist; however, the ministry's scrutiny became especially intense five years later during the filming of *Jadup und Boel* (see below). One of the best publicly documented cases of Stasi intervention, this last picture provides tremendous insight into the nature of the collaboration that existed between top studio management and the secret police. Apparently, the ministry became concerned about the project only after the studio director, Hans Mäde, directed its attention to it.[21] Mäde and other cultural politicians also bore primary responsibility for decisions concerning the disposition of the picture. The Stasi's main responsibility lay in monitoring and persecuting individuals.[22] Overall, the agency actions within the film industry stayed true to its official mission as the "shield and sword" of the Party—more an instrument of policy than its formulator.[23]

Artists such as Plenzdorf and Simon were subject to constant observation by literally dozens of secret informants. In many cases, supposed colleagues and close friends did not shrink from reporting on even the most intimate details of their personal and professional lives. Such horrendous experiences notwithstanding, both of these men managed to continue their creative work. In other cases, the atmosphere of suspicion and fear accompanying Stasi persecution had even more devastating consequences. Younger artists lacking both official protectors within the SED and international renown were particularly vulnerable to the ministry's machinations. One of the most tragic individual cases at DEFA during the eighties was that of Ulrich Weiss, whose career came to a standstill after two highly promising films (see below).[24] Another publicly documented case is that of Hannes and Sibylle Schönemann. Having suffered continued harassment at DEFA, the young couple was arrested after applying for an exit visa and endured over a year of incarceration before receiving permission to depart for the West.[25]

Further compounding a stagnating cultural-political climate were worsening economic conditions in the late GDR. Although technical backwardness and equipment shortages were nothing new at DEFA, they proved increasingly ruinous given the filmmaking's declining importance compared to television. In the late fifties and early sixties, DEFA had considerable success increasing its production and adopting new technologies such as wide-screen cinematography (see Chapter 4). Yet by 1970, well before the GDR's general economic decline became evident, studio management reluctantly concluded that further expansion was out of the question.[26] The studio not only continued to experience shortages in equipment, vehicles, and filmstock throughout the seventies; the overall number of films produced declined as well. The studio gradually was forced to limit its support of a varied palette of film genres, and opportunities for younger directors to realize films became scant. At the same time, the GDR's increasingly dilapidated movie theater network further contributed to a loss in viewership.[27]

An unexpected consequence of Honecker's shift toward satisfying domestic consumer needs was a ballooning foreign deficit. By the late seventies, obtaining additional funds for even relatively small capital investments that required hard currency involved petitioning the highest possible levels. Thus Konrad Wolf turned personally to Erich Honecker in order to obtain a hand-held movie camera from the West.[28] Similarly, the first secretary's intervention was necessary to facilitate a special purchase of Kodak film stock to make up for a production snafu at East Germany's only film factory.[29] The Party granted these requests; nevertheless, the ZK Executive Committee underscored DEFA's declining importance by declining to order any special commemorations for the studio's thirtieth anniversary.[30]

DEFA'S FINAL RENAISSANCE AND THE MÄDE REGIME

Despite such debilitating conditions, DEFA's history hardly ended with the Biermann affair. Indeed, the end of the seventies saw something of a mini-revival in the East German cinema. One factor contributing to this development was a change in management. For most of the decade, the studio had been under the direction of Albert Wilkening, an old DEFA hand well respected for his mastery of filmmaking's technical and organizational aspects. Unfortunately, Wilkening's clout within the Party was limited—a factor that helps explain the studio's vulnerability to the incessant political meddling of which directors complained in their 1975 letter to Hager. In any case, the Party responded to the situation by appointing Hans Mäde studio director in 1977. A member of the ZK, he hardly had a liberal reputation as a cultural politician. Still, he had considerable experience as the general director of a theater in Karl-Marx-Stadt (Chemnitz) and Dresden. Once a protégé of the famous theater director Maxim Valentin, he had even made a short *Stacheltier*, or political satire film, in the fifties. Moreover, he enjoyed the confidence of Party leaders and enough political stature to enforce his own decisions. As a ZK member, he outranked the head of the HV Film within the Party, even if the latter was technically his superior in the state hierarchy.

To aid him in his responsibilities, Mäde brought with him a longtime colleague, the theatrical dramaturge Ursula Püschel, to take over the studio's *Lektorat*, or central review office, which became a support unit for the director. This allowed Mäde to keep tabs on film projects without relying on the studio's dramaturgical staff, whose loyalty was often torn between artists and management. At the same time, the studio director was once again granted authority to approve all stages of film production short of releasing a completed picture for distribution.[31] The result was a measure of autonomy for the studio unprecedented since the Eleventh Plenum. This new situation, filmmakers hoped, would remove the frustrating uncertainty that had plagued the industry in recent years. If nothing else, the studio director's decisions would be binding.

During the first years of his tenure, there was considerable optimism concerning Mäde's appointment. As a goodwill gesture toward filmmakers, Mäde reopened consideration of previously blocked projects, including film adaptations of Johannes Bobrowski's *Levins Mühle*, Günter de Bruyn's *Buridans Esel*, and Brigitte Reimann's *Franziska Linkerhand*. Ultimately, some of these projects may have done Mäde's reputation among filmmakers more harm than good. For example, he solicited proposals for the Reimann novel, which concerns the disappointments of a young, idealistic woman architect, from both Frank Beyer and Rainer Simon before finally allowing Lothar Warneke to realize a rather watered-down adaptation under the title *Unser kurzes Leben* (Our Short Life, 1981). Still, Heiner Carow's realization of Günther Rücker's *Bis dass der Tod euch scheidet* (Until Death Do Us Part, 1979) proved to be both a critical and popular success, although the director had to fight hard to complete this picture about a dysfunctional marriage and divorce in the fashion he saw fit. Predictably, officials objected to scenes of domestic violence and attempted to force Carow to defuse the narrative by placing it in a harmonic social context of helpful colleagues and caring professionals. In contrast, Herrmann Zschoche was able to realize Ulrich Plenzdorf's 1973 screen adaptation of *Buridans Esel* virtually without modification; however, by the time the film appeared in 1980, under the title *Glück im Hinterhaus* (Happiness in the Back Courtyard), it had lost its political edge. Thematically quite similar to Carow and Plenzdorf's *Die Legende von Paul und Paula* (see Chapter 7), Zschoche's picture ironically told the story of an ambitious librarian who starts to question his career and model family life after falling in love with a younger woman.

Without a doubt, the best-known picture from the revival of the late seventies and early eighties was Konrad Wolf and Wolfgang Kohlhaase's *Solo Sunny* (1979). A popular and critical success in the GDR, this also won prizes in the West, including at the Berliniale, thus becoming the first DEFA film ever honored at the famous West Berlin film festival. Wolf's last feature film before his death in 1982 was also a curious conclusion to the career of an artist so loyal to the Communist cause. While the picture's theme, self-realization, placed it in a long line of DEFA productions emphasizing the emancipatory potential of socialist society (see Chapter 4), the work presented the GDR in a rather distressing light. The protagonist, a small-time pop singer, struggles to realize her aspirations in a society profoundly antagonistic to her individuality. Professionally, she is dependent on male colleagues who clearly value her body more than her talents. Her dream of performing solo ends in disappointment when an unappreciative audience treats her passionate performance as mere mood music. Privately, she must contend with an overly intellectual, cold lover, who is incapable of reciprocating her feelings, and with the general rigidity of East German society. Emblematic of the latter are the conditions in Sunny's dilapidated Prenzlauer Berg apartment house. In particular, the building's back courtyard—a setting that traditionally serves as a focal point of proletarian sociability in much German art—takes on a sinister character. Her neighbors use this space to keep Sunny under constant observation. While one files a complaint with the police objecting to her bohemian lifestyle, another masturbates across from her window.

Other important productions produced during Mäde's early years include two additional pictures by Herrmann Zschoche, *Sieben Sommersprossen* (Seven Freckles, 1978) and *Und Nächstes Jahr am Balaton* (And Next Year at the Balaton, 1980), both of which are noteworthy for their frank treatment of teenage sexuality. The last picture even went a step further by combining this theme with that of picaresque adventure and travel in the East Bloc, including a reluctant farewell between the film's East German protagonist and his Dutch paramour at the Bulgarian-Turkish border. Another film from this period that touched on politically sensitive issues was Roland Oehme's *Einfach Blumen aufs Dach* (Just Put Flowers on the Roof, 1979), which made light of GDR's highly hierarchical society by describing the adventures of an ordinary family after purchasing a used government limousine. Similarly, Günter Reisch's *Anton der Zauberer* (Anton the Magician, 1978) told in humorous fashion the story of an ex-confidence man and smuggler, who after returning from prison endears himself as a purchasing agent in a factory by his ability to "organize" all sorts of prized commodities difficult to obtain under socialism. Yet another noteworthy *Alltagsfilm* from this period was Lothar Warneke's *Die Beunruhigung* (The Apprehension, 1982), which, in telling the story of a woman diagnosed with breast cancer, did not shirk from officially suspect themes such as illness and death.

THE "VATER" LETTER

While these films touched on questions of political concern to the regime, their critical potential was hardly explosive. Nevertheless, the regime was less than pleased by the studio's direction under Mäde. In November 1981, a letter appeared in *Neues Deutschland*, the SED's official newspaper. Purportedly written by a worker with the curiously appropriate name of "Vater," or "father," it clearly signaled the Party's displeasure: "I sense in [our recent films] a lack of pride in what the working class and its Party . . . has accomplished in this land during the last decades. Where are the artworks that bring to light the titanic nature . . . of . . . our stable and blooming state of workers and farmers?"[32] The Party ordered no changes in the studio's management in conjunction with the "Vater" letter; however, Mäde had gotten the message. His confidence was shaken, and his willingness to back potentially controversial projects was gone. His rule in the studio, which had begun on an enlightened note, now became simply despotic, since the studio director retained his unprecedented authority.[33]

One picture caught up in the aftermath of the "Vater" letter was Rainer Simon's *Jadup und Boel* (1981/1988), which had then just made it through production despite intense political scrutiny. Seven years would pass before this extraordinary work made it into cinemas. Combining gentle sarcasm with lyrical and even supernatural elements, *Jadup und Boel* painted a picture of the GDR at once affectionate and highly critical. When an ancient house suddenly collapses, Jadup, the middle-aged *Bürgermeister* of a small rural town, comes across a dog-eared copy of an Engels tract in the rubble. This stirs up memories of the immediate postwar period and his first youthful love, a refugee girl named Boel, who later left town, the victim in an unsolved rape case. Jadup himself has feelings of guilt toward her since he interrogated her at the time hoping to disprove rumors of an attack by a Soviet soldier. Now thirty-five years later, gossip circulates that Jadup was the assailant. While the charge is untrue, the authority of the sympathetic mayor is in question. In the end, Jadup takes a moral stand, calling for communication rather than the repression of problems. In a speech to his son's class on the occasion of their *Jugendweihe*—the socialist confirmation ceremony—Jadup departs from his stultifying text and reminds his audience that what counts in life is not the right answers but the willingness to pose honest questions. At the same time, the film did not obscure violent impulses never far from the surface of East German society. In a concluding scene, Jadup looks on powerlessly as the festivities accompanying the *Jugendweihe* conclude with the senseless beating of a man by local youths.

Another picture affected by the change in cultural policy was Herrmann Zschoche's *Insel der Schwäne* (Island of the Swans, 1983). Based on a novel by Benno Pludra adapted for the screen by Ulrich Plenzdorf, the picture concerns Stefan, a teenage boy, whose family moves to a new "satellite city" under construction on the outskirts of Berlin. Clearly problematic from an official perspective was the picture's depiction of its setting. The Honecker regime prided itself on its success in combating the GDR's chronic housing shortage through the creation of hundreds of thousands of modern apartments; however, life in the new projects was anything but appealing. While Stefan's parents admire modern conveniences such as central heating, he finds himself in a Hobbesian world of disenchanted children struggling to survive in the sterile, mazelike housing complex.

As with Simon's work, a major theme of Zschoche's picture is violence as a result of failed social communication. An attempt by Stefan and other young people to preserve an improvised play area finds little understanding among adults. The building superintendent ruthlessly polices public spaces, preventing any play and spontaneity by the children. Particularly controversial was the film's conclusion, in which a bully plunges to his death in an elevator shaft. After considerable wrangling, officials reluctantly permitted the release of the picture, but critics, in what was clearly an orchestrated press campaign, roundly condemned it.

The *Alltag* films of the late seventies and early eighties were hardly the last of their kind. At least numerically, films set in the GDR continued to dominate DEFA's yearly production throughout the eighties. Still, these tended to be very modest in their aspirations, if not downright formulaic and derivative. Directors such as Siegfried Kühn, Bernhard Stephan, and Erwin Stranka, among others, turned out collectively a steady stream of light dramas or romantic comedies concerning relationships and stage-of-life crises among young adults or teenagers. These productions sometimes featured character constellations and plots that would have been all but unthinkable at DEFA in a previous, more prudish era. For example, Roland Oehme's *Meine Frau Inge und meine Frau Schmidt* (My Wife Inge and My Wife Schmidt, 1985) featured a pair of women who decide to share a husband. Still, these pictures rarely touched on sensitive issues. Instead, by focusing on rather stereotyped conflicts within a depoliticized private realm, they tended to present the GDR as a comfortably provincial society where individuals could exercise a measure of control over their lives and achieve self-fulfillment.

The few *Alltagsfilme* that resisted this pattern avoided overt political themes but instead satirized narrative conventions governing other DEFA films. Thus two works by younger directors, Peter Kahane's *Ete und Ali* (1985) and Michael Kann's *Die Entfernung zwischen dir und mir und ihr* (The Distance between You and Me and Her, 1987), were notable for featuring characters who experience little or no personal development. The comic potential of both works derives less from the temporary inversion of societal norms than from positing an ironic distance between such norms and the experience of the protagonists. Kahane's film featured two buddies fresh out of the army. Ali, the more energetic of the Abbott-and-Costello-like pair, persuades Ete to win back his wife, Mary, who during his absence in the army has decided to divorce him. Thanks mainly to Ali's outrageous interventions, Ete succeeds in wooing Mary and building up a respectable existence only to have her and Ali betray him in a spontaneous fit of genuine passion. In a similar vein, Kann's picture is told from the perspective of a self-described schizophrenic, Robert, whose self-deprecating monologue is reminiscent of Woody Allen. The two women in his life are inversions of opposite stock DEFA characters. His ex-wife is a GDR rock star who flaunts all convention, while carefully cultivating her career. In contrast, his girlfriend is a journalist who despite her cynical, conformist demeanor is privately sentimental and vulnerable.

In addition, the eighties saw the emergence of new women filmmakers at the studio, including a couple of female directors. Iris Gusner and Evelyn Schmidt distinguished themselves with several pictures that built on DEFA's tradition of strong female protagonists. Schmidt's *Das Fahrrad* (The Bicycle, 1982), for example, concerns a single mother who is an unskilled worker and who reports her bicycle stolen in order to collect the insurance money. When her well-meaning but rather conventional boyfriend shows little compassion for her predicament, she chooses her own independence over the financial security he offers.[34] Whether the films of Gusner and Schmidt display a distinctly female sensibility remains an open question. Because official ideology had co-opted the cause of women's emancipation, East German women intellectuals generally avoided identifying themselves as feminists in the Western sense. Still, women filmmakers were aware of their anomalous position in a studio long dominated by men.[35] Indeed, at least one film by Gusner and the scriptwriter Gabriele Kotte seems to comment ironically on their male colleagues' fascination with female worker protagonists. *Alle meine Mädchen* (All My Girls, 1980) features a male director in training who sets out to make a documentary about an all-female work brigade in a lightbulb factory, but who soon finds his sovereign position as an outside observer undermined by personal entanglements with the group's members.

ESCAPE INTO HISTORY?

The same political and discursive developments responsible for the relative dearth of innovative *Alltagsfilme* facilitated new directions for historical works during the eighties. After Honecker's accession in 1971, the regime abandoned its previous insistence on rapid progress and began conceiving of the GDR as a nation unto itself. Eventually, the East German state would trace its origins through Prussia back into the mists of time. Meanwhile, the regime showed an increasing tolerance for modes of personal expression such as rock music, sexual liberation, and Western fashions. These developments robbed the notion of *Alltag* of much of its critical potential. What represented a fresh departure in the early seventies was growing stale a decade later.

No less important, East German society in the eighties was in a state of growing ferment. For the first time, independent opposition movements were developing around such issues as nuclear disarmament, civil rights, the environment, and gay liberation. Until the late seventies, most examples of overt political protest were limited either to isolated individuals or to more or less spontaneous mass actions, such as the June 17 uprising of 1953. Ironically, the SED itself was one of the few forums during the

GDR's first two decades where potential critics of official policy could find a hearing. Thus the GDR's most prominent dissidents—Wolf Biermann, Robert Havemann, and Rudolf Bahro among them—arose among the Party faithful.

By the time of the Biermann affair, this situation was changing. Frustrated by the failure of socialist reform, advocates of change began to organize outside the Party. A growing number of voices within the Protestant church—the one major institution in East German society that had retained a measure of autonomy from the state—were calling for constructive engagement with socialism. Even though its hierarchy was loath to provoke the regime, the church offered its protection to a broad spectrum of opposition groups. Otherwise forbidden organizations could hold meetings in relative safety on church property. In this way, an alternative communicative network arose in the GDR during the eighties. Numbering at most a few thousand committed individuals, the East German opposition was small compared to dissident movements in other East Bloc countries. Still, its spokespeople provided leadership and direction to East Germans in the months leading up to the fall of the Wall, thus playing a key role in the final overthrow of the SED.[36]

While DEFA itself did not participate in these developments, the growth of the opposition movement during the eighties influenced the general cultural-political climate, affecting the creative interests and choices of filmmakers. As discussed above, works like Rainer Simon's *Jadup und Boel* or Herrmann Zschoche's *Insel der Schwäne* explicitly addressed the issue of inadequate social communication. Jadup's isolation as a small-town mayor or the inflexibility exhibited by many adults toward children in Zschoche's film pointed to both the conformist pressures of socialist society and the precariousness of state authority.

The political problems these works encountered were a clear signal to artists of the regime's increasing sensitivity concerning the depiction of the present, now that signs of political ferment were growing. Only toward the very end of the SED regime did one or two DEFA projects dealing head-on with controversial social issues see the light of day.

Made in 1989, Heiner Carow's *Coming Out* (the original title is in English) was the first and last East German picture to deal openly with homosexuality. In many ways, its plot was hardly unusual for a DEFA *Alltagsfilm*, since a central theme of its story was *Bildung*, or self-realization, through honesty and openness. The only road to happiness for its protagonist, Philipp, is accepting his homosexuality, whatever the potential cost to his career as a teacher. Notably, the picture features scenes shot at an East Berlin gay bar and appearances by members of East Berlin's gay underground, including the colorful transvestite Charlotte von Mahls-dorf. Although scriptwriter Wolfram Witt proposed the original idea, the picture would probably have never gotten off the ground save for the resourcefulness and courage of its director, Heiner Carow. Realizing that the project stood little chance for approval through normal studio chan-nels, Carow sought endorsement for the film from the Academy of the Arts, before directly approaching Politburo member Kurt Hager. Since the GDR officially did not persecute homosexuals, Hager was hard pressed to turn down the prominent filmmaker's request. Unfortunately, the film's release came too late to have much of an impact on East German society. The date of its premiere, November 9, 1989, coincided with the fall of the Berlin Wall. Despite a warm reception both at home and abroad, the picture was politically immediately obsolete.[37]

A similar fate also awaited Peter Kahane and Thomas Knauf's *Die Archi-tekten* (The Architects, 1990). This film tells the story of a group of frus-trated younger architects who finally receive a chance to realize a public housing project reflecting their own ideals. Predictably, though, bureau-cratic intransigence leads to their hopes being dashed. Once completed, the project is all but identical with the impersonal, cookie-cutter designs that the young architects wished to avoid. The picture presents a devas-tating portrait of the late GDR. Both landscapes and interiors reflect the desolation of its characters. Moreover, Kahane broke long-standing ta-boos surrounding Germany's division and travel restrictions on East Ger-man citizens. The picture even includes a scene in which its main protago-nist says farewell to family members heading West filmed in front of the notorious *Tränenpalast*, or "palace of tears," the customs facility at the Berlin Friedrichstrasse train station.[38] Nevertheless, by May 1990, when *Die Architekten* appeared in theaters, the picture had already been by-passed by events.

In the sensitive political climate of the late eighties, many filmmakers turned to remote times and places in order to find greater creative lati-tude. Further facilitating this development were changes in official atti-tudes. Having long abandoned their millennialism, Party leaders assumed a decidedly self-satisfied and indulgent attitude toward the past. Now that the GDR had officially acquired many of the attributes of a timeless so-ciety, functionaries were less sensitive about how pictures depicted his-tory's inevitable march toward the socialist present. Potentially embar-rassing issues from the GDR's early past, if properly handled, could now be thematized almost sentimentally as minor diversions on the path to a manifestly happy conclusion. Filmmakers were also relatively free to ap-proach other aspects of German history that deviated from the regime's antifascist narrative, as long as they did not directly call that narrative into question.

After the disaster that befell *Jadup und Boel*, Rainer Simon realized a series of films with historical themes, including *Das Luftschiff* (The Dirigible, 1983) and *Die Frau und der Fremde* (The Woman and the Stranger, 1985).[39] Especially the first of these pictures was characterized by an aesthetic license uncommon for DEFA films. Based on a novel by Rudolf Fries, the film tells the story of an inventor who in his obsession to realize his dreams allows himself to be misused by the Nazis. Although the narrative was fully consistent with official antifascism, the picture dispensed with conventions for preserving a linear narrative while freely mixing in fantastic and realistic elements. The result was a phantasmagorical tableau whose very disorder was subversive. The work was less concerned with reproducing an ideological narrative than with wider questions about the nature of creativity and repression. Indeed, nervous officials refused to allow the film to enter international festivals.[40] Similarly, *Die Frau und der Fremde*, while clearly an antimilitaristic film, thematized war's existentially disruptive nature in an unconventional fashion: a POW returning home assumes not only the identity but the persona of a still-missing comrade, persuading the latter's wife that he is in fact her husband.

Other notable DEFA films from the eighties with historical themes included Frank Beyer's *Der Aufenthalt* (The Detention, 1983), Roland Gräf's *Fallada—Letztes Kapitel* (Fallada—The Last Chapter, 1988), and Lothar Warneke's *Einer trage des anderen Last* (Bear Ye One Another's Burdens, 1988). All handled sensitive political topics. Beyer's picture, based on a novel by Hermann Kant, dramatizes the experience of a German soldier who stands falsely accused of wartime atrocities in postwar Poland. Although the picture's theme was unambiguously antifascist, the premise was too much for Polish authorities, who prevented the picture from being entered in the Berliniale Film Festival in West Berlin. Gräf's film concerns the last years of the novelist Hans Fallada, whose works were celebrated by both the Nazis and the SED. Appointed mayor of a small town by the Soviets in the immediate postwar period, the best-selling author is unable to overcome his morphine addiction and dies a moral failure. Warneke's picture is also set in the period after World War II. It tells the story of two tubercular young men, a police officer who is a fanatical Communist and an evangelical minister; they grow to respect each other for their mutually held humanist values while sharing a room in a sanatorium. One of the few positive depictions of the clergy in a DEFA film, the picture had a gala premiere with members of the Politburo and the Protestant Synod in attendance.[41] Clearly, the regime intended to use the work to feign reconciliation with the church.

Despite the greater creative latitude allowed some filmmakers, the regime was still sensitive about depictions of the past that in any way called into direct question the Party's heroic role in resisting fascism. Thus Ulrich Weiss's *Dein unbekannter Bruder* (Your Unknown Brother, 1982) caused its maker considerable grief. Based on a story by the Communist writer Willi Bredel, the picture concerns betrayal among members of the Communist underground during the Third Reich. Some audience members also recognized in the deeply psychological work a parable for the experience of dissidents involved in the GDR's fledgling citizens' rights movement.[42] Aesthetically, the picture marked an unusual return for DEFA to the highly stylized set design and lighting associated with German expressionism.

Initially, the picture's official reception was warm as well. *Neues Deutschland* crooned about the positive response to the picture at the Max Ophuls Film Festival in the West German city of Saarbrücken and about its being subsequently invited to the Cannes Film Festival. The situation, however, changed radically after Politburo member Hermann Axen complained that its depiction of the Communist resistance movement was false.[43] Not only did the film not make it to Cannes, but Weiss's career was permanently compromised.

The injustice suffered by Weiss notwithstanding, the GDR cinema of the eighties was clearly characterized by a highly self-conscious, reflective attitude toward history. This was indeed evident even in works set in contemporary GDR society that interrogated the relationship between past and present. One obvious example is Rainer Simon's *Jadup und Boel* (Jadup and Boel, 1981), a film consciously concerned with history both as a source of political legitimacy and as a disruptive force in the present; a featured character is an antique dealer named *Gewissen*, or "Conscience," who roams about confronting Jadup and others with unpleasant particulars. Similarly, Roland Gräf's *Märkische Forschungen* (Researching the Mark Brandenburg, 1982), based on a Günter de Bruyn novel, contrasts two different approaches toward the past, personified by the picture's principal protagonists, a village teacher and a famous professor. What unites them is a shared passion for an obscure romantic poet; the teacher, however, is motivated by a narrow antiquarian interest in local history, whereas the professor sees history as a political instrument. The two men get along famously, until one day the teacher discovers that the progressive poet used in fact a nom de plume and later, under his own name, became a reactionary Prussian censor!

By the mid-eighties, DEFA had thus come full circle. It was once again a cinema that most comfortably dwelled on the mythic past rather than on the present. Captive to a decaying state and an exhausted ideology, filmmakers found narrowing possibilities of engaging their society critically. A fundamental problem facing East German film was that *Alltag* had indeed triumphed. Dramatizing the rhythms of everyday existence may have once appeared to be an antidote to Communism's self-legitimizing use of history, but it had now become merely another means of celebrating the GDR as a traditional state predicated on a quasi-eternal, natural community. Of course, the critical potential of the realist cinema lay only dormant. As individual films by Heiner Carow, Rainer Simon, Herrmann Zschoche, and others attest, some artists would have undoubtedly contributed to the quiet ferment slowly spreading in East German society during the eighties if their officially sponsored medium had allowed it. Only with the fall of the Berlin Wall in November 1989 would filmmakers enjoy an opportunity to engage themes of immediate political relevance. Alas, by this time, East Germany itself was passing into history. Many of the last DEFA films, despite their hard appraisal of the East German state, could not escape guilt by association with their subject. Artifacts of a rapidly vanishing and discredited world, these works failed to find substantial audiences. The East German cinema was negotiating its final transition. A once living artistic tradition was becoming a contested cultural legacy.

NOTES

ARCHIVAL SOURCE ABBREVIATIONS

BA Berlin:
Bundesarchiv, Berlin
BA Berlin DR117:
DEFA Betriebsarchiv, housed in the Bundesarchiv, Berlin
BA Film:
Bundesarchiv Filmarchiv, Berlin
SAPMO:
Stiftung Archiv Parteien und Massenorganisationen der DDR im
Bundesarchiv, Berlin

INTRODUCTION

1. Examples would include critical artists such as Christa Wolf and Heiner Müller and members of the Citizens Movement such as Bärbel Bohley, Jens Reich, and Konrad Weiss. It should be noted that these individuals by no means represent a unified group. Many younger dissidents viewed older artists such as Müller or Wolf with ambivalence. For a detailed discussion of East German dissidents, see Torpey, *Intellectuals, Socialism, and Dissent.*

2. There were a total of eleven films affected by the Plenum. Two of these, *Der Frühling braucht Zeit* (Günter Stahnke, 1965) and *Spur der Steine* (Frank Beyer, 1966), had premieres before being banned. At least one other film, *Denk bloss nicht, ich heule*... (Frank Vogel, 1965), was shown to test audiences. The remaining films at the time of their production were screened only within the studio or before officials. Postproduction work on many was left uncompleted. These films included *Berlin um die Ecke* (Gerhard Klein, 1966); *Denk bloss nicht, ich heule*...; *Jahrgang '45* (Jürgen Böttcher, 1966); *Das Kaninchen bin ich* (Kurt Maetzig, 1965); *Karla* (Herrmann Zschoche, 1966); *Der verlorene Engel* (Ralf Kirsten, 1966); *Wenn Du gross bist, lieber Adam* (Egon Günther, 1966); *Fräulein Schmetterling* (Kurt Barthel, 1966); and *Hände hoch—oder ich schiesse* (Hans-Joachim Kasprzik, 1966). Of these, the final two films have never been publicly shown and may be beyond reconstruction. *Der verlorene Engel* was released in 1971. *Berlin um die Ecke* experienced a handful of viewings in art cinemas in the late eighties. The remaining seven first premiered publicly after the fall of the Wall.

3. Marlen Köhler, "Wie 'Spur der Steine' verschwand und Spuren in Menschen blieben," *Die Freiheit* (Halle), November 27, 1989.

4. Ulrike Elsner, "Nach 24 Kellerjahren endlich auf der Leinwand," *Lausitzer Rundschau* (Cottbus), March 10, 1990.

5. Gerd Dehnel, "Ein Film traf den Nerv des totalitären Systems," *Berliner Allgemeine*, March 6, 1990.

6. Wilfriede Eichler, "Mit moralischen Anspruch," *Berliner Allgemeine*, February 8, 1990.

7. R. Harold, "Rechtfertigung vor sich selbst?" *Sächsisches Tageblatt*, April 25, 1990.

8. Helmut Ullrich, "Recht ferngerückt schon: 'Berlin um die Ecke'—ein DEFA-Film von 1965," *Neue Zeit*, May 18, 1990.

9. "Aktuell aber leider zu spät," *BZ am Abend*, June 21, 1990.

10. Michael Hanisch, "Eine gefährliche Krankheit: Der einst verbotene DEFA-Film 'Wenn Du gross bist, lieber Adam,'" *Neue Zeit*, October 24, 1990.

11. Compare the introduction by Günter Agde in *Kahlschlag: Das 11. Plenum des ZK der SED 1965*.

12. "Die 'Spur der Steine' und die Last der Erinnerung," *Junge Welt*, November 24, 1989.

13. For example, many "*Alltag*" films from the seventies still presented the GDR as a dynamic society on the move. By the same token, certain "*Gegenwart*" movies from the late fifties and early sixties contain aesthetic elements that strongly anticipate the ahistoricity of later films. In addition, the term "*Gegenwartsfilm*" first seems to have come into routine use in official Party statements after 1956.

14. See Meuschel, *Legitimation und Parteiherrschaft in der DDR*, 283–91, or relevant articles in the *DDR Handbuch*. The precise formulation was that the GDR was one of "zwei Nationen deutscher Ethnizität," whereby it was stressed that ethnicity no longer belonged to the essential defining characteristics of nationhood. A wonderful novel that explores the contradictory resonances and uses of "Heimatpflege" as practiced in the GDR is Günter de Bruyn's *Märkische Forschungen*, originally published in 1978.

15. Hall, "Culture, Community, Nation," 355.

16. As Marc Silberman has emphasized, "A socialist public sphere did not exist [in East Germany] if by that we mean a set of institutions, communication networks and practices which facilitated debate about causes and remedies to political stagnation and economic deterioration and which encouraged the creation of oppositional sites of discourse." Silberman, "Problematizing the 'Socialist Public Sphere': Concepts and Consequences," 4.

17. Here I disagree with Silberman, who states, "Officially *Öffentlichkeit* did not exist in the GDR. The tradition of Marxist analysis views the separation of state and civil society as an invention of the eighteenth century. . . . The ideal of public discourse becomes, consequently, a classic example of ideology." First, according to official ideology, the GDR was a socialist, not a Communist society. The melting away of the state still lay in the future. Indeed, the political system, which included, besides the SED, "bloc" parties supposedly representing the interests of various segments of the population, was theoretically premised on the continued existence of diverse classes. The proletariat had still not become

identical with society as a whole. Second, the maintenance of a huge network of newspapers, including some purporting to speak for groups other than the Party and the workers, suggests the priority attached by the regime to projecting the appearance of a properly functioning public sphere, where truth is produced through the independent convergence of opinion. See also Barck, Langermann, and Requate, "Kommunikative Strukturen, Medien und Öffentlichkeiten in der DDR," 26–27.

18. Bullock, *Hitler: A Study in Tyranny*, 44–45.

19. Bathrick, *The Powers of Speech*, 34–35.

20. Important works emphasizing communication as a key aspect of the nationalist project include Deutsch, *Nations and Communication*; Anderson, *Imagined Communities*; and Gellner, *Nations and Nationalism*.

21. See, for example, Schroeder, *Der SED-Staat*.

22. See, for example, Kocka, "Eine durchherrschte Gesellschaft."

23. See, for example, Meuschel, *Legitimation und Parteiherrschaft in der DDR*; Jarausch, "Care and Coercion: The GDR as Welfare Dictatorship."

24. Lindenberger, "Die Diktatur der Grenzen."

25. See, for example, Hübner, *Konsens, Konflikt und Kompromiss*; Merkel, "Konsumkultur in der DDR"; Rauhut, *Beat in der Grauzone*.

26. Poiger, *Jazz, Rock, and Rebels*, 225.

27. Sobchack, "'Surge and Splendor': A Phenomenology of the Hollywood Historical Epic," 28.

28. Engell, *Sinn und Industrie*, 9–15.

29. Groys, *Gesamtkunstwerk Stalin*.

30. Interview by author, tape recording, Berlin, February 26, 1993.

31. Rolf Richter, the late East German film historian, once estimated that approximately twenty to twenty-two films were banned during the history of the DEFA. See Byg, "What Might Have Been: DEFA Films of the Past and the Future of German Cinema"; Ronneburg, "'Eine Zensur findet nicht statt!': Zulassungsdaten der DDR." It should be noted that the term "banned" is imprecise. It can refer to films that were withdrawn from distribution after having been shown as well as to those which never made it through the postproduction stage. In theory, one could also include all films that, after having had a normal run after their release, were subsequently withdrawn from further distribution (through television, film clubs, and the like) for political reasons. This was often the case if one of the main actors or the director emigrated to the West or where there were references to a Party program that contradicted current policy. If this last category were included, the total number of "banned" films would be much higher.

32. Many such *informelle Mitarbeiter* were blackmailed into service. Others have defended themselves by arguing that their cooperation represented a well-intended tactical maneuver, a desperate attempt to protect friends and colleagues from worse persecution. Prominent cases have also surfaced where the exact relationship between an individual and the Stasi seems never to have been clearly defined. See Gauck, *Die Stasi-Akten*.

33. See the various newspaper articles reprinted in *Akteneinsicht Christa Wolf*.

34. Again, it is necessary to emphasize that such events did not progress in the GDR nearly as far as they did in other East Bloc countries. The developments that are associated with the Eleventh Plenum pale in comparison to those of the Prague Spring two and a half years later. What is ultimately remarkable about the East German case is the speed and finality with which the SED reacted to nascent threats to its authority.

35. In the film industry, Konrad Wolf would be the prime example for this phenomenon. The writer Christa Wolf and the poet Franz Fühmann are similar cases.

CHAPTER ONE

1. See, for example, Jäger, *Kultur und Politik in der DDR.*

2. For example, few if any would have advocated the distribution of Hollywood films in the GDR glorifying U.S. militarism.

3. Groys, *Gesamtkunstwerk Stalin.*

4. For an overview of alternative leftist film in the Weimar period, see Murray, *Film and the German Left in the Weimar Republic.*

5. See, for example, "Bericht des amerikanischen Geheimdienstes über die Einstellungen der deutschen Bevölkerung in der US-Zone" from August 12, 1945, as reproduced in Klessmann, *Die doppelte Staatsgründung,* 372–74.

6. See, for example, the "Kölner Leitsätze der CDU" as reproduced in Klessmann, *Die doppelte Staatsgründung,* 423–24.

7. Klemperer, *LTI.* Klemperer, whose book was published in the East, did not directly criticize the SBZ, but he also did not limit his critique to the West.

8. Jäger, *Kultur und Politik in der DDR,* 1.

9. Quoted in Klessmann, *Die doppelte Staatsgründung,* 438–40.

10. Mann, of course, died in Los Angeles before he could return to East Germany, but his intention to do so was clear. Compare Kantorowicz, *Deutsches Tagebuch,* or documents reprinted in *Die Regierung ruft die Künstler.*

11. See, for example, Pike, *The Politics of Culture in Soviet-Occupied Germany, 1945–1949.* In contrast, Naimark in *The Russians in Germany* emphasizes the highly improvised, often inconsistent, and sometimes downright chaotic nature of Soviet policy, which reflected complex tensions among occupation officials, Soviet political leaders, and German Communists.

12. Quoted in Jäger, *Kultur und Politik in der DDR,* 16.

13. Weber, *DDR: Grundriss der Geschichte 1945–1990,* 50–53.

14. Heimann, "DEFA, Künstler und SED," 83–84.

15. See Jäger, *Kultur und Politik in der DDR,* for a standard account.

16. Alfred Kantorowicz reports in his memoirs, *Deutsche Tagebücher,* that the SMAD offered him far more support in keeping his journal *Ost und West* afloat than the SED, which he describes as constantly trying to sabotage his efforts. Similarly, the SMAD cultural officers, Tulpanow and Dymshits, are generally remembered as relatively tolerant in comparison to German cultural functionaries.

17. Mückenberger, "Zeit der Hoffnungen," 41–42.

18. Harbich migrated to Brazil. Rabenalt made one additional film at DEFA and then continued his career in West Germany.

19. Mückenberger, "Zeit der Hoffnungen," 26–32, 37.

20. For more concerning this episode, see Wilkening, *Betriebsgeschichte des VEB DEFA Studio für Spielfilme*, vol. 1; Byg, "Two Approaches to GDR History in DEFA Film."

21. These were the director Kurt Maetzig; the actor Adolf Fischer; a cultural functionary with practical film experience, Alfred Lindermann; Hans Klering, who had had considerable experience with film during fourteen years of Soviet exile; and the film architects Karl Hans Bergmann and Willi Schiller.

22. Heimann, "DEFA, Künstler und SED," 50–51.

23. Here, Soviet reparation policies did not always work to ease matters. For example, the Agfa film factory in Wolfen, even though quickly brought into operation, produced almost exclusively for the Soviets at first. Heimann, "DEFA, Künstler und SED," 34 n, 43.

24. Heimann, "DEFA, Künstler und SED," 46–52; Kersten, *Das Filmwesen in der sowjetischen Besatzungszone*, 7–12.

25. Heimann, "DEFA, Künstler und SED," 56–57.

26. Ibid., 42.

27. Ibid., 58.

28. Ibid., 34 n. 27, 55, 58.

29. Ibid., 56.

30. These were Alfred Lindemann, Karl Hans Bergmann, and Hans Klering.

31. For example, Anton Ackermann renounced a "special German path to socialism" in the official SED organ, *Neues Deutschland*, on November 24, 1948.

32. See Wilkening, *Betriebsgeschichte*, vol. 1.

33. Ibid., 114.

34. Ibid., 132–33.

35. Heimann, "DEFA, Künstler und SED," 96.

36. Apparently, some confusion exists about exactly how film censorship functioned in the SBZ, although the Soviets obviously could intervene at will and controlled distribution. See Heimann, "DEFA, Künstler und SED," 45–46.

37. Compare ibid., 13–14, 96–98, 121–24.

38. Ibid., 108.

39. Wilkening, *Betriebsgeschichte*, 2:21. See also Heimann, "DEFA, Künstler und SED," 119–20.

40. Wilkening, *Betriebsgeschichte*, 2:22.

41. *Auf neuen Wegen*, 18.

42. Where no other source is given, my figures for film output are based on the published catalog of the former Staatliches Filmarchiv der DDR, *DEFA-Spielfilme 1946–1964: Filmographie*. For purposes of comparison, I am looking at year of completion rather than date of release. The latter yields slightly different figures: eight works in 1951, six in 1952, and seven in 1953. Compare the filmography provided in *Das zweite Leben der Filmstadt Babelsberg*.

43. "Für den Aufschwung der fortschrittlichen deutschen Filmkunst: Resolu-

tion des Politbüros des ZK der Sozialistischen Einheitspartei Deutschlands," *Neues Deutschland*, July 27, 1952.

44. "Für den Aufschwung der fortschrittlichen deutschen Filmkunst," *Neues Deutschland*, August 18, 1952.

45. The official rationale against the film was that it suggested sympathy with its protagonist. The plot concerns a neighborhood butcher who moonlights as an executioner for the Nazis, becomes a social outcast in his working-class community, and commits suicide.

46. In the end, Slatan Dudow and Kurt Maetzig agreed to appear in the credits as "heads" (Leiter) of an "artistic collective." The film's third director, Richard Groschopp, apparently succeeded in having his name not mentioned at all. See Wilkening, *Betriebsgeschichte*, 2:14–15. Other films from this period that had industrial espionage as a theme include *Der Auftrag Höglers* (Gustav von Wangenheim, 1950), *Zugverkehr unregelmässig* (Erich Freund, 1951), and *Geheimakten Solvay* (Martin Hellberg, 1953).

47. See, for example, the following reviews of *Modell Bianka*: H Müller, "Ein Missglücktes Modell," *Neues Deutschland*, June 23, 1951; -ach., "Modell mit Schönheitsfehlern," *Die Union*, June 30, 1951; -d-, "Modell Bianka—etwas zu leicht," *Sonntag*, no. 25, 1951. Other roughly comparable films include *Der Kahn der fröhlichen Leute* (Hans Heinrich, 1950), *Sauere Wochen—Frohe Feste* (Wolfgang Schleif, 1950), *Sein grosser Sieg* (Franz Barrenstein, 1952), *Jacke wie Hosen* (Eduard Kubat, 1953), and *Das kleine und das grosse Glück* (Martin Hellberg, 1953).

48. Compare, for example, Wolfgang Joho, "Der Kampf um unser Glück," *Sonntag*, June 15, 1952; R. Rh.-Gl., "Sind diese Schicksale typisch?," *Neues Deutschland*, December 18, 1952; "'Frauenschicksale im Frauenurteil,'" *Der Morgen*, June 29, 1952.

49. Heimann, "DEFA, Künstler und SED," 141.

50. Heimann, "DEFA, Künstler und SED," 111–21, discusses this problem somewhat but fails to give precise figures.

51. Other directors from the West quite active at the studio included Hans Müller and Artur Pohl.

52. "Für den Aufschwung der fortschrittlichen deutschen Filmkunst: Resolution des Politbüros des ZK der Sozialistischen Einheitspartei Deutschlands," *Neues Deutschland*, July 27, 1952.

53. Heimann, "DEFA, Künstler und SED," 108.

54. Staritz, *Geschichte der DDR*, 78–80.

55. Ibid., 80–84.

56. Mitter and Wolle, *Untergang auf Raten*. For an excellent overview of historiographical approaches to the June 17 uprising, see Spittmann, "Zum 40. Jahrestag des 17. Juni."

57. These were Rudolf Herrnstadt, editor of *Neues Deutschland*, and Wilhelm Zaisser, the internal security minister.

58. Staritz, "Die SED, Stalin, und der 'Aufbau des Sozialismus' in der DDR"; Richard Löwenthal's foreword to Baring, *Der 17. Juni 1953*.

59. Quoted in Staritz, *Geschichte der DDR*, 85.

60. Ibid., 87–88.

61. "Die Erklärung der deutschen Akademie der Künste," reproduced in *Dokumente zur Kunst-, Literatur- und Kulturpolitik der SED*, 1:289–90.

62. "Vorschläge des Kulturbundes für die Entwicklung unseres Kulturlebens," reproduced in *Dokumente zur Kunst-, Literatur- und Kulturpolitik der SED*, 1:290–91.

63. Reproduced in *Dokumente zur Kunst-, Literatur- und Kulturpolitik der SED*, 1:292–96.

64. "Diskussionsbeitrag Bertolt Brechts zur Kunstpolitik," *Neues Deutschland*, August 12, 1953, reproduced in *Dokumente zur Kunst-, Literatur- und Kulturpolitik der SED*, 1:292–96.

65. "Das Volk will echten Realismus—Beobachtungen zum literarischen Leben in der DDR!," *Berliner Zeitung*, July 27, 1953.

66. "Ausprache zwischen Otto Grotewohl und 'führenden Kunst- und Kulturschaffenden der DDR,'" reproduced in *Dokumente zur Kunst-, Literatur- und Kulturpolitik der SED*, 1:313–15.

67. "Einsicht ist gut—Qualität ist besser," *Deutsche Filmkunst* 1, no. 3 (1953): 9–14.

68. From the Sixteenth Plenum of the Central Committee, September 17, 1953. As quoted in Heimann, "DEFA, Künstler und SED," 157.

69. "Einsicht ist gut—Qualität ist besser," *Deutsche Filmkunst* 1, no. 3 (1953): 9–14.

70. Compare articles appearing in *Neues Deutschland* on February 1, 10, and 19, 1953. See also Kersten, *Das Filmwesen in der sowjetischen Besatzungszone*, 80–81.

71. Otto Grotewohl, speech on the occasion of the founding of the Ministry of Culture, January 7, 1954, as reproduced in *Dokumente zur Kunst-, Literatur- und Kulturpolitik der SED*, 1:327–31.

72. Or even approach forty, if films done at its facilities for East German television (DFF) are included.

73. These were *Carola Lamberti—Eine vom Zirkus* (Hans Müller, 1954) and *Das Fräulein von Scuderi* (Eugen York, 1955).

74. Compare Heimann, "DEFA, Künstler und SED," 176.

75. See Kersten, *Das Filmwesen in der sowjetischen Besatzungszone*, 135–40. DEFA's eagerness for political reasons to enter into coproduction, particularly with the French, did not always result in the most favorable financial arrangements for the studio.

76. Examples include *Das Fräulein von Scuderi* (Eugen York, 1955) and *Pole Poppenspäler* (Artur Pohl, 1954). See Kersten, *Das Filmwesen in der sowjetischen Besatzungszone*, 90.

77. Examples include *Rauschende Melodien* (E. W. Fiedler, 1955) and *Zar und Zimmermann* (Hans Müller, 1956). See Kersten, *Das Filmwesen in der sowjetischen Besatzungszone*, 90.

78. *Star mit fremden Feder* (Harald Manl, 1955) and *Alter Kahn und junge Liebe*

(Hans Müller, 1957). Kersten, *Das Filmwesen in der sowjetischen Besatzungszone*, 91.

79. Wolfgang Gersch, "Die Verdoppelung der Ferne: Notizen von der anderen Seite," 104. Indeed, as early as July 17, the regime advised the State Film Committee to alter the previous production goal of 60 percent political films and 40 percent entertainment films to 75 percent entertainment films and only 25 percent political films. See Staatliches Komitee für Filmwesen, "Aktenvermerk," July 17, 1953, SAPMO DY30 IV2/906/26 (ZK Kultur).

80. For the regime, a "profitable" industry was one that did not require annual operating subsidies from the central state budget.

81. See, for example, ZK Abteilung Binnen und Aussenhandlung, "Analyse des Besuches von Westberliner Kinos durch Bewohner unseres Wirtschaftsgebietes," April 23, 1956, SAPMO DY30 IV2/2026/75 (Büro Kurella).

82. See "Vorlage für den Ministerrat," July 1, 1959, SAPMO DY30 IV2/2026/75 (Büro Kurella), where a dramatic downturn in moviegoing is attributed both to the decision to decrease imports from the West as well as to competition from television.

83. Compare, for example, Johannes R. Becher's speech of November 1953, "Unsere Kulturpolitik," as reproduced in *Dokumente zur Kunst-, Literatur- und Kulturpolitik der SED*, 1:316–20.

84. Compare Walter Ulbricht's "Rechenschaftbericht vor dem IV. Parteitag des SED" of April 1954, reproduced in *Dokumente zur Kunst-, Literatur- und Kulturpolitik der SED*, 1:338–42.

85. Heimann, "DEFA, Künstler und SED," 104.

86. For some, nearly the same excitement animated struggles of the past and those of the present. Functionaries volunteered as extras in scenes depicting debates in the German Reichstag. On inspecting the shoot, Minister President Wilhelm Pieck was so taken by the idea that he spontaneously decided to participate himself. See Kurt Maetzig, *Filmarbeit*, 70.

87. *Gefährliche Fracht* (Gustav von Wangenheim, 1954) and *Der Fackelträger* (Johannes Knittel, 1955) were set in the Federal Republic; the film set in the United States was *Hotelboy Ed Martin* (Ernst Kahler, 1955). *Der Fall Dr. Wagner* (Harald Mannl, 1954) was yet another film concerning industrial sabotage.

88. *Heimliche Ehen* (Gustav von Wangenheim, 1956) and *52 Wochen sind ein Jahr* (Richard Groschopp, 1955).

89. The HV film's extremely circumscribed authority in political matters is clearly emphasized in undated notes concerning the agency's founding. "Besprechung mit Genossen Wandel," SAPMO DY30 IV2/906/26 (ZK Kultur).

90. Despite repeated calls for such films, few were ever made, largely because such a subject matter was simply too much of a hot potato.

91. Geiss, *Repression und Freiheit*, 42.

92. This is the opinion of the man originally charged with supervising the former Stasi archives, Joachim Gauck, *Die Stasi-Akten*, 69–75.

93. Please refer to the Epilogue for further discussion of the Stasi's influence at the studio.

94. Greenblatt, *Shakespearean Negotiations*, 30–38.

CHAPTER TWO

1. Kohlhaase, "Er suchte die Poesie, die in den Dingen steckt," 23–24.

2. Indeed, Kohlhaase and Klein's next film, *Der Fall Gleiwitz* (1961), is distinguished through highly formalized, anything but unobtrusive, camera work.

3. HV Film, Abteilung Planung und Statistik, "Ergebnisse von DEFA-Filmen," February 14, 1958, SAPMO DY30 NL 109/94 (Ackermann Nachlass), lf. 78. After seventeen and a half weeks, the film attracted 1,885,765 viewers. Two circumstances make these viewer figures particularly impressive. The film had no special political priority, so it did not benefit from a Party-organized attendance drive; nor did it belong to a popular entertainment genre. At the same time, *Berlin—Ecke Schönhauser*'s success in terms of attendance was by no means unprecedented, even for a "serious" drama set in the GDR. Klein and Kohlhaase's previous film, *Eine Berliner Romanze* (1956), attracted close to 2 million viewers in only fourteen weeks.

4. "Die Kluft zwischen den Generationen: Der Defa-Film 'Berlin—Ecke Schönhauser' uraufgeführt," *Der Morgen*, August 31, 1957.

5. Günther Stahnke, "Nicht nur für die an der Ecke," *Junge Welt*, August 31, 1957.

6. Wolfgang Joho, "Nachkriegsjugend vor der Kamera," *Sonntag*, September 8, 1957.

7. "Eine Strasse, wie sie liebt und lebt," *BZ am Abend*, September 25, 1957.

8. "Schönfärberei wäre unedel: Lesermeinungen zu 'Berlin—Ecke Schönhauser,'" *Junge Welt*, October 5, 1957.

9. Anna Teut, "Unter den Torbögen Ostberlins," *Die Welt*, September 7, 1957.

10. Horst Knietzsch, "Wo wir nicht sind . . . ," *Neues Deutschland*, September 3, 1957.

11. Ibid.

12. Poiger, *Jazz, Rock, and Rebels*, 70–105.

13. Ibid., 101–3.

14. Ibid., 84–85, 94.

15. "Stenographische Niederschrift der Parteiaktivtagung der Parteiorganisation der DEFA am 23. April 1958," SAPMO DY30 IV2/906/227 (ZK Kultur), lf. 68–75.

16. For an example of at least one director distancing himself from neorealism, see Kurt Maetzig, "Der Film als Kunstwerk," *Neue Film-Welt Berlin*, no. 5 (1951): 1; reproduced in Maetzig, *Filmarbeit*, 219–22. In contrast, Maetzig in June 1947 spoke positively of Rossellini's *Rome Open City*; *Filmarbeit*, 177–88.

17. In fact, many of the interior shots were filmed in the studio; however, obsessive attention was paid to verisimilitude. Sets were built with ceilings, even where these do not appear in the frame. Wolfgang Kohlhaase, interview by author, tape recording, Berlin, March 19, 1993.

18. Ernst Schwill, who played Kohle, was an apprentice in the studio's film copying lab. Ilse Pagé, who played Angela, was "discovered" in West Berlin only two days before the filming began. See "Schlussbericht zur Fertigstellung des Filmes 213 'Berlin—Ecke Schönhauser," BA Berlin DR117 A/096.

19. For a good overview of aesthetic debates among German communists, see Gallas *Marxistische Literaturtheorie*; Lunn, *Marxism and Modernism*. More specifically on socialist realism: Clark, *The Soviet Novel*; Dunham, *In Stalin's Time*; Groys, *Gesamtkunstwerk Stalin*; Robin, *Socialist Realism*.

20. Gorky, "Soviet Literature."

21. Lukács, "Critical Realism and Socialist Realism."

22. If anything, neorealism is even a more elastic term than socialist realism. See Marcus, *Italian Film in the Light of Neorealism*. In contrast, Bondanella, *Italian Cinema*, presents a more cohesive view that emphasizes the tension between art and reality thematized in many neorealist films.

23. Bazin, *Qu'est-ce que le cinéma*, 4:15–16. Emphasis in the original.

24. Ibid., 15–16.

25. Ibid., 14–15.

26. My discussion here follows categories proposed in Murray, *Film and the German Left in the Weimar Republic*.

27. Kohlhaase began one autobiographical statement by describing memories of flipping through a Zille album while a child. See "Vernügen stiller Art" in Kohlhaase, *Ortszeit ist immer auch Weltzeit*.

28. Khrushchev, "Speech of Nikita Khrushchev . . . ," 23. Emphasis added.

29. Klein and Kohlhaase were working on separate projects at the beginning of 1956. Heimann, "DEFA, Künstler und SED," 268 n. 191.

30. The HV Film objected to the film before it went into production, but was overruled by the ZK's cultural section. Ibid., 267.

31. Kohlhaase, interview by author, tape recording, Berlin, March 19, 1993. His memory is consistent with the slim paper trail left by the film. See "Schlussbericht zur Fertigstellung des Filmes 213 'Berlin—Ecke Schönhauser,'" BA Berlin DR117 A/096; Klein and Kohlhaase to Wilkening, April 5, 1956, BA Berlin DR117 1924 (Zentrale Analysengruppe); as well as a memo in the same place from the Albrecht technical production group to Wilkening, May 6, 1957. Four brief scenes were added after a review of the rough cut by the studio in April in order to clarify character motivation and to strengthen the plotline. Klein and Kohlhaase to Wilkening, April 5, 1957, BA Berlin DR117 1924. Compare Heimann, "DEFA, Künstler und SED," 267.

32. On May 17, an internal DEFA committee endorsed the work. No record seems to survive of its certification by the State Approval Commission (Abnahme Kommission). ZK Secretary Paul Wandel included the film in a long list of projects that he felt demonstrated the studio's shortcomings during a meeting that same month with DEFA's management and the MfK's top brass. If a screening of the film for members of the Central Board of the FDJ was designed to add to momentum building against the film, the effect was quite the reverse, as only one of the five "Youth Friends" present found serious fault with the film. See Abteilung Filmabnahme und -kontrolle [HV Film], "Protokoll: Am 14.6.57 wurde der DEFA-Film 'Berlin—Ecke Schönhauser' vor Mitgliedern des Zentralrats der FDJ gezeigt," SAPMO DY30 NL 109/97 (Nachlass Ackermann).

33. See the corresponding chapter in Mitter and Wolle, *Untergang auf Raten*.

34. Meuschel, *Legitimation und Parteiherrschaft in der DDR*, 153–55.

35. Ibid., 159; Staritz, *Geschichte der DDR*, 100.

36. Meuschel, *Legitimation und Parteiherrschaft in der DDR*, 141.

37. Staritz, *Geschichte der DDR*, 116.

38. "Aus dem Beschluss 'Über den Kampf um den Frieden für den Sieg des Sozialismus . . . auf dem V. Parteitag der SED, 10.–16. Juli 1958,'" *Dokumente zur Geschichte der SED*, 2:231–52, especially 240 and 252. Also see Meuschel, *Legitimation und Parteiherrschaft in der DDR*, 169–71.

39. Compare Heimann, "DEFA, Künstler und SED," 239–41.

40. Ackermann to Schirdewan, June 5, 1956, SAPMO DY30 NL 109/95 (Nachlass Ackermann).

41. Kersten, *Das Filmwesen in der sowjetischen Besatzungszone*, 26–27. See also Heimann, "DEFA, Künstler und SED," 245.

42. "Die Zeit ist reif," *Deutsche Filmkunst* 2, no. 9 (1956): 257; reproduced in Maetzig, *Filmarbeit*.

43. Anton Ackermann, "Ideologische Klarheit und höhere Leistungen," *Deutsche Filmkunst* 2, no. 1 (1956).

44. See Zentrale Kommission für staatliche Kontrolle, "Bericht über die Themen- und Produktionsplanung sowie die Verpflichtung von Künstlern im VEB DEFA-Studio für Spielfilme in Potsdam-Babelsberg," March 19, 1956, SAPMO DY30 IV2/2026/77 (Büro Kurella).

45. Ackermann to Wilkening, April 27, 1956, SAPMO DY30 NL 109/95 (Nachlass Ackermann).

46. Ibid.; "Einschätzung des vorliegenden Thematischen Planes des VEB Defa-Studios für Spielfilme," November 23, 1956, SAPMO DY30 IV2/2026/87 (Büro Kurella). The functionary who prepared this report, Arno Röder, while complaining about the studio production plan's lack of "political orientation," admitted that it "was based more than all previous plans on the personal suggestions of writers and directors. Thus it is not an 'unrealistic' plan, but a compendium of actually available [literary] materials."

47. Anton Ackermann, "Sozialistischer Realismus, Unverbindlichkeit und Dogmatismus in unserem Filmschaffen," *Deutsche Filmkunst* 3, no. 5 (1957): 129–30.

48. They were explicitly precluded from assuming financial responsibility. In addition, the studio's preexisting structure was to be left intact. See "Erweiterte Rechte und Pflichten für DEFA-Studios," *Deutsche Filmkunst* 3, no. 2 (1957): 33; "Neuregelung der Beziehung zwischen Studios und Hauptverwaltung," BA Berlin DR1 4386 (Abteilung Filmproduktion). Compare Heimann, "DEFA, Künstler und SED," 254.

49. See "Erweiterte Rechte und Pflichten für DEFA-Studios," *Deutsche Filmkunst* 3, no. 2 (1957): 33, and Heimann, "DEFA, Künstler und SED," 254–55. Over the years, the commission's actual composition, and with it the relative representation of artists, fluctuated. The HV Film director usually presided over meetings. Representatives from the ZK apparatus were often invited.

50. Ironically, of twenty-nine projects, the only one he praised, *Sonnensucher*, was eventually banned! "Betr: Beratung beim Genossen Wandel über Probleme der Filmkunst am 23.5.57," 1, SAPMO DY30 IV2/2026/87 (Büro Kurella).

51. Wilhelm Girnus, "Kulturfrage sind Machtfragen: Diskussionsbeitrag von Wilhelm Girnus für die Kulturkonferenz des ZK der SED, 23. und 24. Oktober 1957," *Dokumente zur Kunst-, Literatur- und Kulturpolitik der SED*, 1:508.

52. "Betr: Information über die Sitzung des künstlerischen Rates am 1.2.58," February 3, 1958, signed Konrad Schwalbe, SAPMO DY30 IV2/906/204 (ZK Kultur). Those present included Slatan Dudow, Konrad Wolf, Gerhard Klein, Wolfgang Kohlhaase, Martin Hellberg, and Kurt Maetzig.

53. SAPMO DY30 IV2/906/224, IV2/906/226, IV2/906/225, and IV2/906/227 (ZK Kultur).

54. Siegfried Wagner to Erich Wendt, January 25, 1958, SAPMO DY30 IV2/906/204 (ZK Kultur).

55. Erich Wendt to Siegfried Wagner, February 2, 1958, SAPMO DY30 IV2/906/204 (ZK Kultur).

56. For a more detailed discussion of this film, see Wolfgang Jacobsen, "Cha Cha Bim Bam Bum," in *Babelsberg: Ein Filmstudio 1912–1992*, 279–84.

57. For an interesting discussion of all three of these productions, rich in telling detail, see Schenk, "Mitten im kalten Krieg 1955–1960," 139–42.

58. Other films grouped with the Berlin films were Carl Balhaus's *Ein Mädchen von sechzehneinhalb* (1957) and Kurt Maetzig and Kurt Bartel's comedy *Vergesst mir meine Traudel nicht* (1957).

59. Soviet objections concerned the film's depiction of a uranium mine. This theme was deemed inappropriate in light of the Soviet desire to ease relations with the United States at this time. For an excellent summary of the film's production history, see Reinhard Wagner, "'Sonnensucher': Notizen zur Werkgeschichte."

60. SAPMO DY30 IV2/906/226 (ZK Kultur), lf. 39–40.

61. Ibid., lf. 102–3.

62. Ibid., lf. 1–8.

63. SAPMO DY30 IV2/906/225 (ZK Kultur), lf. 43.

64. SAPMO DY30 IV2/906/224 (ZK Kultur), lf. 60.

65. SAPMO DY30 IV2/906/227 (ZK Kultur), lf. 22–27.

66. SAPMO DY30 IV2/906/224 (ZK Kultur), lf. 46–47.

67. SAPMO DY30 IV2/906/227 (ZK Kultur), lf. 223.

68. Ibid., lf. 222.

69. Ibid., lf. 56–57.

70. SAPMO DY30 IV2/906/224 (ZK Kultur), lf. 60.

71. Ibid., lf. 20.

72. SAPMO DY30 IV2/906/227 (ZK Kultur), lf. 57.

73. SAPMO DY30 IV2/906/226 (ZK Kultur), lf. 97.

74. SAPMO DY30 IV2/906/224 (ZK Kultur), lf. 39–40.

75. SAPMO DY30 IV2/906/226 (ZK Kultur), lf. 104–6.

76. Klein claimed that the film resulted from discussions organized through the FDJ with 17,000 youths; SAPMO DY30 IV2/906/224 (ZK Kultur), lf. 61. Similarly, Kohlhaase insisted that film's purpose was merely to draw attention to an issue that was being ignored; SAPMO DY30 IV2/906/227, lf. 24.

77. In fact, the film's political slogan, "Where we aren't, our enemies are," fits in well with the message of a January 1956 Politburo resolution titled "Our Heart and Help to Youth." *Dokumente der Sozialistischen Einheitspartei Deutschlands,* 6:11–33.

78. Kurt Maetzig, "Die Zeit ist reif," *Deutsche Filmkunst* 4, no. 9 (1956).

79. SAPMO DY30 IV2/906/225 (ZK Kultur), lf. 9–20.

80. SAPMO DY30 IV2/906/224 (ZK Kultur), lf. 64.

81. SAPMO DY30 IV2/906/225 (ZK Kultur), lf. 77–78.

82. SAPMO DY30 IV2/906/224 (ZK Kultur), lf. 44.

83. SAPMO DY30 IV2/906/225 (ZK Kultur), lf. 82.

84. See, for example, Dudow's comments in SAPMO DY30 IV2/906/226 (ZK Kultur), lf. 67–70.

85. SAPMO DY30 IV2/906/227 (ZK Kultur), lf. 3–4.

86. SAPMO DY30 IV2/906/225 (ZK Kultur), lf. 63.

87. Ibid., lf. 60.

88. SAPMO DY30 IV2/906/227 (ZK Kultur), lf. 57–59.

89. SAPMO DY30 IV2/906/225 (ZK Kultur), lf. 33–36.

90. See the report to the Activists' Convention of a special Party *"Arbeitsgruppe"* formed to evaluate the studio. Ibid., lf. 2–8.

91. See the draft proposal prepared by the studio: Direktor für Wirtschaft und Arbeit, "Entwurf über die Bildung von Produktionsgruppen und deren Aufgabe und Rechte im VEB DEFA Studio für Spielfilme," November 16, 1958, SAPMO DY30 IV2/906/204 (ZK Kultur). A plan specifically calling for *künstlerische Arbeitsgruppen* (KAGs) was then approved by the VVB Film on May 4, 1959. See "Protokoll der Leitungssitzung der VVB Film vom 4.5.59—Nr. 8," BA Berlin DR1 4380 (Sekretariats des HV Leiters).

92. See "Thesen zur Vereinfachung des Staatsapparates und zur Änderung der Arbeitsweise der Mitarbeiter des Staatsapparates: Beschluss des Zentralkommittees vom 12. Juli 1957," in *Dokumente der Sozialistischen Einheitspartei Deutschlands,* 6:281–94.

93. SAPMO DY30 102/906/277 (ZK Kultur), lf. 43–53.

94. Alexander Abusch, "Aktuelle Probleme und Aufgaben unserer sozialistischen Filmkunst," *Deutsche Filmkunst* 6, no. 9 (1958): 264. Ironically, Abusch praised Wolf's *Sonnensucher*—which would eventually be banned—with the identical words.

95. *Deutsche Filmkunst* 6, no. 9 (1958): 267–68.

96. Slatan Dudow, "Der Alltag, die Liebe, die Heiterkeit: Zur Filmkonferenz des Ministeriums für Kultur," *Neues Deutschland,* July 1, 1958.

CHAPTER THREE

1. Walter Ulbricht, "Was ist das Wichtigste?," *Sonntag,* November 15, 1959.

2. Slatan Dudow, "Die Heiterkeit und das Schöne," *Sonntag,* January 10, 1960.

3. The secondary literature on Dudow's life is limited. Herlinghaus, *Slatan Dudow*, is still useful despite its tendentious nature. The lengthiest Western treatment of his life is Aubry, "Slatan Dudow 1903–1963."

4. For a discussion of Dudow's relationship to Brecht, see Natew, "Slatan Dudow in den dreissiger und vierziger Jahren."

5. "Die Komödie und ihre gesellschaftliche Bedeutung" was originally published as the introduction to his play *Das Narrenparadies* under the pseudonym Stefan Brodwin. The essay is reprinted, as part of a special issue devoted to Dudow, in *Beiträge zur Film- und Fernsehwissenschaft* 23, no. 5 (1982): 173–87, here 183.

6. See Schenk, "Mitten im kalten Krieg 1955–1960," 118. A script fragment is reproduced in *Beiträge zur Film- und Fernsehwissenschaft* 23, no. 5 (1982).

7. A short-film comedy genre did, however, flourish in East Germany during the fifties and early sixties. The so-called *Stacheltierfilme*, or "porcupine films," were designed to poke gentle fun at socialist society, taking aim in particular at examples of backward-thinking behavior. See Klötzer and Lokatis, "Criticism and Censorship."

8. Films that fall into the first category include *Alter Kahn und Junge Liebe* (Hans Heinrich, 1957) and *Meine Frau macht Musik* (Hans Heinrich, 1957). The second category might have encompassed *Saure Wochen—frohe Feste* (Wolfgang Schleif, 1950), *Modell Bianka* (Richard Groschopp, 1951), and *Junges Gemüse* (Günter Reisch, 1956). Also see the interview with Dudow, "Menschengestaltung, Lebensnähe und Standort des Künstlers," *Deutsche Filmkunst* 5 (1957): 355–56. Here, the director lamented the nearly complete lack of successful DEFA comedies, a circumstance that he attributed to filmmakers not having a sufficiently "light hand." At the same time, Dudow affirmed the need for politically committed art.

9. "Die Komödie und ihre gesellschaftliche Bedeutung," as reprinted in *Beiträge zur Film- und Fernsehwissenschaft* 23, no. 5 (1982): 183.

10. Frye, *Anatomy of Criticism*, 163.

11. Ibid., 185. The sixth phase corresponds to the collapse of that society. Its object is the realm of the ghost stories and gothic romances.

12. Ibid., 185.

13. Ibid., 181–84.

14. HV Film Filmproduktion, unnumbered protocol, October 3, 1959, located in the "Abnahme" file for *Verwirrung der Liebe*, BA Film.

15. Albert Wilkening to the Abnahmekommission, September 26, 1959, BA Berlin DR117 1929 (Zentrale Analysengruppe).

16. See Wilkening to Ernst Hoffmann, director of the VVB film, October 1, 1959, BA Berlin DR117 1929 (Zentrale Analysengruppe).

17. Aktenvermerk, signed Wilkening and Dudow, October 3, 1959, BA Berlin DR117 1929 (Zentrale Analysengruppe).

18. Konrad Schwalbe, interview by author, tape recording, Potsdam, April 24, 1993. Schwalbe was present at the meeting in his capacity as DEFA's chief dramaturge.

19. Konrad Schwalbe, interview by author, tape recording, Potsdam, April 24, 1993.

20. Annekathrin Bürger, who played Sonja, and her husband, Ralf Römer, interview by author, tape recording, Berlin, August 18, 1993. Apparently, Dudow made passes at both his leading ladies while filming *Verwirrung der Liebe*.

21. Agee, *Twelve Years: An American Boyhood in East Germany*, 149–50.

22. See Kurt Starke, "Die Republik der Nackten," *Wochenpost*, July 22, 1993.

23. See "Aktennotiz," October 24, 1959, signed Wilkening and Dudow, BA Berlin DR117 1929 (Zentrale Analysengruppe, Kollege Zunft).

24. *Greif zur Feder, Kumpel*, 100–102.

25. "Rede Walter Ulbrichts vor Schriftstellern, Brigaden der sozialistischen Arbeit und Kulturschaffenden in Bitterfeld, 24. April 1959," reproduced in *Dokumente zur Kunst-, Literatur- und Kulturpolitik der SED*, 1:552.

26. "Die Kunst des guten Lachens: Zu dem DEFA-Film 'Verwirrung der Liebe' von Slatan Dudow," *Neues Deutschland*, November 28, 1959.

27. Letter of Klausdieter Wernecke, *Sonntag*, January 10, 1960.

28. These included Ekkehard Walter, *Junge Welt*, December 1, 1959. See also the letter of Klausdieter Wernecke, *Sonntag*, January 10, 1960.

29. See Slatan Dudow's response to his critics. "Das Heitere ernst betrachtet: Ein kleiner Beitrag zur Entwirrung der Verwirrung," *Forum*, January 21, 1960.

30. Letter of Willy Walther, *Forum*, December 17, 1959.

31. Letter of Hiltrud Oehlschlägel, *Sonntag*, February 21, 1960.

32. Letter of Anni Rafeld, *Sonntag*, February 21, 1960.

33. Horst Knietzsch, "Die Kunst des guten Lachens," *Neues Deutschland*, November 28, 1959.

34. Ibid.

35. Christoph Funke, "Ein Faschingsball und seine Folgen," *Der Morgen*, October 10, 1959.

36. Letter of Ekkehard Walter, *Junge Welt*, December 1, 1959.

37. Letter of Klausdieter Wernecke, *Sonntag*, January 10, 1960.

38. Letter of Magarete Kühnhackl, *Sonntag*, January 10, 1960.

39. Letter of Harry Siebers, *Sonntag*, March 27, 1960.

40. Winfried Junge, "Sind wir so?," *Forum*, December 3, 1959. Junge himself went on to have a distinguished career as a documentarist. He is best known for *Die Kinder von Gotzow*, a series of films following a group of individuals through various life stages from early childhood to adulthood.

41. Fred Seeger and Brigitta Staaman, "Unser Ja zu diesem Film," *Forum*, December 17, 1959.

42. Kurt Starke, "Die Republik der Nackten," *Wochenpost*, July 22, 1993.

43. See Aktennotiz, signed Dudow and Wilkening, October 24, 1959, BA Berlin DR117 1929 (Zentrale Analysengruppe).

44. See Slatan Dudow, "Das Heitere ernst betrachtet," *Forum*, January 21, 1960. I have not yet attempted to research this incident independently.

45. *Das Protokoll des V. Parteitages der Sozialistischen Einheitspartei Deutschlands*, 1:160.

46. Slatan Dudow, "Die Heiterkeit und das Schöne," *Sonntag*, January 10, 1960.

47. Slatan Dudow, "Das Heitere ernst betrachtet," *Forum*, January 21, 1960.

48. Karl-Eduard von Schnitzler, "Vor dem 10. Jahrestag: Einige Gedanken zur Situation des DEFA-Spielfilms," *Deutsche Filmkunst* 7, no. 9 (1959): 258–59.

49. See Slatan Dudow, "Missbrauch der Kritik," *Deutsche Filmkunst* 7, no. 10 (1959): 329.

50. Arno Röder, "Aktennotiz für Gen. Alfred Kurella," December 24, 1959, SAPMO DY30 IV2/906/222 (ZK Kultur).

51. Ibid.

52. VVB Film, Abteilung Filmproduktion, "Abschlussergebnis der Untersuchungen der Kommission der VVB Film über die Verantwortung des Direktionskollektives im Spielfilmstudio für das Filmprojekt 'Verwirrung der Liebe,' " June 30, 1960, BA Berlin DR117 1929 (Zentrale Analysengruppe, Kollege Zunft).

53. See the report of the SED district office: "Bürovorlage: Einschätzung der Abteilung Volksbildung/Kultur zur Bürovorlage der Parteileitung des VEB DEFA-Studio für Spielfilme," December 21, 1959, SAPMO DY30 IV2/906/211 (ZK Kultur).

54. Konrad Schwalbe, interview by author, tape recording, Potsdam, April 24, 1993.

55. See also Slatan Dudow to the Zentral Parteileitung der SED, DEFA-Studio für Spielfilme, October 2, 1961, SAPMO DY30 IV2/906/222 (ZK Kultur).

56. Abteilung Produktionsvorbereitung und Wirtschaftskontrolle, "Bericht über die Prüfung des Spielfilms 'Verwirrung der Liebe,' " n.d., 1–2, BA Berlin DR117 1929 (Zentrale Analysengruppe, Kollege Zunft).

57. Ibid., 4.

58. Ibid., 7–8.

59. Ibid., 2.

60. Slatan Dudow, "Stellungnahme zum Produktionsablauf des Films 'Verwirrung der Liebe,' " June 12, 1960, 4, 7, SAPMO DY30 IV2/906/222 (ZK Kultur).

61. Ibid., 5–6.

62. Ibid., 10–15.

63. Abteilung Filmproduktion, VVB Film, "Abschlussergebnis der Untersuchungen der Kommission der VVB Film über die Verantwortung des Direktionskollektives im Spielfilmstudio für das Filmprojekt 'Verwirrung der Liebe,' " June 20, 1960, BA Berlin DR1 4042 (Abteilung Filmproduktion).

64. "Vorlage für die Zentral Parteileitungssitzung am 28.6.1960," June 27, 1960, BA Berlin DR1 4042 (Abteilung Filmproduktion).

65. Scattered complaints about the union's ineffectiveness can be found in numerous documents from the late 1950s and early 1960s. For example, during a December 16, 1959, studio direction meeting, a union representative complained not only about artists' "underestimating" the union's importance but also about a lack of "clarity between the Party and the union." In the end, his organization always got stuck with "minor tasks, like bringing ashtrays, etc." "Protokoll über die Direktionssitzung am 16. Dezember 1959," December 18, 1958, BA Berlin DR117 A/091. See also similar complaints in the report of the Potsdam SED

office, "Bürovorlage: Einschätzung der Abteilung Volksbildung/Kultur zur Bürovorlage der Parteileitung des VEB DEFA-Studio für Spielfilme," December 21, 1959, SAPMO DY30 IV2/906/211 (ZK Kultur).

66. See Zentrale Kommission für staatliche Kontrolle, "Bericht über die Themen- und Produktionsplanung sowie die Verpflichtung von Künstlern im VEB DEFA-Studio für Spielfilme in Potsdam-Babelsberg," March 19, 1956, SAPMO DY30 IV2/2026/77 (Büro Kurella).

67. VVB Film, Ökonomie und Planung, "Feststellung zum Film 'Verwirrung der Liebe,'" June 30, 1960, BA Berlin DR1 4042 (Abteilung Filmproduktion).

68. *DDR-Handbuch*, 950–51.

69. SED-Betriebsparteiorganisation des DEFA-Studios für Spielfilme, "Betr.: Bisherige Ergebnisse bei der Durchführung des Beschlusses des Politbüros zu Fragen des Spielfilmschaffens in der DDR vom Oktober 1961," April 17, 1962, 4, SAPMO DY30 IV2/906/211 (ZK Kultur).

70. Ibid.

71. Ruth Breitenbach, "Betr: 'Verwirrung der Liebe.' Wo es zur Verkehrung Arbeitsverhtl. Bestimmungen kam," June 29, 1960, BA Berlin DR1 4042 (Abteilung Filmproduktion).

72. APO I, "Über die Ursachen des Zurückbleibens unserer nationalen Filmproduktion," November 2, 1960, 5, SAPMO DY30 IV2/906/211 (ZK Kultur).

73. Konrad Wolf to HV Film, January 31, 1956, BA Berlin DR1 4143 (Sekretariat des Leiters). The film involved was *Genesung*.

74. Slatan Dudow, "Stellungnahme zum Produktionsablauf des Films 'Verwirrung der Liebe,'" June 12, 1960, SAPMO DY30 IV2/906/222 (ZK Kultur).

75. DEFA had essentially a captive market. Its distributors, Progress Filmverleih and DEFA-Aussenhandel, were required to purchase its films at prices determined in the plan. In addition, it is difficult to assess the exact significance of a balance sheet and money in an economy of scarcity where prices were fixed.

76. This figure is derived from the catalog of the former Staatliches Filmarchiv, *DEFA-Spielfilme 1946–1964*, and includes four made-for-television movies produced under contract with the Deutsche Fernsehfunk (DFF). *Das zweite Leben der Filmstadt Babelsberg* lists twenty-seven films for the year exclusive of the DFF productions.

77. VEB DEFA-Studio für Spielfilm, "Künstlerisch-ideologische Perspektivplan bis 1965," 1, BA Berlin DR117 2324 (Hauptdirektor).

78. This was a Bulgarian coproduction, scripted by the Bulgarian writer Angel Wangelstein.

79. VEB DEFA-Studio für Spielfilm, "Künstlerisch-ideologische Perspektivplan bis 1965," 2, BA Berlin DR117 2324 (Hauptdirektor).

80. Ibid.

81. "Anlage Nr. 1 zum Protokoll Nr. 52 vom 9.10.61," 2–3, SAPMO DY30 J IV2/2-794 (PB Sitzungen). Ironically, one of the few *Gegenwartsfilme* praised in the resolution was *Verwirrung der Liebe*, even though this work's production history was hardly in keeping with the Politburo's call for increased efficiency.

82. Other *Auftragsfilme* include *Die Entscheidung des Dr. Ahrendts* (Frank Vogel, 1959), *Kapitäne bleiben am Bord* (Martin Hellberg, 1959), *Senta auf Ab-*

wegen (Martin Hellberg, 1959), *Musterknaben* (Johannes Kittel, 1959), *Ärzte* (Lutz Köhlert, 1960), *Alwin der Letze* (Hubert Hoelzke, 1960), *Kein Ärger mit Cleopatra* (Helmut Schnieder, 1960), and *Zu jeder Stunde* (Heinz Thiel, 1960). See Ralf Schenk, "Mitten im kalten Krieg 1955–1960," 143.

83. Horst Knietzsch, "Die 'Neue Welle' aus den Babelsberger Ateliers," *Neues Deutschland*, October 10, 1959.

84. VEB Progress Film-Vertrieb, "Analyse zum Stand der Planerfüllung im I. Quartal 1959," May 11, 1959, SAPMO DY30 NL 109/96 (Nachlass Ackermann). This report predicted that by 1963 one-third of GDR households would be equipped with televisions. It also noted that television owners tended immediately after making their purchase to avoid movies but eventually returned to cinemas to view films that either were unavailable on television or supplemented the offerings there. The report concluded that recouping audiences lost to television would be possible only through improving the quality of individual motion pictures.

85. Between 1957 and 1958, the number of cinema visits per capita in the DDR declined from 18.1 to 15.8. In 1959, this figure declined again to 14.9. See VVB Film, "Kurze Einschätzung über die Erfüllung der politisch-ideologischen Aufgaben in Filmverleih," February 12, 1960, SAPMO DY30 IV2/906/249 (ZK Kultur).

86. VEB DEFA-Studio für Spielfilm, "Künstlerisch-ideologische Perspektivplan bis 1965," BA Berlin DR117 2324 (Hauptdirektor). Due to the shortage of hard currency, the GDR film industry committed itself to independently developing 70mm production capabilities. This project, after years of trial and error, was a technical success, but a financial disaster.

87. Ernst Hoffmann, "Errichtet neue Höhe in der Filmkunst," *Deutsche Filmkunst* 7, no. 10 (October 1959): 297–98.

88. See VEB DEFA-Studio für Spielfilme, SED Betriebsorganisation, "Bürovorlage," December 21, 1959, SAPMO DY30 IV2/906/211 (ZK Kultur).

89. Konrad Schwalbe, interview by author, tape recording, Potsdam, April 24, 1993; Klaus Wischnewski, interview by author, tape recording, Berlin, March 1 and 15, 1993, and August 2, 1993.

90. VEB DEFA-Studio für Spielfilm, "Künstlerisch-ideologische Perspektivplan bis 1965," 2, BA Berlin DR117 2324 (Hauptdirektor); "Anlage Nr. 1 zum Protokoll Nr. 52 vom 9.10.61," SAPMO DY30 J IV2/2-794 (PB Sitzungen). See also VVB Film, Abteilung Produktion, "Auszug aus dem Protokoll der 13. Kollegiumssitzung am Dienstag dem 8.12.59," BA Berlin DR1 4437.

91. See HV Film, Abteilung Lichtspielwesen, "Studie zur Verwirklichung des neuen ökonomischen Systems der Planung und Leitung in Film- und Lichtspielwesen," section III, BA Berlin DR1 4231.

92. Jochen Mückenberger, interview by author, tape recording, Babelsberg, April 27, 1993; Klaus Wischnewski, interview by author, tape recording, Berlin, March 1 and 15, 1993, and August 2, 1993.

93. Wilkening to Abusch, August 31, 1960, 2, BA Berlin DR117 A/150. It is unclear from this document if such showings actually occurred. Also see the Politburo's 1961 resolution that placed great emphasis on the "materiele Inter-

essiertheit der Filmschaffenden" and on the need for a better system of economic incentive. "Anlage Nr. 1 zum Protokoll Nr. 52 vom 9.10.61," 10, SAPMO DY30 J IV2/2-794 (PB Sitzungen). Attempts at reforming artists' salaries went back to at least 1957. See HV Film, Film Produktion, "Aktennotiz," June 19, 1957, SAPMO DY30 NL 109/97 (Nachlass Ackermann).

94. See "Anlage Nr. 1 zum Protokoll Nr. 52 vom 9.10.61," 6, SAPMO DY30 J IV2/2-794 (PB Sitzungen).

95. Zentrale Parteileitung, "Aufgaben und Stand der Entwicklung der sozialistischen künstlerischen Arbeitsgruppen im VEB DEFA-Studio für Spielfilme," SAPMO DY30 IV2/906/211 (ZK Kultur).

96. Richter, "Zwischen Mauerbau und Kahlschlag," 159.

97. Ibid. In fact, as the star of the popular television series *Liebling Kreuzberg*, Krug later became a major celebrity in the West. Stahl also had a prominent career in the West. The other actors remain popular in the East today.

98. I am indebted to Erika Richter for explaining the history of this genre to me.

99. The two films were *Der geteilte Himmel* (Konrad Wolf, 1964) and *Mir nach, Canaillen* (Ralf Kirsten, 1964). See "Vorlage an das Politbüro des ZKs der SED, betr: Entwicklungsstand, Probleme sowie Hauptaufgaben des Film- und Lichtspielwesens der DDR bis zum Jahre 1970," June 22, 1965, BA Berlin DR117 A/240.

100. "Analyse über die Erfüllung der staatlichen Aufgaben 1965 im Bereich der Hauptverwaltung Film," BA Berlin DR1 4265 (HV Film, Abteilung Filmproduktion). Of course, the damage had already been done. Between 1958 and 1964, overall attendance at DEFA films dropped 60.6 percent. DEFA's market share was also down during this period from 21.5 percent to 17.5 percent of movie tickets sold in the GDR. Ministerrat der DDR, Ministerium der Finanzen, "Analyse über die Entwicklung des Film- und Lichtspielwesens," n.d., BA Berlin DA 1 2977/68.

101. "Stenographische Niederschrift der Parteiaktivtagung der Parteiorganisation der DEFA am 15. April 1958," SAPMO DY30 IV2/906/226 (ZK Kultur), lf. 65–67.

CHAPTER FOUR

1. Hans-Jörg Rother, ". . . und alle Frage offen?," *Forum*, October 1, 1964.

2. Even in its own monopolized market, DEFA by the early sixties was hard pressed to compete with Western films. These routinely dominated the rankings of best-attended movies. For example, the most popular film in the GDR for 1963 was an American western, *The Magnificent Seven*, which had 3,118,309 viewers in just thirteen weeks! See "Filme mit den höchsten Besuchergebnissen 1963/1964," BA Berlin DR1 4329 (HV Film).

3. See, for example, the letters of H. Körner and Ingrid Gimmel, *Sächsische Zeitung*, September 19, 1964.

4. Bergmann's gripe had to do with the choice to use Totalvision, or extra-

wide-screen photography, whose compositional demands, he felt, had led film-makers to neglect other considerations. See "Die Suche nach dem Mass: Erin-nerungen und Fragen eines Kameramannes," *Film und Fernsehen*, no. 12 (1978): 36–38. Hirschmeier expressed the opinion that the picture was "overplanned" and that many images in the film were too "static" and "decorational." Interview by author, tape recording, Babelsberg, July 8, 1993.

5. This theme is developed more extensively in the novel than in the film.

6. Significantly, the brand of the detergent is "Persil"—a reference to the so-called *Persilscheine*, or character references, used in the Western zones during the post–World War II occupation Germany by accused individuals to circumvent denazification proceedings.

7. Konrad Wolf, interview by Ulrich Gregor, 336.

8. Byg, "Geschichte, Trauer und weibliche Identität im Film," 111.

9. Monaco, *Alain Resnais*, 37.

10. Ibid., 42–44; Byg, "Geschichte, Trauer und weibliche Identität im Film," 102–3.

11. Wolf, *Der geteilte Himmel*, 64.

12. Mitter and Wolle, *Untergang auf Raten*, 359.

13. Albert Wilkening to Hans Rodenberg, October 19, 1961, BA Berlin DR1 4038 (HV Film, Abteilung Filmproduktion).

14. "Bericht über die Lage im VEB DEFA-Studio für Spielfilme," September 5, 1961, SAPMO DY30 IV2/906/204 (ZK Kultur).

15. Ibid.

16. VEB DEFA . . . BPO, "Informationsbericht," September 16, 1961, SAPMO DY30 IV2/906/211 (ZK Kultur).

17. "Bericht über die Lage im VEB DEFA-Studio für Spielfilme," September 5, 1961, SAPMO DY30 IV2/906/204 (ZK Kultur).

18. Ibid.

19. VEB DEFA-Studio für Spielfilme Zentrale Parteileitung, "Informations-bericht," August 12, 1961, SAPMO DY30 IV2/906/211 (ZK Kultur).

20. Bericht über die Lage im VEB DEFA-Studio für Spielfilme," September 5, 1961, SAPMO DY30 IV2/906/204 (ZK Kultur).

21. VEB DEFA-Studio für Spielfilme, Kampfgruppe, "Bericht über den Einsatz der Hundertschaft unseres Studios vom 13.8–1.9.61," SAPMO DY30 IV2/ 906/ 211 (ZK Kultur).

22. Kuhn, *Christa Wolf's Utopian Vision*, 4–6. See also Hell, *Post-Fascist Fantasies*.

23. Emmerich, *Kleine Literaturgeschichte der DDR*.

24. Günter Karl, "Experiment im Streitgespräch," *Neues Deutschland*, September 5, 1964.

25. Christoph Funke, "Der geteilte Himmel," *Der Morgen*, September 4, 1964.

26. Günter Sosse, "Der geteilte Himmel," *Berliner Zeitung*, September 29, 1964.

27. Kohlhaase, "Er suchte die Poesie, die in den Dingen steckt," 37.

28. Wolfgang Kohlhaase, interview with author, tape recording, Berlin,

March 19, 1993; Klaus Wischnewski, interview with author, tape recording, Berlin, March 1, 1993.

29. H.U., "Ein Werk voller erregenden Fragen," *Neue Zeit*, September 8, 1964.

30. *Probleme des sozialistischen Realismus in der darstellenden Kunst behandelt am Beispiel des DEFA-Films "Der geteilte Himmel,"* 35–37.

31. Mittenzwei, "Zur Kafka-Konferenz 1963," 85. See also Erbe, *Die verfemte Moderne*, 98–105.

32. Cultural Minister Hans Bentzien to PB candidate Alfred Kurella, July 12, 1961; HV Film director Hans Rodenberg to Kurella, January 24, 1962, SAPMO DY30 IV2/906/100 (ZK Kultur).

33. See, for example, a memo to the HV Film director Hans Rodenberg, "Betr.: Überprüfung von polnischen Filmen," October 23, 1961, SAPMO DY30 IV2/906/100 (ZK Kultur). A related problem, at least before the Wall's construction, was the discussion of films whose import had been banned in the GDR press. See the letter from Decker, Leiter Sektor Filmabnahme und Kontrolle, HV Film, to Arno Röder, ZK Abteilung Kultur, August 25, 1960, SAPMO DY30 IV2/ 906/ 100 (ZK Kultur).

34. Studiodirektor, "Protokoll über die Besprechung bei Prof. Rodenberg am 25.10.1963," Berlin BA DR117 A/0057 (Studiodirektor).

35. Sekretariat Prof. Rodenberg, "Protokoll über eine Beratung zur Vorbereitung der Leitung des VEB DEFA-Studio für Spielfilme," September 17, 1962, SAPMO DY30 IV2/906/100 (ZK Kultur). See also the PB declaration regarding film of October 9, 1961, available as "Anlage Nr. 1 zum Protokoll Nr. 52 vom 9.10.61," SAPMO J IV2/2-794 (PB Sitzungen).

36. Linden, *Khrushchev and the Soviet Leadership, 1957–1964*, 147–49.

37. "Der Gegenwart verplichtet: Bericht über die Diskussion auf der Parteiaktivtagung der DEFA-Studios für Spielfilme," *Filmwissenschaftliche Mitteilungen* 1, no. 1 (1963): 21.

38. Ibid., 7–8.

39. Anna Lawton, "Introduction: An Interpretive Survey," in *The Red Screen: Politics, Society, Art in Soviet Society*, 6.

40. "Aktennotiz über die Aussprache am 5.1.63 bei Gen. Professor Rodenberg über Probleme unter den Künstlern," BA Berlin DR117 A/0057 (Studiodirektor).

41. "Bericht über die Parteiaktivtagung im VEB DEFA-Studio für Spielfilme zur Vorbereitung des VI. Parteitages," December 19, 1962, 3–4, SAPMO DY30 IV2/906/211 (ZK Kultur).

42. Ibid., 1–3.

43. Klaus Wischnewski, interview by author, tape recording, Berlin, March 15, 1993.

44. KAG Heinrich Greif, "Protokoll über die Produktionsversammlung am 8.10.1963 in Halle," BA Berlin DR117 1956 (Zentrale Analysengruppe).

45. See BA Berlin DR117 A/199 (Filmeinschätzungen und Protokolle) and BA Berlin DR117 1956 (Zentrale Analysengruppe).

46. See Anlage 1 from the September 10, 1961, Politburo session, SAPMO

J IV2/2-794 (PB Sitzungen). See also Kohlhaase, "Er suchte die Poesie, die in den Dingen steckt."

47. "Aktennotiz," March 21, 1963, BA Berlin DR117 A/199 (Filmeinschätzungen und Protokolle); Studiodirektor, "Aktennotiz über eine Aussprache mit den Genossen Wolf, Brückner über den Stoff 'Ein Mann kehrt heim,'" October 30, 1962, BA Berlin DR117 A/199 (DEFA Betriebsarchiv, Filmeinschätzungen und Protokolle).

48. *Das zweite Leben der Filmstadt Babelsberg*, 540.

49. The former studio director, Mückenberger, told me that the completed film was so obvious in its political conception that he had no choice but to ban it. Interview by author, tape recording, Babelsberg, April 27, 1993. It remains a mystery as to how this production was made at all.

50. My formulation here is inspired by Patrice Petro's work on the discursive valence attached to women in Weimar Germany. See Petro, "Modernity and Mass Culture in Weimar: Contours of a Discourse on Sexuality in Early Theories of Perception and Representation," 115–46.

51. Heineman, *What Difference Does a Husband Make?*, 176–77.

52. One exception is Frank Beyer's *Eine alte Liebe* (1959). Other films set clearly in the past that featured central female protagonists include *Besondere Kennzeichen keine* (Joachim Kunert, 1956) and *Lissy* (Konrad Wolf, 1957).

53. These male figures also had deep roots in Weimar culture, particularly Communist "production" literature thematizing political struggle within the factory. See Rohrwasser, *Saubere Mädel, starke Genossen: Proletarische Massenliteratur?*

54. These were *Stärker als die Nacht* and *Genesung*, respectively.

55. These include Wolf's *Leute mit Flügeln* (1960) and Beyer's *Fünf Patronenhülsen* (1960) and *Nackt unter Wölfen* (1963).

56. These were Günter Reisch's *Maibowle* (1959) and *Silvesterpunsch* (1960), which are briefly described in Chapter 3.

57. See, for example, the studio's "Künstlerisch-ideologische Perspektivplan bis 1965," circa 1958, 4, BA Berlin DR117 2324, which confirmed, "Stoffe aus dem der Erbauer der sozialistischen Ordnung müssen nach wie vor das Hauptanliegen des neuen Spielfilmschaffens sein." Such calls were generally not gender specific, but they were often paired with demands for films about "authentic heroes" from the history of the working class. While German Communist hagiography did include women—most notably Rosa Luxemburg and Clara Zetkin—men predominated, and most biographical historical dramas that were actually produced featured a male protagonist. Only in the eighties did a film about Zetkin, *Wo andere schweigen* (Ralf Kirsten, 1984), appear.

58. In our interview, Maetzig denied that the seduction theme in *Das Kaninchen bin ich* could be read as a metaphor for artists' relationship with the state. Interview by author, tape recording, Wildkuhl, February 11, 1993.

59. Wolf's preceding work, again in collaboration with Kohlhaase, *Der nackte Mann auf dem Sportplatz* (1974), was also self-reflective about the role of the artist in socialist society, although the protagonist here is a middle-aged sculptor.

60. One of the GDR's few female directors, Iris Güsner, made a film, *Alle*

meine Mädchen (1980), that provided an ironic comment on this phenomenon. Based on a script by Gabriele Kotte, the picture featured a young male documentarist who sets out to make a picture about an all-female work brigade in a lightbulb factory.

61. The major exceptions here are Christa Wolf and Helga Schütz.

62. See also Chapter 2.

63. Wolf's stance during the aftermath of the Eleventh Plenum bears this judgment out. See Chapter 6.

64. For a basic summary of women's social and political positions in East Germany in comparison with West Germany, see Rueschmeyer and Schissler, "Women in the Two Germanies," and Lemke, "Beyond the Ideological Stalemate: Women and Politics in the FRG and GDR in Comparison." For more detailed information, see *Frauen in Deutschland 1945–1992*; Trappe, *Emanzipation oder Zwang?: Frauen in der DDR zwischen Beruf, Familie und Sozialpolitik*. Compare also Heineman, *What Difference Does a Husband Make?*, 176–208.

65. "Einige Frauenprobleme der Kolleginnen des Studios," August 9, 1964, 1, signed "im Auftrag der Frauenkommission," BA Berlin DR117 A/241 (Studiodirektor).

66. There were only three other women directors who completed more than a single feature film at DEFA during the late seventies and eighties: Iris Gusner, Evelyn Schmidt, and Hannelore Unterberg.

67. See Kersten, "The Role of Women in GDR Films since the Early 1970s." A list of films from the seventies and eighties featuring strong female protagonists might include *He, Du!* (Rolf Römer, 1970), *Der Dritte* (Egon Günther, 1972), *Laut und leise ist die Liebe* (Helmut Dziuba, 1972), *Für die Liebe noch zu mager* (Bernhard Stephan, 1974), *Suse, liebe Suse* (Horst Seemann, 1975), *Die unverbesserliche Barbara* (Lothar Warneke, 1977), *Sabine Wulff* (Erwin Stranka, 1978), *Solo Sunny* (Konrad Wolf, 1980), *Unser kurzes Leben* (Lothar Warneke, 1981), *Bürgschaft für ein Jahr* (Herrmann Zschoche, 1981), *Die Beunruhigung* (Lothar Warneke, 1982), *Das Fahrrad* (Evelyn Schmidt, 1982), and *Kaskade rückwärts* (Iris Gusner, 1984). Kersten provides a detailed summary of many of these films.

68. Another important film about an older male figure is Rainer Simon's *Jadup und Boel* (1981). This concerns the likable *Bürgermeister* of a small town, whose reputation is threatened when rumors concerning the rape and disappearance of an adolescent girl directly after the war begin to reemerge.

69. Schieber, "Anfang vom Ende oder Kontinuität des Argwohns 1980 bis 1989," 274.

CHAPTER FIVE

1. Kurt Maetzig, interview by author, tape recording, Wildkuhl (Brandenburg), February 11, 1993.

2. Frank Beyer, interview by author, tape recording, Berlin, February 26, 1993.

3. See Staritz, *Geschichte der DDR*, 147–57.

4. See Eckert, "Die abgebrochene Demokratisierung."

5. Quoted in Staritz, *Geschichte der DDR*, 157.

6. See, for example, Emmerich, *Kleine Literaturgeschichte der DDR*, 172.

7. *Zweite Bitterfelder Konferenz 1964*, 140–49.

8. Staritz, *Geschichte der DDR*, 170–71.

9. For a detailed discussion of the legal reforms referenced in the film, see Soldovieri, "Censorship and the Law: The Case of *Das Kaninchen bin ich*."

10. HV Film, "Studie zur Verwirklichung des neuen ökonomischen Systems der Planung und Leitung im Film- und Lichtspielwesen der DDR," April 29, 1964, I/1, BA Berlin DR1 4231 (Abteilung Lichtspielwesen). My description of these reforms is also based on the following informants: Jochen Mückenberger, interview by author, tape recording, Potsdam-Babelsberg, April 27, 1993; Günter Witt, interview by author, tape recording, Leipzig, May 11, 1993.

11. See "Rechte und Pflichten des Studiodirektors im Verhältnis zu dem Künstlerischen Arbeitsgruppen," June 29, 1964, and "Ordnung über Planung und Planabrechnung der KAGs," BA Berlin DR117 0149 (Studiodirektor).

12. "Arbeitsordnung der Kommission des wissenschaftlich-künstlerischen Beirates der HV Film für die Prädikatisierung von DEFA Spielfilmen und Trickfilmen," BA Berlin DR117 A/241 (Studiodirektor); KAG "Berlin" to Studiodirektor Mückenberger, September 9, 1965, BA Berlin DR117 A/241.

13. Witt, "Wie eine Inquisition."

14. Gert Springfeld HV Film to Genosse Rätz, Büro Hager, "Übersicht über den Ankauf ausländischer Spielfilme und über den Nichteinsatz von Filmen," July 6, 1967, SAPMO DY30 IVA2/2024/19 (Büro Hager).

15. Witt to Otto Gotsche, September 1, 1964, BA Berlin DA 5 6517 (Volkskammer). It is not clear from Witt's proposal to Gotsche whether the closed film series actually took place.

16. As quoted in Rauhut, "DDR-Beatmusik zwischen Engagement und Repression," 53.

17. Staritz, *Geschichte der DDR*, 170–71.

18. Rauhut, "DDR-Beatmusik zwischen Engagement und Repression," 54–55.

19. See Krenzlin, "Vom Jugendkommuniqué zur Dichterschelte."

20. Weber, *DDR: Grundriss der Geschichte 1945–1990*, 108.

21. Stemmler, "Bemerkungen über die Unterhaltungs-Sendungen vom Beginn des DDR-Fernsehens bis zum Ende der fünfziger Jahre."

22. Hoff, "Von 'Da lacht der Bär' über 'Ein Kessel Buntes'—ins 'Aus.'"

23. Christel Gräf, interview by author, tape recording, Babelsberg, March 3, 1993.

24. "Gespräch zwischen Christiane Mückenberger und Kurt Maetzig zu 'Das Kaninchen bin ich,'" in *Prädikat besonders schädlich*, 319.

25. "Theoretischer Teil" of the scenario, "Gedanken zur filmischen Umsetzung des Romans 'Das Kaninchen bin ich' von Manfred Bieler," 4, BA Berlin DR117 A/0100.

26. Kurt Maetzig, "Konzeption für die Entwicklung des Spielfilms nach einem Romanmanuskript von Manfred Bieler," in *Prädikat besonders schädlich*, 308.

27. Such "Umzugsfuhren," or moving carts, were closely associated with proletarian culture in Berlin. Traditionally, they were used by workers to transport their belongings when changing apartments. See the museum exhibit catalog *Berlin! Berlin!: Die Ausstellung zur Geschichte der Stadt*. I am indebted to Reinhard Rürup for drawing my attention to this significant detail.

28. In fact, when Bieler's novel was finally published in the West four years later, critics complained that it presented an all too predictable picture of East Germany.

29. "Theoretischer Teil" of the film's scenario, "Gedanken zur filmischen Umsetzung des Romans 'Das Kaninchen bin ich' von Manfred Bieler," 3, BA Berlin DR117.

30. "Konzeption für die Umarbeitung des Romans von Manfred Bieler," December 8, 1964, BA Berlin DR1 4313.

31. Ibid.

32. Bieler, *Maria Morzeck, oder Das Kaninchen bin ich*, 140.

33. Kurt Maetzig, "Konzeption für die Entwicklung des Spielfilms nach einem Romanmanuskript von Manfred Bieler," in *Prädikat besonders schädlich*, 309.

34. See HV Film, Abteilung Filmproduktion, "Chronologischer Ablauf der Entstehung des Films 'Das Kaninchen bin ich,'" January 17, 1966, BA Berlin DR1 4313.

35. Abt. Filmproduktion, "Stellungnahme zum Drehbuch 'Das kaninchen bin ich' von Manfred Bieler und Prof. Dr. Kurt Maetzig," January 8, 1965, BA Berlin DR1 4313.

36. KAG "Roter Kreis," "Abschlussbericht 'Das Kaninchen bin ich,'" December 9, 1965, BA Berlin DR117 A/0100. See also HV Film, Abteilung Filmproduktion, "Chronologischer Ablauf der Entstehung des Films 'Das Kaninchen bin ich,'" January 17, 1966, BA Berlin DR1 4313.

37. HV Film, Abteilung Filmproduktion, "Chronologischer Ablauf der Entstehung des Films 'Das Kaninchen bin ich,'" January 17, 1966, BA Berlin DR1 4313.

38. Witt to Mückenberger, January 22, 1965, BA Berlin DR117 A/0100.

39. HV Film, Abteilung Filmproduktion, "Chronologischer Ablauf der Entstehung des Films 'Das Kaninchen bin ich,'" January 17, 1966, BA Berlin DR1 4313.

40. Gruppe "Roter Kreis," "Aufgrund vieler Konsultationen und kritischer Beratungen . . . ," February 22, 1965, BA Berlin DR117 A/0100.

41. Günter Karl, Leiter der KAG "Roter Kreis," to Witt, March 18, 1965, BA Berlin DR1 4313. The actor originally assigned to the role, Hans-Peter Minetti, played the role of the opportunist in several DEFA films, including Frank Beyer's *Spur der Steine* (1966).

42. Witt to Mückenberger, May 28, 1965, BA Berlin DR1 4313. Witt's motivations for not sending the letter are indicated in a note written in the margin of the letter.

43. HV Film, "Aktennotiz," June 3, 1965, BA Berlin DR1 4313.

44. Mückenberger to Witt, September 29, 1965, BA Berlin DR117 A/0100.

45. KAG "Roter Kreis," "'Das Kaninchen bin ich,'" October 18, 1965, BA Berlin DR117 A/0100.

46. HV Film, Abteilung Filmproduktion, "Chronologischer Ablauf der Entstehung des Films 'Das Kaninchen bin ich,'" January 17, 1966, BA Berlin DR1 4313.

47. Jochen Mückenberger, interview by author, tape recording, Babelsberg, April 27, 1993.

48. Witt describes these individuals as a "Second Cultural Ministry." See Witt, "Wie eine Inquisition."

49. This incident is described in HV Film, Abteilung Filmproduktion, "Chronologischer Ablauf der Entstehung des Films 'Das Kaninchen bin ich,'" January 17, 1966, BA Berlin DR1 4313.

50. Witt, "Wie eine Inquisition," 259.

51. Ibid., 260; Günter Witt, interview by author, tape recording, Leipzig, May 11, 1993.

52. "Protokoll: KAG-Leiterbesprechung am 12.11.1965," 12, BA Berlin DR117 0149 (Studiodirektor).

53. "Protokoll: Dienstbesprechung am 23.11.1965," BA Berlin DR117 0149 (Studiodirektor).

54. "Protokoll: KAG-Leiterbesprechung am 29.11.1965," 12, BA Berlin DR117 0149 (Studiodirektor).

55. DDR-Handbuch, 804.

56. See Seidel, "Zur Position Erich Apels." For more on Apel's position on trade, see Sodaro, Moscow, Germany, and the West, 79.

57. Scherstjanoi, "'Von der Sowjetunion lernen . . .'"

58. Ibid. See also Linden, Khrushchev and the Soviet Leadership, 1957–1964, 223.

59. Here one might include Bieler's play Zaza or the works of Heiner Müller that were criticized.

60. "Information der Bezirksleitung Berlin an den ZK der SED über einige ideologische Erscheinungen im künstlerischen Bereich," November 19, 1965, SAPMO DY30 IV/2/335 (Vorbereitung zum 11. Plenum).

61. "Information über die Stimmung unter der Künstlerischen Intelligenz," November 23, 1965, SAPMO DY30 IV/1/335 (Vorbereitung zum 11. Plenum). Also in Kahlschlag: Das 11. Plenum des ZK der SED 1965, 309–15.

62. See Erich Honecker's report to the Plenum, "Stenografische Niederschrift der 11. Tagung des Zentralkomitees im Plenarsaal des Hauses des ZK vom 15.–17. Dezember 1965," 72–73, SAPMO DY30 IV2/1/336. Also in Dokumente zur Kunst-, Literatur- und Kulturpolitik der SED, 1:1078.

63. "Kurze Einschätzung von Wolf Biermanns Gedichtband 'Die Drahtharfe,' erschienen in Westberlin," SAPMO DY30 IV/2/335 (Vorbereitung zum 11. Plenum).

64. "Auszug aus einem Bericht über die Situation im Kulturbereich des Deutschen Fernsehfunks," SAPMO DY30 IV/2/335 (Vorbereitung zum 11. Plenum). Also in Kahlschlag: Das 11. Plenum des ZK der SED 1965, 304–9.

65. "Information über den Inhalt der Filmwissenschaftlichen Mitteilungen Nr. 2/1965 . . . 29.11.1965," SAPMO DY30 IV/2/335 (Vorbereitung zum 11. Plenum).

66. "An die 1. Sekretäre der Bezirksleitungen der SED," November 2, 1965,

SAPMO DY30 IV/2/335 (Vorbereitung zum 11. Plenum). Also in *Kahlschlag: Das 11. Plenum des ZK der SED 1965*, 321–22.

67. "Abschrift eines Briefes und eines Aufrufes von 138 Studenten der Theaterhochschule Leipzig an die Redaktion des 'Forum,' Zeitschrift des Zentralrates der FDJ," SAPMO DY30 IV/2/335 (Vorbereitung zum 11. Plenum). Also in *Kahlschlag: Das 11. Plenum des ZK der SED 1965*, 322–25.

68. "Information über die Vorkommnisse im Ernteeinsatz durch Studenten der Humboldtuniversität im Bezirk Neubrandenburg," SAPMO DY30 IV/2/335 (Vorbereitung zum 11. Plenum). Also in *Kahlschlag: Das 11. Plenum des ZK der SED 1965*, 325–29.

69. "Information über den Studenteneinsatz der TU Dresden im VEG Gustävel, Kreis Sternberg," SAPMO DY30 IV/2/335 (Vorbereitung zum 11. Plenum).

70. "Abschrift eines Briefes einer Lehrerin an Genossen Staatssekretär Giessmann," SAPMO DY30 IV/2/335 (Vorbereitung zum 11. Plenum).

71. Erich Honecker's report to the Plenum, "Stenografische Niederschrift der 11. Tagung des Zentralkomitees im Plenarsaal des Hauses des ZK vom 15.–17. Dezember 1965," 66, SAPMO DY30 IV2/1/336. Also in *Dokumente zur Kunst-, Literatur- und Kulturpolitik der SED*, 1:1076.

72. Kurt Hager, "Die Kunst ist immer Waffe im Klassenkampf," in *Dokumente zur Kunst-, Literatur- und Kulturpolitik der SED*, 1:1114.

73. Ibid., 1115.

74. Ibid., 1115–16.

75. Walter Ulbricht, "Schlusswort auf dem 11. Plenum," in *Kahlschlag: Das 11. Plenum des ZK der SED 1965*, 351.

76. Erich Honecker's report to the Plenum, "Stenografische Niederschrift der 11. Tagung des Zentralkomitees im Plenarsaal des Hauses des ZK vom 15.–17. Dezember 1965," 67, SAPMO DY30 IV2/1/336. Also in *Dokumente zur Kunst-, Literatur- und Kulturpolitik der SED*, 1:1077.

77. Ibid.

78. Ingeborg Lange, "Stenografische Niederschrift der 11. Tagung des Zentralkomitees im Plenarsaal des Hauses des ZK vom 15.–17. Dezember 1965," 302–4, SAPMO DY30 IV2/1/336. The television film to which Lange was referring is *Tiefe Furchen*. Based on a novel by Otto Gotsche, this was hardly a subversive broadcast!

79. Walter Ulbricht, "Schlusswort auf dem 11. Plenum," in *Kahlschlag: Das 11. Plenum des ZK der SED 1965*, 350, 352.

80. This interjection occurred during Witt's self-criticism. See "Parteilichkeit in der Filmkunst: Diskussionsbeitrag und Selbstkritik . . . Günter Witts," in *Dokumente zur Kunst-, Literatur- und Kulturpolitik der SED*, 1:1091.

CHAPTER SIX

1. The director Roland Gräf, who served as the cameraman for *Jahrgang '45*, after relating the story of his own father's fall from grace as a local official and subsequent rehabilitation, explained to me, for example, that "ich hatte die

Hoffnung damals, dass so eine Geschichte wie das 11. Plenum irgendwann korrigiert werden würde, dass es einer von diesen Rückfällen, die mir erschienen, zum System zu gehören, da ich aber von '45 bis in diese Zeit hinein doch erlebt habe." Interview by author, tape recording, Babelsberg, August 17, 1993.

2. "Genosse Werthmann—Versammlung der APO I am 5.1.66," SAPMO DY30 IVA2/906/123 (ZK Kultur).

3. "Bericht über eine Parteiversammlung im DEFA-Studio für Spielfilme— APO Künstlerischer Bereich," December 23, 1965, 8, SAPMO DY30 IVA2/906/223 (ZK Kultur).

4. Ibid.

5. Ibid., 4.

6. See, for example, "Kommissionssitzung am 9.3.66," BA Berlin DR117 A/269.

7. In contrast to the other two films directly criticized at the Plenum, *Der Frühling braucht Zeit* did enjoy a short-lived release; however, it found no public resonance. Its style was radical but wooden, and its script was a politically risky but otherwise unimaginative variant of a standard *Produktionsgeschichte*.

8. HV Film, Abteilung Filmproduktion, "Thesen für eine Analyse des Gegenwartsschaffens im Spielfilms," BA Berlin DR1 4539.

9. Ibid.

10. Ibid.

11. Ibid.

12. Ibid.

13. Ibid.

14. Richter, "Zwischen Mauerbau und Kahlschlag 1961 bis 1965," 204.

15. "Zur Problematik des Filmvorhabens 'Fräulein Schmetterling,'" October 30, 1965, SAPMO DY30 IVA2/906/124 (ZK Kultur).

16. *Das zweite Leben der Filmstadt Babelsberg*, 541.

17. HV Film, Abteilung Filmproduktion, "Betr: Stellungnahme zu dem DEFA-Spielfilm 'Der verlorene Engel,'" August 16, 1966, BA Berlin DR1 4294.

18. "Fortsetzung des Diskussionbeitrages des Gen. Prof. Hager auf der APO-Versammlung am 5.1.1965," SAPMO DY30 IVA2/906/223 (ZK Kultur).

19. Transcript of WDR radio broadcast, "Die Artisten von Babelsberg: Zensur und Selbstbehauptung im Film der DDR," May 10, 1990, 14.

20. "Brief des Genossen Walter Ulbricht an Genossen Prof. Dr. Kurt Maetzig," *Neues Deutschland*, January 23, 1966, as reproduced in *Dokumente zur Kunst-, Literatur- und Kulturpolitik der SED*, 1:1140–44.

21. Bruk to Maass, director of the HV Film, April 12, 1966, BA Berlin DR117 A/269. See also the letter from Bruk to ZK Kultur Abteilung director Siegfried Wagner, November 18, 1966, BA Berlin DR117 A/269. Here Bruk argues that reductions in year-end bonuses are "politisch nicht zu vertreten" despite the studio's heavy losses for the year.

22. Abt. Filmproduktion, "Betr.: Stellungnahme zu dem Filmvorhaben 'Fräulein Schmetterling,'" February 10, 1966, BA Berlin DR1 4249.

23. Frank Beyer, interview by author, tape recording, Berlin, February 26, 1993.

24. The story of *Spur der Steine*'s sabotaged release has been related by Beyer and other filmmakers in numerous interviews. See, for example, "Gespräch mit Frank Beyer," interview by Ralf Schenk in *Regie: Frank Beyer*, 8–105, especially 52–61. See also VEB Berliner Filmtheater, Abt. Filmeinsatz/Presse/Werbung, June 29, 1966, and Abt. Kultur, "Aktennotiz," July 14, 1966, both SAPMO DY30 IVA2/2024/36 (Büro Hager).

25. I am very much indebted for this insight as well as the details of my analysis in this paragraph to Rick Le Vert, who made available to me an unpublished essay on Frank Beyer's films of the early sixties.

26. For the standard account of this literature, see Rohrwasser, *Saubere Mädel, starke Genossen*.

27. Emmerich, *Kleine Literaturgeschichte der DDR*, 108–10.

28. "Aktennotiz," October 21, 1964, BA Berlin DR117 0129.

29. Frank Beyer, interview by author, tape recording, Berlin, February 26, 1993.

30. Wischnewski, "Hoffnungen, Illusionen, Einsichten," 35–39.

31. Frank Beyer, interview by author, tape recording, Berlin, February 26, 1993. See also Beyer to Mückenberger, n.d., BA Berlin DR117 274 (KAG Heinrich Greif). Beyer in this letter also proposed minor changes to the film with two goals in mind. In order to lessen tendencies of "naturalism," he promised to shorten three scenes featuring violence, Balla's public drunkenness, and nude bathing. In addition, Beyer suggested minor dialogue changes in order to make Balla's development as a socialist clearer.

32. "Aussprache zum Film 'Spur der Steine' in der Hauptverwaltung Film . . . am 11. März 1966," 7–8, SAPMO DY30 IVA2/2024/36 (Büro Hager).

33. Ibid., 14–15.

34. Frank Beyer, "Betr.: Film 434—'Spur der Steine,'" March 29, 1966, SAPMO DY30 IVA2/2024/36 (Büro Hager). Beyer, however, resisted more radical changes proposed by the studio's newly named chief dramaturge, Schröder. See Chefdramaturg, "Betr. 'Spur der Steine,'" March 15, 1966, SAPMO DY30 IVA2/2024/36 (Büro Hager).

35. Heinz Kimmel, the functionary in the ZK's cultural section responsible for film, asked Hager for permission to arrange a showing of the altered version to the Politbüro in April; however, such a screening did not occur until late June, well after the film had been officially approved. Kimmel to Hager, April 18, 1966, SAPMO DY30 IVA2/906/124 (ZK Kultur).

36. See Abteilung Kultur, "Information über den Verlauf der Beratung des Filmbeirates . . . zum Film 'Spur der Steine,'" August 16, 1966, SAPMO DY30 IVA2/2024/36 (Büro Hager).

37. Wilfried Maass and Horst Brasch to Hager, May 14, 1966, SAPMO DY30 IVA2/2024/36 (Büro Hager).

38. "Protokoll Nr. 73/66," May 27, 1966, "Abnahmeakte" für *Spur der Steine*, BA Film.

39. Beyer was apparently satisfied with the film's final version. In contrast to other Plenum films, *Spur der Steine* did not require reconstruction after the Wall

fell. Moreover, Beyer has never to my knowledge complained that censorship compromised his film essentially.

40. A copy of this bulletin can be found in SAPMO DY30 IVA2/2024/36 (Büro Hager).

41. VEB Berliner Filmtheater, Abt. Filmeinsatz/Presse/Werbung, June 29, 1966, SAPMO DY30 IVA2/2024/36 (Büro Hager).

42. HV Film, "Notizen zur Zulassung des Films 'Spur der Steine,'" June 23, 1966, 4, SAPMO DY30 IVA2/2024/36 (Büro Hager). For Knietzsch's account, see letter to Beyer, January 17, 1994, published in *Regie: Frank Beyer*, 114–15.

43. HV Film, "Notizen zur Zulassung des Films 'Spur der Steine,'" June 23, 1966, 4, SAPMO DY30 IVA2/2024/36 (Büro Hager).

44. "Reinschriftenprotokoll," June 28, 1966, SAPMO DY30 J IV/2/2-1064 (Politbüro). The details of the plan to limit the film's release were then approved by the ZK Sekretariat, essentially the Politburo's executive committee, on the following day. See "Reinschriftenprotokoll," June 29, 1966, SAPMO DY30 J IV2/3-1194 (ZK Sekretariat). See also addendum no. 6 to this transcript, HV Film, "Für den Einsatz des Filmes 'Spur der Steine' werden folgende Massnahmen angewiesen," June 29, 1966.

45. Indeed, the only reference to the screening I found in the archival record is an indirect one. The head of the ZK Cultural Section, Siegfried Wagner, wrote a letter to Hager to assure the latter that he had *not* revealed information about the screening, even when Konrad Wolf had pressed him to explain the sudden reversal concerning the film. See Wagner to Hager, June 30, 1966, SAPMO DY30 IV2/906/224 (ZK Kultur). See "Standpunkt der Abteilung Kultur des ZK zum Film, 'Spur der Steine,'" June 24, 1966, SAPMO DY30 IV2/906/224 (ZK Kultur).

46. "Werktätige gegen 'Spur der Steine,'" July 5, 1966, published in *Regie: Frank Beyer*, 110–12. Significantly, the ZK Cultural Section contains an informational report about the film prepared for Fröhlich by his office that was apparently also routed to Honecker. See SED Bezirksleitung Leipzig, "Information für Genossen Paul Fröhlich," June 24, 1966, SAPMO DY30 IVA2/2024/36 (Büro Hager).

47. "Reinschriftenprotokoll," June 29, 1966, SAPMO DY30 J IV2/3-1194 (ZK Sekretariat).

48. See "Information über eine Beratung der Abteilung Kultur des ZK mit Genossen der Zentralen Parteileitung des DEFA-Studios für Spielfilme," August 24, 1966, SAPMO DY30 IVA2/906/123 (ZK Kultur).

49. See ibid. That Honecker was consulted on this matter is indicated in a letter from Siegfried Wagner to Kurt Hager, September 1, 1966, SAPMO DY30 IVA2/906/124 (ZK Kultur).

50. Franz Bruk to Siegfried Wagner, July 25, 1966, BA Berlin DR117 A/240.

51. Copies of Wolf's letter to the party activist's convention and an official summary of his self-criticism are contained in *Regie: Frank Beyer*, 119–23.

52. See the Epilogue for a discussion of two examples of such films: *Insel der Schwäne* (Herrmann Zschoche, 1983) and *Jadup und Boel* (Rainer Simon, 1982/1988).

1. Abteilung Produktion, "Stellungnahme zum Drehbuch," March 21, 1966, BA Berlin DR1 4249 (HV Film).

2. Abteilung Filmproduktion, "Betr.: Stellungnahme zu dem DEFA-Spielfilm 'Jahrgang '45,'" October 11, 1966, BA Berlin DR1 4249 (Abteilung Filmproduktion).

3. Roland Gräf, interview by author, tape recording, Babelsberg, August 17, 1993. See also KAG "Roter Kreis," "Protokoll der Parteiversammlung des Stabes 'Jahrgang '45' am 18.10.1966," BA Berlin DR117 1155 (DEFA Archiv).

4. Some examples include *Ein Lord am Alexanderplatz* (Günther Reich, 1967), *Der Mord, der nie verjährt* (Wolfgang Luderer, 1968), *Heroin* (Heinz Thiel, Horst E. Brandt, 1968), *Hauptmann Florian von der Mühle* (Werner W. Wallroth, 1968), and *Mit mir nicht, Madam!* (Roland Oehme, Lothar Warneke, 1969).

5. The directors of the film's four episodes were Gerhard Klein, Karlheinz Carpentier, Ulric Thein, and Frank Vogel.

6. See, for example, "Information über die Ergebnisse der Beratung des ZK über den Stand und die Perspektive der Stoffentwicklung im DEFA-Studio für Spielfilme," February 16, 1968, 3, BA Berlin DY30 IVA2/906/122 (ZK Kultur).

7. Dieter Wolf, interview by author, tape recording, Kleinmachnow, November 15, 1996.

8. For the history of East German television, see *Mit uns zieht die neue Zeit: 40 Jahre DDR-Medien, Eine Ausstellung des Deutschen Rundfunk-Museums* and Hoff, *Tägliche Verblödung: Kritiken, Kollegs und Polemiken zum Fernsehen.*

9. Compare Kersten, "Entwicklungslinien," 46–49.

10. This figure is from the private archive of Dr. Dieter Wiedemann, formerly of the Zentral Institut für Jugendforschung in Leipzig.

11. Theater workers, whose annual bonuses depended in part on the success of special attendance drives, had a direct interest in inflating viewership of films deemed ideologically important. Thus attendance figures for such works are at best very approximate. Still, considerable variation in attendance figures among films suggests that these figures were at least partially reflective of actual popularity.

12. See Rolf Liebmann, "Das einfache Thema war uns gerade recht: Gespräch mit dem Regisseur Lothar Warneke und dem Kameramann Roland Gräf," *Sonntag*, no. 39 (1970).

13. Ironically Böttcher himself was able to participate in these developments only indirectly. *Jahrgang '45* proved to be his first and last feature film. Banished from the studio after the political failure of his film, he resumed a career as a documentarist. Despite repeated political run-ins over the next twenty years, he would hone an extreme minimalist, avant-garde style, which in many of his works transforms a fascination with the ordinary into an exposition of pure form.

14. Rolf Liebmann, "Das einfache Thema war uns gerade recht: Gespräch mit dem Regisseur Lothar Warneke und dem Kameramann Roland Gräf," *Sonntag*, no. 39 (1970).

15. Roland Gräf, interview by author, tape recording, Babelsberg, August 17, 1993.

16. Lothar Warneke, "Der dokumentare Spielfilm" (Diplomarbeit, Deutsche Hochschule für Filmkunst, 1964), as partially reprinted in Lothar Warneke, *Film ist eine Art zu Leben*.

17. "Gegenwärtiger Stand der politisch-ideologischen Situation nach dem 11. Plenum des ZK," BA Berlin DR117 A/269 (Sekretariat Studiodirektor, DEFA Archiv).

18. Maetzig's dramaturge, Christel Gräf, remembers that she and Maetzig were poured big glasses of cognac by Siegfried Wagner, head of the ZK Cultural Section, after the showing of the initial cut. Christel Gräf, interview by author, tape recording, Babelsberg, March 3, 1993.

19. See, for example, VEB DEFA-Studio für Spielfilm, "Begründung zum thematischen Produktionsplan," January 1, 1969, BA Berlin DR117 S757 (DEFA Archiv); and VEB DEFA-Studio für Spielfilm, "Bericht des Hauptdirektors über das 1. Halbjahr 1969," BA Berlin DR117 S691a-i (DEFA Archiv).

20. Abteilung Kultur, "Information zur Spielfilmproduktion des Jahres 1968 und über Mangel in der staatlichen Leitung des Spielfilmstudios," January 20, 1969, 3–4, SAPMO DY30 IVA2/906/122 (ZK Kultur).

21. "Berichterstattung des Parteisekretärs im DEFA-Studio für Spielfilme an die Kulturabteilung des ZK zum Stand der politisch-ideologischen Arbeit im Studio," January 26, 1970, 9–10, SAPMO DY30 IVA2/906/123 (ZK Kultur).

22. Jäger, *Kultur und Politik in der DDR*, 140.

23. Meuschel, *Legitimation und Parteiherrschaft in der DDR*, 221–29; Staritz, *Geschichte der DDR*, 198–214.

24. Günther K. Lehmann, "Poesie des Alltäglichen, Bemerkungen zu äesthetischen Fragen der Arbeit," *Sonntag* no. 50 (1973).

25. As quoted in Richter, *Alltag und Geschichte in DEFA-Gegenwartsfilmen der siebziger Jahre*, 16.

26. Abteilung Kultur, "Aktennotiz über ein Gespräch mit den Genossinnen Ittmann und Leberecht von der Abteilung Frauen," December 6, 1971, SAPMO DY30 IVA2/906/24.

27. Egon Günther, interview by author, tape recording, Babelsberg, November 26, 1996.

28. Heiner Carow, interview with author, tape recording, Babelsberg, November 7, 1996.

29. Kersten, "Entwicklungslinien," 49.

30. Carow, "Ich bin einer aus diesem Volk," 20–21.

31. The poem can be translated roughly as follows:

If a person lives only a short time
Everyone says that it's too soon for him to be leaving.
If a person lives a long time
Everyone says that it is time for him to be leaving

Everything has its time
Gather stones, scatter stones

Plant trees, cut down trees
Life and death and peace and war

My girlfriend is beautiful
As I got up, she had already fled
Wake her not until she stirs
I have laid myself down in her shadow

32. Plenzdorf, "Die Legende von Paul und Paula," 170.

33. Andrea Rinke, "The Eternally Feminine of the Anarchy of Lust?" (paper given at the conference "The Cinema of Eastern Germany: The View from North America," Smith College, Northampton, Mass., October 2–5, 1997). Not surprisingly, some Western feminist filmmakers blasted the film at the time as sexist. See Helke Sander and Renée Schlesier, "Die Legende von Paul und Paula: Eine frauenverachtende Schnulze aus der DDR," *Frauen und Film*, no. 2 (1974): 8–47.

34. Plenzdorf, "Die Legende von Paul und Paula."

35. See Protokoll Nr. 343/72, December 6, 1972, BA Film, Abnahme file. The initial official response seems to have been very positive since the film was originally supposed to premiere in March 1973 at the Leipziger Messe, a high-profile annual trade fair.

36. Heiner Carow, interview with author, tape recording, Babelsberg, November 7, 1996.

37. Horst Knietzsch, "Die Legende von Paul und Paula," *Neues Deutschland*, March 31, 1973. See also K.-H. Schmidt, "Paula ringt um ihre grosse Liebe," *Junge Welt*, April 3, 1973.

38. "1973 eingesetze DEFA-Spielfilme," SAPMO DR117 3027b (DEFA Archiv).

39. See Peter Heldt to Kurt Hager, March 29, 1973, and the attached reports from the Sonderschule des ZK "Hans Marchiwitza" and Gewerksschafts-Hochschule in Bernau, BA Berlin DR117 3115 (DEFA Archiv).

40. "Das Kollektiv des Films 'Die Legende von Paul und Paula' hat in der Zeit vom 14. März bis 4. April 1973 eine Reihe . . . ," n.d., 6–8, BA Berlin DR117 3115 (DEFA Archiv).

41. "Besuchermeinungen zu dem Film 'Paul und Paula,' " n.d., 1, BA Berlin DR117 3115 (DEFA Archiv).

42. Ibid., 3.

43. Ibid.

44. Ibid., 1.

45. Ibid.

46. Ibid., 4.

47. Ibid., 3.

48. Ibid. See also Jahne, Leiter der Kulturpolitik, VEB Lichtspielbetrieb Dresden an Werner Beck, Hauptdramaturg, April 13, 1973, BA Berlin DR117 7137 (DEFA Archiv).

49. The attendance figures after the first year of release for *Der Mann der nach der Oma kam, KLK an PTX—Die Rote Kapelle,* and *Reife Kirschen* were 2,064,002, 2,107,093, and 1,120,166 respectively, although the last two films likely benefited from organized attendance drives. Among the DEFA westerns

produced in the early seventies were *Osceoloa* (Konrad Petzold, 1971), *Tecumseh* (Hans Kratzert, 1972), *Apachen* (Gottfried Kolditz, 1973), and *Ulzana* (Gottfried Kolditz, 1974). All but the last of these had more than 2 million in attendance during their first year of release. See the file BA Berlin DR117 3027b (DEFA Archiv).

50. Bisky and Wiedemann, *Der Spielfilm: Rezeption und Wirkung*, 11.

51. Ibid., 13.

52. "Entwicklung der Besucherzahlen, 1972–1974," exact source and date unclear, SAPMO DY30 IVB2/906/80 (ZK Kultur), f. 206.

53. For DEFA attendance statistics from the early seventies, see the tables contained in BA Berlin DR117 3027b (DEFA Archiv).

54. See, for example, Gewerkschaftsgruppe der Regisseure, VEB DEFA-Studio für Spielfilm, "Gedanken zur Situation unseres Spielfilmsschaffens," ca. September 1975, SAPMO DY30 IVB2/906/83 (ZK Kultur).

55. For official reactions to both *Das zweite Leben des Georg Friedrich Wilhelm Platows* and *Eine Pyramide für mich*, see SAPMO DY30 IVB2/906/80 (ZK Kultur).

56. See "Protokoll über die Studioabnahme des Films 'Die Schlüssel am 29.9.1972," October 3, 1972, BA Berlin DR117 4329 (DEFA Archiv); Abteilung Kultur, "Aktennotiz über eine erweiterte Sitzung des Präsidiums des Verbandes der Film- und Fernsehschaffenden der DDR am 18.1.1973," February 5, 1973, SAPMO DY30 IVB2/906/83 (ZK Kultur).

57. Abteilung Kultur, "Information über ein Gespräch mit Genossen Marekwitzsch, Attaché der Botschaft der VR Polen . . . ," June 8, 1973, SAPMO DY30 IVB2/906/80 (ZK Kultur).

58. Gewerkschaftsgruppe der Regisseure, VEB DEFA-Studio für Spielfilm, "Gedanken zur Situation unseres Spielfilmsschaffens," 2, ca. September 1975, SAPMO DY30 IVB2/906/83 (ZK Kultur).

59. "Zur Leitungssituation auf dem Gebiet der Spielfilmproduktion," 2, exact date unclear but probably 1975, SAPMO DY30 IVB2/906/80 (ZK Kultur).

60. Jürschik, "Alltag und Epoche im DEFA-Kinofilm," 172.

61. Ibid.

62. Ibid., 174–75.

63. SED Hausmitteilung, Manfred Banaschak to Kurt Hager, March 17, 1975, SAPMO DY30 IVB2/2024/83 (Büro Hager).

64. See note 23 above.

65. Merkel, "Konsumkultur in der DDR: Über das Scheitern der Gegenmoderne auf dem Schlachtfeld des Konsums." For more on consumer culture in the GDR, refer to *Wunderwirtschaft: DDR-Konsumkultur in den 60er Jahren*.

66. Rauhut, *Beat in der Grauzone: DDR-Rock 1964 bis 1972—Politik und Alltag*, 209–34.

67. Ibid., 235–98.

68. Thinius, "Paul und Paula im Sozialismus," 146.

69. See Ina Merkel, "Die Nackten und die Roten: Zum Verhältnis von Nacktheit und Öffentlichkeit in der DDR," 80–108.

70. For a summary of official policy toward the family and women, see

Trappe, *Emanzipation oder Zwang?: Frauen in der DDR zwischen Beruf, Familie und Sozialpolitik*, 35–80.

71. Merkel, "Leitbilder und Lebensweisen von Frauen," 374.

72. Bertram, "Zur Entwicklung der sozialen Geschlechterverhältnisse in den neuen Bundesländern." See also Heineman, *What Difference Does a Husband Make?*, 239–46.

73. Barck, Langermann, and Requate, "Kommunikative Strukturen, Medien und Öffentlichkeiten in der DDR," 27.

74. Mitter and Wolle, *Untergang auf Raten.*

75. F. Mühlberg, "Konformismus oder Eigensinn?: Eingaben als Quelle zur Erforschung der Alltagsgeschichte der DDR," 331–45. See also Klötzer, "Öffentlichkeit in der DDR?: Die soziale Wirklichkeit im 'Eulenspiegel.'"

76. *Der Spiegel*, no. 27 (1995): 41.

77. For an introduction to some of the sociological literature, see Hradil, "Die Modernisierung des Denkens: Zukunftspotentiale und 'Altlasten' in Ostdeutschland"; Vester, "Deutschlands feine Unterschiede: Mentalitäten und Modernisierung in Ost- und Westdeutschland"; Brahler and Richter, "Deutsche Befindlichkeiten im Ost-West-Vergleich"; and Meulemann, "Aufholtendenzen und Systemeffekte: Eine Übersicht über Wertunterschiede zwischen West- und Ostdeutschland." See also Vester, Hofmann, and Zierke, *Soziale Milieus in Ostdeutschland.*

78. "Sammlung, Ausstellung, Bibliothek," information pamphlet of Dokumentationszentrum Alltagskultur der DDR (Eisenhüttenstadt, 1997).

79. MDR Fernsehdirektion, "Ausgewählte DEFA-Filme im MDR Fernsehen . . . die zwischen 1.1.1992 und 30.9.1997 gelaufen sind"; ORB-Medienforschung, "DEFA-Spielfilme im ORB 3," April 11, 1997. These materials were prepared for me by Ute Frank of MDR and Dr. Annette Mende of ORB respectively. DEFA films typically run on early weekday or weekend evenings. Not surprisingly, their ratings have been far stronger in the East than in the West. According to the limited statistics provided me, the most popular works have been entertainment pictures, particularly DEFA westerns and those featuring popular stars. In Berlin-Brandenburg, for example, over 200,000 viewers tuned in to watch Rolf Herricht's *Geliebte weisse Maus* (1964) as well as the children's film *Das kalte Herz* (1950). In Saxony, Saxony-Anhalt, and Thuringia, another Herricht picture, *Der Baulöwe* (1980), garnered 13 percent of viewers, while the Austrian coproduction *Johann Strauss—Der ungekrönte König* (1987) obtained a 12.2 percent rating. Other popular films in this region included *Der Reserveheld* (1965), 10.6 percent; *Heisser Sommer* (1966), 8.9 percent (as a repeat); *Vergesst mir meine Traudel nicht* (1957), 8.1 percent; and *Mir nach Canaillen!* (1964), 7.8 percent (as a repeat).

80. Perusal of both of Berlin's two major biweekly entertainment guides, *Tip* and *Zitty*, for the mid-nineties confirms this observation.

81. For a detailed discussion of the enduring nature of this pattern for constructing German identity, see Applegate, *A Nation of Provincials.*

82. There is no real equivalent to the *Schrebergarten* in English. It represents something of a cross between a plot in a community garden and a vacation home.

83. Gaus, *Wo Deutschland liegt*, 119 (punctuation modified).

84. Fulbrook, *Anatomy of a Dictatorship*, 141.

85. For a discussion of these West German developments, see Kaes, *From Hitler to Heimat*.

86. See, generally, *The Reemergence of Civil Society in Eastern Europe and the Soviet Union*.

87. See my discussion of Hall in the Introduction.

EPILOGUE

1. "Babelsberg: Das ist ein Wort wie Hollywood," interview of Peter Fleischmann and Volker Schlöndorff by Wolf Donner, *Tip*, 13/92. For detailed discussions of DEFA's final dissolution, see Dalichow, "Das letzte Kapitel," and Naughton, "'We Were the People': Film Culture, Comedy, and the Unification of Germany."

2. Volker Schlöndorff, "Die Vision oder wem gehört Babelsberg: DEFA und Kein Ende: Offene Antwort . . . auf Günter Reisch," *Berliner Zeitung*, November 22, 1997.

3. "Die etwas vereinfachte Gleichung: Offener Brief des Filmregisseurs Günter Reisch an die DEFA-Erben z. Hd. Volker Schlöndorff," *Berliner Zeitung*, November 13, 1993.

4. See, for example, "Sentiment für Babelsberg," interview of Egon Günther by Rosemarie Rehahn, *Wochenpost*, December 18, 1991.

5. Bulgakowa, "Versprengte Szene: Die DDR-Intellektuellen nach der Vereinigung," 143.

6. Bathrick, *The Powers of Speech*, 19.

7. Dalichow, "Das letzte Kapitel," 336.

8. Compare ibid., 338. I have mentioned here only some of the better-known post-*Wende* DEFA films. Far more extensive discussions can be found in Bulgakowa, Dalichow, and Naughton.

9. Bulgakowa, "Versprengte Szene: Die DDR-Intellektuellen nach der Vereinigung," 146–47.

10. Berbig and Karlson, "Leute haben sich als Gruppe erwiesen," 11–12.

11. These included writers such as Jurek Becker, Ulrich Plenzdorf, Klaus Poche, and Helga Schütz and actors such as Angelika Domröse, Jutta Hoffmann, Manfred Krug, Armin Müller-Stahl, Katherina Thalbach, and Hilmar Thate.

12. Emmerich, *Kleine Literaturgeschichte der DDR*, 239.

13. Bathrick, *The Powers of Speech*, 20–21; Emmerich, *Kleine Literaturgeschichte der DDR*, 401–17.

14. Gewerkschaftsgruppe der Regisseure, VEB DEFA-Studio für Spielfilm, "Gedanken zur Situation unseres Spielfilmsschaffens," 2, ca. September 1975, SAPMO DY30 IVB2/906/83 (ZK Kultur).

15. "Gespräch mit Konrad Wolf," April 12, 1975, SAPMO DY30 IVB2/906/80 (ZK Kultur).

16. Wischnewski, "Träumer und gewöhnliche Leute, 1966 bis 1979," 249.

17. Beyer to Hager, ca. 1980, SAPMO DY30 IVB2/2024/110 (Büro Hager).

18. Hager to Honecker, January 13, 1977, SAPMO DY30 IVB2/906/42 (ZK Kultur).

19. Geiss, *Repression und Freiheit*.

20. Walther, *Sicherungsbereich Literatur: Schriftsteller und Staatssicherheit in der Deutschen Demokratischen Republik*.

21. Geiss, *Repression und Freiheit*, 131.

22. Ibid., 130–40. See also Rainer Simon, "Ich hätte meine Filme auch woanders gemacht," interview by Erika and Rolf Simon, *Film und Fernsehen*, no. 3 (1992): 3–7.

23. Geiss, *Repression und Freiheit*, 194–96. This interpretation is consistent with the conclusions in Joachim Walther's far more detailed study of the Stasi and the GDR publishing industry. Walther, *Sicherungsbereich Literatur*, 28–68.

24. Geiss, *Repression und Freiheit*, 148–69.

25. Ibid., 170–80. After 1989, the Schönemanns also made a documentary film about their experience, *Verriegelte Zeit*.

26. VEB DEFA-Studio für Spielfilme, "Begründung zum Perspektivplan 1971–1975," September 17, 1970, BA Berlin DR117 S633 (DEFA Archiv).

27. DEFA-Studio für Spielfilme, BPO, "Diskussionsgrundlage zu den kulturpolitischen Ergebnisse des DEFA-Studios für Spielfilme seit dem VIII. Parteitag," December 1, 1975, 27–28.

28. Konrad Wolf to Erich Honecker, August 7, 1979, SAPMO DY30 IVB2/2024/117 (Büro Hager).

29. Kurt Hager to Erich Honecker, June 26, 1978, SAPMO DY30 IVB2/2024/83 (Büro Hager).

30. Protokoll Nr. 39 der Sitzung des Sekretariats des ZK, April 28, 1976, SAPMO DY30 IV2/1/2442 (ZK Sekretariat).

31. I rely here on an unpublished essay, written after 1989, by a former DEFA dramaturge: Dieter Wolf, ". . . sich selbst als einen der wichtigsten Zensuren betrachten." Compare also Schieber, "Anfang vom Ende oder Kontinuität des Argwohns 1980 bis 1989," 323–24.

32. Hubert Vater, "Was ich mir mehr von unseren Filmemachern wünsche," *Neues Deutschland*, November 17, 1981. Also quoted in Schieber, "Anfang vom Ende oder Kontinuität des Argwohns 1980 bis 1989," 266.

33. Dieter Wolf, interview by author, tape recording, Kleinmachnow, November 15, 1996.

34. For a nuanced interpretation of *Das Fahrrad*, see Rinke, "From Models to Misfits: Women in DEFA Films of the 1970s and 1980s."

35. Gabriele Kotte, interview by author, tape recording, Berlin, August 4, 1997.

36. For a detailed history of the East German opposition, see Neubert, *Geschichte der Opposition in der DDR, 1949–1989*, and Torpey, *Intellectuals, Socialism, and Dissent: The East German Opposition and Its Legacy*.

37. Heiner Carow, interview by author, tape recording, Babelsberg, November 7, 1996.

38. Peter Kahane, interview by author, tape recording, Berlin, July 17, 1997.

39. Further historical films by Simon include *Wengler und Söhne* (1987) and *Die Besteigung der Chimborazo* (1989).

40. Schieber, "Anfang vom Ende oder Kontinuität des Argwohns 1980 bis 1989," 298–99.

41. Ibid., 318–19.

42. Ibid.

43. Ibid., 286–87.

SELECTED BIBLIOGRAPHY

ARCHIVAL SOURCES

Bundesarchiv, Berlin (BA Berlin)

Collection	Files
HV Film	DR1 521, DR1 529, DR1 4019, DR1 4038, DR1 4042, DR1 4062, DR1 4143, DR1 4197, DR1 4198, DR1 4205, DR1 4208, DR1 4212, DR1 4219, DR1 4231, DR1 4234, DR1 4238, DR1 4243, DR1 4249, DR1 4269, DR1 4277, DR1 4296, DR1 4299, DR1 4313, DR1 4320, DR1 4323, DR1 4329, DR1 4335, DR1 4361, DR1 4380, DR1 4399, DR1 4432, DR1 4437, DR1 4466, DR1 4474a, DR1 4539, DR1 4545, DR1 4587, DR1 4605, DR1 4667, DR1 4692.
Staatsrat	DA 5 6500, DA 5 6517.
Volks-kammer	DA 1 2995/68, DA 1 2977/68.

Bundesarchiv Filmarchiv, Berlin (BA Film)
  Newspaper-clippings files and "Abnahme" (approval) files for DEFA films.
DEFA Betriebsarchiv (BA Berlin DR117)
  Files 096, 0149, 0224, 0299, 255, 274, 278, 290, 454–55, 1011, 1149, 1155, 1780, 1838, 1870, 1922, 1924, 1929, 1936, 1956, 2079, 2300, 2324–25, 2874, 3003, 3027, 3109, 3115, 3121, 3190, 3190/4/526, 3191/2/602, 3192/5/746, 4329, 5134, 7137, 8455, A/0057, A/061, A/069, A/091, A/096, A/0100, 0129, A/150, A/0154–155, A/0166, A/0171, A/198–199, A/235, A/240–242, A/248, A/260, A/269, S69, S308, S617, S624, S633–635, S691a-i, S692–693, S695, S743a-s, S757.
Stiftung Archiv der Parteien und Massenorganisationen der DDR im Bundesarchiv, Berlin (SAPMO)

Collection	Files
11. Plenum	DY30 IV2/1/335–339.
Büro Kurt Hager	DY30 IVA2/2024/19, DY30 IVA2/2024/35–36, DY30 IVA2/2024/71, DY30 IVB2/2024/76, DY30 IVB2/2024/83, DY30 IVB2/2024/84, DY30 IVB2/2024/93, DY30 IVB2/2024/105, DY30 IVB2/2024/106, DY30 IVB2/2024/110, DY30 IVB2/2024/114, DY30 IVB2/2024/117, DY30 IVB2/2024/128.

Büro Alfred Kurella	DY30 IV2/2026/75–78, DY30 IV2/2026/80, DY30 IV2/2026/82, DY30 IV2/2026/87.
Nachlass Anton Ackermann	DY30 NL 109/92–98.
Nachlass Hans Rodenberg	DY30 NL 204/49–50, DY30 NL 204/53–55, DY30 NL 204/58–59, DY30 NL 204/77–78.
Nachlass Walter Ulbricht	DY30 NL 182/731, DY30 NL 182/931–932.
Politbüro	DY30 J IV/2/2-794, DY30 J IV/2/2-855, DY30 J IV/2/2-1010, DY30 J IV/2/2-1013, DY30 J IV/2/2-1017, DY30 J IV/2/2-1041, DY30 J IV/2/2-1048, DY30 J IV/2/2-1064, DY30 J IV/2/2-1.132, DY30 J IV/2/2-1.133, DY30 J IV/2/2-1.146.
ZK Kultur	DY30 IV2/906/26, DY30 IV2/906/66–68, DY30 IV2/906/100, DY30 IV2/906/200, DY30 IV2/906/204, DY30 IV2/906/210, DY30 IV2/906/211, DY30 IV2/906/215, DY30 IV2/906/220, DY30 IV2/906/222–227, DY30 IV2/906/241, DY30 IV2/906/249–250, DY30 IVA2/906/122–123, DY30 IVA2/906/125, DY30 IVA2/906/128, DY30 IVA2/906/131–132, DY30 IVB2/906/4, DY30 IVB2/906/18–19, DY30 IVB2/906/21, DY30 IVB2/906/24, DY30 IVB2/906/41–42, DY30 IVB2/906/48, DY30 IVB2/906/52, DY30 IVB2/906/80–84, DY30 IVB2/906/94.
ZK Sekretariat	DY30 J IV2/3/A-1129, DY30 J IV2/3/A-1146, DY30 J IV2/3/A-1149, DY30 J IV2/3/A-1153, DY30 J IV2/3/A-1155, DY30 J IV2/3/A-1158, DY30 J IV2/3/A-1194, DY30 J IV2/3/A-1196, DY30 J IV2/3/A-1197, DY30 J IV2/3/A-1261, DY30 J IV2/3/A-1269, DY30 J IV2/3/A-1.243.

INTERVIEWS

Frank Beyer, director, Berlin, February 26, 1993.
Annekathrin Bürger and Rolf Römer, actors, Berlin, August 18, 1993.
Heiner Carow, director, Babelsberg, November 7, 1996.
Gerd Golde, accountant, Babelsberg, May 18, 1993.
Christel Gräf, dramaturge, Babelsberg, March 3, 1993.
Roland Gräf, director, Babelsberg, August 17, 1993.
Egon Günther, director, Babelsberg, November 26, 1996.

Alfred Hirschmeier, set designer, Babelsberg, July 8, 1993.
Rudolf Jürschik, DEFA chief dramaturge, Berlin, November 13, 1996.
Peter Kahane, director, Berlin, July 17, 1997.
Wolfgang Kohlhaase, scriptwriter, Berlin, March 19, 1993.
Gabriele Kotte, scriptwriter, Berlin, August 4, 1997.
Kurt Maetzig, director, Wildkuhl (Brandenburg), February 11, 1993.
Jochen Mückenberger, DEFA studio director, Babelsberg, February 27, 1993.
Helga Schütz, scriptwriter, Babelsberg, July 20, 1993.
Konrad Schwalbe, DEFA chief dramaturge, Potsdam, February 24, 1993.
Rainer Simon, director, Potsdam, November 19, 1996.
Klaus Wischnewski, DEFA chief dramaturge, Berlin, March 1 and 15, August 2, 1993.
Günter Witt, GDR deputy cultural minister, Leipzig, May 11, 1993.
Dieter Wolf, dramaturge, Kleinmachenow, November 15, 1996.
Herrmann Zschoche, director, Berlin, December 11, 1996.

PUBLISHED SOURCES

Agee, Joel. *Twelve Years: An American Boyhood in East Germany*. New York: Farrar, Straus and Giroux, 1982.
Akteneinsicht Christa Wolf: Zerrspiegel und Dialog. Hermann Vinke, ed. Hamburg: Luchterhand, 1993.
Anderson, Benedict. *Imagined Communities*. London: Verso Editions, 1983.
Andrew, J. Dudley. *Concepts in Film Theory*. Oxford: Oxford University Press, 1984.
——. *The Major Film Theories*. Oxford: Oxford University Press, 1976.
Applegate, Celia. *A Nation of Provincials*. Berkeley: University of California Press, 1990.
Aubry, Yves. "Slatan Dudow 1903–1963." *Anthologie du cinéma* 6 (1971): 385–440.
Auf Neuen Wegen: Fünf Jahren fortschrittlicher deutscher Film. Berlin: Deutscher Film-Verlag, 1951.
Babelsberg: Ein Filmstudio 1912–1992. Wolfgang Jacobsen, ed. Berlin: Argon Verlag, 1992.
Barck, Simone, Martina Langermann, and Siegfried Lokatis. *"Jedes Buch ein Abenteuer": Zensur-System und literarische Öffentlichkeit in der DDR bis Ende der sechziger Jahre*. Berlin: Akademie Verlag, 1997.
Barck, Simone, Martina Langermann, and Jörg Requate. "Kommunikative Strukturen, Medien und Öffentlichkeiten in der DDR." *Berliner Debatte INITIAL*, no. 4/5 (1995): 25–38.
Baring, Arnulf. *Der 17. Juni 1953*. Cologne: Kiepenheuer & Witsch, 1965.
Bathrick, David. *The Powers of Speech*. Lincoln: University of Nebraska Press, 1995.
Baxandall, Michael. *Patterns of Intention: On the Historical Explanation of Pictures*. New Haven and London: Yale University Press, 1985.

Bazin, André. *Qu'est-ce que le cinéma?*, vol. 4. Paris: Editions du Cerf, 1962.

Berbig, Roland, and Holger Jens Karlson. "Leute haben sich als Gruppe erwiesen." In *In Sachen Biermann*, edited by Roland Berbig, 11–28. Berlin: Ch. Links Verlag, 1994.

Berlin! Berlin!: Die Ausstellung zur Geschichte der Stadt. Berlin: Nicolai Verlag, 1987.

Bertram, Barbara. "Zur Entwicklung der sozialen Geschlechterverhältnisse in den neuen Bundesländern." *Aus Politik und Geschichte. Beilage zur Wochenzeitung Das Parlament*, February 5, 1993, 27–38.

Bieler, Manfred. *Maria Morzeck, oder Das Kaninchen bin ich*. Munich: Biederstein, 1969.

Bisky, Lothar, and Dieter Wiedemann. *Der Spielfilm: Rezeption und Wirkung*. Berlin: Henschel Verlag, 1984.

Blunk, Harry. *Die DDR in ihren Spielfilmen: Reproduktion und Konzeption der DDR-Gesellschaft im neueren DEFA-Gegenwartsspielfilm*. Munich: Profil, 1984.

Bondanella, Peter. *Italian Cinema: From Neo-Realism to the Present*. New York: Continuum, 1990.

Brahler, Elmar, and Horst Eberhard Richter. "Deutsche Befindlichkeiten im Ost-West-Vergleich." *Aus Politik und Zeitgeschichte*, September 29, 1995, 13–20.

Brooks, Peter. *The Melodramatic Imagination*. New Haven: Yale University Press, 1976.

Brüche, Krisen, Wendepunkte: Neubefragung von DDR-Geschichte. Jochen Cerny, ed. Leipzig: Urania, 1990.

Bulgakowa, Oskana. "Versprengte Szene: Die DDR-Intellektuellen nach der Vereinigung." In *Film, Staat und Gesellschaft im Europa nach der Wende*, edited by Bernhard Frankfurter, 139–48. Vienna: Promedia, 1995.

Bullock, Alan. *Hitler: A Study in Tyranny*. Rev. ed. New York: Harper & Row, 1964.

Byg, Barton. "Geschichte, Trauer, und weibliche Identität im Film: *Hiroshima mon amour* und *Der geteilte Himmel*." In *Zwischen Gestern und Morgen: DDR Schriftsteller aus amerikanischen Sicht*, edited by Ute Brandes, 95–112. Berlin: Peter Lang Verlag, 1991.

———. "Two Approaches to GDR History in DEFA Film." *Studies in GDR Culture* 10 (1991): 85–104.

———. "What Might Have Been: DEFA Films of the Past and the Future of German Cinema." *Cineaste* 17, no. 4 (1990): 9–15.

Carow, Heiner. "Ich bin einer aus diesem Volk." *Aufsätze und Dokumentationen über Film und Fernsehen* 20, no. 4 (1979): 7–29.

Clark, Katerina. *The Soviet Novel*. Chicago: University of Chicago Press, 1981.

Dalichow, Bärbel. "Das letzte Kapital." In *Das zweite Leben der Filmstadt Babelsberg*, edited by Ralf Schenk, 328–55. Berlin: Henschel-Verlag, 1994.

Die DDR als Geschichte. Jürgen Kocka and Martin Sabrow, eds. Berlin: Akademie Verlag, 1994.

DDR-Handbuch. 3d ed. Hartmut Zimmermann, ed. Cologne: Verlag Wissenschaft und Volk, 1985.

DEFA: East German Cinema, 1946–1992. Seán Allan and John Standford, eds. New York: Berghahn, 1999.

DEFA-Spielfilme 1946–1964: Filmographie. Günter Schulz, ed. Berlin: Staatliches Filmarchiv der DDR, 1989.

DEFA-Spielfilm-Regisseure und ihre Kritiker. 2 vols. Rolf Richter, ed. Berlin: Henschel-Verlag, 1981–83.

Deutsch, Karl. Nations and Communication. 2d ed. Cambridge: MIT Press, 1966.

Deutscher Filmautoren Kongress, 1., Berlin. Der deutsche Film. Berlin: Henschel-Verlag, 1947.

Dietrich, Gerd. Politik und Kultur in der SBZ 1945–1949. Bern: P. Lang, 1993.

Dokumente der Sozialistischen Einheitspartei Deutschlands. Berlin: Dietz, 1958.

Dokumente zur Geschichte der SED, vol. 2. Eckhard Müller, ed. Berlin: Dietz, 1986.

Dokumente zur Kunst-, Literatur- und Kulturpolitik der SED. Elimar Schubbe, ed. Stuttgart: Seewald, 1972.

Dunham, Vera. In Stalin's Time. Durham, N.C.: Duke University Press, 1990.

Eckert, Detlef. "Die abgebrochene Demokratisierung." In Brüche, Krisen, Wendepunkte, edited by Jochen Cerny, 209–27. Leipzig: Urania, 1990.

Emmerich, Wolfgang. Kleine Literaturgeschichte der DDR. Expanded new ed. Leipzig: Kiepenhauer, 1996.

Engell, Lorenz. Sinn und Industrie: Einführung in die Filmgeschichte. Frankfurt a.M.: Campus Verlag, 1992.

Erbe, Günter. Die verfemte Moderne. Opladen: Westdeutscher Verlag, 1993.

Fehrenbach, Heide. Cinema in Democratizing Germany. Chapel Hill: University of North Carolina Press, 1995.

Ferro, Marc. Cinema and History. Detroit: Wayne State University Press, 1988.

Film in der DDR. Peter W. Jansen and Wolfram Schütte, eds. Munich: C. Hanser, 1977.

Filmland DDR: Ein Reader zu Geschichte, Funktion und Wirkung der DEFA. Harry Blunk and Dirk Jungnickel, eds. Cologne: Verlag Wissenschaft und Volk, 1990.

Film und Gesellschaft in der DDR: Material-Sammlung. Manfred Behn and Hans-Michael Bock, eds. Hamburg: Cinegraph, 1988.

Frauen in Deutschland, 1945–1992. Gisela Helwig and Hildegard Maria Nickel, eds. Berlin: Akademie Verlag, 1993.

Frye, Northrop. Anatomy of Criticism. Princeton: Princeton University Press, 1957.

Fulbrook, Mary. Anatomy of a Dictatorship. Oxford: Oxford University Press, 1995.

Gallas, Helga. Marxistische Literaturtheorie: Kontroversen im Bund proletarisch-revolutionärer Schriftsteller. Neuwied: Luchterhand, 1971.

Gauck, Joachim. Die Stasi-Akten. Hamburg: Rowohlt, 1991.

Gaus, Günter. Wo Deutschland liegt: Eine Ortsbestimmung. Hamburg: Hoffmann und Campe Verlag, 1986.

Geiss, Axel. Repression und Freiheit: DEFA-Regisseure zwischen Fremd- und

Selbstbestimmung. Potsdam: Brandenburgische Landeszentrale für Politische Bildung, 1997.

Gellner, Ernst. *Nations and Nationalism*. Ithaca, N.Y.: Cornell University Press, 1983.

Gersch, Wolfgang. "Die Verdoppelung der Ferne: Notizen von der anderen Seite." In *Zwischen Gestern und Morgen*, 100–113. Frankfurt a.M.: Deutsches Filmmuseum, 1989.

Der gespaltene Dichter: Johannes Becher. Carsten Gansel, ed. Berlin: Aufbau-Verlag, 1991.

Gorky, Maxim. "Soviet Literature: Address Delivered to the First All-Union Congress of Soviet Writers, August 17, 1934." In *On Literature: Selected Articles*. Moscow: Foreign Languages Publishing House, n.d.

Gräf, Roland. *Gedanken beim Filmemachen*. Ugla Gräf and Rolf Richter, eds. Aus Theorie und Praxis des Films, no. 4. Berlin: Betriebsschule des VEB DEFA Studio für Spielfilme, 1987.

Greenblatt, Stephen. *Shakespearean Negotiations*. Berkeley: University of California Press, 1988.

Greif zur Feder, Kumpel: Protokoll der Autorenkonferenz der Mitteldeutschen Verlages Halle am 24. April 1959 im Kulturpalast des elektrochemischen Kombinats Bitterfeld. Halle: Mitteldeutscher Verlag, 1959.

Groys, Boris. *Gesamtkunstwerk Stalin*. Munich: C. Hanser, 1988.

Hall, Stuart. "Culture, Community, Nation." *Cultural Studies* 7, no. 3 (1993): 349–61.

Heimann, Thomas. "DEFA, Künstler und SED." Ph.D. diss., Universität Mannheim, 1993.

Heineman, Elizabeth D. *What Difference Does a Husband Make?: Women and Marital Status in Nazi and Postwar Germany*. Berkeley: University of California Press, 1999.

Hell, Julia. *Post-Fascist Fantasies: Psychoanalysis, History, and the Literature of East Germany*. Durham, N.C.: Duke University Press, 1997.

Herlinghaus, Hermann. *Slatan Dudow*. Berlin: Henschel-Verlag, 1965.

Historische DDR-Forschung. Jürgen Kocka, ed. Berlin: Akademie Verlag, 1993.

Hoff, Peter. *Tägliche Verblödung: Kritiken, Kollegs und Polemiken zum Fernsehen*. Frankfurt a.O., 1995.

——. "Von 'Da lacht der Bär' über 'Ein Kessel Buntes'—ins 'Aus.' " In *Mit uns zieht die neue Zeit: 40 Jahre DDR-Medien, Eine Ausstellung des Deutschen Rundfunk-Museums*, edited by Heide Riedel, 86–93. Berlin: Vistas-Verlag, 1993.

Hradil, Stefan. "Die Modernisierung des Denkens: Zukunftspotentiale und 'Altlasten' in Ostdeutschland." *Aus Politik und Zeitgeschichte*, May 12, 1995, 3–15.

Hübner, Peter. *Konsens, Konflikt und Kompromiss: Soziale Arbeiterinteressen und Sozialpolitik in der SBZ/DDR 1945–1970*. Berlin: Akademie Verlag, 1995.

Jäger, Manfred. *Kultur und Politik in der DDR*. Cologne: Verlag Wissenschaft und Politik, 1994.

Jarausch, Konrad H. "Care and Coercion: The GDR as Welfare Dictatorship." In

Dictatorship as Experience: Towards a Socio-Cultural History of the GDR,
edited by Konrad H. Jarausch, 47–72. New York: Berghahn, 1999.

Jürschik, Rudolf. "Alltag und Epoche im DEFA-Kinofilm." *Einheit*, no. 2 (1975): 169–77.

Kaes, Anton. *From Hitler to Heimat*. Cambridge, Mass.: Harvard University Press, 1989.

Kahlschlag: Das 11. Plenum des ZK der SED 1965. Günter Agde, ed. Berlin: Aufbau-Verlag, 1991.

Kantorowicz, Alfred. *Deutsches Tagebuch*. 2 vols. Munich: Kindler, 1959–61.

Kersten, Heinz. "Entwicklungslinien." In *Film in der DDR*, edited by Peter W. Jansen and Wolfram Schütte, 7–56. Munich: C. Hanser, 1977.

———. *Das Filmwesen in der sowjetischen Besatzungszone Deutschlands*. Bonn: Gesamtdeutsches Ministerium, 1963.

———. "The Role of Women in GDR Films since the Early 1970s." *Studies in GDR Culture and Society* 8 (1988): 47–64.

Khrushchev, Nikita. "Speech of Nikita Khrushchev before a Closed Session of the 20th Congress of the Communist Party of the Soviet Union on February 25, 1956." Washington: U.S. Government Document, 1957.

Klein, Gerhard. *Werkstatterfahrungen mit Gerhard Klein*. Hannes Schmidt, ed. Aus Theorie und Praxis des Films, no. 2. Babelsberg: Betriebsakademie der VEB DEFA Studio für Spielfilme, 1984.

Klemperer, Victor. *LTI*. Leipzig: Philip Reclam, 1975.

Klessmann, Christoph. *Die doppelte Staatsgründung*. 5th ed. Bonn: Bundeszentrale für Politische Bildung, 1991.

Klötzer, Sylvia. "Öffentlichkeit in der DDR?: Die soziale Wirklichkeit im 'Eulenspiegel.'" *Aus Politik und Zeitgeschichte*, November 8, 1996, 28–36.

Klötzer, Sylvia, and Siegfried Lokatis. "Criticism and Censorship: Negotiating Cabaret Performance and Book Production." In *Dictatorship as Experience: Towards a Socio-Cultural History of the GDR*, edited by Konrad Jarausch, 241–64. New York: Berghahn, 1999.

Kocka, Jürgen. "Eine durchherrschte Gesellschaft." In *Sozialgeschichte der DDR*, edited by Hartmut Kaelble, Jürgen Kocka, and Hartmut Zwahr, 547–53. Stuttgart: Klett Cotta, 1994.

Kohlhaase, Wolfgang. "Er suchte die Poesie, die in den Dingen steckt." Interview by Hannes Schmidt. In *Werkstatterfahrungen mit Gerhard Klein*, edited by Hannes Schmidt, 6–46. Aus Theorie und Praxis des Films, no. 2. Babelsberg: Betriebsakademie der VEB DEFA Studio für Spielfilme, 1984.

———. *Ortszeit ist immer auch Weltzeit*. Hermann Herlinghaus, ed. Aus Theorie und Praxis des Films, no. 1/2. Babelsberg: Betriebsakademie des VEB DEFA Studio für Spielfilme, 1981.

Krenzlin, Leonore. "Vom Jugendkommuniqué zur Dichterschelte." In *Kahlschlag: Das 11. Plenum des ZK der SED 1965*, edited by Günter Agde, 148–58. Berlin: Aufbau-Verlag, 1991.

Kuhn, Anna. *Christa Wolf's Utopian Vision*. Cambridge: Cambridge University Press, 1988.

Lemke, Christiane. "Beyond the Ideological Stalemate: Women and Politics in the FRG and GDR in Comparison." *German Studies Review* 13 (1990): 87–94.

Leonhard, Sigrun D. "Testing the Borders: East German Film between Individualism and Social Commitment." In *Post–New Wave Cinema in the Soviet Union and Eastern Europe*, edited by Daniel G. Goulding. Bloomington: University of Indiana Press, 1989.

Liehm, Mira, and Antonín Liehm. *The Most Important Art: Eastern European Film after 1945*. Berkeley: University of California Press, 1977.

Linden, Carl A. *Khrushchev and the Soviet Leadership, 1957–1964*. Baltimore: Johns Hopkins University Press, 1966.

Lindenberger, Thomas. "Die Diktatur der Grenzen." In *Herrschaft und Eigen-Sinn in der Diktatur. Studien zur Gesellschaftsgeschichte der DDR*, edited by Thomas Lindenberger, 51–101. Cologne: Böhlau Verlag, 1999.

Literarische Widerspiegelung. Introduction by Dieter Schlenstedt. Berlin: Aufbau-Verlag, 1981.

Lukács, György. "Critical Realism and Socialist Realism." In *Realism in Our Time*. New York: Harper & Row, 1963.

——. *Essays on Realism*. Rodney Livingstone, ed. Cambridge, Mass.: MIT Press, 1980.

Lunn, Eugene. *Marxism and Modernism*. Berkeley: University of California Press, 1982.

Maetzig, Kurt. *Filmarbeit*. Günter Agde, ed. Berlin: Henschel-Verlag, 1987.

Maier, Charles. *Dissolution: The Crisis of Communism and the End of East Germany*. Princeton: Princeton University Press, 1997.

Marcus, Millicent. *Italian Film in the Light of Neorealism*. Princeton: Princeton University Press, 1986.

Merkel, Ina. "Konsumkultur in der DDR: Über das Scheitern der Gegenmoderne auf dem Schlachtfeld des Konsums." *Mitteilungen aus der kulturwissenschaftlichen Forschung* 37 (February 1996): 314–30.

——. "Leitbilder und Lebensweisen von Frauen." In *Sozialgeschichte der DDR*, edited by Hartmut Kaelble, Jürgen Kocka, and Hartmut Zwahr, 359–82. Stuttgart: Klett Cotta, 1994.

——. "Die Nackten und die Roten: Zum Verhältnis von Nackheit und Öffentlichkeit in der DDR." *Mitteilungen aus der kulturwissenschaftlichen Forschung* 18, no. 36 (August 1995): 80–108.

——. . . . *und Du, Frau an der Werkbank*. Berlin: Elefanten Press, 1990.

Meulemann, Heiner. "Aufholtendenzen und Systemeffekte: Eine Übersicht über Wertunterschiede zwischen West- und Ostdeutschland." *Aus Politik und Zeitgeschichte*, September 29, 1995, 21–33.

Meuschel, Sigrid. *Legitimation und Parteiherrschaft in der DDR*. Frankfurt a.M.: Suhrkamp, 1992.

Michalek, Boleslaw, and Frank Turaj. *The Modern Cinema of Poland*. Bloomington: Indiana University Press, 1988.

Mittenzwei, Werner. "Zur Kafka-Konferenz 1963." In *Kahlschlag: Das 11. Plenum des ZK der SED 1965*, edited by Günter Agde, 84–92. Berlin: Aufbau-Verlag, 1991.

Mitter, Armin, and Stefan Wolle. *Untergang auf Raten*. Munich: Bertelsmann, 1993.

Mit uns zieht die neue Zeit: 40 Jahre DDR-Medien, Eine Ausstellung des Deutschen Rundfunk-Museums. Heide Riedel, ed. Berlin: Vistas-Verlag, 1993.

Monaco, James. *Alain Resnais*. New York: Oxford University Press, 1979.

——. *The New Wave*. New York: Oxford University Press, 1976.

Mückenberger, Christiane. "Zeit der Hoffnungen." In *Das zweite Leben der Filmstadt Babelsberg*, edited by Ralf Schenk, 8–49. Berlin: Henschel-Verlag, 1994.

Mückenberger, Christiane, and Günter Jordan. *Sie sehen selbst, Sie hören selbst: Eine Geschichte der DEFA von ihren Anfängen bis 1949*. Marburg: Hitzeroth, 1994.

Mühlberg, Dietrich. "Überlegungen zu einer Kulturgeschichte der DDR." In *Sozialgeschichte der DDR*, edited by Hartmut Kaelble, Jürgen Kocka, and Hartmut Zwahr, 62–94. Stuttgart: Klett Cotta, 1994.

Mühlberg, Felix. "Konformismus oder Eigensinn?: Eingaben als Quelle zur Erforschung der Alltagsgeschichte der DDR." *Mitteilungen aus der kulturwissenschaftlichen Forschung* 19, no. 37 (February 1996): 331–45.

Murray, Bruce. *Film and the German Left in the Weimar Republic*. Austin: University of Texas Press, 1990.

Naimark, Norman. *The Russians in Germany: A History of the Soviet Zone of Occupation, 1945–1949*. Cambridge, Mass.: Harvard University Press, 1995.

Natew, Wesselin. "Slatan Dudow in den dreissiger und vierziger Jahren." *Beiträge zur Film- und Fernsehwissenschaft* 23, no. 5 (1982): 6–46.

Naughton, Leonie. "'We Were the People': Film Culture, Comedy, and the Unification of Germany." Ph.D. diss., Latrobe University, 1996.

Neubert, Ehrhart. *Geschichte der Opposition in der DDR, 1949–1989*. Bonn: Bundeszentrale für Politische Bildung, 1997.

Neutsch, Erik. *Spur der Steine*. Halle: Mitteldeutscher Verlag, 1964.

Niethammer, Lutz. *Die volkseigene Erfahrung*. Berlin: Rowohlt, 1991.

Petro, Patrice. "Modernity and Mass Culture in Weimar: Contours of a Discourse on Sexuality in Early Theories of Perception and Representation." *New German Critique* 40 (1987): 115–46.

Pike, David. *The Politics of Culture in Soviet-Occupied Germany, 1945–1949*. Stanford: Stanford University Press, 1992.

Plenzdorf, Ulrich. "Die Legende von Paul und Paula." In *Filme*. Vol. 1. Rostock: VEB Hinstorff, 1986.

Poiger, Uta G. *Jazz, Rock, and Rebels: Cold War Politics and American Culture in a Divided Germany*. Berkeley: University of California Press, 2000.

Post–New Wave Cinema in the Soviet Union and Eastern Europe. Daniel J. Goulding, ed. Bloomington: University of Indiana Press, 1989.

Prädikat besonders schädlich. Christiane Mückenberger, ed. Berlin: Henschel-Verlag, 1990.

Probleme des sozialistischen Realismus in der darstellenden Kunst behandelt am Beispiel des DEFA-Films "Der geteilte Himmel." Referat und Diskussionsbeiträge der II. Plenartagung der Deutschen Akademie der

Künste zu Berlin vom 30. Juni 1964. Berlin: Deutsche Akademie der Künste, 1964.

Das Protokoll des V. Parteitages der Sozialistischen Einheitspartei Deutschlands. Berlin: Dietz Verlag, 1959.

Rauhut, Michael. *Beat in der Grauzone: DDR-Rock 1964 bis 1972—Politik und Alltag.* Berlin: Basisdruck, 1993.

——. "DDR-Beatmusik zwischen Engagement und Repression." In *Kahlschlag: Das 11. Plenum des ZK der SED 1965,* edited by Günter Agde, 52–63. Berlin: Aufbau-Verlag, 1991.

——. *Schalmei und Lederjacke: Udo Lindenberg, BAP, Underground: Rock und Politik in den achtziger Jahren.* Berlin: Schwarzkopf & Schwarzkopf, 1996.

The Red Screen: Politics, Society, Art in Soviet Society. Anna Lawton, ed. New York: Routledge, 1992.

The Reemergence of Civil Society in Eastern Europe and the Soviet Union. Zbigniew Rau, ed. Boulder, Colo.: Westview Press, 1992.

Regie: Frank Beyer. Ralf Schenk, ed. Berlin: Henschel-Verlag, 1995.

Die Regierung ruft die Künstler: Dokumente zur Gründung der Deutschen Akademie der Künste (DDR) 1945–1953. Petra Uhlmann and Sabine Wolf, eds. Berlin: Henschel-Verlag, 1993.

Rehan, Rosemarie. "Wohin drehst Du, ist Vorsicht der bessere Teil der Filmtapferkeit?" *Wochenpost,* no. 28 (1964): 3–5.

Reimann, Brigitte. *Ankunft im Alltag.* Berlin: Verlag Neues Leben, 1961.

Rentschler, Eric. *The Ministry of Illusion: The Nazi Cinema and Its Afterlife.* Cambridge, Mass.: Harvard University Press, 1996.

Richter, Erika. *Alltag und Geschichte in DEFA-Gegenwartsfilmen der siebziger Jahre.* Filmwissenschaftliche Beiträge, no. 1. Berlin: Institut für Filmwissenschaft, 1976.

——. "Zwischen Mauerbau und Kahlschlag 1961 bis 1965." In *Das Zweite Leben der Filmstadt Babelsberg,* edited by Ralf Schenk, 158–211. Berlin: Henschel-Verlag, 1994.

Rinke, Andrea. "From Models to Misfits: Women in DEFA Films of the 1970s and 1980s." In *DEFA: East German Cinema, 1946–1992,* edited by Seán Allan and John Standford, 183–203. New York: Berghahn, 1999.

Robert Havemann: Dokumente eines Lebens. Dieter Hoffmann, ed. Berlin: Ch. Links Verlag, 1991.

Robin, Régine. *Socialist Realism: An Impossible Aesthetic.* Stanford: Stanford University Press, 1992.

Rohrwasser, Michael. *Saubere Mädel, starke Genossen: Proletarische Massenliteratur?* Frankfurt a.M.: Verlag Roter Stern, 1974.

Ronneburg, Silke. " 'Eine Zensur findet nicht statt!': Zulassungsakten der DDR." *Filmdienst,* December 22, 1992, 4–9.

Rueschmeyer, Marilyn, and Hanna Schissler. "Women in the Two Germanies." *German Studies Review* 13, special issue (1990): 72–85.

Schenk, Ralf. "Mitten im kalten Krieg 1955–1960." In *Das zweite Leben der Filmstadt Babelsberg,* edited by Ralf Schenk, 50–157. Berlin: Henschel-Verlag, 1994.

Scherstjanoi, Elke. "'Von der Sowjetunion lernen . . .'" In *Kahlschlag: Das 11. Plenum des ZK der SED 1965*, edited by Günter Agde, 39–51. Berlin: Aufbau-Verlag, 1991.

Schieber, Elke. "Anfang vom Ende oder Kontinuität des Argwohns 1980 bis 1989." In *Das zweite Leben der Filmstadt Babelsberg*, edited by Ralf Schenk, 264–327. Berlin: Henschel-Verlag, 1994.

Schroeder, Klaus. *Der SED-Staat: Partei, Staat und Gesellschaft*. Munich: Hanser, 1998.

Seidel, Siegfried. "Zur Position Erich Apels." In *Kahlschlag: Das 11. Plenum des ZK der SED 1965*, edited by Günter Agde, 252–57. Berlin: Aufbau-Verlag, 1991.

17. Juni 1953. Ilse Spittmann, ed. Cologne: Verlag Wissenschaft und Politik, 1992.

Silberman, Marc. "Problematizing the 'Socialist Public Sphere': Concepts and Consequences." In *What Remains?: East German Culture and the Postwar Public* (AICGS Research Report, no. 5), edited by Marc Silberman, 1–37. Washington, D.C.: American Institute for Contemporary German Studies, 1997.

——. "Remembering History: The Filmmaker Konrad Wolf." *New German Critique* 49 (Winter 1990): 163–87.

Sobchack, Vivian. "'Surge and Splendor': A Phenomenology of the Hollywood Historical Epic." *Representations* 29 (Winter 1990): 24–49.

Sodaro, Michael J. *Moscow, Germany, and the West: From Khrushchev to Gorbachev*. Ithaca, N.Y.: Cornell University Press, 1990.

Sodovieri, Stefan. "Censorship and the Law: The Case of *Das Kaninchen bin ich*." In *DEFA: East German Cinema, 1946–1992*, edited by Seán Allan and John Standford, 146–63. New York: Berghahn, 1999.

Spielfilme der DEFA im Urteil der Kritik. Lissi Zilinsk, Götz Barndt, Alfred Krautz, Rolf Liebmann, and Gustav Salffner, eds. Berlin: Henschel-Verlag, 1970.

Spielräume: Aus der Werkstatt des Filmszenographen Alfred Hirschmeier. Günter Agde, ed. Berlin: Akademie der Künste, 1989.

Spittmann, Ilse. "Zum 40. Jahrestag des 17. Juni." *Deutschlandarchiv*, no. 6 (1993): 635–39.

Staritz, Dieter. *Geschichte der DDR 1949–1985*. Frankfurt a.M.: Suhrkamp, 1985.

——. "Die SED, Stalin, und der 'Aufbau des Sozialismus' in der DDR." *Deutschlandarchiv*, no. 7 (1991): 686–700.

Stemmler, Wolfgang. "Bemerkungen über die Unterhaltungs-Sendungen vom Beginn des DDR-Fernsehens bis zum Ende der fünfziger Jahre." In *Mit uns zieht die neue Zeit: 40 Jahre DDR-Medien, Eine Ausstellung des Deutschen Rundfunk-Museums*, edited by Heide Riedel, 77–86. Berlin: Vistas-Verlag, 1993.

Thinius, Bert. "Paul und Paul im Sozialismus." *Mitteilungen aus der kulturwissenschaftlichen Forschung* 18, no. 36 (August 1995): 143–69.

Torpey, John. *Intellectuals, Socialism, and Dissent: The East German Opposition and Its Legacy*. Minneapolis: University of Minnesota Press, 1995.

Trappe, Heike. *Emanzipation oder Zwang?: Frauen in der DDR zwischen Beruf, Familie und Sozialpolitik.* Berlin: Akademie Verlag, 1995.

"Umfrage." *Filmwissenschaftliche Mitteilungen*, no. 2 (1965): 281–319.

Vester, Michael. "Deutschlands feine Unterschiede: Mentalitäten und Modernisierung in Ost- und Westdeutschland." *Aus Politik und Zeitgeschichte*, May 12, 1995, 16–27.

Vester, Michael, Michael Hofmann, and Irene Zierke. *Soziale Milieus in Ostdeutschland.* Cologne: Bund-Verlag, 1995.

Wagner, Reinhard. " 'Sonnensucher': Notizen zur Werkgeschichte." *Beiträge zur Film- und Fernsehwissenschaft* 39 (1990): 34–64.

Walther, Joachim. *Sicherungsbereich Literatur: Schriftsteller und Staatssicherheit in der Deutschen Demokratischen Republik.* Berlin: Ch. Links Verlag, 1996.

Warneke, Lothar. *Film ist eine Art zu Leben.* Hermann Herlinghaus, ed. Aus Theorie und Praxis des Films, no. 3. Babelsberg: Betriebsakademie der VEB DEFA Studio für Spielfilme, 1983.

Weber, Hermann. *DDR: Grundriss der Geschichte 1945–1990.* Hannover: Fackelträger, 1991.

Wilkening, Albert. *Betriebsgeschichte des VEB DEFA Studio für Spielfilme.* 2 vols. Babelsberg: Betriebsparteiorganisation der SED im VEB DEFA Studio für Spielfilme, 1981–84.

Wischnewski, Klaus. "Hoffnungen, Illusionen, Einsichten." Interview by Wieland Becker. *Film und Fernsehen*, no. 6 (1990): 228–46.

——. "Träumer und gewöhnliche Leute, 1966 bis 1979." In *Das zweite Leben der Filmstadt Babelsberg 1945–1992*, edited by Ralf Schenk, 212–63. Berlin: Henschel-Verlag, 1994.

Witt, Günter. "Wie eine Inquisition." In *Kahlschlag: Das 11. Plenum des ZK der SED 1965. Studien und Dokumente*, edited by Günter Agde, 258–62. Berlin: Aufbau-Verlag, 1991.

Wolf, Christa. *Der geteilte Himmel.* Halle: Mitteldeutscher Verlag, 1963.

Wolf, Konrad. Interview by Ulrich Gregor. In *Wie sie filmen: Fünfzehn Gespräche mit Regisseuren der Gegenwart*, edited by Ulrich Gregor, 309–38. Gütersloh: Sigbert Mohn Verlag, 1966.

Wunderwirtschaft: DDR-Konsumkultur in den 60er Jahren. Neue Gesellschaft für Bildende Kunst, Berlin, ed. Cologne: Böhlau Verlag, 1996.

Zweite Bitterfelder Konferenz 1964: Protokoll der . . . im Kulturpalast des Elektrochemischen Kombinats Bitterfeld abgehaltenen Konferenz. Berlin: Dietz, 1964.

Das zweite Leben der Filmstadt Babelsberg: DEFA-Spielfilme 1946–1992. Ralf Schenk, ed. Berlin: Henschel-Verlag, 1994.

SELECTED FILMOGRAPHY

The films are listed by title. Credits and year of release follow the filmography in *Das zweite Leben der Filmstadt Babelsberg*. Bracketed years refer to release dates of banned or otherwise interrupted productions. All extant DEFA films are available for viewing at the Bundesarchiv Filmarchiv Berlin. A wide variety of works, many with English subtitles, are available on video through Icestorm International, 78 Main Street, Northampton, MA 01060, ⟨www.icestorm-video.com⟩.

dir = director, sw = scriptwriter

Die Abenteuer des Werner Holt. Joachim Kunert, dir. Claus Küchenmeister, Joachim Kunert, sws. Based on novel of the same title by Dieter Noll. DEFA, 1965.

Abschied. Egon Günther, dir. Egon Günther, Günter Kunert, sws. DEFA, 1968.

Ach, du fröhliche . . . Günter Reisch, dir. Hermann Kant, sw. DEFA, 1962.

Affaire Blum. Erich Engel, dir. Robert A. Stemmle, sw. DEFA, 1948.

Alle meine Mädchen. Iris Gusner, dir. Gabriele Kotte, sw. DEFA, 1980.

Eine alte Liebe. Frank Beyer, dir. Werner Reinowski, Frank Beyer, sws. DEFA, 1959.

Alter Kahn und junge Liebe. Hans Heinrich, dir. Dieter Noll, Frank Vogel, sws. DEFA, 1957.

Alwin der letzte. Hubert Hoetzke, dir. Gerhard Hartwig, sw. DEFA, 1960.

Anton der Zauberer. Günter Reisch, dir. Karl Georg Egel, sw. DEFA, 1978.

Die Architekten. Peter Kahane, dir. Thomas Knauf, sw. DEFA, 1990.

Auf der Sonnenseite. Ralf Kirsten, dir. Heinz Kahlau, Gisela Steineckert, Ralf Kirsten, sws. DEFA, 1962.

Aus unserer Zeit. In four parts. Joachim Kunert, Kurt Maetzig, Helmut Nitzschke, Rainer Simon, dirs. Manfred Freitag, Ralph Knebel, Joachim Kunert, Irene Maetzig, Kurt Maetzig, Joachim Nestler, Helmut Nitzschke, Rainer Simon, sws. DEFA, 1970.

Bankett für Achilles. Roland Gräf, dir. Martin Stephan, sw. DEFA, 1975.

Berlin—Ecke Schönhauser. Gerhard Klein, dir. Wolfgang Kohlhaase, sw. DEFA, 1957.

Eine Berliner Romanze. Gerhard Klein, dir. Wolfgang Kohlhaase, sw. DEFA, 1956.

Berlin um die Ecke. Gerhard Klein, dir. Wolfgang Kohlhaase, sw. DEFA, 1966 [1990].

Beschreibung eines Sommers. Ralf Kirsten, dir. Karl-Heinz Jakobs, Ralf Kirsten, sws. DEFA, 1963.

Die besten Jahren. Günther Rücker, dir. Günther Rücker, Peter Krause, sws. DEFA, 1965.

Die Beunruhigung. Lothar Warneke, dir. Helga Schubert, sw. DEFA, 1982.

Bis dass der Tod euch scheidet. Heiner Carow, dir. Günther Rücker, sw. DEFA, 1979.

Die Buntkarrierten. Kurt Maetzig, dir. Berta Waterstradt, sw. DEFA, 1949.

Bürgermeister Anna. Hans Müller, dir. Richard Nicolas, sw. DEFA, 1950.

Bürgschaft für ein Jahr. Herrmann Zschoche, dir. Gabriele Kotte, sw. Based on a novel of the same title by Tine Schulze-Gerlach. DEFA, 1981.

Chemie und Liebe. Arthur Maria Rabenalt, dir. Marion Keller, Frank Clifford, sws. DEFA, 1948.

Christine. Slatan Dudow, dir. and sw. DEFA, 1963 [1974].

Coming Out. Heiner Carow, dir. Wolfram Witt, sw. DEFA, 1989.

Dein unbekannter Bruder. Ulrich Weiss, dir. Wolfgang Trampe, sw. DEFA, 1982.

Denk bloss nicht, ich heule. Frank Vogel, dir. Manfred Freitag, Joachim Nestler, sws. DEFA, 1965 [1990].

Der Dritte. Egon Günther, dir. Günther Rücker, sw. DEFA, 1972.

Dr. Med. Sommer II. Lothar Warneke, dir. Hannes Hüttner, sw. DEFA, 1970.

Ehe im Schatten. Kurt Maetzig, dir. and sw. DEFA, 1946.

Ehesache Lorenz. Joachim Kunert, dir. Berta Waterstradt, sw. DEFA, 1959.

Einer trage des anderen Last. Lothar Warneke, dir. Wolfgang Held, sw. DEFA, 1988.

Einfach Blumen aufs Dach. Roland Oehme, dir. Rudi Strahl, Roland Oehme, sws. DEFA, 1979.

Die Entfernung zwischen dir und mir und ihr. Michael Kann, dir. Stefan Kolditz, sw. DEFA, 1988.

Erich Kubak. Johannes Arpe, dir. Heinz Hafke, Manfred Streubel, sws. DEFA, 1959.

Ernst Thälmann—Führer seiner Klasse. Kurt Maetzig, dir. Willi Bredel, Michael Tschesno-Hell, sws. DEFA, 1955.

Ernst Thälmann—Sohn seiner Klasse. Kurt Maetzig, dir. Willi Bredel, Michael Tschesno-Hell, sws. DEFA, 1954.

Erscheinen Pflicht. Helmut Dziuba, dir. and sw. DEFA, 1984.

Ete und Ali. Peter Kahane, dir. Waltraud Meienreis, Henry Schneider, sws. DEFA, 1985.

Das Fahrrad. Evelyn Schmidt, dir. Ernst Wenig, sw. DEFA, 1982.

Fallada: Das letzte Kapital. Roland Gräf, dir. Helga Schütz, Roland Gräf, sws. DEFA, 1988.

Der Fall Gleiwitz. Gerhard Klein, dir. Wolfgang Kohlhaase, Günther Rücker, sws. DEFA, 1961.

For Eyes Only. János Veiczi, dir. Harry Thürk, sw. DEFA, 1963.

Frauenschicksale. Slatan Dudow, dir. and sw. DEFA, 1952.

Die Frau und der Fremde. Rainer Simon, dir. and sw. DEFA, 1985.

Freies Land. Milo Harbich, dir. and sw. DEFA, 1946.

Frühling braucht Zeit. Günter Stahnke, dir. Hermann O. Lauterbach, Konrad Schwalbe, Günter Stahnke, sws. DEFA, 1965.

Genesung. Konrad Wolf, dir. Karl Georg Egel, Paul Wiens, sws. DEFA, 1956.

Geschichten jener Nacht. In four parts. Karlheinz Carpentier, Gerhard Klein, Ulrich Thein, Frank Vogel, dirs. Helmut Baierl, Karlheinz Carpentier, Gerhard Klein, Erik Neutsch, Hartwig Strobel, sws. DEFA, 1967.

Der geteilte Himmel. Konrad Wolf, dir. Christa Wolf, Gerhard Wolf, Konrad Wolf, sws. Based on a novel of the same title by Christa Wolf. DEFA, 1964.

Der Hauptmann von Köln. Slatan Dudow, dir. Henryk Keisch, Michael Tschesno-Hell, Slatan Dudow, sws. DEFA, 1956.

Heisser Sommer. Joachim Hasler, dir. Maurycy Janowski, Joachim Hasler, sws. DEFA, 1968.

Ich war neunzehn. Konrad Wolf, dir. Wolfgang Kohlhaase, Konrad Wolf, sws. DEFA, 1968.

Ikarus. Heiner Carow, dir. Klaus Schlesinger, sw. DEFA, 1975.

Im Spannungsfeld. Siegfried Kühn, dir. Helfried Schreiter, sw. DEFA, 1970.

Insel der Schwäne. Herrmann Zschoche, dir. Ulrich Plenzdorf, sw. Based on a novel of the same title by Benno Pludra. DEFA, 1983.

Ein irrer Duft von frischem Heu. Roland Oehme, dir. Rudi Strahl, Roland Oehme, sws. Based on play of the same title by Rudi Strahl. DEFA, 1977.

Jacke wie Hose. Eduard Kubat, dir. Jan Koplowitz, sw. DEFA, 1953.

Jadup und Boel. Rainer Simon, dir. Paul Kanut Schäfer, sw. Based on the novel *Jadup* by Paul Kanut Schäfer. DEFA, 1981 [1988].

Jahrgang '45. Jürgen Böttcher, dir. Klaus Poche, Jürgen Böttcher, sws. DEFA, 1966.

Jakob der Lügner. Frank Beyer, dir. Jurek Becker, sw. DEFA, 1975.

Julia lebt. Frank Vogel, dir. Konrad Schwalbe, Manfred Freitag, Joachim Nestler, sws. DEFA, 1963.

Die Jungen von Kranichsee. Artur Pohl, dir. and sw. DEFA, 1950.

Junges Gemüse. Günter Reisch, dir. Günther Rücker, Kurt Bortfeldt, sws. DEFA, 1956.

Der Kahn der fröhlichen Leute. Hans Heinrich, dir. Richard Nicolas, sw. DEFA, 1950.

Das Kaninchen bin ich. Kurt Maetzig, dir. Manfred Bieler, sw. Based on the novel of the same title by Manfred Bieler. DEFA, 1965 [1989].

Karbid und Sauerampfer. Frank Beyer, dir. Hans Oliva, sw. DEFA, 1963.

Karla. Herrmann Zschoche, dir. Ulrich Plenzdorf, Herrmann Zschoche, sws. DEFA, 1966 [1990].

Kennen Sie Urban? Ingrid Reschke, dir. Ulrich Plenzdorf, sw. DEFA, 1971.

Der Kinnhaken. Heinz Thiel, dir. Manfred Krug, Horst Bastian, sws. DEFA, 1962.

Das Kleid. Konrad Petzold, dir. Egon Günther, sw. DEFA, 1961 [1991].

KLK an PTX—Die Rote Kapelle. Horst E. Brandt, dir. Wera Küchenmeister, Klaus Küchenmeister, sws. DEFA, 1971.

Königskinder. Frank Beyer, dir. Edith Gorrisch, Walter Gorrisch, sws. DEFA, 1962.

Das Land hinter dem Regenbogen. Herwig Kipping, dir. and sw. DEFA, 1992.

Leben zu zweit. Herrmann Zschoche, dir. Gisela Steineckert, sw. DEFA, 1968.

Die Legende von Paul und Paula. Heiner Carow, dir. Ulrich Plenzdorf, sw. DEFA, 1973.

Letztes aus der DaDaeR. Jorg Fürth, dir. Steffen Mensching, Hans-Eckardt Wenzel, sws. DEFA, 1990.

Leute mit Flügeln. Konrad Wolf, dir. Karl Georg Egel, Paul Wiens, sws. DEFA, 1960.

Die Liebe und der Co-Pilot. Richard Groschopp, dir. Lothar Creutz, Carl Andriessen, Richard Groschopp, sws. DEFA, 1961.

Lissy. Konrad Wolf, dir. Alex Wedding, Konrad Wolf, sws. DEFA, 1957.

Looping. Kurt Tetzlaff, dir. Manfred Freitag, Joachim Nestler, sws. DEFA, 1975.

Lots Weib. Egon Günther, dir. Egon Günther, Helga Schütz, sws. DEFA, 1965.

Das Luftschiff. Rainer Simon, dir. Fritz Rudolf Fritz, Rainer Simon, sws. DEFA, 1983.

Das Mädchen auf dem Brett. Kurt Maetzig, dir. Ralph Knebel, sw. DEFA, 1967.

Der Mann der nach der Oma kam. Roland Oehme, dir. Maurycy Janowski, Lothar Kusche, sws. DEFA, 1972.

Männer ohne Bart. Rainer Simon, dir. Inge Wüste, Rainer Simon, sws. DEFA, 1971.

Der Mann mit dem Objektiv. Frank Vogel, dir. Paul Wiens, sw. DEFA, 1961.

Märkische Forschungen. Roland Gräf, dir. and sw. Based on a novel of the same title by Günter de Bruyn. DEFA, 1982.

Meine Frau Inge und meine Frau Schmidt. Roland Oehme, dir. Joachim Brehmer, Roland Oehme, sws. DEFA, 1985.

Meine Frau macht Musik. Hans Heinrich, dir. Walter Niklaus, sw. DEFA, 1958.

Mein lieber Robinson. Roland Gräf, dir. Klaus Poche, sw. DEFA, 1971.

Mir nach, Canaillen! Ralf Kirsten, dir. Joachim Kupsch, Ulrich Plenzdorf, sws. DEFA, 1964.

Modell Bianka. Richard Groschopp, dir. Erich Conradi, sw. DEFA, 1951.

Die Mörder sind unter uns. Wolfgang Staudte, dir. and sw. DEFA, 1946.

Motivsuche. Dietmar Hochmuch, dir. Henry Scheider, sw. DEFA, 1990.

Der nackte Mann auf dem Sportplatz. Konrad Wolf, dir. Wolfgang Kohlhaase, sw. DEFA, 1974.

Nackt unter Wölfen. Frank Beyer, dir. Bruno Apitz, Frank Beyer, sws. Based on a novel of the same title by Bruno Apitz. DEFA, 1963.

Netzwerk. Ralf Kirsten, dir. Ralf Kirsten, Eberhard Panitz, sws. DEFA, 1970.

Professor Mamlock. Konrad Wolf, dir. Karl Georg Egel, Konrad Wolf, sws. DEFA, 1961.

Eine Pyramide für mich. Ralf Kirsten, dir. Karl-Heinz Jakobs, Ralf Kirsten, sws. DEFA, 1975.

Der Rat der Götter. Kurt Maetzig, dir. Friedrich Wolf, Philipp Gecht, sws. DEFA, 1950.

Reife Kirschen. Horst Seemann, dir. Manfred Richter, Horst Seemann, sws. DEFA, 1972.

Reise ins Ehebett. Joachim Hasler, dir. Maurycy Janowski, Joachim Hasler, Claus Hammel, sws. DEFA, 1966.

Reportage 1957. János Veiczi, dir. Lothar Dutombé, sw. DEFA, 1959.

Roman einer jungen Ehe. Kurt Maetzig, dir. Bodo Uhse, Kurt Maetzig, sws. DEFA, 1952.

Rotation. Wolfgang Staudte, dir. and sw. DEFA, 1949.

Rückwärtslaufen kann ich auch. Karl Heinz Lotz, dir. Manfred Wolter, sw. DEFA, 1990.

Die Russen kommen. Heiner Carow, dir. Claus Küchenmeister, Heiner Carow, sws. DEFA, 1968 [1988].

Sabine Wulff. Erwin Stranka, dir and sw. Based on the novel *Gesucht wird die freundliche Welt* by Heinz Kruschel. DEFA, 1978.

Schlösser und Katen. Kurt Maetzig, dir. Kurt Bartel, sw. DEFA, 1957.

Die Schlüssel. Egon Günther, dir. Helga Schütz, sw. DEFA, 1974.

Septemberliebe. Kurt Maetzig, dir. Herbert Otto, sw. DEFA, 1961.

Sheriff Teddy. Heiner Carow, dir. Benno Pludra, Heiner Carow, sws. DEFA, 1957.

Sieben Sommersprossen. Herrmann Zschoche, dir. Christa Kozik, sw. DEFA, 1978.

Silvesterpunsch. Günter Reisch, dir. Marianne Reinke, Gerhard Weise, sws. DEFA, 1960.

Die Söhne der grossen Bärin. Josef Mach, dir. Liselotte Welskopf-Henrich, sw. Based on a novel of the same title by Liselotte Welskopf-Henrich. DEFA, 1966.

Solange Leben in mir ist. Günter Reisch, dir. Michael Tschesno-Hell, Günter Reisch, Hermann Herlinghaus, sws. DEFA, 1965.

Solo Sunny. Konrad Wolf, dir. Wolfgang Kohlhaase, sw. DEFA, 1980.

Sonnensucher. Konrad Wolf, dir. Karl Georg Egel, Paul Wiens, sws. DEFA 1958 [1972].

Sonntagsfahrer. Gerhard Klein, dir. Karl Georg Egel, Wolfgang Kohlhaase, sws. DEFA, 1963.

Spur der Steine. Frank Beyer, dir. Karl Georg Egel, Frank Beyer, sws. Based on novel of the same title by Erik Neutsch. DEFA, 1966.

Stärker als die Nacht. Slatan Dudow, dir. Jeanne Stern, Kurt Stern, sws. DEFA, 1954.

Stein. Egon Günther, dir. Helga Schütz, Egon Günther, sws. DEFA, 1992.

Sterne. Konrad Wolf, dir. Angel Wagenstein, sw. DEFA, 1959.

Der Tangospieler. Roland Gräf, dir and sw. DEFA, 1991.

Tatort Berlin. Joachim Kunert, dir. Joachim Kunert, Jens Gerlach, sws. DEFA, 1958.

Till Eulenspiegel. Rainer Simon, dir. and sw. DEFA, 1975.

Der Traum von Hauptmann Loy. Kurt Maetzig, dir and sw. Based on novel of the same title by Wolfgang Schreyer. DEFA, 1961.

Treffen in Travers. Michael Gwisdek, dir. Thomas Knauf, sw. DEFA, 1989.

. . . und deine Liebe auch. Frank Vogel, dir. Paul Wiens, sw. DEFA, 1962.

Und nächstes Jahr am Balaton. Herrmann Zschoche, dir. Inge Wüste-Heym, sw. DEFA, 1980.

Unser kurzes Leben. Lothar Warneke, dir. Regine Kühn, sw. Based on the novel *Franziska Linkerhand* by Brigitte Reimann. DEFA, 1981.

Der Untertan. Wolfgang Staudte, dir. Wolfgang Staudte, Fritz Staudte, sws. DEFA, 1951.

Vergesst mir meine Traudel nicht. Kurt Maetzig, dir. Kurt Bartel, Kurt Maetzig, sws. DEFA, 1957.

Der verlorene Engel. Ralf Kirsten, dir. Joachim Nestler, Manfred Freitag, sws. DEFA, 1966 [1971].

Das Versteck. Frank Beyer, dir. Jurek Becker, sw. DEFA, 1978.

Das verurteilte Dorf. Martin Hellberg, dir. Jeanne Stern, Kurt Stern, sws. DEFA, 1952.

Verwirrung der Liebe. Slatan Dudow, dir. and sw. DEFA, 1959.

Weisses Blut. Gottfried Kolditz, dir. Harald Hauser, Gottfried Kolditz, sws. DEFA, 1959.

Weite Strasse—stille Liebe. Herrmann Zschoche, dir. Ulrich Plenzdorf, sw. DEFA, 1969.

Wenn Du gross bist, lieber Adam. Egon Günther, dir. Helga Schütz, Egon Günther, sws. DEFA, 1966 [1990].

Wo der Zug nicht lange hält. Joachim Hasler, dir. Joachim Hasler, Horst Beseler, sws. DEFA, 1960.

Zeit zu leben. Horst Seemann, dir. Wolfgang Held, sw. DEFA, 1969.

Zum Beispiel Josef. Erwin Stranka, dir. Günter Karl, Erwin Stranka, sws. DEFA, 1974.

Das zweite Leben des Georg Friedrich Wilhelm Platow. Siegfried Kühn, dir. Helmut Baierl, sw. DEFA, 1973.

INDEX